J598
G929
V.5

W9-AOD-042

WILDER BRAN
7140 E. SEVEN MILE RD.
DETROIT, MI 48234

SEP - - 2008
W1

grzimek's
Student Animal Life Resource

• • • •

grzimek's
Student Animal Life Resource

• • • •

Birds
volume 5

Monarch Flycatchers to Crows

THOMSON

GALE

Detroit • New York • San Francisco • San Diego • New Haven, Conn. • Waterville, Maine • London • Munich

Grzimek's Student Animal Life Resource
Birds

Project Editor
Melissa C. McDade

Editorial
Julie L. Carnagie, Madeline Harris, Heather Price

Indexing Services
Synapse, the Knowledge Link Corporation

Rights and Acquisitions
Sheila Spencer, Mari Masalin-Cooper

Imaging and Multimedia
Randy Bassett, Michael Logusz, Dan Newell, Chris O'Bryan, Robyn Young

Product Design
Tracey Rowens, Jennifer Wahi

Composition
Evi Seoud, Mary Beth Trimper

Manufacturing
Wendy Blurton, Dorothy Maki

© 2005 Thomson Gale, a part of The Thomson Corporation.

Thomson and Star Logo are trademarks and Gale and UXL are registered trademarks used herein under license.

For more information, contact
Thomson Gale
27500 Drake Rd.
Farmington Hills, MI 48331-3535
Or you can visit our Internet site at
http://www.gale.com

ALL RIGHTS RESERVED
No part of this work covered by the copyright hereon may be reproduced or used in any form or by any means—graphic, electronic, or mechanical, including photocopying, recording, taping, Web distribution, or information storage retrieval systems—without the written permission of the publisher.

For permission to use material from this product, submit your request via Web at http://www.gale-edit.com/ permissions, or you may download our Permissions Request form and submit your request by fax or mail to:

Permissions
Thomson Gale
27500 Drake Rd.
Farmington Hills, MI 48331-3535
Permissions Hotline:
248-699-8006 or 800-877-4253, ext. 8006
Fax: 248-699-8074 or 800-762-4058

While every effort has been made to ensure the reliability of the information presented in this publication, Thomson Gale does not guarantee the accuracy of the data contained herein. Thomson Gale accepts no payment for listing; and inclusion in the publication of any organization, agency, institution, publication, service, or individual does not imply endorsement of the editors or publisher. Errors brought to the attention of the publisher and verified to the satisfaction of the publisher will be corrected in future editions.

LIBRARY OF CONGRESS CATALOGING-IN-PUBLICATION DATA

Grzimek's student animal life resource. Birds / Melissa C. McDade, project editor.
    p. cm.
  Includes bibliographical references and index.
  ISBN 0-7876-9235-2 (set hardcover : alk. paper) — ISBN 0-7876-9236-0 (volume 1) — ISBN 0-7876-9237-9 (volume 2) — ISBN 0-7876-9238-7 (volume 3) — ISBN 0-7876-9239-5 (volume 4) — ISBN 0-7876-9240-9 (volume 5)
  1. Birds—Juvenile literature.   I. Grzimek, Bernhard. II. McDade, Melissa C.
  QL673.G79 2005
  598—dc22   2004015729

ISBN 0-7876-9402-9 (21-vol set), ISBN 0-7876-9235-2 (Birds set),
ISBN 0-7876-9236-0 (v.1), ISBN 0-7876-9237-9 (v.2), ISBN 0-7876-9238-7 (v.3),
ISBN 0-7876-9239-5 (v.4), ISBN 0-7876-9240-9 (v.5)

This title is also available as an e-book
Contact your Thomson Gale sales representative for ordering information.

Printed in Canada
10 9 8 7 6 5 4 3 2 1

Contents

BIRDS: VOLUME 4

BIRDS: VOLUME 5

Reader's Guide

Grzimek's Student Animal Life Resource: Birds offers readers comprehensive and easy-to-use information on Earth's birds. Entries are arranged by taxonomy, the science through which living things are classified into related groups. Order entries provide an overview of a group of families, and family entries provide an overview of a particular family. Each entry includes sections on physical characteristics; geographic range; habitat; diet; behavior and reproduction; animals and people; and conservation status. Family entries are followed by one or more species accounts with the same information as well as a range map and photo or illustration for each species. Entries conclude with a list of books, periodicals, and Web sites that may be used for further research.

ADDITIONAL FEATURES

Each volume of *Grzimek's Student Animal Life Resource: Birds* includes a pronunciation guide for scientific names, a glossary, an overview of birds, a list of species in the set by biome, a list of species by geographic location, and an index. The set has 640 full-color maps, photos, and illustrations to enliven the text, and sidebars provide additional facts and related information.

NOTES

The classification of animals into orders, families, and even species is not a completed exercise. As researchers learn more about animals and their relationships, classifications may change. In some cases, researchers do not agree on how or whether to make a change. For this reason, the heading "Number of species" in the introduction of an entry may read "About 36 species" or "34 to 37 species." It is not a question of whether some animals exist or not, but a question of how they are classified. Some researchers are more likely to "lump" animals into the same species classification, while others may "split" animals into separate species.

Grzimek's Student Animal Life Resource: Birds has standardized information in the Conservation Status section. The IUCN Red List provides the world's most comprehensive inventory of the global conservation status of plants and animals. Using a set of criteria to evaluate extinction risk, the IUCN recognizes the following categories: Extinct, Extinct in the Wild, Critically Endangered, Endangered, Vulnerable, Conservation Dependent, Near Threatened, Least Concern, and Data Deficient. These terms are defined where they are used in the text, but for a complete explanation of each category, visit the IUCN web page at http://www.iucn.org/themes/ssc/redlists/RLcats2001booklet.html.

ACKNOWLEDGEMENTS

Special thanks are due for the invaluable comments and suggestions provided by the *Grzimek's Student Animal Life Resource: Birds* advisors:

- Mary Alice Anderson, Media Specialist, Winona Middle School, Winona, Minnesota
- Thane Johnson, Librarian, Oklahoma City Zoo, Oklahoma City, Oklahoma
- Debra Kachel, Media Specialist, Ephrata Senior High School, Ephrata, Pennsylvania
- Nina Levine, Media Specialist, Blue Mountain Middle School, Courtlandt Manor, New York
- Ruth Mormon, Media Specialist, The Meadows School, Las Vegas, Nevada

COMMENTS AND SUGGESTIONS

We welcome your comments on *Grzimek's Student Animal Life Resource: Birds* and suggestions for future editions of this work. Please write: Editors, *Grzimek's Student Animal Life Resource: Birds*, U•X•L, 27500 Drake Rd., Farmington Hills, Michigan 48331-3535; call toll free: 1-800-877-4253; fax: 248-699-8097; or send e-mail via www.gale.com.

Pronunciation Guide for Scientific Names

Acanthisitta chloris uh-kan-thuh-SIT-tuh KLOR-is

Acanthisittidae uh-kan-thuh-SIT-tuh-dee

Acanthiza chrysorrhoa uh-KAN-thih-zuh KRIH-soh-ROH-uh

Acanthizidae uh-kan-THIZ-uh-dee

Accipitridae ak-sip-IT-ruh-dee

Aceros cassidix AH-ser-uhs KAS-sid-iks

Acridotheres tristis AK-rid-uh-THER-eez TRIS-tis

Actenoides concretus ak-TEN-oi-deez con-CREE-tuhs

Actinodura sodangorum AK-tin-uh-DYOOR-uh soh-dan-GOH-rum

Actophilornis africanus ak-tuh-FIL-or-nis AF-rih-kan-uhs

Aechmophorus occidentalis ek-MOH-for-uhs OK-sih-DEN-tal-is

Aegithalidae ee-jih-THAL-uh-dee

Aegithina tiphia ee-JIH-thin-uh TIF-ee-uh

Aegotheles insignis ee-GO-thel-eez IN-sig-nis

Aegothelidae ee-go-THEL-uh-dee

Agelaioides badius ah-jeh-LAY-oid-eez BAD-ee-uhs

Agelaius phoeniceus ah-jeh-LAY-ee-uhs fee-nih-SEE-uhs

Aix sponsa AKS SPON-suh

Ajaia ajaja ah-JAH-ee-uh AH-jah-juh

Alaemon alaudipes al-EE-mon ah-LAUD-ih-peez

Alaudidae ah-LAUD-uh-dee

Alcedinidae al-sed-IN-uh-dee

Alcidae AL-suh-dee

Amytornis striatus am-IT-or-nis stry-AH-tuhs

Anas platyrhynchos AH-nuhs PLA-tee-RIN-koz

Anatidae ah-NA-tuh-dee

Andigena hypoglauca an-DIH-jin-uh HI-poh-GLO-kuh

Anhima cornuta AN-him-uh KOR-nyoo-tuh

Anhimidae an-HIM-uh-dee

Anhinga anhinga AN-hin-guh AN-hin-guh

Anseriformes an-ser-uh-FORM-eez

Anthus spragueii AN-thuhs SPRAG-ee-eye

Aphelocoma californica uh-fel-uh-KOH-muh kal-uh-FORN-ik-uh

Apodidae a-POD-uh-dee

Apodiformes a-pod-uh-FORM-eez

Aptenodytes forsteri ap-ten-uh-DIE-teez FOS-ter-eye

Apterygidae ap-ter-IJ-uh-dee

Apteryx australis AP-ter-iks au-STRA-lis

Ara macao AR-uh MUH-kow

Aramidae ar-UH-muh-dee

Aramus guarauna AR-uh-muhs GWAR-aw-nuh

Ardea herodias AR-dee-uh hir-OH-dee-uhs

Ardeidae ar-DEE-uh-dee

Arenaria interpres ar-en-AIR-ee-uh IN-ter-preez

Artamidae ar-TAM-uh-dee

Artamus cyanopterus AR-tam-uhs SIGH-an-OP-ter-uhs

Astrapia mayeri as-truh-PEE-uh MAY-er-eye

Atrichornis rufescens a-TRIK-or-nis ROO-fehs-sens

Atrichornithidae a-trik-or-NITH-uh-dee

Attagis gayi AT-uh-jis GAY-eye

Auriparus flaviceps aw-RIP-ar-uhs FLAV-uh-seps

Balaeniceps rex bal-EEN-uh-seps REX

Balaenicipitidae BAL-een-uh-sip-IH-tuh-dee

Balearica regulorum BAL-ih-AR-ik-uh reg-YOO-lor-um

Batis capensis BAT-is KAP-en-sis

Bombycilla cedrorum bom-bih-SILL-uh SEED-roh-rum

Bombycillidae bom-bih-SILL-uh-dee

Botaurus stellaris BOH-tor-uhs STEL-lar-is

Branta canadensis BRAN-tuh kan-uh-DEN-sis

Bubo sumatranus BYOO-boh SOO-mah-TRAN-uhs

Bucconidae buck-ON-uh-dee

Bucerotidae byoo-ser-UH-tuh-dee

Bucorvus leadbeateri BYOO-kor-vuhs LED-bet-er-eye

Buphagus erythrorhynchus BYOO-fag-uhs eh-RITH-roh-RIN-kuhs

Burhinidae bur-HIN-uh-dee

Callaeas cinerea cal-LEE-uhs sin-EAR-ee-uh

Callaeidae cal-LEE-uh-dee

Calypte anna kuh-LIP-tee AN-nuh

Campephagidae kam-pee-FAJ-uh-dee

Campephilus principalis KAM-pee-FIL-uhs PRIN-sih-PAL-is

Campylorhamphus trochilirostris KAM-pie-luh-RAM-fuhs TRO-kil-ih-ROS-tris

Campylorhynchus brunneicapillus KAM-pie-luh-RIN-kuhs BROO-nee-kap-ILL-uhs

Capitonidae kap-ih-TON-uh-dee

Caprimulgidae kap-rih-MUL-juh-dee

Caprimulgiformes kal-rih-mul-juh-FORM-eez

Caprimulgus indicus KAP-rih-MUL-juhs IN-dih-kuhs

Caprimulgus vociferus KAP-rih-MUL-juhs voh-SIF-er-uhs

Carduelis tristis KAR-doo-lis TRIS-tis

Cariama cristata KAR-ee-ah-muh KRIS-tah-tuh

Cariamidae kar-ee-AH-muh-dee

Casuariidae kas-oo-ar-EYE-uh-dee

Casuarius casuarius kas-oo-AR-ee-uhs kas-oo-AR-ee-uhs

Cathartidae kath-ART-uh-dee

Cephalopterus ornatus SEFF-uhl-OP-ter-uhs AWR-nah-tuhs

Cercomacra cinerascens SIR-koh-MAK-ruh si-NEAR-ass-enz

Certhia americana SIR-thee-uh uh-mer-uh-kAN-uh

Certhiidae sirth-EYE-uh-dee

Chaetura pelagica KEE-tur-uh peh-LAJ-ik-uh

Chalcoparia singalensis kal-kuh-PAIR-ee-uh sin-GAHL-en-sis

Chamaea fasciata kam-EE-uh fah-she-AH-tuh

Chamaepetes unicolor kam-ee-PEET-eez YOO-nih-KUH-luhr

Charadriidae kar-ad-RYE-uh-dee

Charadriiformes kar-ad-rye-uh-FORM-eez

Charadrius vociferus kar-ad-REE-uhs voh-SIF-er-uhs

Chionidae ky-ON-uh-dee

Chionis minor KY-on-is MY-ner

Chiroxiphia linearis ky-roh-ZIF-ee-uh lin-EE-air-is

Chlamydera maculata klam-EE-der-uh mak-yoo-LAH-tuh

Chlidonias niger klih-DON-ee-uhs NY-jer

Cicinnurus regius sih-SIN-yoor-uhs RAY-jee-uhs

Ciconia ciconia SIK-uh-nee-uh SIK-uh-nee-uh

Ciconiidae sik-uh-NYE-uh-dee

Ciconiiformes sik-uh-nee-uh-FORM-eez

Cinclidae SIN-kluh-dee

Cinclosoma punctatum sin-cluh-SOH-muh PUNK-tah-tum

Cinclus cinclus SIN-kluhs SIN-kluhs

Cinclus mexicanus SIN-kluhs MEK-sih-KAN-uhs

Cinnyris asiaticus SIN-ny-ris AY-zhi-AT-ik-uhs

Cissa chinensis SIS-suh CHIN-en-sis

Cisticola juncidis sis-tuh-KOH-luh JUNK-id-is

Climacteridae kly-mak-TER-uh-dee

Climacteris rufa kly-MAK-ter-is ROO-fuh

Colibri coruscans KOH-lee-bree KOR-us-kans

Coliidae kol-EYE-uh-dee

Coliiformes kol-eye-uh-FORM-eez

Colinus virginianus KOL-eye-nuhs ver-JIN-ee-an-nuhs

Colius striatus KOL-ee-uhs stry-AH-tuhs

Columba livia KUH-lum-buh LIV-ee-uh

Columbidae kuh-LUM-buh-dee

Columbiformes kuh-lum-buh-FORM-eez

Coracias garrulus kor-UH-see-uhs GAR-oo-luhs

Coraciidae kor-uh-SIGH-uh-dee

Coraciiformes kor-uh-sigh-uh-FORM-eez

Coracina typica kor-uh-SEE-nuh TIP-ik-uh

Corvidae KOR-vuh-dee

Corvus corax KOR-vuhs KOR-aks

Corythaeola cristata kor-ih-thee-OH-luh KRIS-tah-tuh

Corythaixoides concolor kor-ih-THAKS-oi-deez CON-kuh-luhr

Cotinga cayana KOH-ting-guh KAY-ah-nuh

Cotingidae koh-TING-guh-dee

Cracidae KRA-suh-dee

Cracticidae krak-TIK-uh-dee

Cracticus torquatus KRAK-tik-uhs TOR-kwah-tuhs

Crax globulosa KRAKS glob-yoo-LOH-suh

Crex crex CREKS CREKS

Cuculidae kyoo-KYOO-luh-dee

Cuculiformes kyoo-kyoo-luh-FORM-eez

Cuculus canorus KYOO-kyoo-luhs KAN-or-uhs

Cyanocitta cristata SIGH-an-uh-SIT-tuh KRIS-tah-tuh

Cyclarhis gujanensis SIGH-klar-is GOO-jan-en-sis

Cygnus olor   SIG-nuhs OH-lor

Cymbirhynchus macrorhynchos   SIM-bih-RIN-kuhs ma-crow-RIN-kuhs

Cypsiurus parvus   sip-SIH-yoor-uhs PAR-vuhs

Dacelo novaeguineae   DAY-sel-oh NOH-vee-GIN-ee-ee

Dendrocolaptidae   den-droh-koh-LAP-tuh-dee

Dendroica kirtlandii   DEN-droy-kuh KIRT-land-ee-eye

Dendropicos goertae   den-droh-PEE-kuhs GER-tee

Dicaeidae   die-SEE-uh-dee

Dicaeum ignipectus   DIE-see-um IG-nih-PEK-tuhs

Dicruridae   die-KRU-ruh-dee

Dicrurus ludwigii   DIE-kru-ruhs LOOT-vig-ee-eye

Dicrurus paradiseus   DIE-kru-ruhs par-uh-DIE-see-uhs

Diomedea cauta eremite   DIE-uh-MED-ee-uh CAW-tuh ER-ih-mite

Diomedea immutabilis   DIE-uh-MED-ee-uh im-myoo-TUH-bil-is

Diomedeidae   die-uh-med-EYE-dee

Donacobius atricapillus   don-uh-KOH-bee-uhs ay-trih-kap-ILL-uhs

Drepanididae   dre-pan-ID-uh-dee

Drepanorhynchus reichenowi   DRE-pan-uh-RIN-kuhs RYE-keh-now-eye

Dromadidae   droh-MAD-uh-dee

Dromaiidae   droh-MAY-uh-dee

Dromaius novaehollandiae   DROH-may-uhs NO-vee-hol-LAND-ee-ee

Dromas ardeola   DROH-muhs ar-dee-OH-luh

Drymodes brunneopygia   dry-MOH-deez BROO-nee-oh-PIJ-ee-uh

Dulidae   DYOO-luh-dee

Dulus dominicus   DYOO-luhs duh-MIN-ih-kuhs

Dumetella carolinensis   dum-uh-TELL-uh kar-uh-LINE-en-sis

Eclectus roratus   EK-lek-tuhs ROH-rat-uhs

Egretta ibis   EE-gret-uh EYE-bis

Emberizidae   em-ber-IZ-uh-dee

Epthianuridae   ep-thy-an-YOOR-uh-dee

Epthianura tricolor   ep-thy-an-YOOR-uh TRY-kuh-luhr

Eremophila alpestris   ER-em-uh-FIL-uh al-PES-tris

Esacus magnirostris   EH-sak-uhs MAG-nuh-ROS-tris

Estrilda astrild   ES-tril-duh AS-trild

Estrildidae   es-TRIL-duh-dee

Eudyptes chrysolophus   YOO-dip-teez krih-soh-LOH-fuhs

Eupetidae   yoo-PET-uh-dee

Euplectes orix   YOO-plek-teez OR-iks

Eupodotis caerulescens   yoo-pod-OH-tis see-ROO-less-sens

Eurylaimidae   yoo-rih-lay-IM-uh-dee

Eurypyga helias   yoo-RIH-pij-uh HEE-lee-uhs

Eurypygidae   yoo-rih-PIJ-uh-dee

Eurystomus orientalis   yoo-rih-STOH-muhs or-ih-EN-tal-is

Falco peregrinus   FAL-koh PEHR-eh-GRIN-uhs

Falco rusticolis   FAL-koh rus-TIH-kol-is

Falconidae   fal-KON-uh-dee

Falconiformes   fal-kon-uh-FORM-eez

Ficedula basilanica   fih-SEH-duh-luh bas-ill-AN-ik-uh

Formicariidae   for-mih-kar-EYE-uh-dee

Fratercula arctica   frah-TER-kuh-luh ARK-tik-uh

Fregata magnificens   FREH-gah-tuh mag-NIH-fih-sens

Fregatidae   freh-GAH-tuh-dee

Fringilla coelebs   frin-JILL-uh SEE-lebz

Fringillidae   frin-JILL-uh-dee

Fulmarus glacialis   FULL-mar-uhs glay-SHE-al-is

Furnariidae   fur-nar-EYE-uh-dee

Furnarius rufus   fur-NAR-ee-uhs ROO-fuhs

Galbula pastazae   GAL-bull-uh PAS-tah-zee

Galbula ruficauda   GAL-bull-uh roo-fee-KAW-duh

Galbulidae   gal-BULL-uh-dee

Gallicolumba luzonica   gal-ih-KUH-lum-buh loo-ZON-ik-uh

Galliformes   gal-uh-FORM-eez

Gallinago nigripennis   gal-uh-NAY-go NY-gruh-PEN-is

Gavia immer   GAV-ee-uh IM-mer

Gavia stellata   GAV-ee-uh STEL-lah-tuh

Gaviidae   gav-EYE-uh-dee

Gaviiformes   gav-eye-uh-FORM-eez

Geococcyx californiana   GEE-oh-COCK-siks kal-uh-FORN-uh-kuh

Glareola pratincola   glar-ee-OH-luh prat-in-KOH-luh

Glareolidae   glar-ee-OH-luh-dee

Glaucis hirsuta   GLO-kis her-SOO-tuh

Grallina cyanoleuca   GRAL-line-uh SIGH-an-uh-LYOO-kuh

Grallinidae gral-LINE-uh-dee

Gruidae GROO-uh-dee

Gruiformes groo-uh-FORM-eez

Grus canadensis GROOS kan-uh-DEN-sis

Grus japonensis GROOS jap-ON-en-sis

Gymnogyps californianus JIM-nuh-jips kal-uh-FORN-uh-kuhs

Haematopodidae hee-muh-toh-POD-uh-dee

Haematopus unicolor hee-muh-TOH-puhs YOO-nih-KUH-luhr

Harpactes oreskios hahr-PAK-teez or-es-KEE-uhs

Heliornis fulica hee-LEE-or-nis FUL-ik-uh

Heliornithidae hee-lee-or-NITH-uh-dee

Hemiprocne coronata HEMI-prok-nee koh-roh-NAH-tuh

Hemiprocnidae hemi-PROK-nuh-dee

Himantopus himantopus hih-MAN-tuh-puhs hih-MAN-tuh-puhs

Himatione sanguinea hih-MAY-shun-ee san-GWIN-ee-uh

Hirundinidae hir-un-DIN-uh-dee

Hirundo pyrrhonota HIR-un-doh pir-uh-NOH-tuh

Hirundo rustica HIR-un-doh RUS-tik-uh

Hydrobatidae hi-droh-BAT-uh-dee

Hydrophasianus chirurgus hi-droh-fay-SEE-an-uhs KY-ruhr-guhs

Hypocolius ampelinus hi-poh-KOL-ee-uhs am-peh-LINE-uhs

Hypothymis azurea hi-poh-THY-mis az-YOOR-ee-uh

Hypsipetes madagascariensis hip-sih-PEET-eez mad-uh-GAS-kar-EE-en-sis

Icteria virens ik-TER-ee-uh VY-renz

Icteridae ik-TER-uh-dee

Icterus galbula IK-ter-uhs GAL-bull-uh

Indicator archipelagicus in-dih-KAY-ter AR-kih-peh-LAJ-ik-uhs

Indicatoridae in-dih-kay-TER-uh-dee

Irena puella eye-REEN-uh poo-ELL-uh

Irenidae eye-REEN-uh-dee

Jacanidae juh-KAN-uh-dee

Jynx torquilla JINKS tor-KWILL-uh

Lagopus lagopus LAG-uh-puhs LAG-uh-puhs

Laniidae lan-EYE-uh-dee

Lanius ludovicianus lan-ee-uhs LOO-doh-vih-SHE-an-uhs

Laridae LAR-uh-dee

Larus saundersi   LAR-uhs SON-ders-eye

Laterallus jamaicensis   lat-er-ALL-uhs ja-MAY-sen-sis

Leipoa ocellata   LYE-poh-uh os-ELL-ah-tuh

Liosceles thoracicus   lye-OS-sel-eez tho-RAS-ik-uhs

Lonchura punctulata   LON-chur-uh punk-TOO-lah-tuh

Loxia curvirostra   LOK-see-uh KUR-vih-ROS-truh

Macrocephalon maleo   ma-crow-SEFF-uh-lon MAL-ee-oh

Macronyx ameliae   MA-cron-iks am-EEL-ee-ee

Maluridae   mal-YOOR-uh-dee

Malurus splendens   MAL-yoor-uhs SPLEN-denz

Megaceryle alcyon   MEG-uh-ser-EYE-lee al-SIGH-on

Megapodiidae   meg-uh-pod-EYE-uh-dee

Megalaima haemacephala   meg-uh-LAY-muh hee-muh-SEFF-ah-luh

Melanocharis versteri   mel-uh-NOH-kar-is VER-ster-eye

Meleagris gallopavo   mel-ee-AY-gris gal-uh-PAY-voh

Melichneutes robustus   mel-ik-NOO-teez ro-BUHS-tuhs

Meliphagidae   mel-ih-FAJ-uh-dee

Melospiza melodia   mel-uh-SPY-zuh meh-LOH-dee-uh

Menura alberti   MEN-yoor-uh AL-bert-eye

Menuridae   men-YOOR-uh-dee

Meropidae   mer-OP-uh-dee

Meropogon forsteni   mer-uh-POH-gon FOR-sten-eye

Merops apiaster   MER-ops ay-PEE-as-ter

Mesitornis variegata   meh-SIT-or-nis VAIR-ree-uh-GAH-tuh

Mesitornithidae   meh-sit-or-NITH-uh-dee

Microeca fascinans   my-CROW-ek-uh FAS-sin-ans

Mimidae   MIH-muh-dee

Mirafra javanica   MIR-af-ruh jah-VAH-nik-uh

Mniotilta varia   ny-OH-til-tuh VAIR-ee-uh

Moho bishopi   MOH-hoh BISH-up-eye

Mohua ochrocephala   MOH-hyoo-uh OH-kruh-SEFF-ah-luh

Momotidae   moh-MOH-tuh-dee

Momotus momota   MOH-moh-tuhs MOH-moh-tuh

Monarchidae   mon-ARK-uh-dee

Montifringilla nivalis   mon-tih-frin-JILL-uh NYE-val-is

Morus bassanus   MOR-uhs BASS-an-uhs

Motacilla cinerea   moh-tuh-SILL-uh sin-EAR-ee-uh

Motacillidae   moh-tuh-SILL-uh-dee

Muscicapidae   mus-kih-KAP-uh-dee

Muscicaps striata   MUS-kih-kaps stry-AH-tuh

Musophagidae   mus-oh-FAJ-uh-dee

Musophagiformes   mus-oh-faj-uh-FORM-eez

Mycteria americana   mik-TER-ee-uh uh-mer-uh-KAN-uh

Nectariniidae   nek-tar-in-EYE-uh-dee

Neodrepanis coruscans   nee-oh-DREH-pan-is KOR-us-kans

Neophron percnopterus   NEE-oh-fron perk-NOP-ter-uhs

Nesomimus macdonaldi   NEZ-oh-MIH-muhs mak-DON-uld-eye

Nonnula ruficapilla   NON-nuh-luh roo-fih-kap-ILL-uh

Notharchus macrorhynchos   NOTH-ark-uhs ma-crow-RIN-kuhs

Nothocercus bonapartei   NOTH-uh-SER-kuhs BOH-nuh-PART-eye

Nucifraga caryocatactes   NYOO-sih-FRAG-uh KAR-ee-oh-KAT-ak-teez

Numenius americanus   nyoo-MEN-ee-uhs uh-mer-uh-KAN-uhs

Numida meleagris   NYOO-mid-uh mel-ee-AY-gris

Numididae   nyoo-MID-uh-dee

Nyctea scandiaca   NIK-tee-uh skan-DEE-uh-kuh

Nyctibiidae   nik-tih-BYE-uh-dee

Nyctibius griseus   nik-TIB-ee-uhs GRIS-ee-uhs

Oceanites oceanicus   OH-shih-NYE-teez OH-shih-AN-uh-kuhs

Odontophoridae   OH-don-tuh-FOR-uh-dee

Opisthocomidae   op-is-thuh-KOM-eh-dee

Opisthocomiformes   op-is-thuh-kom-eh-FORM-eez

Opisthocomus hoazin   op-is-thuh-KOM-uhs HOH-ah-sin

Oriolidae   or-ih-OH-lu-dee

Oriolus oriolus   or-ih-OH-luhs or-ih-OH-luhs

Ortalis vetula   OR-tal-is VET-uh-luh

Orthonychidae   or-thuh-NIK-uh-dee

Orthonyx temminckii   OR-thon-iks TEM-ink-ee-eye

Otididae   oh-TID-uh-dee

Otis tarda   OH-tis TAR-duh

Otus asio   OH-tuhs AS-ee-oh

Oxyruncidae   ok-sih-RUN-kuh-dee

Oxyruncus cristatus   OK-sih-RUN-kuhs KRIS-tah-tuhs

Pachycephala pectoralis   pak-ih-SEFF-ah-luh pek-TOR-al-is

Pachycephalidae   pak-ih-seff-AL-uh-dee

Pachyramphus aglaiae PAK-ih-RAM-fuhs ag-LAY-ee-ee

Pandion haliaetus PAN-die-on HAL-ee-ee-tuhs

Parabuteo unicinctus par-uh-BYOO-tee-oh YOO-nih-SINK-tuhs

Paradisaeidae par-uh-die-SEE-uh-dee

Pardalotidae par-duh-LOT-uh-dee

Pardalotus striatus par-duh-LOT-uhs stry-AH-tuhs

Paridae PAR-uh-dee

Parulidae par-YOOL-uh-dee

Parus major PAR-uhs MAY-jur

Passer domesticus PASS-er doh-MES-tuh-kuhs

Passerculus sandwichensis pass-ER-kyoo-luhs SAND-wich-en-sis

Passeridae pass-ER-uh-dee

Passeriformes pass-er-uh-FORM-eez

Pelecanidae pel-uh-KAN-uh-dee

Pelecaniformes pel-uh-kan-uh-FORM-eez

Pelecanoides urinatrix pel-uh-KAN-oi-deez yoor-in-AY-triks

Pelecanoididae pel-uh-kan-OI-duh-dee

Pelecanus erythrorhynchos pel-uh-KAN-uhs eh-RITH-roh-RIN-kuhs

Pelecanus occidentalis pel-uh-KAN-uhs ok-sih-DEN-tal-is

Pericrocotus igneus per-ih-CROW-kot-uhs IG-nee-uhs

Petroicidae pet-ROY-kuh-dee

Phacellodomus ruber fay-sell-uh-DOH-muhs ROO-ber

Phaethon lepturus FEE-thon LEPT-yoor-uhs

Phaethontidae fee-THON-tuh-dee

Phalacrocoracidae fal-uh-crow-kor-AY-suh-dee

Phalacrocorax carbo fal-uh-crow-cor-aks KAR-boh

Pharomachrus mocinno far-uh-MAK-ruhs MOH-sin-noh

Phasianidae fay-see-AN-uh-dee

Philepittidae fil-uh-PIT-tuh-dee

Phoenicopteridae FEE-nih-kop-TER-uh-dee

Phoenicopteriformes FEE-nih-KOP-ter-uh-FORM-eez

Phoenicopterus ruber FEE-nih-KOP-ter-uhs ROO-ber

Phoeniculidae FEE-nih-KYOO-luh-dee

Phoeniculus purpureus fee-NIH-kyoo-luhs purh-PURH-ee-uhs

Phyllastrephus scandens FIL-uh-STRE-fuhs SKAN-denz

Phylloscopus borealis FIL-uh-SKOH-puhs BOHR-ee-al-is

Phytotoma raimondii fye-toh-TOH-muh RAY-mund-ee-eye

Phytotomidae fye-toh-TOH-muh-dee

Picathartes oreas PIK-uh-THAR-teez OR-ee-uhs

Picoides borealis PIK-oy-deez BOHR-ee-al-is

Picidae PIS-uh-dee

Piciformes pis-uh-FORM-eez

Pinguinus impennis PIN-gwin-uhs IM-pen-is

Pipra filicauda PIP-ruh fil-eh-KAW-duh

Pipridae PIP-ruh-dee

Pitangus sulphuratus PIT-an-guhs sul-FUR-ah-tuhs

Pitohui kirhocephalus PIT-oo-eey kir-uh-SEFF-ah-luhs

Pitta angolensis PIT-tuh an-GOH-len-sis

Pitta sordida PIT-tuh SOR-dih-duh

Pittidae PIT-tuh-dee

Pityriasis gymnocephala pit-ih-RYE-uh-sis jim-nuh-SEFF-ah-luh

Plectoryncha lanceolata PLEK-tuh-RIN-kuh LAN-see-oh-LAH-tuh

Plectrophenax nivalis PLEK-troh-FEN-aks NYE-val-is

Ploceidae ploh-SEE-uh-dee

Ploceus cucullatus PLOH-see-uhs kyoo-KYOO-lah-tuhs

Ploceus philippinus PLOH-see-uhs fil-ih-PINE-uhs

Podargidae pod-AR-juh-dee

Podargus strigoides POD-ar-guhs STRI-goy-deez

Podiceps cristatus POD-ih-seps KRIS-tah-tuhs

Podicipedidae pod-ih-sih-PED-uh-dee

Podicipediformes pod-ih-sih-ped-uh-FORM-eez

Poecile atricapilla PEE-suh-lee ay-trih-kap-ILL-uh

Pogoniulus chrysoconus po-go-NYE-uh-luhs KRIS-oh-KON-uhs

Polioptila caerulea poh-lih-OP-til-uh see-ROO-lee-uh

Polyborus plancus pol-ih-BOHR-uhs PLAN-kuhs

Pomatostomidae poh-may-tuh-STOH-muh-dee

Pomatostomus temporalis poh-may-tuh-STOH-muhs tem-PER-al-is

Prionops plumatus PRY-on-ops PLOO-mah-tuhs

Procellariidae pro-sell-ar-EYE-uh-dee

Procellariiformes pro-sell-ar-eye-uh-FORM-eez

Promerops cafer PRO-mer-ops KAF-er

Prunella modularis proo-NELL-uh mod-YOO-lar-is

Prunellidae proo-NELL-uh-dee

Psaltriparus minimus sol-TRI-par-uhs MIN-ih-muhs

Psittacidae sit-UH-suh-dee

Psittaciformes sit-uh-suh-FORM-eez

Psittacula krameri sit-UH-kuh-luh KRAY-mer-eye

Psittacus erithacus SIT-uh-kuhs eh-RITH-uh-kuhs

Psittirostra cantans SIT-uh-ROS-truh KAN-tanz

Psophia crepitans SOH-fee-uh KREP-ih-tanz

Psophiidae soh-FYE-uh-dee

Pterocles namaqua TER-oh-kleez nah-MAH-kwuh

Pteroclididae ter-oh-KLID-uh-dee

Pterocliformes ter-oh-cluh-FORM-eez

Pterocnemia pennata ter-ok-NEE-mee-uh PEN-ah-tuh

Ptilonorhynchidae TIL-on-oh-RIN-kuh-dee

Ptilonorhynchus violaceus TIL-on-oh-RIN-kuhs vee-o-LAY-see-uhs

Ptiloris victoriae TIL-or-is vik-TOR-ee-ee

Ptyonoprogne rupestris TY-on-oh-PROG-nee ROO-pes-tris

Puffinus puffinus PUFF-in-uhs PUFF-in-uhs

Pycnonotidae pik-noh-NOH-tuh-dee

Pycnonotus barbatus pik-noh-NOH-tuhs BAR-bat-uhs

Rallidae RALL-uh-dee

Ramphastidae ram-FAS-tuh-dee

Ramphastos toco RAM-fas-tuhs TOH-coh

Raphidae RAF-uh-dee

Raphus cucullatus RAF-uhs kyoo-KYOO-lah-tuhs

Recurvirostra americana re-CURV-ih-ROS-truh uh-mer-uh-KAN-uh

Recurvirostridae re-CURV-ih-ROS-truh-dee

Remizidae rem-IZ-uh-dee

Rhabdornis mysticalis RAB-dor-nis mis-TIH-kal-is

Rhabdornithidae rab-dor-NITH-uh-dee

Rheidae REE-uh-dee

Rhinocryptidae RYE-noh-KRIP-tuh-dee

Rhinoplax vigil RYE-noh-plaks VIH-jil

Rhipidura albicollis rip-ih-DYOOR-uh ahl-bih-KOLL-is

Rhipidura leucophrys rip-ih-DYOOR-uh LYOO-kuh-frees

Rhipiduridae rip-ih-DYOOR-uh-dee

Rhynochetidae rye-noh-KEE-tuh-dee

Rhynochetos jubatus rye-noh-KEE-tuhs JOO-bat-uhs

Rostratula benghalensis ros-TRAT-uh-luh ben-GOL-en-sis

Rostratulidae ros-trat-UH-luh-dee

Rupicola rupicola roo-pih-KOH-luh roo-pih-KOH-luh

Sagittariidae saj-ih-tar-EYE-uh-dee

Sagittarius serpentarius saj-ih-TAR-ee-uhs ser-pen-TAR-ee-uhs

Sarcoramphus papa sar-KOH-ram-fuhs PAH-pah

Sarothrura elegans sar-oh-THROO-ruh EL-eh-ganz

Saxicola torquata sax-ih-KOH-luh TOR-kwah-tuh

Sayornis phoebe SAY-ro-nis FEE-bee

Schetba rufa SKET-buh ROO-fuh

Scolopacidae skoh-loh-PAY-suh-dee

Scopidae SKOH-puh-dee

Scopus umbretta SKOH-puhs UM-bret-tuh

Semnornis ramphastinus SEM-nor-nis ram-FAS-tin-uhs

Sialia sialis sigh-AL-ee-uh SIGH-al-is

Sitta canadensis SIT-tuh kan-uh-DEN-sis

Sitta europaea SIT-tuh yoor-uh-PEE-uh

Sittidae SIT-tuh-dee

Smithornis capensis SMITH-or-nis KAP-en-sis

Somateria spectabilis soh-muh-TER-ee-uh spek-TAB-ih-lis

Sphecotheres vieilloti sfek-UH-ther-eez VYE-ill-oh-eye

Spheniscidae sfen-IS-kuh-dee

Sphenisciformes sfen-is-kuh-FORM-eez

Spheniscus magellanicus SFEN-is-kuhs maj-eh-LAN-ik-uhs

Sphyrapicus varius sfir-AP-ik-uhs VAIR-ee-uhs

Steatornis caripensis stee-AT-or-nis kar-IH-pen-sis

Steatornithidae stee-at-or-NITH-uh-dee

Stercorarius parasiticus ster-koh-RARE-ee-uhs par-uh-SIT-ik-uhs

Stiltia isabella STILT-ee-uh IZ-uh-BELL-uh

Strigidae STRIJ-uh-dee

Strigiformes strij-uh-FORM-eez

Struthio camelus STROO-thee-oh KAM-el-uhs

Struthionidae stroo-thee-ON-uh-dee

Struthioniformes stroo-thee-on-uh-FORM-eez

Sturnidae STURN-uh-dee

Sturnus vulgaris STURN-uhs VUL-gar-is

Sula nebouxii SUL-uh NEB-oo-ee-eye

Sulidae SUL-uh-dee

Sylviidae sil-VYE-uh-dee

Syrrhaptes paradoxus SIR-rap-teez PAR-uh-DOKS-uhs

Taeniopygia guttata tee-nee-uh-PIJ-ee-uh GUT-tah-tuh

Terpsiphone viridis terp-SIF-oh-nee VIR-id-is

Thamnophilus doliatus THAM-nuh-FIL-uhs dol-EE-ah-tuhs

Thinocoridae thin-uh-KOR-uh-dee

Threskiornis aethiopicus THRES-kih-OR-nis EE-thi-OH-pi-kuhs

Threskiornithidae thres-kih-or-NITH-uh-dee

Timaliidae tim-al-EYE-uh-dee

Tinamidae tin-AM-uh-dee

Todidae TOH-duh-dee

Todus multicolor TOH-duhs MULL-tee-KUH-luhr

Tragopan satyra TRAG-uh-pan SAT-eye-ruh

Trichoglossus haematodus TRIK-uh-GLOS-uhs HEE-muh-TOH-duhs

Trochilidae trok-ILL-uh-dee

Troglodytes aedon trog-luh-DIE-teez EE-don

Troglodytes troglodytes trog-luh-DIE-teez trog-luh-DIE-teez

Troglodytidae trog-luh-DIE-tuh-dee

Trogonidae troh-GON-uh-dee

Trogoniformes troh-gon-uh-FORM-eez

Turdidae TUR-duh-dee

Turdus migratorius TUR-duhs my-gruh-TOR-ee-uhs

Turnicidae tur-NIS-uh-dee

Turnix sylvatica TUR-niks sil-VAT-ik-uh

Turnix varia TUR-niks VAIR-ee-uh

Tyrannidae tie-RAN-uh-dee

Tyto alba TIE-toh AHL-buh

Tytonidae tie-TON-uh-dee

Upupa epops UP-up-uh EE-pops

Upupidae up-UP-uh-dee

Uria aalge YOOR-ee-uh AHL-jee

Vanellus vanellus vah-NELL-uhs vah-NELL-uhs

Vangidae VAN-juh-dee

Vireo atricapillus VIR-e-oh ay-trih-kap-ILL-uhs

Vireonidae vir-e-ON-uh-dee

Volatinia jacarina vol-uh-TIN-ee-uh jak-uh-REE-nuh

Zenaida macroura ZEN-ay-duh ma-crow-YOOR-uh

Zosteropidae zos-ter-OP-uh-dee

Zosterops japonicus ZOS-ter-ops jap-ON-ik-uhs

Words to Know

Acacia: A thorny tree, or any of several trees, shrubs, or other plants of the legume family that tend to be ornamental.

Adaptation: Any structural, physiological, or behavioral trait that aids an organism's survival and ability to reproduce in its existing environment.

Adaptive evolution: Changes in organisms over time that allow them to cope more efficiently with their biomes.

Adaptive shift: An evolutionary process by which the descendants of an organism adapt, over time, to ecological niches, or natural lifestyles, that are new to that organism and usually filled in other places by much different organisms.

Aftershaft: The secondary feather that branches from the base of the main feather.

Algae: Tiny plants or plantlike organisms that grow in water and in damp places.

Alpine: Used to refer to the mountainous region of the Alps, or to describe other areas related to mountains.

Altitude: The height of something in relation to the earth's surface or sea level.

Altricial: Chicks that hatch at an early developmental stage, often blind and without feathers.

Anisodactyl: Toe arrangement with three toes pointing forward and one toe facing backward.

Anting: A behavior birds use to interact with ants, either by rolling in an ant hill or placing ants into their feathers.

Aphrodisiac: Anything that intensifies or arouses sexual desires.

Aquatic: Related to water.

Arachnid: Eight-legged animals, including spiders, scorpions, and mites.

Arboreal: Living primarily or entirely in trees and bushes.

Arthropod: A member of the largest single animal phylum, consisting of organisms with segmented bodies, jointed legs or wings, and exoskeletons.

Asynchronous hatching: A situation in which the eggs in a nest hatch at different times, so that some chicks (the older ones) are larger and stronger than others.

Australasia: Region consisting of Australia, New Zealand, New Guinea, and the neighboring islands of the South Pacific.

Avian: Relating to birds.

Aviary: Large enclosure or cage for birds.

B

Barb: Stiff filament that forms the framework of a feather.

Bib: Area under the bill of a bird, just above the breast.

Biodiversity: Abundance of species in a particular biome or geographical area.

Biparental: Both male and female of the species incubate, feed, and fledge their young.

Bower: Shady, leafy shelter or recess.

Brackish: Water that is a mix of freshwater and saltwater.

Bromeliads: A family of tropical plants. Many bromeliads grow high on the branches and trunks of trees rather than in the soil.

Brood: Young birds that are born and raised together.

Brood parasite: An animal species, most often a bird, in which the female lays its own eggs in the nests of other bird species. The host mother raises the chick as if it were her own. This behavior has also been observed in fish.

Brushland: Habitat characterized by a cover of bushes or shrubs.

Burrow: Tunnel or hole that an animal digs in the ground to use as a home.

C

Cache: A hidden supply area.

Camouflage: Device used by an animal, such as coloration, allowing it to blend in with the surroundings to avoid being seen by prey and predators.

Canopy: The uppermost layer of a forest formed naturally by the leaves and branches of trees and plants.

Cap: Patch on top of bird's head.

Carcass: The dead body of an animal. Vultures gather around a carcass to eat it.

Carnivore: Meat-eating organism.

Carrion: Dead and decaying animal flesh.

Caruncle: A genetically controlled outgrowth of skin on an animal, usually for dominance or mating displays.

Casque: A horny growth on the head of a bird resembling a helmet.

Cavity: Hollow area within a body.

Churring: Referring to a low, trilled, or whirring sound that some birds make.

Circumpolar: Able to live at the North and South Pole.

Clutch: Group of eggs hatched together.

Collagen: A type of protein formed within an animal body that is assembled into various structures, most notably tendons.

Colony: A group of animals of the same type living together.

Comb: Fleshy red crest on top of the head.

Coniferous: Refers to evergreen trees, such as pines and firs, that bear cones and have needle-like leaves that are not shed all at once.

Coniferous forest: An evergreen forest where plants stay green all year.

Continental margin: A gently sloping ledge of a continent that is submerged in the ocean.

Convergence: In adaptive evolution, a process by which unrelated or only distantly related living things come to resemble one another in adapting to similar environments.

Cooperative breeding: A social organization of breeding where several birds (not just the parents) feed a group of hatchlings.

Courtship: Behaviors related to attracting a mate and preparing to breed.

Courtship display: Actions of a male and female animal that demonstrate their interest in becoming or remaining a pair for breeding.

Covert: Term derived from the word for something that is concealed, and used to describe the small feathers that cover the bases of the larger feathers on a bird's wing and tail.

Crèche: A group of young of the same species, which gather together in order to better avoid predators.

Crepuscular: Most active at dawn and dusk.

Crest: A group of feathers on the top or back of a bird's head.

Critically Endangered: A term used by the IUCN in reference to a species that is at an extremely high risk of extinction in the wild.

Crop: A pouch-like organ in the throat where crop milk is produced.

Crop milk: A cheesy, nutritious substance produced by adult pigeons and doves and fed to chicks.

Crown: Top of a bird's head.

Cryptic: To be colored so as to blend into the environment.

D

Deciduous: Shedding leaves at the end of the growing season.

Deciduous forest: A forest with four seasons in which trees drop their leaves in the fall.

Decurved: Down-curved; slightly bent.

Defensive posture: A position adopted to frighten away potential predators.

Deforestation: Those practices or processes that result in the change of forested lands to non-forest uses, such as human settlement or farming. This is often cited as one of the major causes of the enhanced greenhouse effect.

Distal: Away from the point of attachment.

Distraction display: Behaviors intended to distract potential predators from the nest site.

Diurnal: Refers to animals that are active during the day.

Domesticated: Tamed.

Dominant: The top male or female of a social group, sometimes called the alpha male or alpha female.

Dormant: Not active.

Dorsal: Located in the back.

Dung: Feces, or solid waste from an animal.

E

Ecological niche: The role a living creature, plant or animal, plays in its community.

Ecotourist: A person who visits a place in order to observe the plants and animals in the area while making minimal human impact on the natural environment.

Elevation: The height of land when measured from sea level.

Endangered: A term used by the U.S. Endangered Species Act of 1973 and by the IUCN in reference to a species that is facing a very high risk of extinction from all or a significant portion of its natural home.

Endemic: Native to or occuring only in a particular place.

Epiphyte: Plant such as mosses that grows on another plant but does not depend on that host plant for nutrition.

Estuary: Lower end of a river where ocean tides meet the river's current.

Eucalyptus: Tall, aromatic trees.

Evolve: To change slowly over time.

Extinct: A species without living members.

Extinction: The total disappearance of a species or the disappearance of a species from a given area.

Eyespot: Colored feathers on the body that resemble the eyes of a large animal, which function in helping to frighten away potential predators.

F

Family: A grouping of genera that share certain characteristics and appear to have evolved from the same ancestors.

Feather tract: Spacing of feathers in a pattern.

Feces: Solid body waste.

Fermentation: Chemical reaction in which enzymes break down complex organic compounds into simpler ones. This can make digestion easier.

Fledgling: Bird that has recently grown the feathers necessary to fly.

Flightless: Species that have lost the ability to fly.

Flock: A large group of birds of the same species.

Forage: To search for food.

Frugivore: Animal that primarily eats fruit. Many bats and birds are frugivores.

G

Gape: The width of the open mouth.

Genera: Plural of genus.

Generalist feeder: A species that eats a wide variety of foods.

Genus (pl. genera): A category of classification made up of species sharing similar characteristics.

Granivore: Animal that primarily eats seeds and grains.

Grassland: Region in which the climate is dry for long periods of the summer, and freezes in the winter. Grasslands are characterized by grasses and other erect herbs, usually without trees or shrubs, and occur in the dry temperate interiors of continents.

Gregarious: Used to describe birds that tend to live in flocks, and are very sociable with other birds. The word has come to be used to describe people who are very outgoing and sociable, as well.

H

Habitat: The area or region where a particular type of plant or animal lives and grows.

Hallux: The big toe, or first digit, on the part of the foot facing inwards.

Hatchling: Birds that have just hatched, or broken out of the egg.

Hawking: Hunting for food by sitting on a perch, flying out and capturing the food, and returning to the perch to eat.

Heath: Grassy and shrubby uncultivated land.

Herbivore: Plant eating organism.

Heterodactyl: With toes pointed in opposite directions; usually with first and second inner front toes turned backward and the third and fourth toes turned forward.

Homeotherm: Organism with stable independent body temperature.

Host: A living plant or animal from which a parasite takes nutrition

I

Igapó: Black waters of the Amazon river area.

Incubation: Process of sitting on and warming eggs in order for them to hatch.

Indicator species: A bird or animal whose presence reveals a specific environmental characteristic

Indigenous: Originating in a region or country.

Insectivore: An animal that eats primarily insects.

Introduced: Not native to the area; brought in by humans.

Invertebrate: Animal lacking a spinal column (backbone).

Iridescent: Having a lustrous or brilliant appearance or quality.

IUCN: Abbreviation for the International Union for Conservation of Nature and Natural Resources, now the World Conservation Union. A conservation organization of government agencies and nongovernmental organizations best known for its Red Lists of threatened an

K

Keel: A projection from a bone.

Keratin: Protein found in hair, nails, and skin.

Kleptoparasite: An individual that steals food or other resources from another individual.

L

Lamellae: Plural of lamella; comb-like bristles inside a flamingos bill.

Larva (pl. larvae): Immature form (wormlike in insects; fish-like in amphibians) of an organism capable of surviving on its own. A larva does not resemble the parent and must go through metamorphosis, or change, to reach its adult stage.

Lek: An area where birds come to display courtship behaviors to attract a mate (noun); to sing, flutter, hop and perform other courtship behaviors at a lek (verb).

Lerp: Sugary lumps of secretions of psillid insects, small plant-sucking insects living on Eucalyptus trees.

Lichen: A complex of algae and fungi found growing on trees, rocks, or other solid surfaces.

Litter: A layer of dead vegetation and other material covering the ground.

M

Mandible: Upper or lower part of a bird's bill; jaw.

Mangrove: Tropical coastal trees or shrubs that produce many supporting roots and that provide dense vegetation.

Mantle: Back, inner-wing, and shoulder area.

Mesic: Referring to any area that is known to be wet or moist.

Midstory: The level of tropical forests between ground level (understory) and treetops (overstory).

Migrate: To move from one area or climate to another as the seasons change, usually to find food or to mate..

Mixed-species flock: A flock of birds that includes multiple species.

Mobbing: A group of birds gathering together to defend themselves from another large bird by calling loudly and flying at the intruder.

Molt: The process by which an organism sheds its outermost layer of feathers, fur, skin, or exoskeleton.

Monogamous: Refers to a breeding system in which a male and a female mate only with each other during a breeding season or lifetime.

Montane forest: Forest found in mountainous areas.

Mutualism: A relationship between two species where both gain something and neither is harmed.

N

Nape: Back part of the neck.

Near Threatened: A category defined by the IUCN suggesting that a species could become threatened with extinction in the future.

Nectar: Sweet liquid secreted by the flowers of various plants to attract pollinators (animals that pollinate, or fertilize, the flowers).

Neotropical: Relating to a geographic area of plant and animal life east, south, and west of Mexico's central plateau that includes Central and South America and the West Indies.

Nest box: A small, human-made shelter intended as a nest site for birds. Usually a rectangular wooden box with a round entrance hole.

Nestling: Young bird unable to leave the nest.

New World: Made up of North America, Central America, and South America; the western half of the world.

Niche: A habitat with everything an animal needs.

Nictating membranes: Clear coverings under the eyelids that can be moved over the eye.

Nocturnal: Occuring or active at night.

O

Omnivore: A plant- and meat- eating animal.

Opportunistic feeder: One that is able to take advantage of whatever food resources become available.

Overstory: The level of tropical forests nearest treetops.

P

Palearctic: The area or subregion of Europe, Africa, and the Middle East, that is north of the Tropic of Cancer, and the area north of the Himalayas mountain range.

Pampas: Open grasslands of South America.

Parasite: An organism that lives in or on a host organism and that gets its nourishment from that host.

Pelagic: To live on the open ocean.

Permafrost: Permanently frozen lands.

Plain: Large expanse of land that is fairly dry and with few trees.

Plumage: Feathers of a bird.

Pneumatic: Air-filled cavities in the bones of birds.

Poisonous: Containing or producing toxic materials.

Pollen: Dust-like grains or particles produced by a plant that contain male sex cells.

Pollinate: To transfer pollen from the male organ to the female organ of a flower.

Polyandry: A mating system in which a single female mates with multiple males.

Polygamy: A mating system in which males and females mate with multiple partners.

Polygynous lek: A mating system in which several males display together for the attention of females. A female, after watching the displaying males, may mate with one or more males in the lek.

Polygyny: A mating system in which a single male mates with multiple females.

Precocial: Young that hatch at an advanced stage of development, with feathers and able to move.

Predator: An animal that eats other animals.

Preen: To clean and smooth feathers using the bill.

Preen gland: A gland on the rear of most birds which secretes an oil the birds use in grooming.

Prey: Organism hunted and eaten by a predator.

Primary forest: A forest characterized by a full-ceiling canopy formed by the branches of tall trees and several layers of smaller trees. This type of forest lacks ground vegetation because sunlight cannot penetrate through the canopy.

Promiscuity: Mating in which individuals mate with as many other individuals as they can or want to.

Pupae: Plural of pupa; developing insects inside cocoon.

Q

Quill: Hollow feather shaft.

R

Rainforest: An evergreen woodland of the tropics distinguished by a continuous leaf canopy and an average rainfall of about 100 inches (250 centimeters) per year.

Raptor: A bird of prey.

Regurgitate: Eject the contents of the stomach through the mouth; to vomit.

Resident: Bird species that do not migrate.

Retrices: Plural of retrix; paired flight feathers of the tail, which extend from the margins of a bird's tail.

Rictal bristles: Modified feathers composed mainly of the vertical shaft.

Riparian: Having to do with the edges of streams or rivers.

Riverine: Located near a river.

Roe: Fish eggs.

Roost: A place where animals, such as bats, sit or rest on a perch, branch, etc.

S

Savanna: A biome characterized by an extensive cover of grasses with scattered trees, usually transitioning between areas dominated by forests and those dominated by grasses and having alternating seasonal climates of precipitation and drought.

Scavenger: An animal that eats carrion.

Scrub forest: A forest with short trees and shrubs.

Secondary forest: A forest characterized by a less-developed canopy, smaller trees, and a dense ground vegetation found on the edges of fores

Sedentary: Living in a fixed location, as with most plants, tunicates, sponges, etc. Contrast with motile.

Semi-precocial: To be born in a state between altricial and precocial. Semi-precocial chicks can usually leave the nest after a few days.

Sequential polyandry: A mating system in which a female mates with one male, leaves him a clutch of eggs to tend, and then mates with another male, repeating the process throughout the breeding season.

Serial monogamy: Mating for a single nesting then finding another mate or mates for other nestings.

Serrated: Having notches like a saw blade.

Sexual dichromatism: Difference in coloration between the sexes of a species.

Sexual dimorphism: Differences in size and in shapes of body or body parts between sexes of a species.

Sexually mature: Capable of reproducing.

Sheath: Tubular-shaped covering used to protect a body part.

Snag: A dead tree, still standing, with the top broken off.

Social: Species in which individuals are found with other individuals of the same species.

Solitary: Living alone or avoiding the company of others.

Specialist feeder: A species that eats only one or a few food items.

Species: A group of living things that share certain distinctive characteristics and can breed together in the wild.

Squab: Young pigeons and doves.

Steppe: Wide expanse of semiarid relatively level plains, found in cool climates and characterized by shrubs, grasses, and few trees.

Sternum: The breastbone.

Subalpine forest: Forest found at elevations between 9,190 and 10,500 feet (2,800 and 3,200 meters).

Sub-canopy: Below the treetops.

Subordinate: An individual that has lower rank than other, dominant, members of the group.

Subspecies: Divisions within a species based on significant differences and on genetics. Subspecies within a species look different from one another but are still genetically close to be considered separate species. In most cases, subspecies can interbreed and produc

Subtropical: Referring to large areas near the tropics that are not quite as warm as tropical areas.

Syndactyly: A condition in which two bones (or digits) fuse together to become a single bone.

Syrinx (pl. syringes): Vocal organ of birds.

T

Taiga: Subarctic wet evergreen forests.

Tail coverts: The short feathers bordering the quills of the long tail feathers of a bird. They may be over-tail or under-tail (i.e., top or bottom).

Tail streamer: A central part of a bird's tail that is longer than other parts.

Talon: A sharp hooked claw.

Taxonomy: The science dealing with the identification, naming, and classification of plants and animals.

Temperate: Areas with moderate temperatures in which the climate undergoes seasonal change in temperature and moisture. Temperate regions of the earth lie primarily between 30 and 60° latitude in both hemispheres.

Terrestrial: Relating to the land or living primarily on land.

Territorial: A pattern of behavior that causes an animal to stay in a limited area and/or to keep certain other animals of the same species (other than its mate, herd, or family group) out of the

Tetrapod: Any vertebrate having four legs or limbs, including mammals, birds, reptiles, and others.

Thermal: Rising bubble of warm air.

Thicket: An area represented by a thick, or dense, growth of shrubs, underbrush, or small trees.

Threat display: A set of characteristic motions used to communicate aggression and warning to other individuals of the same species.

Threatened: Describes a species that is threatened with extinction.

Torpor: A short period of inactivity characterized by an energy-saving, deep sleep-like state in which heart rate, respiratory rate and body temperature drop.

Tropical: The area between 23.5° north and south of the equator. This region has small daily and seasonal changes in temperature, but great seasonal changes in precipitation. Generally, a hot and humid climate that is completely or almost free of frost.

Tundra: A type of ecosystem dominated by lichens, mosses, grasses, and woody plants. It is found at high latitudes (arctic tundra) and high altitudes (alpine tundra). Arctic tundra is underlain by permafrost and usually very wet.

U

Understory: The trees and shrubs between the forest canopy and the ground cover.

V

Vertebra (pl. vertebrae): A component of the vertebral column, or backbone, found in vertebrates.

Vertebrate: An animal having a spinal column (backbone).

Vocalization: Sound made by vibration of the vocal tract.

Vulnerable: An IUCN category referring to a species that faces a high risk of extinction.

W

Wattle: A fold of skin, often brightly colored, that hangs from the throat area.

Wetlands: Areas that are wet or covered with water for at least part of the year and support aquatic plants, such as marshes, swamps, and bogs.

Wingbars: Stripes of coloration on the wing.

Wingspan: The distance from wingtip to wingtip when the wings are extended in flight.

X

Xeric forest: Forest adapted to very dry conditions.

Z

Zygodactyl: Two pairs of toes, with two toes pointing forward and two toes facing backward.

Getting to Know Birds

FEATHERS

It is easy to tell that an animal is a bird. If it has feathers, it is one of the more than 8,600 kinds of birds in the world. Birds can also be recognized by their bills, wings, and two legs, but feathers are what make them different from every other animal.

First feathers

Scientists are not sure when feathers first appeared on animals. They might have begun as feather-like scales on some of the dinosaurs. In 1861, fossils of a feathered animal, *Archaeopteryx* (ar-key-OP-tuh-rix), were found in Germany. These are the first animals known to scientists that were covered with feathers. These crow-sized animals with heads like lizards lived on the Earth about 150 million years ago.

How birds use different types of feathers

Feathers in most birds' wings and tail help them fly. Each of these flight feathers has a stiff shaft that goes from one end to the other. Flight feathers are light, but they are surprisingly strong. Birds that can fly can escape enemies and get to food sources and nesting places they wouldn't be able to walk to.

Feathers have many other uses in addition to flight. The outer feathers on a bird's body give it color and shape and help to waterproof the bird. Outer feathers with patterns are useful for camouflaging some birds, and colorful feathers send messages. For example, male birds show off their bright feathers to impress females or wave them as warnings to others. Downy inner feathers trap air to keep the bird warm.

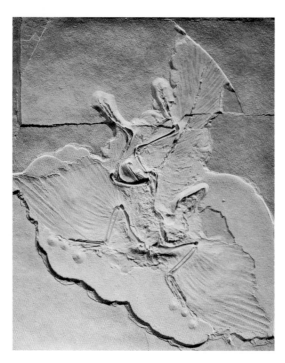

Archaeopteryx is the first animal known to be covered with feathers. (© François Gohier/Photo Researchers, Inc. Reproduced by permission.)

Scientists have names for different types of feathers and also for groups of feathers according to where they grow on a bird's body.

Flight

Most birds' bodies are built for flight. Air sacs in their chests and hollow bones keep them light. They have powerful chest muscles that move their wings. The wing and tail feathers are tough, and birds can turn some of them for steering. A bird usually shuts its wing feathers to trap the air as its wings go down. This lifts the bird into the air and pushes it forward. Then, as it raises the wings, it fans the feathers open to let the air through.

How birds fly depends somewhat on the shape of their wings. Vultures and seabirds have long, narrow wings that are great for soaring high on air currents or gliding over the ocean. Songbirds have short, broad wings that are made for flapping as the birds fly among trees. Falcons have narrow, pointed wings that curve backward. These wings help them fly fast and steer well. But all birds flap their wings at times and glide at other times, depending on what they are doing and how the wind is blowing.

Some birds use their wings in unusual ways. Hummingbirds can flap their wings about fifty times every second. This allows them to hover at one spot as they lap nectar from flowers. Flipper-like wings help penguins to "fly" through the water, and even ostriches use their wings to keep their balance as they run.

The wing of a bird is rounded on top and flat on the bottom, similar to the wing of an airplane. This shape is what gives the bird the lift it needs to stay up in the air.

Birds take off and land facing the wind. Small birds (up to the size of pigeons) can jump up from the ground and fly right off into the air. Larger birds have to jump off something high or run along the ground or the water to get going.

BIRDS' BODIES

Different, but the same

A 400-pound (181-kilogram) ostrich may seem very different from a tiny bee hummingbird that weighs less than an ounce (about 2 grams). But all birds have many things in common besides having feathers. They have bills, two legs, a backbone, they are warm-blooded (keep an even body temperature), and they lay hard-shelled eggs.

Body shapes

Birds have many different shapes. Wading birds such as flamingos have long necks and long legs. Eagles have short necks and legs. But both kinds of birds are able to find their food in the water. Falcons and penguins have sleek, torpedo-shaped bodies that are perfect for catching speedy prey. Turkeys' heavier bodies are just right for their quiet lives in the forest searching for acorns and insects.

Bill shapes

Bird bills come in a wide variety of shapes. They use their bills to gather food, build nests, fix their feathers, feed their young, attract mates, and attack their enemies. The type of food a bird eats depends on its bills' shape. For example, the sturdy bills of sparrows are good for cracking seeds, and hawks' hooked beaks are perfect for tearing up prey.

Legs and feet

Bird legs and feet fit their many different lifestyles. For example, hawks have sharp talons for hunting and ducks have webbed feet to help them swim. Some of the birds that spend most of their lives in the air or on the water are not good at walking. Most birds have four toes, but some have three, and ostriches have only two.

BIRDS' SENSES

Sight

For most birds, sight is their best sense. They can see much better than humans, and they can see in color, unlike many mammals.

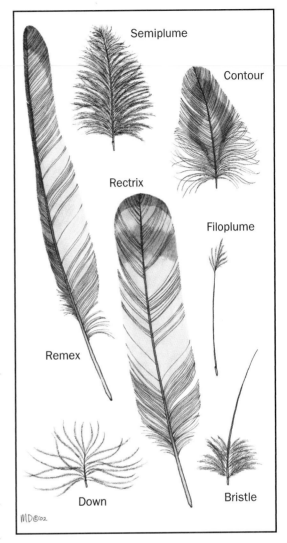

A bird's stiffest feathers are the remex feathers of the wing and the retrix feathers of the tail. The outside of a bird's body is covered with contour feathers that give the body shape and waterproof the bird. Underneath the contour feathers are the semiplume and down feathers that help keep the bird warm. Filoplumes lie alongside the contour feathers and help the bird tell if its feathers are in place. Some birds have bristles around their beaks that allow them to feel insects in the air. (Illustration by Marguette Dongvillo. Reproduced by permission.)

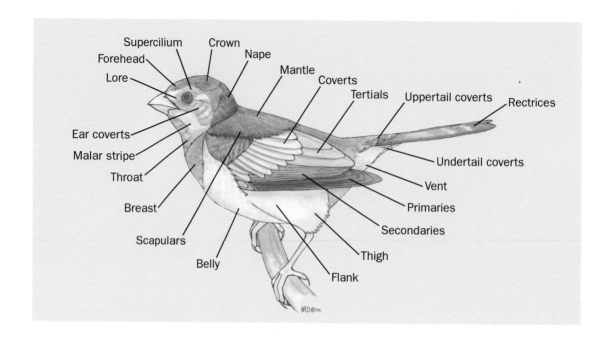

Labels on illustration:
Forehead, Supercilium, Crown, Nape, Mantle, Coverts, Tertials, Uppertail coverts, Rectrices, Lore, Ear coverts, Malar stripe, Throat, Breast, Scapulars, Belly, Flank, Thigh, Secondaries, Primaries, Vent, Undertail coverts

MD©'02

Scientists have names for groups of feathers according to where they grow on a bird's body. (Illustration by Marguette Dongvillo. Reproduced by permission.)

A bird's eyes are big and are usually set on the sides of its head. The eyes focus independently, so that the bird sees two different things at the same time. This gives the bird a very wide view and helps it to watch for predators in most directions. Most birds cannot roll their eyes, but they can turn their heads farther around than mammals can. Owls and other birds of prey have forward-facing eyes that usually work together. This helps them judge distance as they swoop down on prey.

Hearing

Birds have a good sense of hearing—they can hear about as well as mammals. The sound goes in through a little opening near each eye. The holes are usually covered with feathers. They lead to the bird's middle and inner ear, which are very sensitive to sounds. Because owls hunt at night, hearing is especially important to them. Some owls have a disc of stiff feathers on the face. The disc catches sounds, such as the squeaks of a mouse, and leads them to the ears.

Touch

Birds have many nerve endings, which shows that they have a good sense of touch. They can also feel pain, hot, and cold.

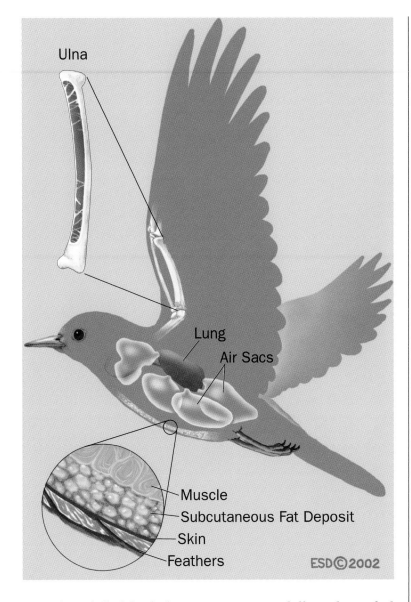

Ulna

Lung

Air Sacs

Muscle

Subcutaneous Fat Deposit

Skin

Feathers

ESD©2002

Birds' bodies have adaptations for flight, including air sacs in the chest and hollow bones to keep them light, and strong chest muscles. (Illustration by Emily Damstra. Reproduced by permission.)

Some long-billed birds have very sensitive bills and can feel their prey in muddy water.

Smell and taste

Most birds' sense of smell seems to be poorly developed. But kiwis, turkey vultures, and several other birds are able to find food by sniffing it. Although birds do not have many taste buds on their tongues, they can often taste well enough to avoid eating harmful foods.

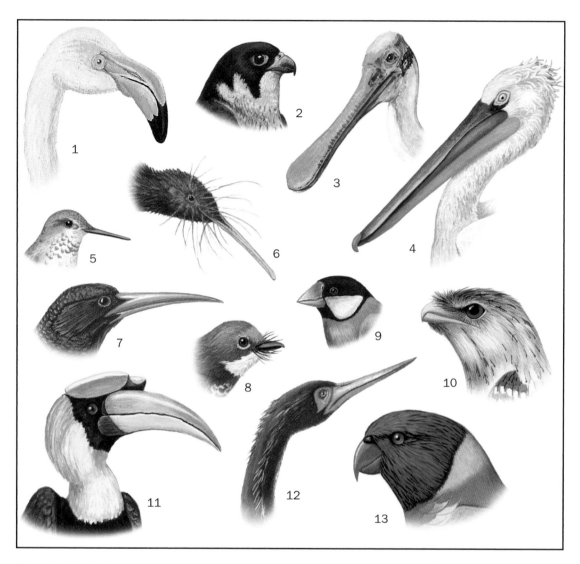

Bills are different shapes and sizes for different eating methods: 1. The greater flamingo filters microorganisms from water; 2. A peregrine falcon tears its prey; 3. Roseate spoonbills sift water for fish; 4. The Dalmation pelican scoops fish in its pouch; 5. Anna's hummingbird sips nectar; 6. The brown kiwi probes the soil for invertebrates; 7. The green woodhoopoe probes bark for insects; 8. Rufous flycatchers catch insects; 9. Java sparrows eat seeds; 10. Papuan frogmouths catch insects; 11. The bicornis hornbill eats fruit; 12. American anhingas spear fish; 13. Rainbow lorikeets crack nuts. (Illustration by Jacqueline Mahannah. Reproduced by permission.)

WHAT'S INSIDE?

Organs and muscles

Birds have many of the same organs that humans have, but they have special features that help with flight and keep them light. Their biggest, strongest muscles control their wings. Birds

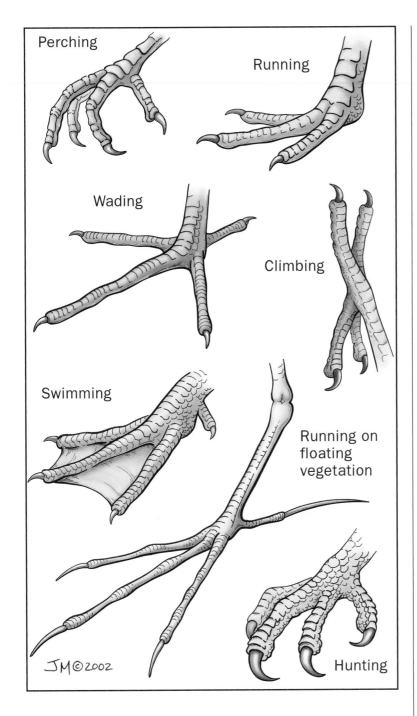

Perching

Running

Wading

Climbing

Swimming

Running on floating vegetation

Hunting

JM©2002

The number of toes, and the arrangement of their toes and feet fit birds' different lifestyles. (Illustration by Jacqueline Mahannah. Reproduced by permission.)

When a bird perches, its ankle
bends and contracts (pulls
together) the tendons in its
foot, forcing its foot to close
around the perch (B).
(Illustration by Jacqueline
Mahannah. Reproduced by
permission.)

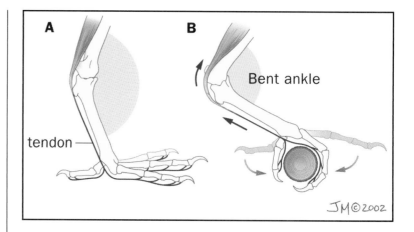

do not have a heavy jaw with teeth to grind their food. Instead, it is ground up in a muscular stomach called a gizzard, and they swallow gravel to help with the grinding. To get the energy they need for flight, birds digest their food quickly. Their fast digestion also keeps them from being weighed down for long by the food they have eaten.

Skeleton

A birds' skeleton is strong, even though it light. Many of the bones are hollow, and some of them are joined together to give the skeleton extra strength. (Loons and other diving birds have some solid bones to help the birds sink in the water.) The breastbone, or sternum, of a flying bird has a part called the keel. The bird's big flight muscles are attached to the keel. What looks like a backward-bending knee on a bird is really its ankle. The bird's knee is hidden high up inside its body feathers.

Body temperature

Birds are warm-blooded, which means their bodies stay at an even temperature no matter how warm or cold it is outside. They make their own heat from the food that they eat. Some birds cope with cold weather by growing extra feathers or a layer of fat, fluffing their feathers to trap more air, and huddling together with other birds. When birds can't find enough food to keep warm, they fly to warmer places. In hot weather, they cool down by panting, swimming in cool water, sitting in the shade, and raising their wings to catch a breeze.

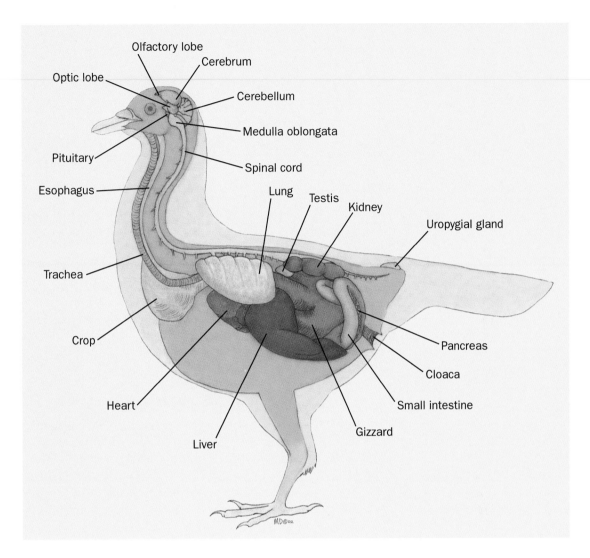

Labels on illustration:

Olfactory lobe
Cerebrum
Optic lobe
Cerebellum
Medulla oblongata
Pituitary
Spinal cord
Esophagus
Lung
Testis
Kidney
Uropygial gland
Trachea
Crop
Heart
Liver
Gizzard
Small intestine
Cloaca
Pancreas

MD©'02

FAMILY LIFE

Singing

Singing is one of the most important ways that songbirds communicate. Birds do not sing just because they are happy. Instead, a male songbird sings to say that he "owns" a certain territory, and he warns birds of the same species to stay away. Songbirds do not have to see each other to know who is nearby. Birds can recognize the songs of their neighbors, because each bird of the same species sounds a little different. Male birds show off to females by singing the most complicated songs they can. Often the best singers are the strongest, healthiest males.

Though birds may look different on the outside, they have the same organs on the inside. (Illustration by Marguette Dongvillo. Reproduced by permission.)

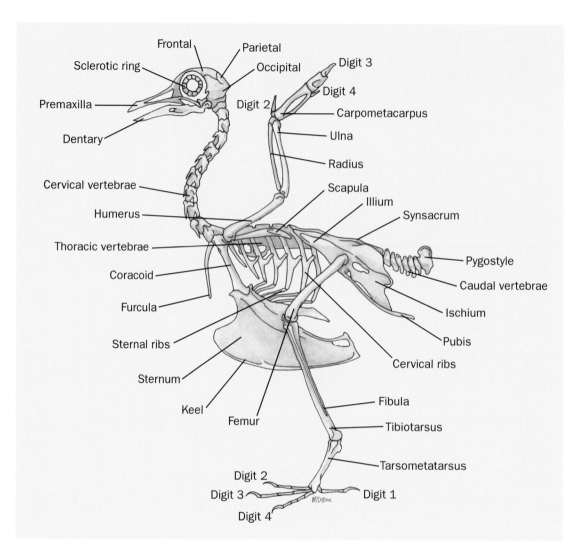

Frontal　　　Parietal
Sclerotic ring
　　　　　　　　　　Occipital
　　　　　　　　　　　　　Digit 3
　　　　　　　　　　　　　Digit 4
Premaxilla　　　　　Digit 2
　　　　　　　　　　　Carpometacarpus
Dentary
　　　　　　　　　　　Ulna
　　　　　　　　　　　Radius
Cervical vertebrae
　　　　　　　　　Scapula
Humerus　　　　　Illium
　　　　　　　　　　　　Synsacrum
Thoracic vertebrae
Coracoid　　　　　　　　　　　Pygostyle
　　　　　　　　　　　　　Caudal vertebrae
Furcula
　　　　　　　　　　　　　Ischium
Sternal ribs
　　　　　　　　　　　　　Pubis
Sternum　　　　　　　Cervical ribs
Keel　　　　　　　Fibula
Femur　　　　　Tibiotarsus
　　　　　　　　　Tarsometatarsus
Digit 2
Digit 3　　　　　　Digit 1
Digit 4

Birds have a strong, light skeleton. (Illustration by Marguette Dongvillo. Reproduced by permission.)

When a female songbird hears her mate singing, her brain tells her body to make hormones (special chemicals). These hormones make eggs start to grow inside her body.

Other ways birds communicate

Singing is just one of the many ways that birds communicate with each other. They have warning calls that tell other birds that a predator is nearby. They chirp to say, "I am here, where are you?" And young birds sometimes beg noisily to be fed. At breeding time, birds have a variety of courtships displays that ask, "Will you be mine?" and state, "We belong together." These include bowing, flight displays, and calling together. Male birds

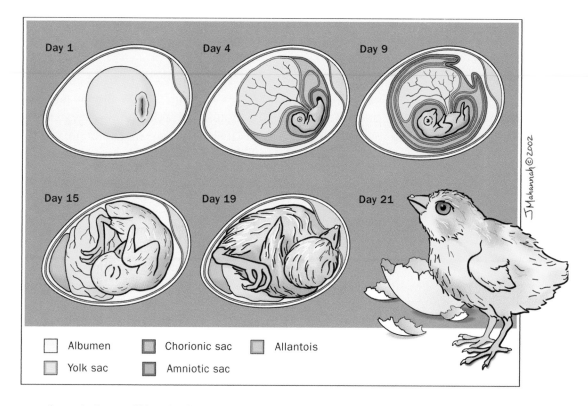

Day 1   Day 4   Day 9

Day 15   Day 19   Day 21

J.Mahannah © 2002

- [ ] Albumen
- [ ] Chorionic sac
- [ ] Allantois
- [ ] Yolk sac
- [ ] Amniotic sac

parade and show off bright feathers or blow up colorful throat sacs to impress females.

Nests

When a bird has found a mate, it is nest-building time. Birds lay their hard-shelled eggs where they can be protected from predators and rain. There are many different kinds of nests. Some birds lay their eggs right on the ground or on the sides of cliffs, some use tree holes or burrows, and some weave complicated stick nests. A few kinds of birds even bury their eggs in mounds of soil and leaves.

Eggs and hatching

Eggs come in many different sizes and colors. Those laid on the ground usually have camouflage colors, and eggs laid in hidden places are often white. The female bird usually incubates the eggs (keeps them warm), especially if she has duller, harder-to-see feathers than the male. Sometimes males and females take turns, and occasionally the males incubate by themselves. Some birds, such as cowbirds, lay their eggs in the nests of other bird species and let the other birds incubate them.

An egg is a perfect package for the chick developing inside it. The albumen (egg white) and yolk provide all the food and water it needs, and are used up as the bird develops. Air moves in and out through hundreds of tiny holes in the shell. Waste from the developing chick is stored in a sac called the allantois (uh-LAN-tuh-wus). The chorionic (kor-ee-AHN-ik) sac lines the inside of the shell, and the amniotic sac surrounds the chick. Time spent in the egg is different for each species, but for this chick, feathers have started to grow by Day 15, and the chick begins making noises by Day 19. There is a little egg tooth on the tip of the chick's bill that it uses to break out of the shell on Day 21. (Illustration by Jacqueline Mahannah. Reproduced by permission.)

Growth of young birds

There are two main types of newly hatched birds. Young chickens, ducks, geese, turkeys, and ostriches are precocial (pre-KOH-shul). Precocial chicks are covered with down feathers and can run or swim after their parents soon after hatching. Before long, they learn to find their own food, but the parents usually protect them for a while longer. Altricial (al-TRISH-ul) birds are helpless when they hatch. Songbirds, seabirds, owls, parrots, and woodpeckers are some of the altricial birds. They are naked, blind, and weak, and they need to be fed by adults at least until they leave the nest.

HABITATS, HABITS, AND PEOPLE

Surviving in a habitat

In order to live in a habitat, birds need food, water, and shelter (such as a hedge to hide in). At breeding time, they also need a place to raise their young. Many different kinds of birds can live in the same habitat because they eat different foods and nest in different places. Some birds, such as crows, can often adapt to changes in their habitat, but other birds are very particular and have to leave if something changes.

Staying alive and keeping fit

Birds have to have their feathers in flying shape at all times so that they can escape predators. Well-cared-for feathers are also necessary for keeping the birds warm and waterproof. Birds often have to stop what they are doing and take time out to fix their messed-up feathers. Sometimes they start with a bath. But they always finish by preening. To preen, the birds nibble along each feather to remove dirt and tiny pests. Most birds also get oil on their beaks from a gland near their tails. They spread the oil on each feather and straighten it by zipping it through their beaks. The oil keeps the feathers from drying out and waterproofs them. When a feather gets too worn, it either falls out or gets pushed out by a new feather growing in its place.

Migration

Migration is one way birds cope with natural changes in their habitats. When the weather gets cold and insects get scarce in fall, for example, insect-eating birds fly to warmer places where

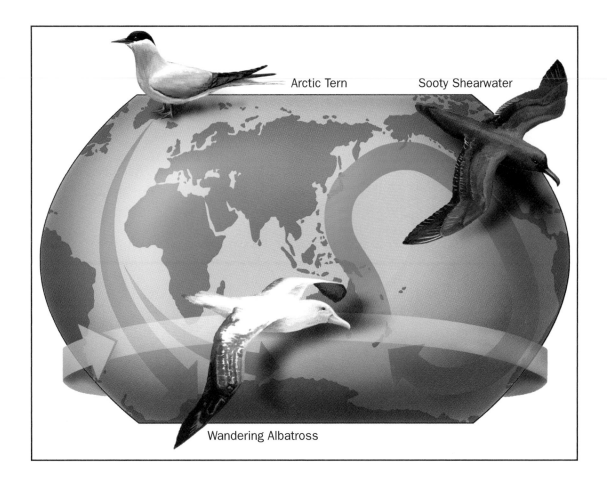

Arctic Tern   Sooty Shearwater

Wandering Albatross

they will be able to find the food they need. Their bodies are programmed to tell them that when the days start getting shorter, they have to eat more so they will have enough fuel for the journey. They follow the same migration routes year after year, and they know the general direction they should go and where to stop. The migrating birds are guided by the stars and by the direction the sun moves across the sky. Birds have a built-in compass and are able to follow magnetic fields in the earth. Some birds also rely on landmarks such as rivers and mountains to follow, and some may use sounds and smells to help them find their way.

Birds and people

Birds are some of the most visible wild animals on Earth, and they play an important part in people's lives. Humans

Seabirds have some of the longest migrations. The arctic tern migrates about 25,000 miles (40,000 kilometers) round-trip each year. The sooty shearwater breeds around New Zealand and the southern tip of South America and migrates in the spring to the northern Pacific and Atlantic Oceans. The wandering albatross moves around the Earth from west to east over the oceans south of the tips of the southern continents. (Illustration by Emily Damstra. Reproduced by permission.)

learned about flight from birds, they eat birds and their eggs, and they keep birds as pets. They appreciate the way birds eat insect pests and weed seeds, and they enjoy watching and listening to birds. Sometimes people kill the birds that eat fish or destroy their crops. People have also harmed birds unintentionally by polluting their habitats or turning them into farms and cities.

Humans now take the disappearance of birds from an area as a warning—there may be harmful poisons in the air or water. Many people are working hard to preserve natural places for birds and all wild animals. They are also having some success with fixing habitats that have been destroyed, but fixing them is much harder than preserving them in the first place.

FOR MORE INFORMATION

Books

Johnson, Jinny. *Children's Guide to Birds*. New York: Simon & Schuster, 1996.

MacKay, Barry Kent. *Bird Sounds*. Mechanicsburg, PA: Stackpole Books, 2001.

Markle, Sandra. *Outside and Inside Birds*. New York: Bradbury Press, 1994.

Perrins, Christopher M. *The Illustrated Encyclopedia of Birds*. New York: Prentice Hall Press, 1990.

Proctor, Noble S., and Patrick J. Lynch. *Manual of Ornithology, Avian Structure and Function*. New Haven, CT: Yale University Press, 1993.

Reid, Struan. *Bird World*. Brookfield, CT: The Millbrook Press, 1991.

Rupp, Rebecca. *Everything You Never Learned About Birds*. Pownal, VT: Storey Communications, Inc., 1995.

Sibley, David Allen, Chris Elphick, and John B. Dunning, Jr., eds. *National Audubon Society: The Sibley Guide to Bird Life & Behavior*. New York: Alfred A. Knopf, 2001.

Taylor, Kim. *Flight*. New York: John Wiley & sons, Inc., 1992.

Periodicals

Able, Kenneth P. "The Concepts and Terminology of Bird Navigation." *Journal of Aviation Biology* 32 (2000): 174–182.

Berger, Cynthia. "Fluffy, Fancy, Fantastic Feathers." *Ranger Rick* (January 2001): 2–10.

Greij, Eldon. "Happy Returns: Landing Safely Is Every Bit as Tricky as Flying." *Birders World* (February 2003): 58–60.

Kerlinger, Paul. "How High? How High a Bird Flies Depends on the Weather, the Time of Day, Whether Land or Water Lies Below—and the Bird." *Birder's World* (February 2003): 62–65.

Miller, Claire. "Guess Where They Nest." *Ranger Rick* (March 1996): 19–27.

Pennisi, Elizabeth. "Colorful Males Flaunt Their Health." *Science* (April 4, 2003): 29–30.

Web sites

"Act for the Environment." National Wildlife Federation. http://www.nwf.org/action/ (accessed on May 3, 2004).

"All About Birds." Cornell Lab of Ornithology. http://www.birds.cornell.edu/programs/AllAboutBirds/ (accessed on May 3, 2004).

American Bird Conservancy. http://www.abcbirds.org (accessed on May 3, 2004).

American Ornithologists' Union. http://www.aou.org (accessed on May 3, 2004).

"Bird and Wildlife Information Center." National Audubon Society. http://www.audubon.org/educate/expert/index.html (accessed on May 3, 2004).

BirdLife International. http://www.birdlife.net (accessed on May 3, 2004).

"Birdlife Worldwide." Birdlife International. http://www.birdlife.net/worldwide/index.html (accessed on May 3, 2004).

National Audubon Society. http://www.Audubon.org (accessed on May 3, 2004).

National Wildlife Federation. http://www.nwf.org (accessed on May 3, 2004).

The Nature Conservancy. http://nature.org (accessed on May 3, 2004).

MONARCH FLYCATCHERS
Monarchidae

Class: Aves

Order: Passeriformes

Family: Monarchidae

Number of species: 96 species

phylum

class

subclass

order

monotypic order

suborder

▲ **family**

PHYSICAL CHARACTERISTICS

Monarch flycatchers are small to medium birds that are 5 to 21 inches (13 to 53 centimeters) long. Their tails can be relatively short compared to their body length but some species have tails that measure 6 inches (15 centimeters). Monarch flycatchers have wide, bluish gray bills with bristles characteristic of insect eaters. They have short legs, long wings, and sharp, curved claws.

Coloring is often quite striking, with most species having no difference between males and females. In those that do show gender variations in color, many have very dramatic differences.

GEOGRAPHIC RANGE

Monarch flycatchers can be found in southern Africa, India and Southeast Asia, Indonesia, and the southern tip of Saudi Arabia. Indonesia is the home of thirty species that nest in the archipelagoes, or groups of tiny islands.

HABITAT

Monarch flycatchers prefer forest habitats, living in clearings and along the edges of the forest growth. They also can be found nesting in fruit plantations, formal gardens, and parks.

DIET

These birds are insect eaters. Most members of this family catch flying insects on the wing, while in the air. Others, however, will find insects among the leaves of trees and shrubs.

THE GUAM FLYCATCHER AND SNAKES

Guam flycatchers, also known as Guam boatbills, were exterminated, killed off, by the introduction of brown tree snakes. Guam has no native snakes, so these snakes quickly multiplied and began to feed on native birds, including Guam flycatchers. The native birds did not have time to develop a defensive strategy as they would have done if they had been exposed to other predatory snakes in their territories over a long period of time.

BEHAVIOR AND REPRODUCTION

Monarch flycatchers usually mate for life and forage, search for food, alone with their mates. Some prefer the company of small groups of their kind and may even have other birds help a mated pair raise their young. Though most species prefer solitude, the males are noisy and make elaborate displays when they wish to attract mates.

Females lay two to four eggs in small, cup-shaped nests, made of plant fibers, lichens (LIE-kenz), moss, and even spider webs. These nests are anchored in the forks of tree branches. Both parents usually incubate the eggs, or sit on them until they are hatched. After fourteen days, the plain brown chicks hatch. Their striking coloring appears after they molt, shed their feathers.

MONARCH FLYCATCHERS AND PEOPLE

Monarch flycatchers are potential attractions for ecotourism, an industry based on attracting tourists to view birds, animals, and environments.

CONSERVATION STATUS

Five species of monarch flycatcher are Critically Endangered, facing an extremely high risk of extinction in the wild, and six are Vulnerable, facing a high risk of extinction in the wild. Fourteen are Near Threatened, in danger of becoming threatened with extinction, and two are Extinct, no longer exist.

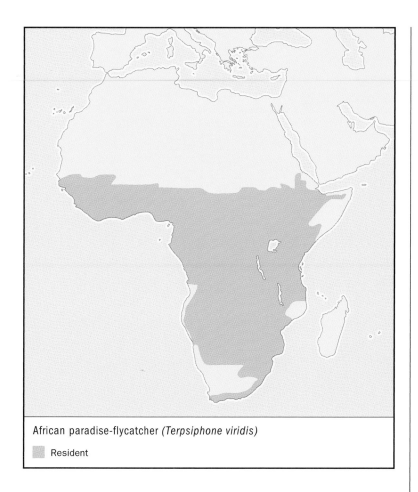

African paradise-flycatcher (*Terpsiphone viridis*)

▨ Resident

AFRICAN PARADISE-FLYCATCHER
Terpsiphone viridis

Physical characteristics: African paradise-flycatchers are the largest paradise-flycatchers in Africa. They have a tail that is twice as long as their body. The head and crest are bluish black, and they have a bright blue ring around the eye. The back and the outside of their tails are reddish brown, with a gray belly. There is either a black or a white stripe on each wing, depending on the subspecies. The tail has two long white feathers that can be as long as 3.5 inches (9 centimeters) in the male. Females have similar coloring but are duller than and not as glossy as males. Subspecies that live in savanna

The African paradise-flycatcher's tail is twice as long as its body. (© W. Tarboton/VIREO. Reproduced by permission.)

woodlands, characterized by thorny scrub, mopane trees, and grass, are usually all black or all white.

Geographic range: The African paradise-flycatcher is found only in sub-Saharan Africa.

Habitat: Very adaptable, African paradise-flycatchers can be found in almost every habitat in their region, except where it is very dry. They avoid dense forest but will nest along the forest edge, in clearings, and in savanna woodlands. Sometimes the birds are found in orchards, parks, and gardens as high up as 8,200 feet (2,500 meters). Some populations will move from one habitat to another during the dry season.

Diet: These birds eat insects, especially flying ants, termites, butterflies, moths, beetles, and caterpillars.

Behavior and reproduction: African paradise-flycatchers grab flying insects on the wing, and will perch and dive to capture food. Some subspecies search for insects among the leaves of trees, flitting, moving about rapidly, from branch to branch. Rather solitary, they are found alone or in pairs. Males defend their territory at sunrise and sunset with loud songs and calls. Males also use their long tail and crest as courtship displays to attract a female. Sometimes, males will shiver their wings and do a dance on a branch. The female lays two to three white eggs in a cup-shaped nest that is anchored to the fork of a branch with spider webs. Both the male and the female incubate the eggs for fifteen days. The young birds are fed by the parents for eleven to fifteen days, but stay nearby for another week.

African paradise-flycatchers and people: Because of their striking beauty, African paradise-flycatchers are potential attractions for ecotourism.

Conservation status: African paradise-flycatchers are quite common throughout Africa and their numbers are healthy. However African paradise-flycatchers in East Africa are rapidly disappearing due to the population explosion of crows, which were imported into the country in 1891. Crow numbers have become so large that in Dar es Salaam, the capital of Tanzania, alone there are nearly 500,000 crows. These birds attack native birds, livestock, and domestic pets. Crows attack African paradise-flycatchers outright and eat them. Working in pairs, one crow often distracts the bird away from its nest while another crow steals the eggs. African flycatchers are no longer found in the city. Though African paradise-flycatcher numbers elsewhere are numerous, they will become even more threatened as the crows move inland. ■

Black-naped monarch (*Hypothymis azurea*)

Resident

BLACK-NAPED MONARCH
Hypothymis azurea

Physical characteristics: Also called Pacific monarchs, black-naped monarchs are only 6 inches (16 centimeters) long. Their legs and feet are so weak they sit in a squatting pose when they perch. Both the male and the female have bright blue coloring on their heads, necks, backs, and chests, with grayish white bellies. Females, though blue, have grayish brown tones on their backs and more blue on their tails and wings. Males also have a round black spot on the back of their head, or nape. The Chinese name for this bird means, "black pillow," and refers to this black spot. In addition, males have a black stripe that encircles their throat. Because of their small size and their bright blue coloring, these birds have been nicknamed the "blue fairies of the forest."

Most black-naped monarchs prefer the lower to middle levels of the forest canopy and nest close to the ground, but the population in Taiwan prefers the upper and middle levels of the forest canopy and are not usually seen on the ground. (Illustration by Emily Damstra. Reproduced by permission.)

Geographic range: This species can be found in India, Southeast Asia, southern China, Taiwan, the Philippines, and Indonesia.

Habitat: Black-naped monarchs are common in mixed forests of pine and hardwoods below 4,265 feet (1,300 meters), as well as in stands of bamboo in river valleys. Though many black-naped monarchs prefer the lower to middle levels of the forest canopy and will nest close to the ground, the population in Taiwan prefers the upper and middle levels of the forest canopy and are not usually seen on the ground. They will migrate to cooler, higher elevations when the temperatures get too warm.

Diet: Black-naped monarchs eat insects, including butterflies, moths, and crickets.

Behavior and reproduction: The call of the black-naped monarch is a series of short whistles or trills. Sometimes, they give out loud chirps when they vocalize.

Territorial birds, they remain close to their ranges in pairs or alone. They will gather in small flocks or with other species when it is not mating season. These birds begin searching for mates at the end of the spring and on through the middle of summer. Females lay two to three cream or buff eggs that have reddish brown spots in their deep woven nests. Built into the forks of tree branches, these nests are made of plant materials, bark, moss, and spider webs.

Black-naped monarchs and people: These birds have no special significance to people.

Conservation status: Black-naped monarchs are very common and are not threatened with extinction. ■

FOR MORE INFORMATION

Books:

Barlow, Clive, and Tim Wacher. *A Field Guide to the Birds of the Gambia and Senegal.* New Haven, CT and London: Yale University Press, 1998.

Perrins, Christopher. *Firefly Encyclopedia of Birds.* Richmond Hill, Canada: Firefly Books, 2003.

Robbins, Michael. *Birds: Fandex Family Field Guides.* New York: Workman Publishing Company, 1998.

Urban, E. K., H. D. Fry, and S. Keith. *The Birds of Africa,* vol. 5. London: Academic Press, 1997.

Weidensaul, Scott. *Birds: National Audubon Society First Field Guides.* New York: Scholastic Trade, 1998.

Class: Aves
Order: Passeriformes
Family: Petroicidae
Number of species: 35 species

family
CHAPTER

phylum

class

subclass

order

monotypic order

suborder

▲ **family**

PHYSICAL CHARACTERISTICS

Australian robins are small, plump birds with large heads and short tails. They have long legs and strong feet, which allow the birds to have an upright stance. They have small bills with bristles on them, which helps them catch insects. Most of them have short tails, but the scrub robins have longer ones to help them balance as they feed on the ground. The scrub robin is also the only species that nests and forages, searches for food, on the ground.

The coloring of Australian robins differs among species. Some are all black or black with distinctive white stripes on their lower backs. Others are gray with yellow or red undersides. Still others have grayish brown backs and whitish undersides.

GEOGRAPHIC RANGE

Australian robins can be found in India, Southeast Asia, Micronesia, Indonesia, New Zealand, and Australia.

HABITAT

Most Australian robins live in forests and woodlands, but scrub robins live in semi-arid scrub, dry areas with short trees and shrubs. Some species live in mangroves and eucalyptus (yoo-kah-LIP-tus) forests. Some Australian robins can be found nesting in trees and bushes along cultivated fields.

DIET

Australian robins eat insects, spiders, earthworms, and sometimes even leeches, crabs, and mollusks.

FAMILY HISTORY

Australian robins are not related to the robins of the New World, the Western Hemisphere, which are actually thrushes. Though they resemble some Old World flycatchers due to similar adaptations to the environment, they are not related to this family either, nor do they behave like them. They do not normally find their food while they are flying. An ancient family, Australian robins are more closely related to Australian lyrebirds and honeyeaters.

BEHAVIOR AND REPRODUCTION

Australian robins live with a mate or in small family groups. They usually stay within their territories and do not migrate. They may move to a different altitude, which is usually not far away. Their territories can be as small as 1 acre (0.5 hectare) or as large as 10 acres (4 hectares).

The songs of this family are composed of whistling or piping notes. These birds give harsh alarm calls when they feel threatened.

Most Australian robins feed by diving from a perch to grab food they spot on the ground. Scrub robins forage on the ground.

Generally, this species mates for life. Some species allow helpers to raise the young with them. The female builds a cup-shaped nest in the fork of a tree branch. Bark or lichen (LIE-ken) is often placed over the top of the nest in order to hide it from predators, animals that hunt them for food. The female lays one to three eggs and incubates them, or sits on them until they hatch, for fifteen to nineteen days, depending on the species. The male of some species will feed the female while she incubates the eggs. The young are fed by the parents for nine to fourteen days; this also varies among species.

AUSTRALIAN ROBINS AND PEOPLE

Their bright colors and pleasant songs make them popular among bird watchers.

CONSERVATION STATUS

One species is Endangered, facing a very high risk of extinction, or dying out, in the wild. Two subspecies are Vulnerable, facing a high risk of extinction in the wild, and one subspecies is Near Threatened, in danger of becoming threatened with extinction. Many species have experienced declining population due to habitat loss because of extreme clearing of land for agricultural use. Australian robins are also vulnerable to larger birds that prey on them.

Jacky winter *(Microeca fascinans)*

Resident

JACKY WINTER
Microeca fascinans

Physical characteristics: Also called brown flycatchers, jacky winters are part of the subfamily Petroicinae. They are 5 to 5.5 inches (12.5 to 14 cm) long and weigh 0.5 to 0.65 ounces (14 to 18 grams). These birds have sand colored crowns and backs, white and brownish gray wings and tails, and white throats and undersides. Their eyes are striking, bearing a white ring over their eyes. A stripe that looks like the stroke of an artist's paintbrush in black runs from the beak, over the eye, and to the edge of the white eye ring.

Geographic range: Jacky winters are found in Australia and around Port Moresby in New Guinea. They occupy nearly all of Australia except for the desert regions, Tasmania, Kangaroo Island, and Cape York in the north.

Jacky winters usually dive for insects from a perch and take them either on the wing while in the air or by scooping them up as they fly low over the ground. (Illustration by Emily Damstra. Reproduced by permission.)

Habitat: Jacky winters prefer woodlands and scrub where there are trees and an abundance of insects. They will nest in gardens and on the edges of farmlands.

Diet: These birds eat flying insects, beetles, worms, and insect larvae (LAR-vee), the newly hatched wingless form of insects.

Behavior and reproduction: Jacky winters are not noisy birds. They stay within their local territories and often can be heard singing their repeated "peter-peter" or "jacky-jacky" songs or making whistling calls. They will often wag their tails from side to side or spread their tail feathers as a display when they feel threatened.

Jacky winters dive for insects from a perch and take them either on the wing while in the air or by scooping them up as they fly low over the ground. Sometimes, they will stand and pounce onto their food.

This species mates in the spring and summer months of the Southern Hemisphere, July through December. The female lays two to three light blue eggs that are blotched with lavender and brown. The nest, made of grass and roots, is built in a fork of a branch of a tree that is either living or dead. The eggs are incubated for sixteen to seventeen days. Both parents feed the young birds for fourteen to seventeen days.

Jacky winters and people: Jacky winters are popular songbirds among birdwatchers.

Conservation status: Jacky winters are quite common, and their numbers are generally healthy. However, in farming areas, their populations are declining as native vegetation is cleared for more agricultural use. ∎

Southern scrub robin *(Drymodes brunneopygia)*

Resident

SOUTHERN SCRUB ROBIN
Drymodes brunneopygia

Physical characteristics: The southern scrub robin is 8 to 9 inches (21 to 23 centimeters) long and weighs 1.25 to 1.35 ounces (36 to 38 grams). They have white to buff bellies with dark brown wings and white tipped tails. The wings have light grayish brown undersides.

Geographic range: This species lives in extreme southwestern Australia, along the south central coast into Victoria, and the southwestern part of New South Wales.

Habitat: As their name suggests, southern scrub robins live in the semi-arid scrub forests along the southern regions of Australia. Some populations live in the tea tree thickets along the southern coast. They also can be found in eucalyptus groves and acacia (uh-KAY-shah), short thorny shrubs and trees, scrub.

The southern scrub robin female builds a cup-shaped nest on or near the ground. Females lay one egg and incubate it. Both parents feed the young birds for nine to twelve days. (Illustration by Emily Damstra. Reproduced by permission.)

Diet: Southern scrub robins eat primarily insects, especially beetles, termites, and ants. Occasionally, they will eat fruit from low bushes.

Behavior and reproduction: Southern scrub robins find insects on the ground, foraging through leaf litter.

These birds are territorial and very shy. Their call is either a soft "pee, pee" or a more musical "chip, chip, par-ee."

The southern scrub robin mates in Australia's spring and summer from July to December. The female builds a cup-shaped nest on or near the ground. Females lay one pale green egg, blotched with black and brown and incubate it for sixteen days. Both parents feed the young birds for nine to twelve days. If threatened, the male will whistle and draw predators away from the nest and the eggs or young.

Southern scrub robins and people: There is no known significance between southern scrub robins and people.

Conservation status: This species is quite common and is not threatened. Their numbers, however, have declined because of extensive land clearing for agricultural use. ■

FOR MORE INFORMATION

Books:

Higgins, P. J., and J. M. Peter, eds. *Handbook of Australian New Zealand and Antarctic Birds: Pardalotes to Shrike-thrushes.* Melbourne: Oxford University Press, 2003.

Perrins, Christopher. *Firefly Encyclopedia of Birds.* Richmond Hill, Canada: Firefly Books, 2003.

Robbins, Michael. *Birds: Fandex Family Field Guides.* New York: Workman Publishing Company, 1998.

Schodde, R. *Directory of Australian Birds: Passerines.* Collingwood, Australia: CSIRO Publishing, 1999.

Simpson, K., and N. Day. *A Field Guide to the Birds of Australia.* Ringwood, Australia: Penguin Books Australia Ltd., 1996.

Stattersfield, A. J., David R. Capper, and Guy C. L. Dutson. *Threatened Birds of the World.* Barcelona and Cambridge, U.K.: Lynx Edicions and Birdlife International, 2000.

Weidensaul, Scott. *Birds: National Audubon Society First Field Guides.* New York: Scholastic Trade, 1998.

WHISTLERS

Pachycephalidae

Class: Aves

Order: Passeriformes

Family: Pachycephalidae

Number of species: 52 to 59
species

family

CHAPTER

phylum

class

subclass

order

monotypic order

suborder

▲ family

PHYSICAL CHARACTERISTICS

Whistlers range from 5 to 11 inches (12.5 to 28 cm) in length and weigh 0.8 to 3.84 ounces (12.5 to 110 grams). They have sturdy bodies and large, round heads, giving this family of birds the name "thickheads." They have small, round wings and strong feet and legs, making them more suited to hopping about on tree branches, rather than flying and diving. Their bills are thick and strong with a hook at the tip, allowing them to grasp insects and other small invertebrates. Some species have powerful jaws and bills that are shorter and fuller so that they can pry up bark to look for insects. Other species have small crests on the backs of their heads.

Most species are subdued brown, reddish brown, gray, or olive-gray for both males and females. However, there are some species that have bright markings in yellows, whites, and reds for males; females have duller coloring. Young birds are usually reddish brown.

GEOGRAPHIC RANGE

Whistlers are found in Southeast Asia, the Philippines, Indonesia, Micronesia, New Guinea, New Zealand, Australia, and islands in the southwest Pacific. New Guinea and Australia, in particular, have the greatest number of different species in their regions.

HABITAT

Some whistler species live in dense rainforests in the tropics or the forests and woodlands of temperate zones, and others occupy mangrove swamps and mallee, or eucalyptus (yoo-kah-LIP-tus) trees that grow in semi-arid regions. The sandstone shrike-thrush builds its nest on sandstone escarpments, steep cliffs, that have few trees.

DIET

Whistlers eat insects, larvae (LAR-vee), and small invertebrates, animals without a backbone. The white-breasted whistler includes small crabs and mollusks in its diet. The large shrike-thrushes eat small vertebrates, animals with a backbone, baby birds, and eggs. Some birds will take fruit, especially berries, and the mottled whistler eats fruit exclusively.

BEHAVIOR AND REPRODUCTION

Members of this family are called whistlers because their songs are composed of whistling sounds, with each species having a distinctly different variation. The song of the crested bellbird is deep and bell-like. Pitohuis often sing duets. When startled by loud noises like thunder, whistlers will burst into song. They also sing during mating season to mark their territories.

Whistlers forage for insects alone by looking among leaves and bark. Shrike-tits forage in small groups, and pitohuis will congregate with birds of different species or families that look like they do. The crested bellbird and the larger shrike-thrushes find food on the ground and will stand and pounce. The shrike-tits and the ploughbill remove bark from branches and look underneath for insects.

These birds generally stay in their territories. Those along the southeastern coast of Australia, however, will migrate to lower elevations during the winter.

Whistlers choose mates in the dry season and rear their young as the rainy season begins in the Southern Hemisphere's spring and summer. Those species that live in arid areas, however, will mate whenever climate conditions permit.

Males and females share nest-building and child-rearing duties, although this practice varies among species. Some males will even incubate, or sit on the eggs until they hatch. Females in other species will build the nest and incubate the eggs, but will receive help feeding chicks from males and, sometimes, from other members of a group who help with child rearing. This is called cooperative breeding.

Cup or bowl-shaped nests, made from twigs and bark, are built in a tree branch or shrub. In regions with tall forests, the

POISONOUS BIRD

In 1989, biologist Jack Dumbacher recorded the first instance of natural toxicity, or poison, in a bird. The bright orange-and-black hooded pitohui and four others in this genus (JEE-nus), group of related birds, have a neurotoxin, or poison that affects the nerves, in their skin, feathers, and flesh. This neurotoxin produces numbness when touched and is the same poison found in the poison dart frogs of Central and South America. Scientists have not been able to figure out how the birds, or the frogs, make the poison, or how these animals are able to survive with the poison in their systems.

nest can be as high as 33 feet (10 meters) from the ground. In more arid regions where tree growth is limited, the nests will be placed in shrubs and low vegetation within 3 feet (100 centimeters) of the forest floor. The sandstone shrike-thrush, which lives in a region with few trees, will build its nest on a cliff edge or in a rock crevice. Oddly, the crested bellbird places paralyzed caterpillars along the rim of the nest when the eggs are incubated.

Generally, whistlers have only one brood, or set of eggs hatched at the same time, each season, although some species will try to raise two or three. Females lay two to four speckled or blotched eggs that are incubated fourteen to twenty-one days and fed in the nest for fourteen to twenty-one days.

WHISTLERS AND PEOPLE

The whistlers' songs have made them favorites of bird watchers. Some species like the gray shrike-thrush will even build its nest among the foliage of potted plants outside homes.

CONSERVATION STATUS

The piopio is Extinct, or died out. The Sangihe shrike-thrush is Critically Endangered, facing an extremely high risk of extinction, due to loss of its forest habitat on the tiny Indonesian island of Sangihe.

The yellowhead is Vulnerable, facing a high risk of extinction, because its population in New Zealand has been preyed upon by stoats (ermines) that were introduced into the birds' territory. Stoats have eaten not only eggs and newly-hatched birds, but adult females as well.

The red-lored whistler of Australia, the white-bellied pitohui of New Guinea, and the Tongan whistler are Near Threatened, in danger of becoming threatened with extinction, due to habitat loss and foreign animals that were introduced into whistler territory.

Golden whistler (*Pachycephala pectoralis*)

- Resident

GOLDEN WHISTLER
Pachycephala pectoralis

Physical characteristics: Also called the golden-breasted whistler, this bird is small, measuring 5.9 to 7.5 inches (15 to 19 centimeters) and weighing 0.8 to 0.96 ounces (21 to 28 grams). It has a black bill, head, and band below a white throat. The back and wings of the male are olive green, and the undersides are sulfur yellow. The female has a muted olive gray body with a pale yellow belly. Both sexes have reddish brown eyes. Young birds of both sexes are reddish, changing to the muted colors of the female. When they are fully mature, male birds will display bright plumage.

Geographic range: Over seventy subspecies of golden whistlers live in Indonesia, New Guinea, Tasmania, and the southern and eastern coasts of Australia, as well as small Pacific Islands such as Fiji and the Solomon Islands.

Habitat: Golden whistlers have adapted to a variety of habitats that support trees, ranging from the dry mallee to the wet mangrove

Both golden whistler parents feed their chicks after they've hatched. (© Eric Lindgren/Photo Researchers, Inc. Reproduced by permission.)

swamps. Occasionally, these birds will occupy trees in orchards and parks. Golden whistlers nest below 6,900 feet (2,100 meters).

Diet: This species eats mainly insects, spiders, and berries.

Behavior and reproduction: Golden whistlers mate in the spring of the southern hemisphere, September to January, and only have one brood. Both the male and the female build a cup-shaped nest from bark and twigs, lashed together with spider webs and lined with fine grass. Placed in the fork of a branch or nestled deep in a shrub, the nest can be as high up as 20 feet (6 meters). The female lays one to three spotted eggs of varying colors. The eggs can be cream, buff, salmon, or pale olive green with spots or blotches of greenish brown, or reddish brown, gray, or lavender. Sometimes, these blotches collect around the larger end of the egg like a cap. Both parents incubate the eggs, usually fourteen to seventeen days. The young birds are fed by their parents for ten to thirteen days.

This species forages among tree branches in the middle story of the forest canopy, only searching the lower level when necessary. Sometimes, golden whistlers will hawk, or dive, for insects they see, but usually they settle on a branch and glean insects and berries from their perches.

These birds are quiet, except when mating, and are not social, living alone or with a mate. Their song is melodious "wi-wi-wi-tu-whit." Generally, they stay within their territories, though some southeastern

Australian birds will migrate to the north or west during the winter or descend to lower elevations.

Golden whistlers and people: The golden whistler is appreciated by bird watchers.

Conservation status: Though this species was once quite common, it is now a protected bird in some areas of Australia and efforts are being made to ensure that these birds can increase their population numbers.

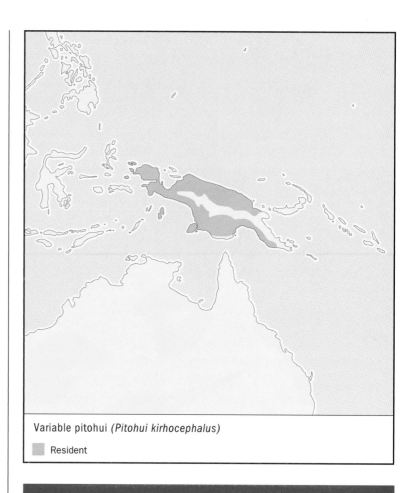

Variable pitohui *(Pitohui kirhocephalus)*

Resident

VARIABLE PITOHUI
Pitohui kirhocephalus

Physical characteristics: A medium-sized bird, the variable pitohui is 9 to 10 inches (23 to 25.5 cm) long and weighs 3 to 3.5 ounces (85 to 100 grams). It has a black head and wings, a reddish back, an orange breast and belly, and black legs. This general coloring, however, varies among its twenty subspecies.

Geographic range: This species can be found in New Guinea and neighboring islands.

Habitat: The variable pitohui nests in thick undergrowth at the edge of forests up to 4,950 feet (1,500 meters). It can even live in forests that have been greatly disturbed.

Although it generally hides in dense vegetation with its mate, the variable pitohui will forage with other birds, including birds of other species. (Illustration by Emily Damstra. Reproduced by permission.)

Diet: This species eats insects and berries.

Behavior and reproduction: Though it generally hides in dense vegetation with its mate, the variable pitohui will forage with other birds, including many that aren't its own species. Its song is musical and pleasant. Mated pairs will often sing duets together. Little is known about the mating behavior of this species.

The variable pitohui and people: This bird has been rarely hunted for food because of its unpleasant taste. In some cases, it is extremely poisonous.

Conservation status: The variable pitohui is not in danger of dying out. However, it is common in some areas, and rare in others.   ∎

FOR MORE INFORMATION

Books:

Higgins, P. J., and J. M. Peter, eds. *Handbook of Australian, New Zealand and Antarctic Birds.* Vol. 6, *Pardalotes to Shrike-thrushes.* Melbourne: Oxford University Press, 2003.

Perrins, Christopher. *Firefly Encyclopedia of Birds.* Richmond Hill, Canada: Firefly Books, 2003.

Robbins, Michael. *Birds (Fandex Family Field Guides).* New York: Workman Publishing Company, 1998.

Schodde, R. *Directory of Australian Birds: Passerines.* Collingwood, Australia: CSIRO, 1999.

Simpson, K., and N. Day. *A Field Guide to the Birds of Australia.* Ringwood, Australia: Penguin Books Australia Ltd., 1996.

Weidensaul, Scott. *Birds (National Audubon Society First Field Guides).* New York: Scholastic Trade, 1998.

PSEUDO BABBLERS
Pomatostomidae

Class: Aves

Order: Passeriformes

Family: Pomatostomidae

Number of species: 5 species

family

C H A P T E R

PHYSICAL CHARACTERISTICS

Pseudo babblers are medium-sized birds, measuring 7 to 10.5 inches (18 to 27 centimeters) long, and weighing 1.6 to 3.2 ounces (45 to 90 grams). They have short wings, long fan-shaped tails, and thin, pointed bills that are ideal for probing and digging into the ground or bark. Their long, powerful legs and dark, strong feet allow them to hop for long periods along the forest floor and among low tree branches. Their bodies are mainly a solid rust color or a dull brown highlighted with white brows, throat, and tail tip. There is no difference in color between males and females or between young and mature birds. The only change that comes with adulthood is a longer bill. The rufous babbler and the gray-crowned babbler, however, change the color of their eyes on adulthood, from the normally brown eyes of this family of birds to pale cream.

GEOGRAPHIC RANGE

Australia and lowland New Guinea.

HABITAT

Pseudo babblers of New Guinea live in regions up to 1,500 feet (500 meters). Members of this family can also be found in the western Papuan Islands and throughout Australia. They avoid the desert regions of the central and northwest and the southeastern and southwestern seacoasts. Mostly, pseudo babblers forage under eucalyptus (yoo-kah-LIP-tus) trees and in clearings among acacia (uh-KAY-shah) trees. In New Guinea, they occupy rainforests. Where the foraging territories overlap,

phylum

class

subclass

order

monotypic order

suborder

▲ **family**

COMMUNAL BREEDING

The survival of the gray-crowned babbler depends on the number of helper birds in each social group. These birds are critical to the rearing of the young and the defense of the group's territory. Helpers in these social groups usually are the siblings of the primary mating pair or the pair's own grown offspring. Unlike bees, which also have a highly developed social structure, helper birds are able to breed and do so when the primary pair has died and a new primary pair takes over leadership of the group.

different species of pseudo babblers do not divide the resources between groups; they openly compete for the same foods in the same areas.

DIET

This family of birds eats mainly insects and spiders but sometimes will eat seeds, buds, and fruit, and even small reptiles.

BEHAVIOR AND REPRODUCTION

Social birds, pseudo babblers live and forage in communal groups of twelve or more birds. These groups consist of one primary breeding pair, their offspring, and even their siblings. They will roost, feed, rest, and preen together. They constantly call out to each other as they move about the forest floor as if to keep in hearing range of one another. At night, they all cluster together in large, sturdy dormitory nests to sleep.

These birds forage in permanent territories of approximately 124 acres (50 hectares), using their long bills to shift through the litter on the forest floor. Sometimes, they will dig into the ground or poke into the trunks and branches of trees. If they find a large insect or small reptile, they will share the food with the group.

Depending on the location and the species, breeding occurs in the spring and early summer of the Southern Hemisphere. In New Guinea, however, breeding occurs whenever the conditions within the region can support the young. The primary breeding pair builds the dome-shaped nest, made from twigs and plant fibers and lined with animal hair and finer plant materials. These nests are constructed in the upper branches of shrubs and trees up to 6.6 to 16.2 feet (2 to 8 meters) above the ground. Rufous babblers in New Guinea anchor their nests on the tips of palm fronds.

The primary female lays two to five pale gray eggs that are covered with dark lines. While she incubates, or sits on the eggs until they hatch, for sixteen to twenty-three days, she is fed by all of the members of the social group. The group will also help feed the young hatchlings for twenty to twenty-one days.

PSEUDO BABBLERS AND PEOPLE

Pseudo babblers have no known significance to humans.

CONSERVATION STATUS

Pseudo babblers in some areas of Australia are threatened, or at a risk of extinction, or dying out. They have disappeared from some regions altogether. This is a result of habitat loss due to clearing land for agriculture and the introduction of invasive plants and livestock grazing.

Gray-crowned babbler *(Pomatostomus temporalis)*

☐ Resident

GRAY-CROWNED BABBLER
Pomatostomus temporalis

Physical characteristics: The gray-crowned babbler is also called the chatterbox, the happy family, the red-breasted cackler, and the happy jack. It is the largest of the pseudo babblers, measuring 9.5 to 10.5 inches (24 to 27 centimeters) long and weighing 2.2 to 3.2 ounces (65 to 90 grams). This bird has a dull brown body with the characteristic pseudo babbler white markings. It displays a reddish patch on its outer wings when it flies, and its undersides range from dull brown to deep russet brown. It has a brown bill, black feet, and pale cream-colored eyes. The back and center crowns of the head are gray, giving the bird one of its names.

Geographic range: The gray-crowned babbler can be found mainly in northern and eastern Australia, and is also located in a small region in southern New Guinea.

Gray-crowned babblers live in groups, and if there are several breeding pairs within the group, they will use the same nest and share incubation duties. (Illustration by Marguette Dongvillo. Reproduced by permission.)

Habitat: The gray-crowned babbler lives in trees of moderate height and sometimes in shrubs. It prefers eucalyptus, cypress, and paperbark trees. Since much of its habitat has been cleared for agriculture, this species has been limited to clusters of trees along roadways in their territories. They stay within these narrow bands of trees because they are not strong fliers and are reluctant to fly over open land.

Diet: This species eats mainly insects.

Behavior and reproduction: The gray-crowned babbler is not afraid of heights. It will forage as far as 66 feet (20 meters) up a tree, turning over leaves and poking into crevices in bark. In drier regions where trees do not grow as tall, this bird will also sift through the litter on the forest floor and even scratch in the dirt, looking for food. Sometimes, it will try to catch flying termites on the wing.

This species is rather social, foraging in groups of twelve to fifteen over 25 to 37 acres (10 to 15 hectares) and sleeping together in dormitory nests. Their loud "yahoo yahoo" calls mark territory but also warn of predators and act as a means of staying in touch with all members of the social group.

These birds find mates not only in the Australian spring and summer, but also in the fall. Two to four eggs are laid in huge, messy, dome-shaped nests made from twigs that are built in the forks of branches of shrubs or trees 9.8 to 32.8 feet (3 to 10 meters) high.

The female incubates the eggs for eighteen to twenty-three days. The young are fed in the nest for twenty to twenty-two days. If there are several breeding pairs within the group, they will use the same nest and share incubation duties. Sometimes, there are as many as ten or more eggs in these communal nests.

Gray-crowned babblers and people: There is no known significance to humans.

Conservation status: The gray-crowned babbler has seriously reduced its numbers and is already extinct in South Australia and in Victoria. Its territory has been reduced because of clearing nearly 90 percent of their habitat for agricultural use and to build roads. Overuse of the land because of irrigation practices has raised the ground water level and caused serious changes in the bird's habitat. In addition, the introduction of invasive weeds and grazing livestock has led to continued destruction of the native vegetation. Complicating this scenario are competitors such as noisy miners that have further stressed the food supply and species including the Australian raven that are competing for nesting sites. Because of these factors that reduce available food sources and restrict nesting to certain areas, population numbers for this species have dropped dramatically since the 1960s. It is, therefore, listed as endangered, or at high risk of becoming extinct, by the Australian government, though it is not listed by the World Conservation Union (IUCN). ■

FOR MORE INFORMATION

Books:

Higgins, P. J., and J. M. Peter, eds. *Handbook of Australian, New Zealand and Antarctic Birds*. Vol. 6, *Pardalotes to Shrike-thrushes*. Melbourne: Oxford University Press, 2003.

Perrins, Christopher. *Firefly Encyclopedia of Birds*. Richmond Hill, Canada: Firefly Books, 2003.

Robbins, Michael. *Birds (Fandex Family Field Guides)*. New York: Workman Publishing Company, 1998.

Schodde, R. *Directory of Australian Birds: Passerines*. Collingwood, Australia: CSIRO, 1999.

Simpson, K., and N. Day. *A Field Guide to the Birds of Australia*. Ringwood, Australia: Penguin Books Australia Ltd., 1996.

Weidensaul, Scott. *Birds (National Audubon Society First Field Guides)*. New York: Scholastic Trade, 1998.

AUSTRALIAN CREEPERS
Climacteridae

Class: Aves
Order: Passeriformes
Family: Climacteridae
Number of species: 8 species

PHYSICAL CHARACTERISTICS

Australian creepers, or treecreepers, tend to be small birds about the same size as sparrows. They average in length from 5.7 to 6.9 inches (14.5 to 17.5 centimeters), with an average weight of 0.75 to 1.15 ounces (21 to 32 grams). Their legs are short, with long toes that have claws that are curved and long. They have short necks, and long decurved, downward curved, bills. Their color varies from a reddish brown, to brown, to almost black. Each species displays a streak, either white, black, or brown, on their undersides, and display an off-white to rufous, red, bar across their flight feathers that are noticeable when they are in flight. Some species have white throats, for instance, the white-throated treecreeper. Brows range in color from a pale buff, as in the case of the brown treecreeper; to red, in the red-browed treecreeper; to white, as shown in the white-browed treecreeper. The difference between males and females is slight. Orange patches on the neck, throat, or breast usually distinguishes the female from the male.

GEOGRAPHIC RANGE

Australian treecreepers are distributed throughout Australia, except in the sandy and stony deserts, or grasslands. One of the eight species, the Papuan treecreeper, is native to New Guinea, where it is found in some of the mountains. However they are unexplainably absent from an area of approximately 250 miles (400 kilometers) in central New Guinea. The island of Tasmania, off the southeastern coast of Australia, has no treecreepers despite the fact that it has a natural environment

phylum

class

subclass

order

monotypic order

suborder

 family

GREAT AUSTRALASIAN RADIATION

The Great Australasian Radiation refers to the period of time when many different birds evolved across Australia and Asia—the birds evolved in isolation for eons. Australian treecreepers are part of that radiation. Data has indicated that they are related to lyrebirds, scrub-birds, and bowerbirds. The birds' behavior had originally placed them near the northern treecreepers, spotted creepers of Africa and India, and Philippine creepers. But they are not related to any of these birds. Their tree-climbing is an example of convergent evolution, where species develop similar characteristics although they are not related.

suitable to the birds—rainforests, eucalyptus forests, and woodlands. The explanation that has been suggested for this is that Tasmania did not have the extensive forest before it became isolated from the mainland, and treecreepers are poor fliers, so have not colonized Tasmania since then.

HABITAT

Australian treecreepers live in various environments throughout the continent, preferring eucalyptus forest, dry savanna, or semi-arid mulga, an evergreen shrub, that inhabits Australia's interior. Brown treecreepers and rufous treecreepers can also be found in mallee—low woodland with eucalyptus (yoo-kah-LIP-tus) that are multi-stemmed. As a rule, these treecreepers do not inhabit areas that have a dense understory, vegetation under the forest canopy.

DIET

Australian treecreepers are primarily insectivores, insect eaters, with ants composing the biggest portion of their diet. They forage, search for food, for ants and other insects along the trunks and branches of trees they have climbed, especially trees that have rough bark. Treecreepers are known to peel bark, or dig into fissures, cracks, in order to find their prey. Their long claws make it possible for them to hang onto a trunk or branch in an upside down position, but they seldom move downward on a tree. The other insects they eat include beetles, larvae, and spiders. Rarely, a treecreeper might take nectar or seeds in addition to insects.

BEHAVIOR AND REPRODUCTION

Australian treecreepers are usually found in pairs, family groups, or alone. When they are found in pairs, or family groups, territorial defenses are more obvious, such as chasing and calling. Otherwise, the birds tend to be sedentary, stay in one place. Only in some young birds does any migration, travel, occur, and then it is only within several miles or kilometers.

Most species have a voice that consists of shrill, high-pitched whistles. Their display includes tail clicking and flicking.

Some species breed in pairs. Those include the white-throated treecreeper in Australia and New Guinea. Most are co-operative breeders, where young males from previous breedings help care for and protect the current chicks. Those species that breed cooperatively include the red-browed treecreeper, the black-tailed treecreeper, the brown treecreeper, and the rufous treecreeper. Neighboring groups of treecreepers often have close relationships with each other, with males going only one or two territories away from their homes to live. The breeding season is from August to January, with many attempts to breed. It is not uncommon for Australian treecreepers to have two broods a year. The nests are built deep into tree hollows, or sometimes in a hollow log or other cavity. Nests are made of grasses, plant down, soft bark, and animal fur. The female is known to sweep snakeskin, insect wings, and even plastic around the entrance to the nest. One or more males assist the female in incubation, the process of sitting on eggs to provide warmth for development. Eggs are found in clutches of two or three and are white to pinkish in color with brown markings. The incubation takes place over fourteen to twenty-four days, with fledging at twenty-five to twenty-seven days.

AUSTRALIAN CREEPERS AND PEOPLE

There is no special significance between Australian treecreepers and people.

CONSERVATION STATUS

Due to the clearing and breakdown of woodland, some species have declined in numbers. Three subspecies have been categorized as Near Threatened, in danger of becoming threatened with extinction.

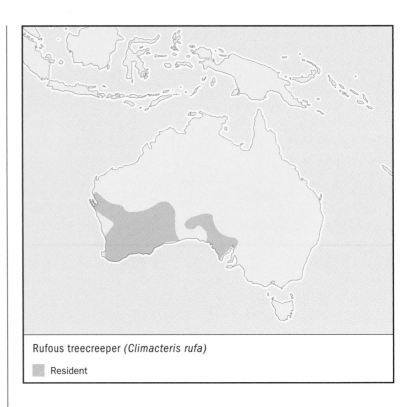

Rufous treecreeper *(Climacteris rufa)*

Resident

RUFOUS TREECREEPER
Climacteris rufa

Physical characteristics: Rufous treecreepers have faces that are cinnamon-rufous, reddish brown, with rufous brows, and cheeks that have a black eye stripe. Their undersides are rufous with white streaks for the female, and black with white streaks on the male. Their upperparts are gray-brown. Their length averages 6.7 inches (17 centimeters). These birds weigh between 1.1 and 1.2 ounces (30 and 33 grams).

Geographic range: Rufous treecreepers can be found throughout southwestern Australia and on the Eyre Peninsula of South Australia.

Habitat: Australian treecreepers live in eucalyptus forest and accompanying woodland, and in the mallee, dense thickets formed by various shrubby species of Australian eucalyptus.

Rufous treecreepers build their nests deep into the hollows of tree branches, stumps, and fallen logs. (© G. Reynard/ VIREO. Reproduced by permission.)

Diet: Rufous treecreepers, like other species of Australian treecreepers forage for their food along the trunks and lower branches of eucalyptus and casuarinas, and on the ground. They are primarily insectivores, with ants as their preference; but also eat centipedes, snails, small reptiles, and seeds.

Behavior and reproduction: The rufous treecreeper lives in family groups that are made up of the breeding pair and its offspring from previous breedings. They tend to be sedentary, and make peeping and churring calls at their predators. Their voice is like the brown treecreeper with short, staccato notes and harsh rattles, with chuckling songs, but they are higher in pitch.

This bird has a breeding season from August to January. Their nests, like those of other Australian treecreepers, are built deep into the hollows of tree branches, stumps, and fallen logs. A clutch has one to three eggs that the female incubates for seventeen days. The young are fed by both parents, and by helpers, usually the young of previous breedings. At twenty-six days they fledge with a great success rate—one study in western Australia showed that 78 percent of attempts succeeded.

Rufous treecreepers and people: There is no known significance between rufous treecreepers and people.

Conservation status: As a species, the rufous treecreeper is not threatened. Populations have declined, with extinction in some local areas of the wheat growing region of western Australia where the land has been cleared extensively. ■

FOR MORE INFORMATION

Books:

Campbell, Bruce, and Elizabeth Lack, eds. *A Dictionary of Birds.* Vermillion, SD: Buteo Books, 1985.

Garnett, S. T., and G. M. Crowley. *The Action Plan for Australian Birds 2000.* Canberra, Australia: Environment Australia, 2000.

Higgins, P. J., J. M. Peter, and W. K. Steele, eds. *Handbook of Australian, New Zealand and Antarctic Birds. Tyrant-flycatchers to Chats,* vol. 5. Melbourne, Australia: Oxford University Press, 2001.

Sibley, C. G. *Birds of the World.* On diskette, Windows version 2.0. Santa Rosa, CA: Charles G. Sibley, 1996.

Sibley, C. G., and J. E. Ahlquist. *Phylogeny and Classification of Birds: A Study of Molecular Evolution.* New Haven, CT: Yale University Press, 1990.

Simpson, Ken, and Nicolas Day. *The Birds of Australia.* Dover, NH: Tanager Books, 1984.

Periodicals:

"The Demography and Cooperative Breeding Behaviour of the Rufous Treecreeper, *Climacteris rufa.*" *Australian Journal of Zoology* (December 2001): 515–537.

Web sites:

"Austral-Papuan Tree-creepers." Treecreepers, Lyrebirds, Bowerbirds and Fairy Wrens of the World. http://camacdonald.com/birding/Sampler6_TreecreepersLyrebirdsBowerbirdsFairyWrens.htm#Treecreepers (accessed on June 18, 2004).

"Australian Treecreepers, Climacteridae." Bird Families of the World. http://www.montereybay.com/creagrus/treecreepers.html (accessed on June 18, 2004).

"Australian Treecreepers." Birds of the World. http://www.eeb.cornell.edu/winkler/botw/climacteridae.html (accessed on June 18, 2004).

"Rainforest understory." Rainforest Education. http://www.rainforesteducation.com (accessed on June 18, 2004).

LONG-TAILED TITMICE

Aegithalidae

Class: Aves
Order: Passeriformes
Family: Aegithalidae
Number of species: 8 species

PHYSICAL CHARACTERISTICS

Long-tailed titmice range in length from 3.5 to 6.3 inches (8.9 to 16 centimeters) and weigh 0.14 to 0.32 ounces (4 to 9 grams). The birds derive their name from their characteristic long tails, with the longest tail belonging to the long-tailed tit, whose tail makes up half of its length. Both male and female adults tend to be alike in their feathers, with dark gray or brown, and sometimes lighter shades, on top, and with white underneath. Some species have what looks like a black mask. Some have pink tints to their feathers on their tails and shoulders. Their feathers are arranged loosely all over their bodies, giving them a fluffy look. Given their size and appearance, they are often a favorite with birdwatchers.

GEOGRAPHIC RANGE

One species of titmice, the bushtits, can be found in western North America, from the northernmost parts of British Columbia to the southern regions of Mexico. Five species are found in the Himalayas, and mountainous regions of western China. Long-tailed tits, the species that is most common, have a range from Western Europe and Asia, to China and Japan. Pygmy tits, the smallest titmice species, can only be found on the Indonesian island of Java.

HABITAT

Long-tailed titmice can be found primarily inhabiting the shrub layers and edges of forests and woodlands among the leafy trees and dense thickets. Those inhabiting the Himalayas and mountains in China are normally found at elevations between 4,000 and 8,860 feet (1,200 to 2,700 meters). White-throated tits can be found living in the mountains at elevations as high as 13,100 feet (4,000 meters), up to the top of the tree line, the elevation where trees do not grow. North American bushtits are also at home in suburbs, parks, and gardens.

DIET

Long-tailed titmice are primarily insectivores, eating insects, their larvae, the newly hatched wingless form of insects, and eggs, spiders, and other invertebrates, animals without backbones, and sometime eating fruit, primarily berries, and seeds. They show remarkable skill in the use of their bodies and limbs. These titmice are at ease even when hanging from the thinnest branches, as they hold their food with one claw and nibble at it with their stubby bill.

BEHAVIOR AND REPRODUCTION

Most of the species of long-tailed titmice live most of the time in flocks of their own species. These small flocks usually number between five and ten birds. Occasionally, they might also be found in flocks of composed of related birds. The birds of this family tend to be sociable. Their chatter is usually heard before they are visible to observers. Some groups can be observed flying in a line of single birds from between the bushes. At night the birds roost, sleep, together, lining up on a branch, and huddling in order to preserve body heat. In that case, the birds that are the largest of the flock are most likely found in the middle of the line, the point at which most of the heat is held. Long-tailed tits can sometimes be found roosting in ground holes.

Long-tailed titmice have a breeding season from January to July. The pygmy tit of Java breeds from August to November. During the breeding season, the flocks break down into individual pairs, though if it is cold, the largest group still might roost together. If the nest has been built already, the individual pair roosts alone in their nest.

Long-tailed titmice build nests that are an enclosed oval shape, or possibly a more elongated structure. They are made from moss, lichen, spider silk, and plant material. The light color of the nests are most likely an attempt to protect the nest by making them the same color as the light background breaks in the tree canopy, upper layer of the forest. A hole is put at the top of the nest to serve as an entrance. Nests have been constructed with a soft lining that might include more than 2,000 feathers. These nests are usually found low in the woodland shrub layer, held up off the ground by branches. Clutch size, the number of eggs laid at the same time, is between two and twelve eggs. The clutch is incubated for a period of twelve to eighteen days. Both males and females, and sometimes other members of the flock will feed the young. Fledging, growing feathers needed for flight, occurs within three weeks of hatching. Chicks remain with the parents' flock for the first winter. The birds raise two broods, a group of birds raised at the same time, a year. The bird has a life span of up to eight years.

LONG-TAILED TITMICE AND PEOPLE

Bushtits are common visitors to garden feeders. Other long-tailed titmice do not visit feeders, but are often observed in garden trees and in parks and remain popular with birdwatchers.

CONSERVATION STATUS

Long-tailed titmice can be found in large numbers throughout their habitat range, and are not classified as a threatened bird family. However, up to 80 percent of the population can die during a hard winter. The species native to the Himalayas and Chinese mountains are also common locally, except for two species, the sooty tit and the white-throated tit. They are both listed as Near Threatened, close to becoming threatened with extinction. The pygmy tits of Java are also very common, however, the continual danger of deforestation, cutting down of forest, might be a concern for their survival in the future. As a species that relies on the dense forests for their habitat, the loss of such forests would definitely pose a threat.

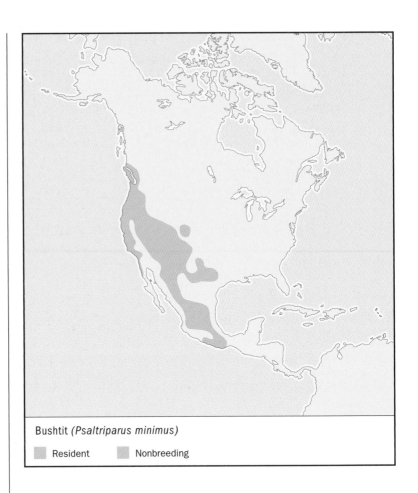

Bushtit (*Psaltriparus minimus*)

▨ Resident   ▨ Nonbreeding

BUSHTIT
Psaltriparus minimus

Physical characteristics: Bushtits range in length from 4 to 4.5 inches (10 to 11.4 centimeters), with an average weight of 0.18 to 0.21 ounces (5 to 6 grams). They are tiny birds, and like other long-tailed titmice have loose feathers that can result in a fluffy appearance, especially when spreading their plumage. The bushtits that inhabit the interiors of their range are usually gray on top with paler gray undersides; the coastal birds have brown caps. Southwestern members of this species have black masks that go all the way to their ears. This variety was once considered a separate species, the black-eared bushtit, but is no longer categorized separately. Female bushtits

Bushtits are social birds that tend to live and travel in large flocks. (© R. & N. Bowers/ VIREO. Reproduced by permission.)

are known for their cream to yellowish eyes, different from the males and young that have dark brown eyes.

Geographic range: The bushtit is commonly found in western North America, along the west coast from Mexico through the United States, and to the northern parts of British Columbia.

Habitat: The bushtit most commonly inhabits deciduous forests, where trees undergo seasonal change, and mixed woodlands, as well as parks and gardens. They can be found in suburbs and even in cities within their range.

Diet: As with other family members, the bushtit is primarily an insectivore, feeding on insects and spiders, as well as occasionally eating fruit and berries.

Behavior and reproduction: Bushtits are social birds that tend to live and travel in large flocks. They roost together, especially during the winter when they attempt to conserve body heat by huddling together. When spring arrives, the young leave the larger flock to establish their own colonies in another territory. Their song is a high thin call that resembles a buzzy, excited twittering sound. Some also are known to have a thin, trilled sort of call.

Breeding occurs from January to June, with courtships, mating behaviors, that are brief and include posturing, posing, and calling, with no particular song yet discovered. The nests they create are elaborate—a pendant nest that resembles a pocket. They can take from two weeks to almost two months to complete. Nests are hung from a hood of a woven spider web, which is hanging from a branch. They are monogamous (muh-NAH-guh-mus), having only one mate, with both male and female building the nest. Should the pair be disturbed while they are in the process of nest building, or laying or incubating, sitting on, eggs, it is not uncommon that they leave the nest site, even change mates, and build a new nest. The incubation of the eggs lasts for twelve days and is done by both sexes, with both of the pair roosting on the eggs in the nest at night. Each clutch averages five to seven eggs. The young are altricial (al-TRISH-uhl), helpless, blind and naked when hatched. The young stay in the nest for fourteen to fifteen days and are fed by both sexes. Sometimes helpers are present in caring for the young, but rarely are they from a previous brood. They have two broods a year.

Bushtits and people: Bushtits provide interesting entertainment to people and birdwatchers due to their cute appearance and fluffing of their feathers.

Conservation status: This species is not threatened, and has been known to be increasing in population in certain areas of its range. ■

FOR MORE INFORMATION

Books:

Alsop, Fred J. III. *Birds of North America.* London and New York: DK Publishing, 2001.

Campbell, Bruce, and Elizabeth Lack, eds. *A Dictionary of Birds.* Vermillion, SD: Buteo Books, 1985.

Elphick, Chris, John B. Dunning Jr., and David Allen Sibley, eds. *The Sibley Guide to Bird Life & Behavior.* New York: Alfred A. Knopf, Inc., 2001.

Web sites:

"Bushtit *Psaltriparus minimus.*" BirdWeb: Seattle Audubon's Online Guide to the Birds of Washington State. http://www.birdweb.org/birdweb/species.asp?id=332 (accessed on June 20, 2004).

"Family Aegithalidae (Long-tailed Tits)." University of Michigan Museum of Zoology Animal Diversity Web. http://animaldiversity. ummz.umich.edu/ site/accounts/classification/Aegithalidae.html (accessed on June 20, 2004).

"Long-tailed Tits (Aegithalidae)." Bird Families of the World. http://www. montereybay.com/creagrus/longtailedtits.html (accessed on June 20, 2004).

Michaels, Patricia A. "Bushtit (Aegithalidae) Picture and ID." Green Nature. http://greennature.com/article908.html (accessed on June 20, 2004).

PENDULINE TITMICE
Remizidae

Class: Aves

Order: Passeriformes

Family: Remizidae

Number of species: 10 species

phylum

class

subclass

order

monotypic order

suborder

▲ **family**

PHYSICAL CHARACTERISTICS

Penduline titmice (sometimes called penduline tits) are small passerines (PASS-uh-reenz; perching songbirds) with short wings and tails, delicate heads, and straight bills. Plumage (feathers) is the same over the entire body, being dull-colored in both males and females. But the actual body color and shape differs widely among species. Upperparts range from pale grays, whites, and yellows to chestnut and olive green, and underparts range from white to yellow. Some adult species have black masks on the head and deep chestnut on the back. A few species are bright yellow or red. Tail length also varies: some are very short while others are relatively long. Their feet have four toes, all at the same level. The hind toe points backward, allowing them to firmly grip slender perches. One of the more constant features of penduline tits is the bill, which is shaped like a cone with a needle-like point, more sharply pointed than in other titmice. Penduline tits are 3.0 to 4.3 inches (7.5 to 11 centimeters) long and weigh between 0.16 and 0.44 ounces (4.6 and 12.5 grams).

GEOGRAPHIC RANGE

Penduline tits are widely found from Africa through Europe and into Asia. One species, the verdin, is located in North America, specifically in southwest United States and northern Mexico.

HABITAT

Penduline tits are found in a large range of open country habitats including deserts, large reed beds in marshes and along riverbanks, and scrublands and forests.

DIET

Penduline tits eat many invertebrates (animals without backbones), fruits, and small seeds. They grasp food with one foot while pecking at it with their bill. The birds often search in spider's nests and crevices (cracks) in trees.

BEHAVIOR AND REPRODUCTION

Penduline tits are very active and quick birds. They are usually found in pairs or in small groups for most of the year. Species that live in forests are found in the tree canopy (treetops). Because of their ability to move quickly and skillfully, penduline tits easily move through branches and the undersides of twigs and branches. They often roost in groups at night. Penduline tits that live in northern temperate (mild) climates migrate during the breeding season. Others that live in warmer climates are generally sedentary (tend not to migrate, move seasonally). The birds are fairly quiet but do sometimes give out high-pitched calls and songs that range from various notes to others that only repeat certain notes. They sometimes sound a "ti ti ti" followed by a short whistle.

During the breeding season, penduline tits are territorial, but only defend a small area just around the nest. Since the birds use only a small nesting area, other penduline tits will nest close by in a colony-type arrangement; that is where large numbers of birds nest together. The mating system is very complex. Penduline tits can be monogamous (muh-NAH-guh-mus; having one mate) or polygamous (puh-LIH-guh-mus; having more than one mate). Breeding takes place from April to July in northern temperate climates, while in African species, breeding depends on local climates (with some species breeding during the wet season and others breeding during the dry season).

The nests of penduline tits are "pendulous" (meaning that they hang loosely from a base). Nests are found in many different locations such as branches of trees and shrubs and reeds along waters. The shape of nests are usually teardrop or pearlike with a hole near the top; except for one species that builds a cup-shaped nest, which does not hang. A ledge is sometimes built near the entrance, which is fastened together for protection from its enemies. Penduline tits make nests from plant matter that is pressed flat to produce a strong outside covering. It is lined inside with soft grasses, mosses, and lichens (plants growing on rocks).

PENDULINE TITMICE NESTS ARE PENDULOUS

Penduline titmice get their name because their nests are pendulous. Pendulous means to hang loosely, which is how their nests are constructed. Male penduline tits build elaborate bag-like nests of feathers and soft plant fibers. Nests hang suspended, usually from tree branches or off of reeds above water.

Females lay white eggs with red spots, except for the species verdin, whose eggs are bluish green. Females lay two to nine eggs. The incubation period (time it takes to sit on eggs before hatching) is between thirteen and seventeen days, and the nestling period (time necessary to take care of young birds before they can leave the nest) is about eighteen days. The caring of the chicks is performed by both parents, with some species using helpers to assist the parents.

PENDULINE TITMICE AND PEOPLE

People show little interest toward penduline tits other than admiring them for their complicated construction of nests. In the past, their nests have been used in eastern Europe as slippers for children and in Africa as purses within certain tribes.

CONSERVATION STATUS

Penduline tits are not considered to be threatened. Some species, however, are declining in numbers due to increasing amounts of farming and general human development of their habitat.

Verdin *(Auriparus flaviceps)*

Breeding

VERDIN
Auriparus flaviceps

Physical characteristics: Tiny, rounded short-tailed verdins have a dull yellow head and throat; chestnut shoulder patch; dark gray upperparts, and light gray underparts. They have stout but sharply pointed black bills and strong legs. Males and females look alike. Adults are 4 to 4.5 inches (10 to 11 centimeters) long and weigh between 0.21 and 0.29 ounces (6.0 to 8.2 grams).

Geographic range: Verdin are found in the southwestern United States and Mexico. It is the only species within the family Remizidae that lives in the New World (within the Americas).

Unlike other penduline tits, which make pendulous nests, the verdins' nests are made in the shape of a sphere. (© A. Morris/VIREO. Reproduced by permission.)

Habitat: Verdins prefer arid lowland and hilly scrub desert that contains scattered thorny bushes and cacti (KAK-tie or KAK-tee); they especially like mesquite and creosote bushes.

Diet: Verdins eat invertebrates (such as insects and their larvae and eggs, and spiders), seeds, and fruits such as wild berries. Much of their water is obtained through the eating of fruits and insects. They actively forage for food among twigs, leaves, and buds, sometimes hanging upside down while clinging to twigs and leaves.

Behavior and reproduction: Verdins are usually found in singles or pairs, and in family groups after the breeding season. They do not migrate, being more solitary than other penduline tits. During the winter, they may join other species of birds while foraging. Verdins are very active, flittering about and constantly flicking their tails up. Songs of verdins consist of a gloomy-sounding, three-note series of "tswee-swee, tswee", with the second note higher. Their call is a high-pitched "tseewf" or a lower-pitched "tee-too-too" or "tee-too-tee-tee."

Verdins breed from March to June. They are monogamous and solitary nesters. Nests, which are unique from other penduline tits, are made in the shape of a sphere (ball-like), and constructed by adding several layers of thorny and non-thorny twigs, finally lining the inside with softer materials (such as leaves, grasses, feathers, plant down, and spider's silk). The finished nest is around 8 inches (20 centimeters) in diameter, and may consist of as many as two thousand twigs. Nests are usually near the end of a low limb, or in the fork of a bush or tree, and normally from 2 to 20 feet (0.6 to 6.1 meters) above the ground. Nests are also built 10 or more miles (16 or more kilometers) away from water sources. Males may build several nests within a territory, with the female selecting one of them, which may be then used for several years. The thick walls protect them from the hot desert sun and the cold desert nights. Nests built early in the breeding season have side entrances facing away from cool winds to conserve heat, while those built toward the end of the breeding season face the cooling wind during hot weather.

Females lay a clutch (number of eggs hatched together) of between two and four bluish green eggs (sometimes with reddish brown speckles). Young are brownish gray in coloring, and lack the yellow head and chestnut shoulder patch of adults. The incubation period is fourteen to seventeen days, with the fledging period (time necessary for chicks to grow feathers in order to fly) being from seventeen to nineteen days. Females may have up to two broods (young birds that are born and raised together) a year.

Verdins and people: Verdins have no special significance to humans.

Conservation status: Verdins are not threatened; they are common and increasing in numbers within their habitat. ■

FOR MORE INFORMATION

Books:

Alsop, Fred J. III. *Birds of North America.* New York: DK, 2001.

del Hoyo, Josep, Andrew Elliott, Jordi Sargatal, Jose Cabot, et al., eds. *Handbook of the Birds of the World.* Barcelona: Lynx Edicions, 1992.

Dickinson, Edward C., ed. *The Howard and Moore Complete Checklist of the Birds of the World,* 3rd ed. Princeton, NJ and Oxford, U.K.: Princeton University Press, 2003.

Field Guide to the Birds of North America, 4th ed. Washington, DC: National Geographic Society, 2002.

Forshaw, Joseph, ed. *Encyclopedia of Birds,* 2nd ed. San Diego, CA: Academic Press, 1998.

Harrison, Colin James Oliver. *Birds of the World.* London and New York: Dorling Kindersley, 1993.

Kaufman, Kenn, et al. *Birds of North America.* New York: Houghton Mifflin, 2000.

Perrins, Christopher M., and Alex L. A. Middleton, eds. *The Encyclopedia of Birds.* New York: Facts on File, 1985.

Sibley, David. *The Sibley Guide to Birds.* New York: Alfred A. Knopf, 2000.

Stattersfield, Allison J., and David R. Capper, eds. *Threatened Birds of the World: The Official Source for Birds on the IUCN Red List.* Cambridge, U.K.: BirdLife International, 2000.

Terres, John K. *The Audubon Society Encyclopedia of North American Birds.* New York: Knopf, 1980.

TITMICE AND CHICKADEES
Paridae

Class: Aves

Order: Passeriformes

Family: Paridae

Number of species: 55 to 58 species

family
CHAPTER

PHYSICAL CHARACTERISTICS

Titmice and chickadees are perching songbirds that are small and compact with short, stout bills. The bill's shape can vary depending upon the habitat and the type of food the birds eat. In most species, the bill, legs, and iris (colored part of eye) are dark and dull. However, in a few species the iris is pale yellow. Generally, the birds have brightly colored, soft, thick plumage (feathers), with striking differences in plumage features depending on the species. In fact, many plumage differences occur within species if they have wide areas in which they roam. Females and males are similar in characteristics, with females usually a bit smaller than males. They are well adapted to living in trees, having short, rounded wings and tails, and short but strong legs and feet. Titmice (sometimes shortened to tits) and chickadees have little difference in size within the family. They are 3.9 to 8.0 inches (10.0 to 20.5 centimeters) and weigh between 0.2 and 1.7 ounces (5 and 49 grams).

GEOGRAPHIC RANGE

Titmice and chickadees are located in Europe, Asia, the far north and most parts of central and southern Africa, North America, and Mexico.

HABITAT

Titmice and chickadees are found in all habitats except those in the treeless Arctic zone, South America, the desert areas of Asia and Africa, and Australasia (region consisting of Australia, New Zealand, New Guinea, and the neighboring islands of the

South Pacific). Titmice and chickadees are specifically found in a wide variety of woodland areas from conifers and evergreen broad-leaved woodlands to deciduous broad-leaved woodlands. They are also found in parks, gardens, hedgerows, orchards, vineyards, open woodlands, and scrublands. The birds inhabit a range in altitudes from sea level to 14,764 feet (4,500 meters).

DIET

Titmice and chickadees eat many types of invertebrates (animals without backbones). They also eat seeds, nuts, fruits, and nectar (sweet liquid that flowering plants produce). Most species forage (search for food) in the canopies (uppermost layer of vegetation) of trees and scrubs. Some species forage on the ground. Titmice and chickadees in the northern regions of their habitats regularly store food (mostly insects and seeds).

BEHAVIOR AND REPRODUCTION

All titmice and chickadees are quick and acrobatic in movement, often flying with daring maneuvers. They fly on short, quick flights that may be straight or in a slight up-and-down motion, regularly hopping from branch to branch and often hanging upside down in order to pry food from under tree bark. Some species of titmice and chickadees are able to regulate their nightly body temperature to conserve energy.

Most species live in pairs or small groups during breeding periods, being very territorial. They often join other species' flocks when they are not in breeding periods. Some species display aggressive behaviors when competing for food in flocks. Two such displays are a heads-up posture in species with black chests and crest-raising in crested species. Songs are rare among the birds, but they do make a wide variety of loud and frequent calls.

The birds nest mostly in tree cavities, holes, but also between rocks, in walls, on raised ground, and in artificially made materials such as pipes and nesting boxes. Birds use various soft nesting materials to line their nests. Most species nest between March and July, but others nest year-round or seasonally. Clutch size (group of eggs hatched together) varies between the various groups of titmice and chickadees, but generally ranges from four to ten eggs. Eggs are usually white or blushed pink with some red-brown spotting at the larger end of the egg. The incubation period (time to hatch eggs) is about fourteen days, and the brood period (time to raise young) is between fourteen and twenty-four days.

TITMICE, CHICKADEES, AND PEOPLE

Titmice and chickadees have no known significance to humans, other than with respect to bird watching. The birds are relatively tame in the presence of humans and will nest in boxes made for them.

CONSERVATION STATUS

Most titmice and chickadees are common in most of their distributions. However, the white-naped tit is listed as Vulnerable, facing a high risk of extinction; while three species (the Palawan tit, the white-fronted tit, and the yellow tit) are listed as Near Threatened, in danger of becoming threatened with extinction.

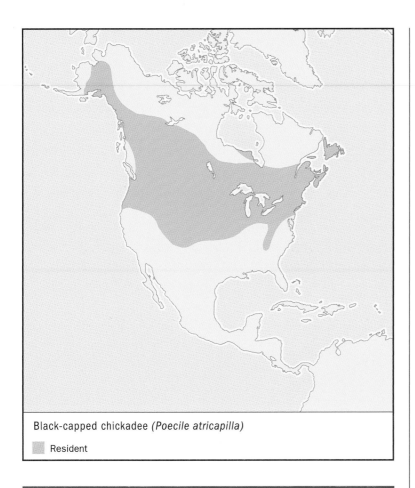

Black-capped chickadee (Poecile atricapilla)

▨ Resident

BLACK-CAPPED CHICKADEE
Poecile atricapilla

Physical characteristics: Black-capped chickadees have white outer tail feathers (longer than other chickadees), light gray on the upperparts, white under parts, white cheeks, deep brownish buff sides and flanks, rather large, round heads with black caps (patch on top of head) and bibs (chest). They also have strong feet and claws that are blackish gray, as well as short black bills. Males and females are similar in physical features. They are 4.8 to 5.7 inches (12.3 to 14.6 centimeters) long and weigh between 0.3 and 0.5 ounces (10 to 14 grams).

Geographic range: They range throughout the northern part of the United States and throughout the southern parts of Canada, up

Black-capped chickadees are common throughout North America. (© T. Vezo/VIREO. Reproduced by permission.)

to the northwestern part of Canada and the south and central parts of Alaska.

Habitat: Black-capped chickadees are found in deciduous, coniferous, and mixed woodlands, including open areas such as gardens and parks, willow and cottonwood thickets, and small groves of trees and suburban gardens.

Diet: Black-capped chickadees eat a great number of different invertebrates such as insects and their larvae (LAR-vee), caterpillars, spiders, beetles, ants, sawflies, millipedes, snails, and small amphibians (land animals that breed in water), along with wild fruits, seeds (such as of conifers and bayberries), and bark during winter months. They forage throughout the tree canopy, but prefer low branches and rarely go to the ground. They often hold large seeds between their feet on a perch and pound the seed coat open with their beak. They store food in preparation for winter.

Behavior and reproduction: Black-capped chickadees fly slowly but can be quick-moving around pine cones, twigs, and branches. They do not generally migrate except for the ones that live in mountainous regions, where they move to lower elevations during colder months. Outside of the breeding season, the birds form groups of several bird species. During breeding season, they are territorial. Their song is a simple, high "fee-bee" with the second note lower than the first, or "fee-bee-be." They have a variety of calls, including a loud "chick-a-dee-dee-dee."

The chickadees nest in the cavities of rotted birch or pine trees that are usually 1 to 10 feet (0.3 to 3.0 meters) off the ground, often with both males and females digging their own hole but sometimes using natural holes or abandoned woodpecker holes. Nests are cup-shaped consisting of plant fibers, feathers, and hairs that are set on top of a moss base. Females lay white eggs that are dotted with brown from mid-April to late May (sometimes into July). Usually a single clutch of five to thirteen (but usually six to eight) eggs is laid each year. Incubation period is eleven to thirteen days, and brooding period is from twelve to eighteen days.

Black-capped chickadees and people: Black-capped chickadees are attracted to gardens in which sunflower seeds, peanuts, or suet is available. There is no other special significance to humans.

Conservation status: Black-capped chickadees are not threatened, being common and very widespread with around 0.6 pairs per acre (0.25 pairs per hectacre). ■

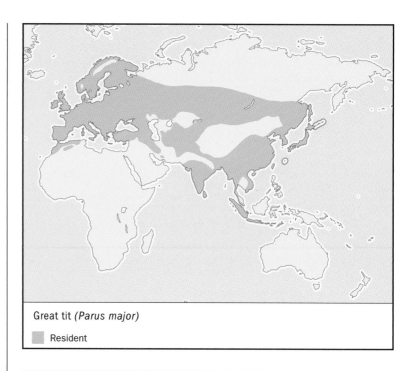

Great tit *(Parus major)*

Resident

GREAT TIT
Parus major

Physical characteristics: Great tits are larger than other titmice. They have a yellow underside, with a powerful-looking head and bill. Plumage varies with specific physical location, but generally has a black throat, crown, and vertical breast stripe, white cheeks, green back, blue rump, wings, and tail with a yellow breast. They are about 5.5 inches (14 centimeters) long, and weigh between 0.5 and 0.8 ounces (14 and 22 grams). The sexes look alike, but males are generally larger in size than females.

Geographic range: They range across Eurasia and into Southeast Asia and northern China. The species is generally considered the most widely spread of all the titmice and chickadees.

Habitat: They occur over a wide range of different woodland types, but prefer to live in lowland, broad-leaved deciduous woodlands, especially those with plenty of shrub growth. Great tits stay away from conifer forests. They are also found in open and semi-open woodland areas, including gardens, parks, and cemeteries.

Great tits often use the same nest from year to year. (Illustration by Emily Damstra. Reproduced by permission.)

Diet: Great tits eat many different types of invertebrates (mostly insects), seeds, nuts, and fruits. They forage within all parts of trees and shrubs, but prefer to be among the leaves. Their strong bill is able to open seeds as large as hazel nuts. They do not store food for the winter.

Behavior and reproduction: Great tits migrate out of mountainous altitudes for the winter months, but otherwise are considered non-migratory. They can sometimes be territorial during the year, but also join flocks of many bird species outside of the breeding season. The loud, repetitive singing of great tits has many variations, especially within males.

Nests, frequently used for several seasons, occur in cavities of trees, walls, and burrows; and sometimes in nest boxes placed by people. The cup-type nest is lined with fine grasses. Females begin to lay eggs in February in southern populations and can continue as late as May in northern populations. Two clutches are often laid each year, with three clutches seldom occurring. Clutch size varies widely from three to eighteen eggs. The incubation period is twelve to fifteen days and only the females incubate the eggs. The fledging period is between sixteen and twenty-two days.

Great tits and people: Some cultural significance exists, especially with Europeans, who maintain close associations with the birds. Great tits are often believed to be the most studied wild bird in the world.

Conservation status: Great tits are very common, but some populations are very small in number. ∎

FOR MORE INFORMATION

Books:

Alsop, Fred J. III. *Birds of North America.* New York: DK, 2001.

Baughman, Mel M., ed. *Reference Atlas to the Birds of North America.* Washington, DC: National Geographic, 2003.

del Hoyo, Josep, Andrew Elliott, Jordi Sargatal, Jose Cabot, et al, eds. *Handbook of the Birds of the World.* Barcelona: Lynx Edicions, 1992.

Dickinson, Edward C., ed. *The Howard and Moore Complete Checklist of the Birds of the World,* 3rd ed. Princeton, NJ and Oxford, U.K.: Princeton University Press, 2003.

Field Guide to the Birds of North America, 4th ed. Washington, DC: National Geographic Society, 2002.

Harrison, Colin James Oliver. *Birds of the World.* London and New York: Dorling Kindersley, 1993.

Forshaw, Joseph, ed. *Encyclopedia of Birds,* 2nd ed. San Diego, CA: Academic Press, 1998.

Kaufman, Kenn, with collaboration of Rick and Nora Bowers and Lynn Hassler Kaufman. *Birds of North America.* New York: Houghton Mifflin, 2000.

Perrins, Christopher M., and Alex L. A. Middleton, eds. *The Encyclopedia of Birds.* New York: Facts on File, 1985.

Sibley, David. *The Sibley Guide to Birds.* New York: Alfred A. Knopf, 2000.

Terres, John K. *The Audubon Society Encyclopedia of North American Birds.* New York: Knopf, 1980.

Class: Aves

Order: Passeriformes

Family: Sittidae

Number of species: About
27 species

CHAPTER

PHYSICAL CHARACTERISTICS

Nuthatches and wall creepers consist of three groups: typical nuthatches, sittellas, and wall creepers. They are small and stocky, large-headed, short-tailed perching birds. Nuthatches are 3.5 to 7.5 inches (8.5 to 19.0 centimeters) long. They have a compact body, large head, short neck, and a thin, chisel-shaped, slightly upturned bill. Their long, pointed wings have ten primary feathers each, they have a short, squared tail, short legs and strong, long toes that have sharp claws. Nuthatches have blue-gray upperparts (blue in some tropical species) and white, pale gray, or reddish brown underparts. The crown on the top of the head is dark and there is a white stripe over the eye.

Sittellas are 4.3 to 4.8 inches (11 to 12 centimeters) long. They have a compact body, large head, thin, chisel-shaped bill and a short tail. They also have a brown-streaked or black body with a red face. Wall creepers are about 6.5 inches (16 centimeters) long. They have a compact body and strong, slightly down-turned bill, a rather long claw on its hind toe and a short tail. Sittellas have brownish upperparts, white underparts (with brown streaks), a white throat, and a brownish yellow patch around the eyes.

GEOGRAPHIC RANGE

Nuthatches and wall creepers are distributed throughout North America, Eurasia, Africa, Southeast Asia, and Australasia (region consisting of Australia, New Zealand, New Guinea, and the neighboring islands of the South Pacific).

HABITAT

They inhabit mostly coniferous, deciduous, and mixed forests and woodlands, while others live in rocky scrublands.

DIET

Nuthatches and wall creepers eat mostly invertebrates (animals without backbones) such as insects, snails, spiders, and other similar animals. They forage (look for food) by climbing up and down on trees while using their bills to pick loose bark away in order to locate their prey on the surface and crevices (narrow cracks) of tree trunks. Nuthatches and wall creepers are the only tree-trunk foraging birds that climb up trees with their head downwards instead of upwards (thus, finding food missed by other birds such as woodpeckers). They climb back down by holding themselves with one foot on the bark while moving with the other, switching feet positions as they zigzag in their path. Foraging on rocks and in epiphytic mosses and lichens (plants that grow on another) also occurs. Arthropods (invertebrate animal with jointed limbs) are sometimes found in foliage from the ground or while in flight. During the winter, they also eat small fruits and seeds. Nuthatches and wall creepers use their bills to crack open seeds by wedging the seed into a small crevice and hitting it with the top of their bill. When food is plentiful, they store it for later use.

BEHAVIOR AND REPRODUCTION

Nuthatches and wall creepers fly in an up-and-down motion. Most birds are not migratory. Adult pairs are monogamous (muh-NAH-guh-mus; having one mate) and occupy a permanent territory throughout their lives. Nests are made in natural cavities in trees or in cavities that were dug out and abandoned by woodpeckers. When previously used nests are used, they will often narrow the opening with mud, dung (solid excrement of animals), and other sticky substances in order to keep predators and competitors out. Some nests are made in rock cavities with substances such as bark flakes and leaves. Many sittellas build open nests in trees rather than using holes. Females lay four to ten white eggs that are flecked with brown or red. Only females sit on the eggs, but both males and females feed the chicks. Most birds produce only one brood each year.

NUTHATCHES, WALL CREEPERS, AND PEOPLE

People do not have any direct, significant relationship with nuthatches and wall creepers, other than the enjoyment that birdwatchers receive from viewing them. They often nest in bird-houses built by people and eat out of provided feeding stations.

CONSERVATION STATUS

Two species in this family are considered Endangered, facing a very high risk of extinction; two species are considered Vulnerable, facing a high risk of extinction; and two species are considered Near Threatened, in danger of becoming threatened with extinction.

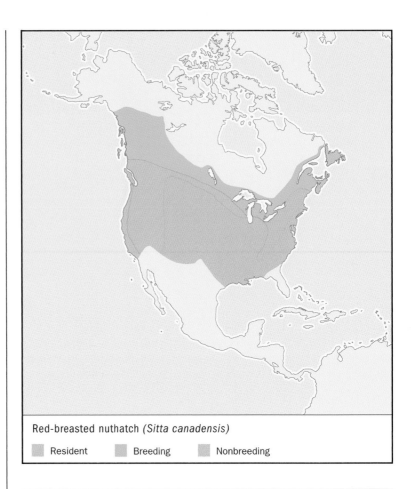

Red-breasted nuthatch *(Sitta canadensis)*

■ Resident ■ Breeding ■ Nonbreeding

RED-BREASTED NUTHATCH
Sitta canadensis

Physical characteristics: Male red-breasted nuthatches have blue-gray upperparts (back, shoulders, wings, and rump) with red-brown to buffy orange under parts. They have a black cap and nape (back part of neck), a white throat, a white stripe over the eyes and a black stripe through them. The male nuthatches also have a blue-grey short tail (which shows a white band near the ends). Females are similar to males except for a dark gray crown and nape, and lighter buff under parts that are rustier on the sides of the lower body and the feathers beneath the wings. They are 4.0 to 4.7 inches (10.2 to 11.9 centimeters) long, with wings that are 8.0 to 8.5 inches (20.3 to 21.6 centimeters) wide. They weigh about 0.35 ounces (10 grams).

Geographic range: Red-breasted nuthatches are found throughout southern and northwestern Canada and most of the United States (and found very infrequently in Florida and the southern parts of the Southwest, usually only during the winter months).

Habitat: Red-breasted nuthatches inhabit dense coniferous forests (such as balsam fir and spruce), mixed coniferous-deciduous forests, and along rivers within such forests, moving northward into the high mountains during breeding season. They may also be found in other types of forests, especially during their fall migration.

Diet: They eat invertebrates such as beetles, wasps, caterpillars, insect eggs, and crane flies from tree bark and foliage. In winter, they also eat fruits, nuts, and seeds (especially of pines, spruces, firs, and other conifers). The birds wedge food in tree bark crevices with their bills, and then break off pieces before eating them. They use the head-down movement as they climb trees, as opposed to the normal way of climbing trees head first (head-up).

Red-breasted nuthatches eat a number of invertebrate species. In winter, they also eat fruits, nuts, and seeds, especially of pines, spruces, firs, and other conifers. (© H.P. Smith Jr./ VIREO. Reproduced by permission.)

Behavior and reproduction: Red-breasted nuthatches are rather quiet and tame birds. They are normally found as pairs who defend a breeding territory. Considered an irregular migratory bird, they sometimes spend winters in breeding areas when food is plentiful. At other times during the fall, large numbers of the birds move south together and into lowlands, especially when food supplies are low. They produce calls that sound like a nasal "hennk-jemml," which is quite high-pitched but soft. Other calls include "it-it-it" and "ank-ank-ank." Their song is a high-pitched "wa-wa-wa-wa-wa" or "eeeen-eeeen-eeeen."

Males court females by feeding them. The male's courtship rituals also include turning his back to her, and then lifting his head and tail, raising back feathers and drooping wings, and swaying from side to side. The monogamous breeding pair uses cavities of trees (often pine and cottonwood) for their nests, along with old woodpecker holes and bird boxes. Nests are from 5 to 100 feet (1.5 to 30.5 meters) off the ground but usually 15 feet (4.5 meters). The inside of the nest is lined with grasses, mosses, rootlets, shredded bark, and plant fibers. Females lay four to seven eggs (which are peppered and spotted with different shades of brown) from April to June. Females sit on the eggs for an incubation period (time of sitting on eggs) of about twelve days, but males join females in feeding of the young. Fledging period (time it takes for the young to grow flying feathers) is eighteen to twenty-one days.

Red-breasted nuthatches and people: Red-breasted nuthatches will often eat out of the hands of people who feed them.

Conservation status: Red-breasted nuthatches are not threatened, being fairly common to common in most of its range. Its eastern breeding range is expanding southward. ■

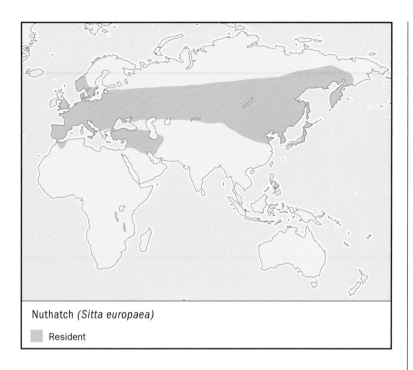

Nuthatch *(Sitta europaea)*

Resident

NUTHATCH
Sitta europaea

Physical characteristics: Nuthatches have blue-gray upperparts, rusty under parts, brown to white undersides, a blue-gray crown, a white throat, and a black line through the eyes with a white line above them. Coloration varies greatly due to the species' very large range. Females and juveniles have a duller head coloring and paler under parts. They are 5.5 inches (14 centimeters) long, with a short tail, and weigh 0.7 to 0.9 ounces (20 to 25 grams).

Geographic range: The birds range widely in temperate Eurasia, from the western coast of the Atlantic Ocean to the eastern coast of the Pacific Ocean. They have the most extensive range of all nuthatches.

Habitat: Nuthatches are located in mature temperate forests, from deciduous to coniferous ones.

Diet: Nuthatches eat invertebrates, such as insects, from tree bark and foliage, especially from branches. They also eat fruits, nuts, and

Pairs of nuthatches live together and defend a territory against other nuthatches. (Illustration by John Megahan. Reproduced by permission.)

seeds during winter months. Nuts are wedged into crevices and then broken open with hits from the bird's bill.

Behavior and reproduction: Nuthatches are often seen running along tree branches or up and down trunks in search of insects. They occur as pairs that defend a breeding territory. The birds do not migrate. During the nonbreeding season, nuthatches are seen in flocks with many different species. Pairs nest in cavities and holes of trees. Nests are cup-shaped and made of bark flakes. The entrance to the nest is often plastered with mud to reduce its size to the width of the female's body, in order to deter enemies. Females sit on the eggs, but both sexes feed the chicks.

Nuthatches and people: People and nuthatches have no known significant relationship.

Conservation status: Nuthatches are not threatened, being common throughout their habitat. ■

FOR MORE INFORMATION

Books:

Alsop, Fred J. III. *Birds of North America.* New York: DK, 2001.

Baughman, Mel M., ed. *Reference Atlas to the Birds of North America.* Washington, DC: National Geographic, 2003.

del Hoyo, Josep, Andrew Elliott, Jordi Sargatal, Jose Cabot, et al, eds. *Handbook of the Birds of the World.* Barcelona: Lynx Edicions, 1992.

Dickinson, Edward C., ed. *The Howard and Moore Complete Checklist of the Birds of the World,* 3rd ed. Princeton, NJ and Oxford, U.K.: Princeton University Press, 2003.

Field Guide to the Birds of North America, 4th ed. Washington, DC: National Geographic Society, 2002.

Harrison, Colin James Oliver. *Birds of the World.* London, U.K. and New York: Dorling Kindersley, 1993.

Forshaw, Joseph, ed. *Encyclopedia of Birds,* 2nd ed. San Diego, CA: Academic Press, 1998.

Kaufman, Kenn, with collaboration of Rick and Nora Bowers and Lynn Hassler Kaufman. *Birds of North America.* New York: Houghton Mifflin, 2000.

Sibley, David. *The Sibley Guide to Birds.* New York: Alfred A. Knopf, 2000.

Terres, John K. *The Audubon Society Encyclopedia of North American Birds.* New York: Knopf, 1980.

TREECREEPERS
Certhiidae

Class: Aves
Order: Passeriformes
Family: Certhiidae
Number of species: 7 species

family

CHAPTER

phylum
class
subclass
order
monotypic order
suborder
▲ family

PHYSICAL CHARACTERISTICS

Treecreepers are small, mostly brown birds that have long, slightly curved bills, long, slender tails with twelve stiff, pointed feathers, a narrow, teardrop-shaped body, and short legs with long toes and highly curved claws. They possess coloration that allows them to blend into their forest habitat in order to protect themselves from predators, animals that hunt them for food. Plumage (feathers) varies among species. However, upperparts are generally shades of brown with streaks of black, under parts are white or buff with shades of mostly rufous (reddish) or cinnamon, but sometimes of gray, and a stripe above the eye is buff or white. Males and females are similar in both size and color. In the first year, young birds have duller and streakier looking upperparts than adults, but look more like adults after the first year. Adults are 5 to 6 inches (12 to 15 centimeters) long.

GEOGRAPHIC RANGE

They range widely across the Northern Hemisphere, and in many areas of central and southwest Africa.

HABITAT

Treecreepers inhabit mature pine-oak woodlands and open pine forests. Depending on the species, treecreepers are found anywhere from sea level to mountainous regions and from temperate (mild) to tropical climates.

DIET

Treecreepers eat primarily small insects, spiders, and other small invertebrates. They use their thin bill to explore beneath the tree bark. During the winter, they also eat seeds and nuts, especially when other prey is scarce. Food is not normally stored for future use.

BEHAVIOR AND REPRODUCTION

All treecreepers, except for one species, use their tails to help them climb. Their short legs, long toes, and strong claws help them to cling tightly to the side of trees while foraging (searching for food). They forage singly, in pairs, and in flocks of many different bird species. Foraging rituals consist of flying to the base of a tree and then searching and probing under the bark for insects while climbing the trunk. They also look for food while clinging to the undersides of limbs, creeping outward from the trunk almost to the tip of the main branch. They climb in a jerky, spiral motion. Songs of treecreepers are quiet sounding trills, and calls are high-pitched and thin. Such sounds are used to establish and defend their breeding territory.

Most treecreepers construct nests under loose pieces of bark on dying or dead trees. Once in a while, treecreepers build nests on walls of buildings, in crevices (narrow cracks or openings) of trees, in heavy vegetation such as ivy, and within nesting boxes. Nests are built from 1.5 to 52 feet (0.5 to 16 meters) off the ground, with such a range of heights due to differences in species. Most females lay four to six white and faintly spotted red or reddish brown eggs. Females perform all of the incubation (sitting on eggs) duties, but both males and females feed their young. The brooding period (time to raise young together) is thirteen to seventeen days, with sometimes two broods each year. After the young are old enough to fly off, they will often remain as a family group for two to three weeks.

TREECREEPERS AND PEOPLE

There is no known significant relationship between treecreepers and people.

CONSERVATION STATUS

Treecreepers are not threatened, but some species have seen slight decreases in their populations.

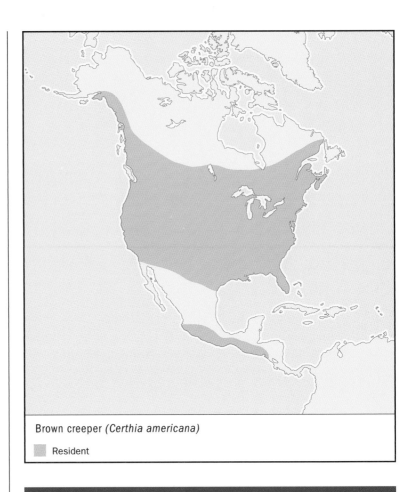

Brown creeper (*Certhia americana*)

▨ Resident

BROWN CREEPER
Certhia americana

Physical characteristics: Brown creepers vary in plumage within different populations. They generally have dark brownish upperparts that are spotted and streaked with white, buff, or pale gray, cinnamon rump and undertail coverts (small feathers around base of quill), white to buff under parts, pale eyebrows, and a rusty base on the long tail that contains stiff pointed feathers at the end. There is a bold, buffy band on the wings that is noticeable above and below during flight. Wings are also edged and tipped with buff and white. The bill of the brown creeper is thin and curved, and its claws are sharp. Western populations are relatively small, dark, and long-billed, while eastern populations are slightly larger, paler, and shorter-billed. The isolated population in Central America is darker and smaller than the northern population. Females and males look alike, and most juveniles look very much like adults. Brown creepers are about 5.25 inches (13.4 centimeters) long, with a wing span of 7 to 8 inches (17.8 to 20.3 centimeters) and a weight of about 0.29 ounces (8.4 grams).

Geographic range: Brown creepers range through North America (western and central Canada and most of the United States) and Central America (south to Nicaragua). Northern populations winter in southeastern United States and northern Mexico.

Habitat: Brown creepers live in mature coniferous, deciduous, mixed (coniferous/deciduous), or swampy forests and woodlands. They are usually located in lowlands.

Diet: Brown creepers forage by flying to the base of a tree. They are adapted for climbing ("creeping") on tree trunks and large branches in search

To hide from predators, brown creepers hold their body against a tree, spread their wings and tail, and remain motionless. Their coloration blends in with the tree bark. (Ilustration by Michelle Meneghini. Reproduced by permission.)

for food with the use of their stiff tail that is placed against the bark for both support and balance. They also use their strong toes and claws for grabbing onto tree bark. The birds search and probe within bark crevices with their bill for insects while climbing either in a spiraling (like ascending a spiral staircase) or in a somewhat straight path up the trunk and large tree branches. They eat spiders, insects, larvae (LAR-vee), and other invertebrates, along with seeds and nuts. Once reaching the top of the tree, they fly down to the base of the next tree to repeat their foraging technique. Brown creepers are unable to climb head down, which is most likely why they fly from the top of previously foraged trees to the base of its next tree to be searched.

Behavior and reproduction: Brown creepers are usually not seen when observers are looking at trees, because their coloration is so similar to that of the tree bark. To hide from predators, they hold their body against a tree, spread their wings and tail, and remain motionless. They are generally solitary birds, but may join flocks of nuthatches, titmice, warblers, chickadees, and other small birds in the winter (during the nonbreeding season). Brown creepers are unable to move sideways or upside down. Their direct flights are usually of short duration, using rapid shallow beats of their wings. Their call is a high, reedy "tseeeee." Eastern birds have a call that is a very high, thin, quavering "seee" or "sreee," while the western birds' call is a buzz-like, often doubled "teesee." Their song is a thin, high series of quickly sounding notes "tee see see, teesyew, seee" (but the pattern may vary). For instance, eastern populations may begin singing with two long, high notes followed by an irregular low note "seee sooo sideeda sidio," while the song of western birds generally ends on a high note "seee sitsweeda sowit-see."

Before breeding, they build pocket-shaped nests of bark flakes, plant fibers, twigs, conifer needles, mosses, and silks, which are placed behind loose sheets of bark, in a split-out tree, or behind a heavy growth of ivy. Nests are lined inside with feathers and shredded bark. Monogamous (muh-NAH-guh-mus) partners (having one mate) build nests usually 5 to 50 feet (1.5 to 15 meters) above the ground. The nest is built away from other nests and birds. Females lay four to eight eggs, which are lightly flecked with reddish brown. The incubation period is thirteen to seventeen days, which is performed only by the female. The nestling period (time period necessary to take care of young before ready to fly off) is thirteen to sixteen days. Both parents feed the young birds, with only one brood per year.

Brown creepers and people: People enjoy putting out a mixture of nuts, peanut butter, suet, and cornmeal in feeders for brown creepers and watching them feed.

Conservation status: It is believed that brown creepers are declining in numbers, but so far they are not threatened. Their nesting areas are declining due to the cutting down of forest habitats.   ■

FOR MORE INFORMATION

Books:

Alsop, Fred J. III. *Birds of North America.* New York: DK, 2001.

Baughman, Mel M., ed. *Reference Atlas to the Birds of North America.* Washington, DC: National Geographic, 2003.

del Hoyo, Josep, Andrew Elliott, Jordi Sargatal, et al, eds. *Handbook of the Birds of the World.* Barcelona: Lynx Edicions, 1992.

Dickinson, Edward C., ed. *The Howard and Moore Complete Checklist of the Birds of the World,* 3rd ed. Princeton, NJ and Oxford, U.K.: Princeton University Press, 2003.

Field Guide to the Birds of North America, 4th ed. Washington, DC: National Geographic Society, 2002.

Harrison, Colin James Oliver. *Birds of the World.* London and New York: Dorling Kindersley, 1993.

Forshaw, Joseph, ed. *Encyclopedia of Birds,* 2nd ed. San Diego, CA: Academic Press, 1998.

Kaufman, Kenn, with collaboration of Rick and Nora Bowers and Lynn Hassler Kaufman. *Birds of North America.* New York: Houghton Mifflin, 2000.

Sibley, David. *The Sibley Guide to Birds.* New York: Alfred A. Knopf, 2000.

Terres, John K. *The Audubon Society Encyclopedia of North American Birds.* New York: Knopf, 1980.

PHILIPPINE CREEPERS

Rhabdornithidae

Class: Aves

Order: Passeriformes

Family: Rhabdornithidae

Number of species: 3 species

family

phylum

class

subclass

order

monotypic order

suborder

▲ **family**

PHYSICAL CHARACTERISTICS

Philippine creepers are a small group of medium-sized, very similar looking, arboreal (living in trees) birds found only in the Republic of the Philippines. They are similar in physical appearances to treecreepers. The perching birds have long, slender bills and brush-tipped tongues. The bird group consists of three species, the greater rhabdornis, the stripe-breasted rhabdornis, and the stripe-headed rhabdornis.

As a group, Philippine creepers are very similar in size and color. However, there is little known about the specific details of the family's size and color. Philippine creepers are marked and shaded with black, brown, red-browns, gray, and white; colors that help them to blend into the forests in which they live. The birds have dark brown streaks on their upperparts, white on the under parts and flanks (with blackish streaks), and lighter streaks on the other parts of their body. They have a long, slender, pointed, down-curved bill and brush-like tongue. Philippine creepers are 6 to 7 inches (15 to 17 centimeters) long and weigh between 3 and 4 ounces (80 to 95 grams).

GEOGRAPHIC RANGE

Philippine creepers are limited to the range of the major Philippine Islands of Luzon, Samar, Leyte, Mindanao, Negros, and Panay and of the minor islands of Catanduanes, Masbate, Calicoan, Dinagat, Basilan, and Bohol.

HABITAT

Philippine creepers inhabit deep, dense, tropical primary and secondary lowland and mountainous forests, along with the edges of forests. They specifically prefer the upper levels, including the canopy (uppermost level of vegetation of the forest) and the crown (top part of the forest) of trees and the middle story (middle part) of the forest.

DIET

Philippine creepers run across the tops of tree branches, hop and jump between branches on trees, and crawl on tree bark found on the trunks and main limbs of trees during their foraging for food within the forest. They search on the bark of tree trunks and branches and even among flowers. Philippine creepers eat mostly insects, but also nectar (sweet liquid produced by flowering plants), fruits, and seeds. Their long, slender bill allows them to easily remove insects from bark, while their brush-tipped tongue enables them to quickly feed on nectar.

PHILIPPINE HABITAT DESTRUCTION

About 572 species of birds, including the Philippine creepers, are known to occur within the 7,100 islands that comprise the country of the Republic of the Philippines. Scientists believe that of these 572 species, about 172 bird species are not found in any other place on Earth. Many of these unique birds, however, are endangered as the result of high levels of habitat destruction in the Philippine forests. Their continued existence will depend in part on how successful conservation and protection measures will be in the future.

BEHAVIOR AND REPRODUCTION

In most of the recent past, these birds have been grouped with the northern creepers (family Certhidae), which is why they are often called Philippine creepers. Although they are called "creepers," their behavior is not very creeper-like. In fact, they act more like chickadees and titmice while in flocks of mixed species of birds. Philippine creepers are diurnal (active during the day) and arboreal (living in trees). They do not migrate (move between habitats) other than with regards to local movements in their permanent territory. They are very social birds, often found foraging with a flock of birds both within and outside of their family. Other specific behaviors with other birds are not known for certain due to a lack of adequate study and research. Their songs and calls are also unknown. At dusk, groups of the birds roost in the upper branches of trees. Little information is known about the reproduction activities of Philippine creepers. It is known that they nest in tree crevasses (cracks), but it is unknown what type of nesting material is used inside the nest. Also unknown is specific information about the number and coloring of eggs laid by the birds. Breeding probably begins in March but may occur at other times during the year.

PHILIPPINE CREEPERS AND PEOPLE

Philippine creepers have no special significance to people.

CONSERVATION STATUS

Philippine creepers are not threatened. The stripe-breasted rhabdornis and the stripe-headed rhabdornis are common throughout their ranges, while the greater rhabdornis is relatively rare and confined to the mountainous regions in Luzon (within the Philippines). As the native forests of the Philippines are increasingly destroyed, the size of their habitat (home environment and territory) is being decreased and the condition of their habitat is being severely degraded. Because of this, Philippine creepers have a weakened ability to grow in numbers.

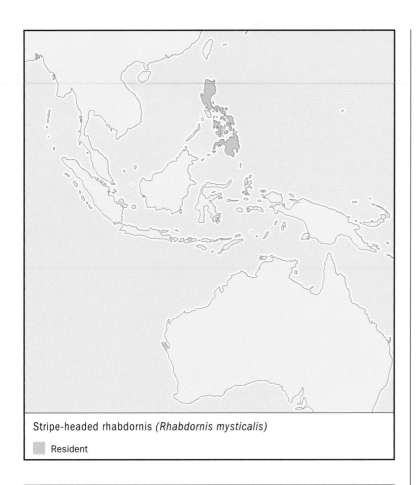

Stripe-headed rhabdornis *(Rhabdornis mysticalis)*

■ Resident

STRIPE-HEADED RHABDORNIS
Rhabdornis mysticalis

Physical characteristics: Stripe-headed rhabdornises (sometimes called the stripe-sided rhabdornises) are 5.7 to 6.2 inches (14.5 to 15.8 centimeters) long, and weigh between 2.75 and 3.00 ounces (78 to 85 grams). Both sexes are colored in a similar way, but males are larger in size than females. Generally, stripe-headed rhabdornises have black bills, dark brown eyes, and dark legs. Adult males have a blackish brown crown (top part of the head) and nape (back part of the neck) with many white streaks, a broad strip through the eye, while the face and the rest of the neck are blackish brown. Adult females differ from males in having a lighter brown crown and face. Both sexes have a striated head (marked with narrow parallel bands).

Stripe-headed rhabdornises are active during the day, and often flock together in groups of up to twenty-five individuals. (Illustration by John Megahan. Reproduced by permission.)

Geographic range: Stripe-headed rhabdornises range in the Philippine Islands of Luzon, Negros, Panay, Masbate, Contanduenes, Leyte, Mindanao, Samar, Basilan, Bohol, Calicoan, and Dinagat.

Habitat: Stripe-headed rhabdornises live throughout the major Philippine Islands in tropical forests from sea level up to an elevation of about 3,900 feet (1,200 meters). They generally prefer lowland forests and second growth forests, and are usually found within the canopy or middle story of the trees.

Diet: Stripe-headed rhabdornises primarily eat insects, along with nectar, fruits, and seeds found within their forest habitat. Stripe-headed rhabdornises forage (search for food) along limbs, checking crevices with their thin pointed, down-curved bills in order to remove insects from tree bark. They then use their brush-tipped tongues for the removal of nectar within flowers.

Behavior and reproduction: Stripe-headed rhabdornises are very active during the day. They occupy the canopy and middle story of primary forests, forest edges, and secondary growth. Groups of the birds themselves or groups of the birds along with other bird species often flock together in numbers up to twenty-five individuals. At dusk, they usually roost in large groups of up to several hundreds of birds. The call of the stripe-headed rhabdornises is an uninteresting, high-pitched "tsee tsee WICK tsee," with the "tsee" called out softly but the "WICK" spoken sharp and loud. The reproduction habits of the birds are largely unknown. They are believed to nest in cavities (hollow areas) and holes of trees.

Stripe-headed rhabdornises and people: Stripe-headed rhabdornises have no special significance to people.

Conservation status: Stripe-headed rhabdornises are not threatened. They are commonly found throughout a restricted range of the Philippine islands. However, as the native forests of the Philippines decrease due to increased and continuing activities of humans, the size and condition of the habitat of the birds is being negatively affected. Stripe-headed rhabdornises, thus, are less able to adequately cope with their changing environment.   ▪

FOR MORE INFORMATION

Books:

del Hoyo, Josep, Andrew Elliott, Jordi Sargatal, et al, eds. *Handbook of the Birds of the World.* Barcelona: Lynx Edicions, 1992.

Dickinson, Edward C., ed. *The Howard and Moore Complete Checklist of the Birds of the World,* 3rd ed. Princeton, NJ and Oxford, U.K.: Princeton University Press, 2003.

Harrison, Colin James Oliver. *Birds of the World.* London and New York: Dorling Kindersley, 1993.

Forshaw, Joseph, ed. *Encyclopedia of Birds,* 2nd ed. San Diego, CA: Academic Press, 1998.

Perrins, Christopher M., and Alex L. A. Middleton, eds. *The Encyclopedia of Birds.* New York: Facts on File, 1985.

Web sites:

Birdwatch.ph. The Official Website of the Wild Bird Club of the Philippines. http://www.birdwatch.ph/gallery/stripeheadedrhabdornis.html (accessed on April 19, 2004).

FLOWERPECKERS
Dicaeidae

Class: Aves
Order: Passeriformes
Family: Dicaeidae
Number of species: 52 species

CHAPTER

phylum

class

subclass

order

monotypic order

suborder

▲ **family**

PHYSICAL CHARACTERISTICS

Flowerpeckers consist of the true flowerpeckers and the berrypeckers. Some researchers consider only the true flowerpeckers as members of the family Dicaeidae, with the berrypeckers sometimes in dispute among scientists as to their membership in the family.

All six groups of birds are very small, dumpy-looking, often brightly colored with short, usually straight bills and short stubby tails. Upperparts are dark and glossy, and under parts are lighter. In species with dull plumage (feathers), no difference between males and females occurs. In those species with bright plumage, males have patches of bright colors; those patches are missing in females. In some species, females appear duller and larger than males. They are 2.2 to 8.3 inches (5.6 to 21.0 centimeters) long and weigh between 0.14 and 2.80 ounces (4 to 80 grams).

True flowerpeckers are small birds with short bills and short, stubby tails. The outer third of the upper bill is serrated (having notches). Their tongues have frilly outer edges, termed fimbriations.

Berrypeckers have simple tongues, long, straight bills, and lack specializations of the gut (abdomen) that are contained in true flowerpeckers.

GEOGRAPHIC RANGE

Flowerpeckers and berrypeckers are found on the Indian subcontinent, Sri Lanka, Myanmar, Thailand, Vietnam, Cambodia,

Laos, southern China, Hainan Island, Taiwan, the Malay Peninsula, Indonesia, the Philippines, Sulawesi, the Moluccas, New Guinea and its surrounding islands, and Australia.

HABITAT

Flowerpeckers reside in tall forests, from sea level up to more than 12,000 feet (3,700 meters) in altitude where little vegetation grows. The birds range from rainforests, secondary growth forests, and woodlands to cultivated farmlands and urban areas.

DIET

Food for flowerpeckers consists mostly of berries from shrubs, trees, and vines (especially mistletoe berries); fruits; nectar; and pollen; but also small insects and spiders. The birds do a funny-looking dance while trying to separate the fleshy part of the mistletoe berries from their large seeds. Smaller fruits are eaten whole, while insects and spiders are caught as they fly through the air.

BEHAVIOR AND REPRODUCTION

Flowerpeckers easily twist and turn while roaming among foliage. They actively move their wings and sharply call out while feeding. The birds are territorial, with males chasing intruders in weaving flight over their territory. The birds are usually found singly, in pairs, or small groups, but sometimes join with different types of birds. They often sit quietly on perches for long periods of time. When vocal, they give out simple, faint metallic chirps and clicks, and high-pitched twittering. Some species produce a series of rapid back-and-forth notes.

Reproduction behavior of flowerpeckers is not known very well. Courtship rituals include flitting around females, calling out to them, and fanning their tails. They generally nest in pairs. The description of eggs is still unknown in some species. Males and females share duties on the construction of nests, incubation (process of sitting on eggs before hatching) of eggs, and feeding of the young. Open nests are hung from thick bushes, shrubs, or trees, and are made in the shape of a cup or pendant with a narrow side entrance near the top. Nest materials

PECKING AT FLOWERS

Flowerpeckers are named for their tendency to peck at flowers with their bills for nectar, seeds, and small insects. One species of flowerpecker native to Australia is the mistletoebird, which pecks on mistletoe berries. Within a half an hour after eating the berry, it is excreted. Because mistletoe is considered a parasitic plant on trees, the mistletoe bird is sometimes considered a pest.

consist of vegetable material, dried flowers, lichen, feathers, grass, or small roots, all of which are held together with cobwebs and lined with vegetable down. Some nests are decorated with insect waste matter or other debris. Most eggs are white, but a few species lay spotted ones. The female lays usually two eggs, but one to four eggs are possible. The incubation period is about 15 days, and the nestling period (time necessary to take care of young birds unable to leave nest) is also about 15 days.

FLOWERPECKERS AND PEOPLE

People consider some species to be pests because they deposit seeds of mistletoe, which is a parasite (organism living on another) on trees that are used in the lumber industry and for other economic purposes. The crested berrypecker is often caught for food in the highlands of New Guinea.

CONSERVATION STATUS

The Cebu flowerpecker is Critically Endangered, facing an extremely high risk of extinction, with a population of less than fifty birds. The black-belted or Visayan flowerpecker and the scarlet-collared flowerpecker are both Vulnerable, facing a high risk of extinction. Five other species are Near Threatened, in danger of becoming threatened with extinction.

Fire-breasted flowerpecker (*Dicaeum ignipectus*)

Resident

FIRE-BREASTED FLOWERPECKER
Dicaeum ignipectus

Physical characteristics: Fire-breasted flowerpeckers have a black crown (top part of the head); black upperparts with dark brown cheeks, a scarlet breast, and buff belly and throat. They are about 3.5 inches (8.9 centimeters) long, and weigh between 0.14 and 0.28 ounces (4 and 8 grams).

Geographic range: Fire-breasted flowerpeckers range throughout most of Southeast Asia including Mindanao, Negros, and Samar (within the Philippines), Sumatra (within Indonesia), Cambodia, northeast and southeast Thailand, Taiwan, Kashmir, northeast India, Nepal, Bhutan, Sikkim, northern Myanmar, northern Indochina, southern China, and southeast Tibet.

Habitat: These birds live in mountainous forests, oak woodlands, and cultivated lands. They also live near rhododendrons (an ornamental evergreen shrub of the heath family).

Fire-breasted flowerpeckers are very active birds, and join other birds within their species and other bird species during the nonbreeding season. (Illustration by Bruce Worden. Reproduced by permission.)

Diet: Nectar, fruits, mistletoe berries, insects, and spiders are eaten by fire-breasted flowerpeckers.

Behavior and reproduction: Fire-breasted flowerpeckers are very active birds, especially around treetops. They join other birds within their species and other bird species during the nonbreeding season.

Fire-breasted flowerpeckers and people: People and fire-breasted flowerpeckers have no especially significant relationship.

Conservation status: Fire-breasted flowerpeckers are not threatened.   ■

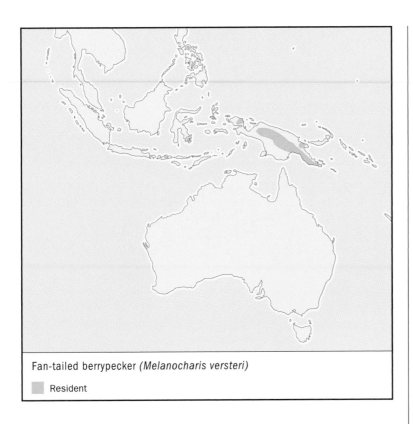

Fan-tailed berrypecker (*Melanocharis versteri*)

■ Resident

FAN-TAILED BERRYPECKER
Melanocharis versteri

Physical characteristics: Fan-tailed berrypeckers have whitish underparts and side feathers on a very long tail. The white tail patches are very noticeable while they fly. They are 5.5 to 6.0 inches (14 to 19 centimeters) long. Females are larger and heavier than males, with a wing length of 2.6 to 2.8 inches (6.6 to 7.1 centimeters) and a weight of between 0.56 and 0.70 ounces (16 and 20 grams). Males have a wing length of 2.32 to 2.52 inches (5.9 to 6.4 centimeters) and a weight of between 0.44 and 0.53 ounces (12.5 and 15.0 grams).

Geographic range: Fan-tailed berrypeckers are found in the mountains of New Guinea; both in Indonesia and Papua New Guinea. The birds are usually found in lands that lie 4,500 to 10,800 feet (1,400 to 3,300 meters) in altitude.

The fan-tailed berrypecker has a distinctive, long tail. (© W. Peckover/VIREO. Reproduced by permission.)

Habitat: Fan-tailed berrypeckers occupy mountainous forests, tree-fern heaths (grassy and shrubby uncultivated land), and alpine thickets. They generally prefer undergrowth but sometimes are found in the middle strata of forests.

Diet: Small berries and insects are usually eaten by fan-tailed berrypeckers. Berries and insects are taken from the undergrowth and eaten whole. The bird often hovers to pluck berries or to take insects from the foliage.

Behavior and reproduction: Fan-tailed berrypeckers are shy birds, usually found singly or in pairs. They are active feeders. While flying in an acrobatic (with daring maneuvers) manner, they show white coloring in the tail. They have a harsh song and their calls are often heard in squeaks and nasal scold-like tones.

Nests are built much larger than necessary for the size of the birds. A neat, sturdy, and deep cup is constructed that is usually 3 inches (8 centimeters) in diameter and about 4 inches (10 centimeter) high. Nests are made of fibers torn from ferns, lined with lichens, and usually placed in the fork of a tree or on a horizontal branch. Fan-tailed berrypeckers build the nests so predators cannot easily find them.

Fan-tailed berrypeckers and people: People and fan-tailed berrypeckers have no known significant relationship.

Conservation status: Fan-tailed berrypeckers are not threatened.   ■

FOR MORE INFORMATION

Books:

del Hoyo, Josep, Andrew Elliott, Jordi Sargatal, et al, eds. *Handbook of the Birds of the World.* Barcelona: Lynx Edicions, 1992.

Dickinson, Edward C., ed. *The Howard and Moore Complete Checklist of the Birds of the World,* 3rd ed. Princeton, NJ and Oxford, U.K.: Princeton University Press, 2003.

Forshaw, Joseph, ed. *Encyclopedia of Birds,* 2nd ed. San Diego, CA: Academic Press, 1998.

Harrison, Colin James Oliver. *Birds of the World.* London and New York: Dorling Kindersley, 1993.

Perrins, Christopher M., and Alex L. A. Middleton, eds. *The Encyclopedia of Birds.* New York: Facts on File, 1985.

PARDALOTES
Pardalotidae

Class: Aves
Order: Passeriformes
Family: Pardalotidae
Number of species: 8 species

phylum
class
subclass
order
monotypic order
suborder
▲ **family**

PHYSICAL CHARACTERISTICS

Pardalotes (PAR-dah-lohts) are small- to medium-sized birds, with some species being very small in size. They are fairly bright colored, beautiful birds. Pardalotes have a short and plump body; a short, stumpy, scoop-shaped black bill; a short tail; nine long, stiff primary feathers (with a tenth feather barely visible), nine secondary feathers (with some species having a tenth shortened one); short pointed wings; and strong legs and feet. All species have brightly colored plumage (feathers), with many combinations including yellow, brown, and black colorings and white spots or streaking. The color combination is often called "sparkling," which has given them the popular name "diamond bird." Their backs are slate to olive, while the head and wings are black with white spots or stripes and with patches of bright yellow or orange. Females are duller in color than males in some species. They are 3 to 5 inches (8 to 12 centimeters) long, and weigh between 0.3 and 0.5 ounces (8 to 13 grams).

GEOGRAPHIC RANGE

Pardalotes are found only on the continent of Australia.

HABITAT

Pardalotes inhabit areas of woodlands and forests, mostly living alongside eucalyptus (yoo-kah-LIP-tus; tall, aromatic trees) and acacia (uh-KAY-shah; flowering trees). They range from the wet coasts to the arid interior of the continent, missing only from certain small areas of the southern desert.

DIET

The diet of pardalotes consists of a wide variety of small, soft-bodied invertebrates (animals without a backbone), including small wasps, spiders, weevils (a destructive beetle with a snout), and termites. They also eat lerps (sugary lumps of secretions made by a particular insect). Pardalotes move quickly around the outer parts of foliage in search of prey from leaves and twigs, which they pick up with their scoop-shaped bills. They frequently hang upside down when foraging. They are not restricted to tree trunks or cones in their foraging, but roam throughout the foliage.

BEHAVIOR AND REPRODUCTION

Pardolotes spend most of their time high in the outer foliage of trees, feeding mostly on lerps, as well as insects and spiders. Their feeding on lerp infestations in eucalyptus forests is significant to maintaining the health of the forest ecosystem. They nest in pairs, only combining in groups during winters, migrations, and after breeding periods. They sometimes come together into flocks after the breeding season. Several species are migratory and make large seasonal movements. They often forage in flocks of several species during the winter. When feeding, they make clicking sounds from their bills while removing lerps from the foliage.

Female and male partners defend their nesting territories with two- to five-note whistles that are also repeated over and over again. Breeding partners mate for life (that is, they are monogamous [muh-NAH-guh-mus]). Nests are built in shapes of cups, sometimes with domes on top. Nests are usually built in hollows or burrows. Deep horizontal tunnels that lead to the nests are burrowed into earthen banks or horizontally into the ground, and are usually dug 16 to 28 inches (40 to 70 centimeters) long. At other times, nests are made in tree hollows. The external size of the nest is usually no bigger than a mouse hole, but the tunnel can be up to 3 feet (1 meter) in length. The nests are made with various plant fibers. Females lay three to five eggs that are 0.6 by 0.5 inches to 0.7 by 0.6 inches (1.6 by 1.3 centimeters to 1.9 by 1.5 centimeters). The incubation period (time necessary to sit on eggs before hatching) is fourteen to sixteen days, while the nestling period (time necessary to take care of young birds unable to leave the nest) is about twenty-five days.

PARDOLOTES AND PEOPLE

People and pardolotes have no special relationship between them.

CONSERVATION STATUS

The forty-spotted pardalote is Endangered, facing a very high risk of extinction. The species has been studied in great detail with regards to a detailed plan to increase its numbers that are confined to southeastern Tasmania. Other species of pardolotes are widely spread around and are not considered threatened. Their primary threats are from land clearing, overgrazing, and degradation and fragmentation of habitat.

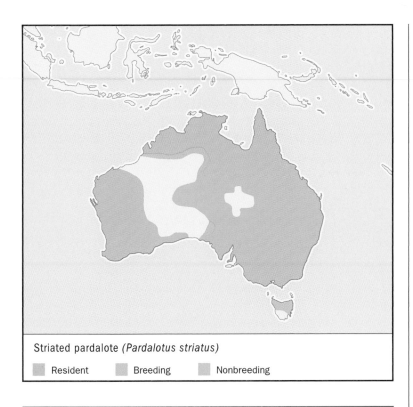

Striated pardalote *(Pardalotus striatus)*

■ Resident   ■ Breeding   ■ Nonbreeding

STRIATED PARDALOTE
Pardalotus striatus

Physical characteristics: Striated pardalotes are the largest of the pardalotes. They are small, brightly colored birds that are easily identified by the bright yellow patch above the eyes. They have considerable variation in plumage characteristics across the geographical range of their species. All birds have white eyebrows, olive-gray backs, and a white stripe on the wings. In different parts of the country, the wing stripe may be narrower or wider, the colored spot at the front end of this stripe may be red or yellow, and the black crown (top part of the head) may have narrow white stripes. Both male and female are similar in plumage. They are 3.5 to 4.5 inches (9.0 to 11.5 centimeters) long and weigh about 0.42 ounces (12 grams). Females and males are similar in plumage, but juveniles are much paler, particularly on the crown and face.

Geographic range: Striated pardalotes are located throughout Australia except for desert sections of the interior of the country. Like

Striated pardalotes eat a number of insects and their larvae that they pick from outer twigs and leaves in the tops of trees. (© R. Brown/VIREO. Reproduced by permission.)

other species of pardalotes, they are found only in Australia.

Habitat: Striated pardalotes are found in almost every territorial habitat that contains trees or shrubs. They are widely distributed through woodlands and forests filled with eucalyptus, but are also found in rainforests and mangroves (tropical evergreen trees of tidal coasts). They often are found near and about water courses.

Diet: Striated pardalotes eat a number of invertebrates, including insects (and their larvae [LARvee; active immature insects]) that they pick from the surfaces of foliage in the tops of trees, such as outer twigs and leaves, mostly from eucalyptus and acacia trees. They sometimes come close to the ground and feed among low shrubs. Feeding takes place in small groups, with the birds maintaining contact with each other with soft sounding trills.

Behavior and reproduction: Striated pardalotes are very active and curious in their overall behavior. They form flocks of birds during winter. Some species are nomadic or migratory, while others tend to be sedentary (tending not to migrate). They do not defend their breeding territory, except for the immediate area surrounding the nest. They are loud sounding birds with a repetitious two- to three-note call, such as the "tchip tchip." When not breeding, the birds form flocks that feed together. While feeding they utter constant, short calls.

The breeding season takes place between the months of June and January. They form breeding pairs or small groups of up to six birds. Striated pardalotes build nests close to the ground, often in earthen burrows, or in tree hollows or tunnels. They sometimes use artificial objects built by people for their nests. The completed nests are cup-shaped, either partially or completely domed. They are made with plant fibers, such as tree bark and grass, and lined with finer materials. Nests are located at the end of a tunnel, or in a tree hollow. The birds appear regularly at the entrance to the nest, aggressively guarding the area around the nest from other pardalotes and predators. Females usually lay three to five white eggs, which are incubated by both the male and female of breeding pair. Other members of the breeding group also help with feeding the young.

Striated pardalotes and people: People and striated pardalotes have no special relationship between them.

Conservation status: Striated pardalotes are not threatened, being plentiful in a broad range of environments and across a wide geographic area. ■

FOR MORE INFORMATION

Books:

del Hoyo, Josep, Andrew Elliott, Jordi Sargatal, Jose Cabot, et al., eds. *Handbook of the Birds of the World.* Barcelona: Lynx Edicions, 1992.

Dickinson, Edward C., ed. *The Howard and Moore Complete Checklist of the Birds of the World,* 3rd ed. Princeton, NJ and Oxford, U.K.: Princeton University Press, 2003.

Forshaw, Joseph, ed. *Encyclopedia of Birds,* 2nd ed. San Diego, CA: Academic Press, 1998.

Harrison, Colin James Oliver. *Birds of the World.* London and New York: Dorling Kindersley, 1993.

Perrins, Christopher M., and Alex L. A. Middleton, eds. *The Encyclopedia of Birds.* New York: Facts on File, 1985.

Pizzey, Graham. *Field Guide to the Birds of Australia.* Sydney, Australia: Angus and Robertson, 1997.

SUNBIRDS

Nectariniidae

Class: Aves

Order: Passeriformes

Family: Nectariniidae

Number of species: About 124 species

family

phylum

class

subclass

order

monotypic order

suborder

▲ **family**

PHYSICAL CHARACTERISTICS

Sunbirds are very small birds, 3 to 7 inches (8 to 16 centimeters) long, resembling New World hummingbirds. The males of most sunbird species are brilliantly colored with combinations of iridescent, metallic green, purple, blue and black along with spots and patches of yellow, orange and red. Males of a few species are more drab, as are the females of nearly all sunbird species, although females of some species bear a metallic sheen. Outside of the breeding season, males molt and revert to less gaudy plumage (feathers) resembling that of the female of the species.

Sunbirds can easily be mistaken for the New World hummingbirds, but the sunbirds are strictly Old World birds and are not in any way related to hummingbirds. Sunbirds and hummingbirds are vivid examples of convergence, through adaptive evolution, by which unrelated species come to resemble each other due to similar environmental pressures over long stretches of time. In the case of sunbirds and hummingbirds, feeding on nectar has been the major adaptive molding factor in the two families.

Many single species are confined to some small islands off Africa, India, or in Indonesia. Examples include the Seychelles sunbird, found only on the Seychelles Islands, and the São Tomé sunbird, found on São Tomé.

Sunbirds in the genus *Nectarinia* have long, thin, downcurved bills for reaching into flowers to sip nectar, much like the bills of hummingbirds and other nectar-feeding bird species among the asity-sunbirds (family Philepittidae) and Hawaiian honeycreepers. Species in genus *Anthreptes*, considered the most primitive of the genera, have short, straight bills and chiefly feed by gleaning (plucking) insects from leaves, although they add nectar and fruits to their diets. Species of the genus *Aethopyga* have short bills and are among the most brilliantly colored animals alive. Species of genus *Arachnothera*, the spiderhunters, have low-key green, yellow, and gray plumage and most have very long, downcurved bills.

GEOGRAPHIC RANGE

Sunbirds live in tropical Africa, Madagascar, tropical Southeast Asia, Indonesia, Philippine Islands, Australia, and New Guinea.

HABITAT

Sunbirds can be found in lowland and mountain tropical rainforest, savanna with open woodlands, gallery forests (along rivers in dry country), thornscrub, and mangrove.

DIET

Sunbirds eat mostly nectar but also fruit, insects, spiders and related creatures.

BEHAVIOR AND REPRODUCTION

Sunbirds are active, energetic creatures. Individuals may forage alone, in monogamous (muh-NAH-guh-mus) pairs (with just one mate), or in groups. Some species, among them the olive sunbird, collared sunbird, and Bates' sunbird, forage in groups in the canopies of dense primary tropical forest.

The most common sort of nest built by sunbirds is oval, purse-like, and hung from a small tree branch. Sunbirds form monogamous pairs to mate and breed. The female constructs the nest and incubates the eggs, while both sexes care for the chicks. The female lays two or three eggs.

SPIDERHUNTERS

The ten species of spiderhunters are an obscure, little-studied group of small, mostly arboreal birds scattered through the tropical forests of Southeast Asia and some of the Indonesian islands. They feed on spiders and insects. Beaks of all the spiderhunters are thin and downcurved, more or less like those of sunbirds, but more robust. The beak of the gray-breasted spiderhunter is so long and robust that it borders on the grotesque.

SUNBIRDS AND PEOPLE

Sunbirds are not harmful to humankind in any way. They are a delight wherever they live, and a tourist draw for bird-watchers and people interested in exotic things.

CONSERVATION STATUS

The World Conservation Union (IUCN) lists two species of sunbird as Endangered, facing a very high risk of extinction; four as Vulnerable, facing a high risk of extinction; and eight as Near Threatened, in danger of becoming threatened with extinction.

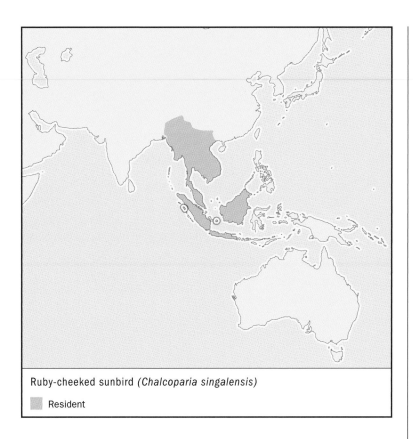

Ruby-cheeked sunbird (*Chalcoparia singalensis*)

Resident

RUBY-CHEEKED SUNBIRD
Chalcoparia singalensis

Physical characteristics: The adult body length is around 3.9 to 4.3 inches (10 to 11 centimeters). The bill is short and not down-curved. The male is iridescent green above, yellow below, with vivid crimson patches on the cheeks. Females and young are duller but the female shares the male's orange throat.

Geographic range: Northern India to northern Indochina, Sumatra, Java, and Borneo.

Habitat: Lowland and mountain tropical rain forest; also open forest, scrub forest, gardens.

Diet: Ruby-cheeked sunbirds feed on nectar and insects.

Behavior and reproduction: Ruby-cheeked sunbirds forage in tropical forests, in the canopy and at mid-level, usually in groups of five to ten. They also visit gardens for foraging. The call is a loud "chirp." Breeding follows the usual pattern among sunbirds: monogamous breeding pairs, purse-like nests, female incubating eggs, and both parents caring for the chicks.

Ruby-cheeked sunbirds and people: There is little significant interaction between ruby-cheeked sunbirds and humans, other than human appreciation of the exotic beauty of this and other sunbird species.

Ruby-cheeked sunbirds forage in tropical forests and sometimes gardens, usually in groups of five to ten. (Illustration by Barbara Duperron. Reproduced by permission.)

Conservation status: This species is not threatened. ■

Purple sunbird (*Cinnyris asiaticus*)

☐ Resident

PURPLE SUNBIRD
Cinnyris asiaticus

Physical characteristics: Adult body length is 3.9 inches (10 centimeters). Males are dark, glossy bluish purple above, with yellowish underparts. The female is less colorful, with a yellow and gray upper body, but has yellow underparts much like the male's. The beak is thin and downcurved and the tongues are tubular with brushy tips (of flesh), because of their adaptation to a diet of mainly nectar.

Geographic range: These birds live from Pakistan through India to Southeast Asia. This is the most common sunbird species in India.

Habitat: Purple sunbirds live in forests, often visiting gardens.

Diet: These sunbirds eat nectar and insects.

Purple sunbirds forage for nectar and insects in forests and often visit gardens specifically to seek out nectar. (Illustration by Barbara Duperron. Reproduced by permission.)

Behavior and reproduction: Purple sunbirds forage for nectar, insects, and related creatures in forests and often visit gardens to seek out nectar. The call can be rendered as a humming "zit zit" and "swee swee." Breeding follows the usual pattern among sunbirds: monogamous breeding pairs, purse-like nests, female incubating eggs, and both parents caring for the chicks.

Purple sunbirds and people: There is little significant interaction between purple sunbirds and humans, other than human appreciation and awe of these jewel-like birds.

Conservation status: These birds are not threatened. ∎

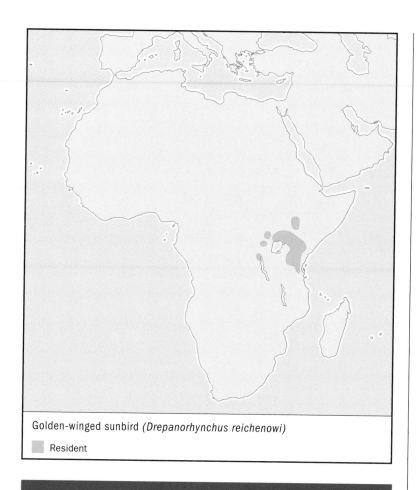

Golden-winged sunbird (*Drepanorhynchus reichenowi*)

■ Resident

GOLDEN-WINGED SUNBIRD
Drepanorhynchus reichenowi

Physical characteristics: Adult male body length is about 4.7 inches (12 centimeters) without the tail, which adds another 4.7 inches (12 centimeters). The tail and wings are bright yellow, the shoulders are dark gray, the dark gray extending to the nape and throat, while the head and downturned beak are lighter gray. The tail is long and ends in two long, very narrow parallel feathers.

Geographic range: These birds are found in East Africa; Kenya, Tanzania, and Uganda.

Habitat: Golden-winged sunbirds live in grassland, bamboo thickets, and tropical mountain forest.

Groups of golden-winged sunbirds defend the area where they feed against other birds that might feed on the nectar. They feed when the nectar has built up to a level so that the whole group can feed. (A. J. Deane/Bruce Coleman Inc. Reproduced by permission.)

Diet: These sunbirds eat mainly nectar, with some insect fare.

Behavior and reproduction: Golden-winged sunbirds are of special interest to ethologists (scientists who study animal behavior) because a typical foraging flock of related individuals guards its major source of nectar outside the breeding season, when nectar is their main food source. They actively chase other birds, including others of their own species, away from the nectar source, usually a patch of shrubbery or other plants bearing flowers and nectar. The effect is to increase the amount of nectar available in a flower patch by letting it collect throughout the day, undisturbed by other nectivores (animals that feed on nectar). The more nectar per flower, the less foraging time the sunbirds have to spend on sipping enough for their needs. In addition, the sunbirds wait for nectar in a flower patch to accumulate to a level adequate for feeding the group before making the sipping rounds.

Breeding follows the usual pattern among sunbirds: monogamous breeding pairs, purse-like nests, female incubating eggs, and both parents caring for the chicks.

Golden-winged sunbirds and people: There is little if any interaction between golden-winged sunbirds and humans. They are valuable to science for their resource-defending behavior, the study of which promises more understanding of avian biology and behavior.

Conservation status: These birds are not threatened. ◼

FOR MORE INFORMATION

Books:

Cheke, Robert A., Clive E. Mann, and Richard Allen. *A Guide to the Sunbirds, Flowerpeckers, Spiderhunters, and Sugarbirds of the World.* New Haven, CT: Yale University Press, 2001.

Christy, P., and W. V. Clarke. *Guide des Oiseaux de São Tomé & Príncipe.* Libreville, Gabon: Ecofac, 1998.

Goodman, Steven M., and Jonathan P. Benstead. *The Natural History of Madagascar.* Chicago: University of Chicago Press, 2003.

Kavanagh, James. *African Birds.* Chandler, AZ: Waterford Press, 2001.

Strange, Morten. *Birds of Southeast Asia: A Photographic Guide to the Birds of Thailand, Malaysia, Singapore, the Philippines and Indonesia.* London: New Holland, 1998.

Strange, Morten. *A Photographic Guide to Birds of Malaysia and Singapore: Including Southeast Asia, the Philippines and Borneo.* Singapore: Periplus, 2000.

Sinclair, Ian, et al. *Illustrated Guide to the Birds of Southern Africa.* Princeton, NJ: Princeton University Press, 1995.

Stevenson, Terry. *Field Guide to the Birds of East Africa: Kenya, Tanzania, Uganda, Rwanda, Burundi.* Princeton, NJ: Princeton University Press, 2001.

Van Perlo, Ber. *Birds of Western & Central Africa.* Princeton, NJ: Princeton University Press, 2003.

Periodicals:

Gill, F. B., and L. L. Wolf. "Economics of Feeding Territoriality in the Golden-winged Sunbird." *Ecology* 56 (1975): 333–345.

Irwin, M. P. S. "The Genus *Nectarinia* and the Evolution and Diversification of Sunbirds: An Afrotropical Perspective." *Honeyguide* 45, no. 1 (1999): 45–58.

Irwin, M. P. S. "What Sunbirds Belong to the Genus *Anthreptes?*" *Honeyguide* 39, no. 4 (1993): 211–215.

Kennedy, R. S., P. C. Gonzales, and H. C. Miranda. "New *Aethopyga* Sunbirds (Aves: Nectariniidae) From the Island of Mindanao, Philippines." *Auk* 114 (1997): 1–10.

Pyke, G. H. "The Economics of Territory Size and Time Budget in the Golden-winged Sunbird." *American Naturalist* 114 (1979): 131–145.

Showler, D. A., and P. Davidson. "The Socotra Sunbird *Nectarinia balfouri.*" *Sandgrouse* 17 (1996): 148–150.

Web sites:

Sugarbirds, Flowerpeckers, Sunbirds and Spiderhunters of the World (photo gallery). http://www.camacdonald.com/birding/Sampler7_SunbirdsFlowerpeckers.htm (accessed on July 20, 2004).

WHITE-EYES

Zosteropidae

Class: Aves

Order: Passeriformes

Family: Zosteropidae

Number of species: 86 species

phylum

class

subclass

order

monotypic order

suborder

▲ **family**

PHYSICAL CHARACTERISTICS

The white-eyes are small perching birds that look very similar across the species. They have slightly rounded wings; short, pointed bills; a brush-tipped tongue that has four sides and is bordered with hairs both at the sides and at the tip; and black legs and feet. Some species have a distinct ring of tiny, dense, pure-white feathers around each eye (which appears early in life) that is divided by black feathers found between the eyes and bill. The name "white-eye" was given to the birds because of the silky white rings around their eyes. Eye color ranges from gray to brown. Overall, plumage (feathers) vary in shades of yellow-green. The upperparts of the birds are green to greenish yellow, with a gray upper back in some species. Underparts are yellowish from throat to undertail coverts (small feathers around the base of quills on wings, tail, or other parts of bird) in some species while other species are grayish to white. The color of the sides of the body varies from light gray to dark brown. Males and females are similar throughout the year, although males are larger in some species. In addition, males in some species can be more brightly colored than females when in colder climates.

Their short, thin bill is blackish, slightly decurved, curved downward, and sharply pointed. Legs are grayish to brownish. Fledglings (birds that have recently grown the feathers necessary to fly from the nest) and old birds have a pinkish color, while one-year-old birds are darker in color. Older birds molt (phase after breeding where feathers are shed and later grown back) into longer wing and tail feathers.

Continental species are generally 4.0 to 5.5 inches (10 to 14 centimeters) long, have wingspans of 2.2 to 2.6 inches (55 to 65 centimeters), and weigh between 0.3 and 0.5 ounces (9 and 15 grams). Those living in higher latitudes tend to be larger, while island species also tend to have bills, legs, and bodies that are larger than normal.

GEOGRAPHIC RANGE

White-eyes are found widely in sub-Saharan Africa, southern Asia, New Guinea, Australia, and the smaller islands of the Pacific Islands. They have been introduced in Hawaii and Tahiti.

HABITAT

White-eyes are found in almost every kind of wooded habitat including woodlands, forest edges and canopies (uppermost layer of vegetation of forest, treetops), and bushes within parks and gardens. They are found from sea level to altitudes of about 9,800 feet (3,000 meters).

DIET

White-eyes have developed highly specialized tongues, which allow them to feed on nectar. They also feed on fruits (especially in winter) and small insects. The birds hunt for insects and spiders by picking them from foliage, probing into small crevices, and sometimes catching them as they fly. They often forage in gardens, orchards, and at the edges of forests. White-eyes are very aggressive when fighting over food. They often flutter their wings and fight in the air with other birds while clattering loudly.

BEHAVIOR AND REPRODUCTION

White-eyes are very social birds, living in wandering groups when not breeding. White-eyes that live on continents migrate regularly to lower latitudes, though sometimes some of the population remains behind. When breeding, they will drop out of the flock, returning after breeding is finished. They are often seen huddling, resting, foraging, bathing, and roosting together, while sunning is done alone. Breeding mates, parent-offspring, young siblings, and prospective partners often preen each other (grooming of feathers with the bill). Wing fluttering and bill clattering are part of their daily activities, which shows rank and status in flocks and decides who has the better chance to reproduce and to survive. Their warbles sound like a rich melody, and are similar across all species. Calls of both sexes are long and sad sounding. Other calls are high-pitched and short, with constant exchanges just before dawn between birds of a flock that are migrating. Other specialized calls include ones for alarm, roosting, begging, huddling, aggression, and distress. Bills are often clattered when aggression is showed.

Courtship involves horizontal wing quivering and some activities that portray nest building (without actually building a nest). Male birds sing for up to twenty minutes at dawn throughout the breeding season, while some singing is also performed at dusk and occasionally throughout the day. Males also have a courtship warble that is softer sounding than the warble sounded during nonbreeding times.

Breeding season usually begins at the start of the summer rains in September or October, and ends six months later. Birds usually mate for life, and breed in small territories. Information about nests and eggs are known for only about half of the species. What is known is that nests are cup-shaped and constructed from plant fibers. They are usually slung from a small fork under the cover of vegetation at any height. The glossy eggs are colored from whitish to pale blue or bluish green, with a few species having spotted eggs. Eggs measure 0.55 by 0.43 inches (14 by 11 millimeters) to 0.79 by 0.59 inches (20 by 15 millimeters). Females lay from one to five eggs, with three being average. The incubation period (time that it takes to sit on eggs before they hatch) last ten to twelve days. Both parents help in the construction of the nest, in incubation, and with feeding of the young. The chicks are about 0.07 ounces (2 grams) when first hatched. They are fed insects at first, but are given fruits at about the time of fledgling. Up to five clutches (group of eggs hatched together) can be laid in one breeding season. A new nest is usually constructed for each clutch. Parents often take care of two clutches at a time. The nestling period (time necessary to take care of young birds unable to leave nest) is eleven to thirteen days.

WHITE-EYES AND PEOPLE

People often keep white-eyes as pets, often for their beautiful songs. They are considered pests in vineyards and orchards in southern Africa and Australia. However, they are also considered beneficial because they eat aphids and other pest insects.

CONSERVATION STATUS

Of the eighty-six species of white-eyes, six species are considered Critically Endangered, facing an extremely high risk of extinction; one species is considered Endangered, facing a very high risk of extinction; and fourteen species are Vulnerable, facing a high risk of extinction. Two species have recently been classified as Extinct.

Japanese white-eye (*Zosterops japonicus*)

  Resident

JAPANESE WHITE-EYE
Zosterops japonicus

Physical characteristics: Japanese white-eyes have an olive-green back, pale gray underparts, and lemon-yellow throat and undertail coverts. They are about 4.7 inches (12 centimeters) long, and weigh about 0.4 ounces (11 grams). Their wing size is between 20.5 and 25.6 inches (52 and 65 centimeters), and the tail length is between 13.4 and 18.1 inches (34 and 46 centimeters).

Geographic range: Japanese white-eyes are distributed in the Japanese islands, China, Taiwan, Hainan Island, and the Philippines. They have been introduced into Hawaii and Bonin Island.

During the breeding season, each breeding pair of Japanese white-eyes defends a small nesting territory. After the breeding season, the birds form small flocks of numerous species. (Illustration by Wendy Baker. Reproduced by permission.)

Habitat: Japanese white-eyes live in broadleaf evergreen forests and deciduous forests on lowlands and foothills of mountains. They are found from sea level to the upper canopies of forests. The birds are also found on cultivated lands and gardens.

Diet: The diet of Japanese white-eyes consist of arthropods (invertebrate animal with jointed limbs), soft fruits, berries, and nectar.

Behavior and reproduction: After breeding season, the birds form small flocks of numerous species, often for foraging. They are partially migratory birds, moving to villages and suburban gardens in the winter. Males sing beautiful songs. Japanese white-eyes breed in the spring, with each breeding pair defending a small nesting territory. Cup-shaped nests are hung from a fork of shrubs. Females lay three to four eggs, which are incubated for about eleven days.

Japanese white-eyes and people: People keep males in cages in order to enjoy their songs. The birds are often found in Japanese literature.

Conservation status: Japanese white-eyes are not threatened. They are common in most parts, but in some remote areas the birds are vulnerable. ∎

FOR MORE INFORMATION

Books:

del Hoyo, Josep, Andrew Elliott, Jordi Sargatal, et al., eds. *Handbook of the Birds of the World.* Barcelona: Lynx Edicions, 1992.

Dickinson, Edward C., ed. *The Howard and Moore Complete Checklist of the Birds of the World,* 3rd ed. Princeton, NJ and Oxford, U.K.: Princeton University Press, 2003.

Forshaw, Joseph, ed. *Encyclopedia of Birds,* 2nd ed. San Diego, CA: Academic Press, 1998.

Harrison, Colin James Oliver. *Birds of the World.* London and New York: Dorling Kindersley, 1993.

Perrins, Christopher M., and Alex L. A. Middleton, eds. *The Encyclopedia of Birds.* New York: Facts on File, 1985.

Class: Aves
Order: Passeriformes
Family: Meliphagidae
Number of species: 182 species

family
C H A P T E R

phylum

class

subclass

order

monotypic order

suborder

▲ **family**

PHYSICAL CHARACTERISTICS

Australian honeyeaters differ with respect to their outward appearance. They are mostly small birds with some tiny species and others as large as jays. They are longish birds with long, pointed wings, strong legs and feet, sharp claws, and rather long, down-curved and sharply-pointed bills (which vary from this basic shape, based on diet differences). They are usually dull colored, mostly greenish, olive, or brown. The smaller species often have yellow on their under parts. Some of the smaller species are black and white, while some of the larger species are black, gray, dark green, or streaked brown. Most Australian honeyeaters have colored bare skin around the eyes; a somewhat swollen mouth area; fancy wattles (skin that hangs from the throat); and a head that is bald. Such characteristics often change in color as they get older or seasonally as they breed.

In most species, the bill and legs are easily noticed due to their bright color. The bill varies in shape and size, sometimes being short and straight, slightly decurved, or quite long and markedly decurved. All birds have a unique tongue structure, being deeply notched and finely edged with bristles at the tip, forming four parallel brushes. Some of the juveniles have plumage (feathers) that differs greatly from adults, but most differences are small. Adults are 3 to 20 inches (7 to 50 centimeters) long and weigh between 0.25 and 7.0 ounces (7 and 200 grams).

GEOGRAPHIC RANGE

Australian honeyeaters are found throughout Australia (except for dense grasslands without trees and shrubs),

New Guinea, Melanesia, Moluccas, and Lesser Sundas, west to Bali, Micronesia, New Caledonia, and New Zealand; through Polynesia to the Hawaiian Islands. Two species occur in southern Africa.

HABITAT

Australian honeyeaters inhabit tropical, subtropical, and temperate (mild) rainforests, eucalyptus (yoo-kah-LIP-tus) forests (tall, aromatic trees), monsoonal forests, woodlands that contain eucalyptus, casuarinas (trees with needle-shaped leaves that form whorls on short branches), native pines, and acacias (uh-KAY-shuhz; flowering trees). They can also be found in semi-arid woodlands and scrublands, desert shrub-steppes, coastal and upland heathlands (shrubby uncultivated land), and parks and gardens.

DIET

All Australian honeyeaters eat nectar and invertebrates (animals without a backbone), especially insects. They regularly fly to native and exotic flowers. They also eat honeydew (a sticky substance from bugs, called lerp) and sap from trees. Smaller sized Australian honeyeaters consume tiny insects captured in flight, as well as caterpillars and beetles taken from foliage. Species with extra-strong bills probe beneath bark for insects and honeydew. Infrequently eaten foods are spiders, crustaceans (hard-shelled creatures), and small lizards. Some of the largest species eat eggs and nestlings (young birds unable to leave the nest) of other birds. In wetter climates, fruits are a major part of the diet.

BEHAVIOR AND REPRODUCTION

They are active birds, sometimes noisy and aggressive. Australian honeyeaters are seldom found alone, but often seen in family groups or loose flocks. Species that migrate usually occur in large flocks. Some species that inhabit arid and semi-arid habitats are nomadic as they regularly move to different locations. When feeding on large nectar supplies, many birds will come together in noisy groups that chase each other. Species of larger sizes will often dominate smaller birds, taking over better feeding spots. They are often seen probing among flowers for nectar. During breeding and molting (the phase after breeding), the birds are often quiet and difficult to find due to little activity.

Their songs and calls range from beautiful to harsh. Species of smaller sizes have twittering, musical songs, and whistling calls. Medium-sized birds have many different songs and calls. Larger birds emit harsh cackling and coughing calls.

Most Australian honeyeaters are monogamous (muh-NAH-guh-mus; having one mate), although polygamy (puh-LIH-guh-mee; having more than one mate) and a mixed mating system also occurs. It is thought that about one-third of the species are cooperative breeders, their roles ranging from occasional helpers to members of complicated colonies. Most of the birds have long breeding seasons that last for six or more months. Breeding occurs most frequently in late winter to late spring (August to October).

Nests are built from low bushes nearly on the ground to the tops of tall trees. Most nests are located in forks of trees or suspended from foliage. The woven nests are made of spider webs, animal hair, plant down, wool, artificial materials, feathers, and human hair. Some species build hollow nests.

Females lay eggs that range in color from white to pale pink or buff, with purple, red, brown, or black spots and blotches. The average number of eggs is two, but some species lay only one egg. Other species lay up to three or four eggs. The female does most of the incubation (process of sitting on and warming the eggs), which usually lasts from twelve to seventeen days. Both parents feed the young, which usually consists of insects but can be nectar in some species. The fledgling period (the time it takes for a bird to grow feathers necessary to fly) ranges from eleven to twenty days, but can be as long as thirty-two days in the hollow-nesting species.

AUSTRALIAN HONEYEATERS AND PEOPLE

People often find Australian honeyeaters in parks and gardens. A few species are regarded as pests to fruit farmers. People hunt some of the larger species for food. The birds regularly scatter seeds throughout the forest, helping to maintain forest growth. They also help to pollinate many native plants.

CONSERVATION STATUS

Of the various species of Australian honeyeaters, one species and four subspecies are Near Threatened, in danger of becoming threatened with extinction; two species are Endangered, facing a very high risk of extinction; two species and one subspecies are

Critically Endangered, facing an extremely high risk of extinction; and five species are Vulnerable, facing a high risk of extinction. There is not much information on many Indonesian species. Many species have declined in numbers due to the clearing of forests and woodlands for farming and habitation by humans and to the destruction of their habitat in other ways.

Bishop's oo *(Moho bishopi)*

▉ Resident

BISHOP'S OO
Moho bishopi

Physical characteristics: Bishop's oos have a smoky black neck, back, and underparts with narrow white shaft lines on the feathers. The wings and tail are black. Males have a long, graduated tail with yellow feathers on the wing, neck, and tail coverts (small feathers around quill base). At the ear coverts, undertail, and axillary are clumps of golden feathers. They are about 12 inches (31 centimeters) long.

Geographic range: Bishop's oos are found on the island of Maui in the Hawaiian Islands.

Habitat: They inhabit dense rainforests in mountains.

Diet: They eat nectar from lobelia flowers (plants with two-lipped blue, red, or white flowers), but also eat insects from the forest's upper canopy.

Behavior and reproduction: Bishop's oos are curious birds, but are also timid. They have a very loud call "owow, owow-ow." The long tail and yellow feathers on the male's wing, neck, and tail coverts are used to attract females. Reproductive activities are not known, other than it is believed that they build hollow nests.

Bishop's oos and people: Native Hawaiians have caught Bishop's oos for their yellow plumes, which were used for ceremonial cloaks.

Conservation status: Bishop's oo is considered Critically Endangered. ■

Bishop's oos live in rainforests in the mountains of Maui, one of the Hawaiian Islands. (Illustration by Emily Damstra. Reproduced by permission.)

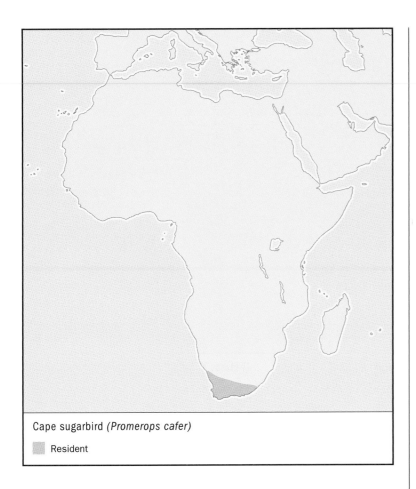

Cape sugarbird *(Promerops cafer)*

Resident

CAPE SUGARBIRD
Promerops cafer

Physical characteristics: Cape sugarbirds have rufous (reddish) head and breast. They have a distinctive long bill and long, brownish tail feathers. The chin is white with a moustache-looking dark streak. The abdomen is whitish, vent (waste opening) yellow. Females are 9.5 to 11.5 inches (24 to 29 centimeters) long, and males are 14.5 to 17.0 inches (37 to 44 centimeters) long, including the long tail. Both weigh about 1.5 ounces (42 grams).

Geographic range: Cape sugarbirds are found in South Cape Province, South Africa.

Cape sugarbirds are usually found alone or in pairs, but occasionally in small flocks. (© G. Olioso/VIREO. Reproduced by permission.)

Habitat: Their habitat includes scrublands of the Western Cape area of South Africa. The scrubs consist generally of shrubs that resemble heaths (low evergreen shrubs) with hard leaves.

Diet: Their diet consists of nectar and insects captured in flight or picked from plants.

Behavior and reproduction: Cape sugarbirds are usually found alone or in pairs, but occasionally in small flocks. In order to attract females, males fly with both wings clapped together and keep their tail held high. Both sexes defend against other sugarbirds and sunbirds. Their song is a jumble of unpleasant notes.

They breed from February to August, depending mostly on when local vegetation flowers. A deep cup-shaped nest is placed in a bush or low tree. It is constructed from grass and twigs, and lined with plant down. Females lay buff to reddish eggs with brown spots, streaks, and blotches.

Cape sugarbirds and people: Cape sugarbirds are not known to have a special significance to people.

Conservation status: These birds are not threatened. ■

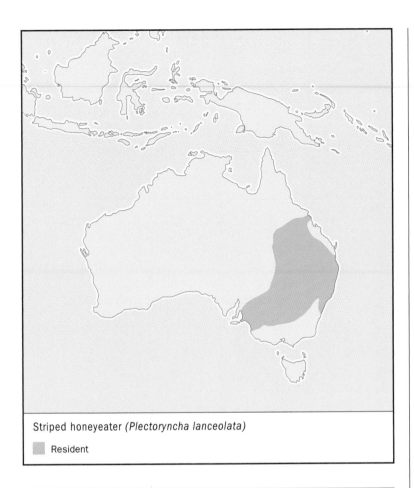

Striped honeyeater (*Plectoryncha lanceolata*)

■ Resident

STRIPED HONEYEATER
Plectoryncha lanceolata

Physical characteristics: Striped honeyeaters are about 8.5 inches (22 centimeters) long and weigh about 1.4 ounces (40 grams). Their cheeks and the area from the forehead to the nape (back part of the neck) is dark with white stripes. Their underparts are a pinkish buff, and upperparts and tail are grayish.

Geographic range: The birds are located in eastern Australia, from mid-north Queensland to northern Victoria and west to the York Peninsula, especially inland from the Great Dividing Range.

Habitat: They live in riparian (along the riverbank) woodlands with casuarina (a type of tree) and mallee (shrubby eucalyptus) and other

Striped honeyeaters eat nectar from eucalyptus, mistletoes, and other plants, and sometimes eat fruits and seeds. (Illustration by Emily Damstra. Reproduced by permission.)

semiarid woodlands with eucalyptus, acacia, and native pine.

Diet: Striped honeyeaters eat nectar from eucalyptus, mistletoes, and other plants, and sometimes eat fruits and seeds. They also occasionally eat insects and spiders that they capture from foliage and tree bark or that they catch in the air.

Behavior and reproduction: Striped honeyeaters are usually found in pairs or small groups. They sound an attractive whistling song. The generally do not migrate, but do show local movements. The species breeds from August to January. Nests are suspended off of drooping foliage. They tend to like to build nests near gray butcherbird nests. Females lay from two to five eggs, with three being average. Both parents incubate the eggs. After hatching, both parents feed the young, but sometimes have helpers feed the chicks. The time it takes to hatch the eggs is sixteen to seventeen days, while the fledgling period is also sixteen to seventeen days.

Striped honeyeaters and people: People sometimes regard them as pests in orchards.

Conservation status: Striped honeyeaters are not threatened. ■

FOR MORE INFORMATION

Books:

del Hoyo, Josep, Andrew Elliott, Jordi Sargatal, Jose Cabot, et al., eds. *Handbook of the Birds of the World.* Barcelona: Lynx Edicions, 1992.

Dickinson, Edward C., ed. *The Howard and Moore Complete Checklist of the Birds of the World,* 3rd ed. Princeton, NJ and Oxford, U.K.: Princeton University Press, 2003.

Forshaw, Joseph, ed. *Encyclopedia of Birds,* 2nd ed. San Diego, CA: Academic Press, 1998.

Harrison, Colin James Oliver. *Birds of the World.* London and New York: Dorling Kindersley, 1993.

Perrins, Christopher M., and Alex L. A. Middleton, eds. *The Encyclopedia of Birds.* New York: Facts on File, 1985.

Class: Aves
Order: Passeriformes
Family: Vireonidae
Number of species: 43 species

family
CHAPTER

phylum

class

subclass

order

monotypic order

suborder

▲ **family**

PHYSICAL CHARACTERISTICS

Vireos and peppershrikes are small, plain-colored songbirds with a somewhat heavy to very heavy, pointed bill that has a small hook at the end. For most species, the wings are either rounded at the end or are more pointed. Their legs are short but strong. Vireos and peppershrikes are commonly olive brown, olive gray, greenish, or yellowish on the upper parts, and white, light gray, yellow, or yellow-washed on the breast and abdomen. A black line runs through the eyes of most species, but sometimes a white strip goes above the eye while in other species a light-colored eye ring is present. A pale wing-bar is usually seen. Females and males are colored almost the same. They are 4.0 to 6.25 inches (10 to 16 centimeters) long and weigh between 0.3 and 1.5 ounces (8 and 40 grams).

GEOGRAPHIC RANGE

The family ranges widely over the Americas including most of the continental United States, all but the northern-most parts of Canada, Mexico, and Central America, most of South America including as far south as Uruguay, northern Argentina, and northern Chile.

HABITAT

Vireos and peppershrikes are found in boreal (northern), temperate, and tropical habitats including woodlands, scrublands, and forests. Some prefer the forest canopy (treetops), while others like dense undergrowth, forest edges, or mangroves (tropical evergreen tree of tidal coasts).

DIET

Their diet consists of insects, spiders, and other invertebrates (animals without a backbone) taken from foliage, flowers, bark, and other plant surfaces. Small berries and other fruits are also eaten.

BEHAVIOR AND REPRODUCTION

Vireos and peppershrikes are usually solitary but active birds, but sometimes appear as a breeding pair or family group. During the nonbreeding season, they are sometimes found in foraging flocks of many different species of birds. Their song is heard often, even during the hottest parts of the day when most birds are quiet, and it usually is loud and melodic, but seldom is it considered beautiful. The song generally consists of several repeated phrases. Different species range from about ten to more than 100 song types. Males sing most frequently, being vocal especially during foraging. Males commonly sing while sitting on the nest. Northern species of the birds migrate, while southern species do not. The trip may vary from 100 miles (160 kilometers) to 3,000 miles (4,800 kilometers).

After migration is complete, birds pair up soon after arriving in their spring breeding territory. Males defend the territory with their song. Open, cup-shaped nests are woven from spider and silkworm webbing, grass stems, other plant fibers, lichens, mosses, and feathers. In species where both sexes build the nests, males construct a rough bag, and females make the lining. Birds locate the nest at the fork of a tree branch, usually suspended by the rim from the bark. The nests are usually located close to the ground or high in the forest canopy.

Females lay two to five whitish to speckled or spotted eggs of various colors. Both females and males perform incubation and caring for the young. The incubation period (time it takes to sit on and warm the eggs before hatching) is usually twelve to fourteen days, and the nestling period (time necessary to take care of young unable to leave nest) is usually nine to eleven days. Fledglings cannot fly well when first leaving the nest, but are good at running along branches and within shrubs. Both parents feed them for about three weeks after leaving the nest. Migratory species usually have two to three clutches (group of eggs hatched together) each year.

VIREOS, PEPPERSHRIKES, AND PEOPLE

Vireos and peppershrikes have no special relationship with people.

CONSERVATION STATUS

One species is listed as Critically Endangered, facing an extremely high risk of extinction, dying out; one species is listed as Endangered, facing a very high risk of extinction; one species is listed as Vulnerable, facing a high risk of extinction; two species are listed as Near Threatened, in danger of becoming threatened with extinction. In all cases, the species are at risk due to loss of habitat as a result of converting native lands to agriculture, thinning out or elimination of forests due to logging, and other detrimental human activities.

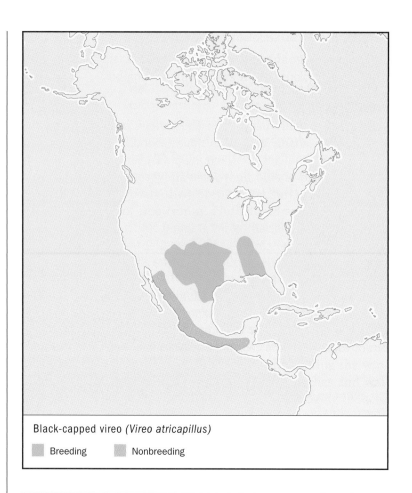

Black-capped vireo *(Vireo atricapillus)*

■ Breeding   ■ Nonbreeding

BLACK-CAPPED VIREO
Vireo atricapillus

Physical characteristics: Black-capped vireos are small vireos with olive-colored upperparts. Males have white under parts, yellow wash beneath the wings, yellowish-white wing-bars, reddish eyes, a blackish bill, a glossy black head, and blue-gray legs and feet. They also have white eye-rings that look like broken eyeglasses. Females are similar except for a slate gray to bluish gray head, white eye-rings, pale lemon-yellow wing bars, buffy white under parts, and yellowish wash on the sides and flanks. Juvenile females have plumage that is more buff-colored. Adults are about 4.5 inches (12 centimeters) long, with a wingspan of about 8 inches (20.3 centimeters) and a weight of about 0.3 ounces (8.5 grams).

Male and female black-capped vireos feed their chicks after they've hatched. (© S. & S. Rucker/VIREO. Reproduced by permission.)

Geographic range: During cold months, black-capped vireos are found on the west coast of Mexico. During the warm months when the birds breed, they are located in parts of Texas, New Mexico, Oklahoma, Missouri, and north-central Mexico.

Habitat: Black-capped vireos inhabit open, grassy woodlands that contain clumps of shrubs and trees, especially oak scrublands and dense low thickets. Within that environment, they are usually found around low-lying vegetation.

Diet: They feed mostly on invertebrates such as insects, their larvae (LAR-vee; active immature insects), and eggs, taken from the deep cover among leaves of trees and shrubs. Other food sources are small spiders, small fruits, and berries.

Behavior and reproduction: Black-capped vireos are solitary birds. They migrate short distances between breeding and nonbreeding seasons, often going southwest, wintering along the western coast of Mexico. The birds defend breeding territories. Their song is a hurried string of husky-sounding two- or three-note phrases that is repeated slowly, such as "grrtzeepidídid, prididzeegrrt . . . " Their call is a "ji-dit" or "tsidik."

The birds are monogamous (muh-NAH-guh-mus; having one mate). Males court females with fluttering display flights. The male then sings a courtship song, often with the spreading of his wings. The mating pair builds a cup-shaped nest that is made of twigs, bark, and leaves, surrounded with silk and lined with fine grasses. The nest hangs down from a branch fork of a shrub or low tree, about 1 to 15 feet (0.3 to 4.6 meters) off the ground in scrub oak or other short deciduous trees. Females lay three to four white, unmarked eggs. The incubation period is fourteen to nineteen days, which is shared by male (alternating with female during the day) and female (during the night). Both birds feed the young. Two broods are produced each year.

Black-capped vireos and people: There is no known significant relationship between people and black-capped vireos.

Conservation status: Black-capped vireos are not listed as threatened internationally, however, some populations face habitat loss from mining, agriculture, flood-control projects, and reservoir construction. Because of these problems, the U.S. Fish and Wildlife Service placed the bird on the U.S. Endangered Species List. Black-capped vireos are also hurt by cowbirds, which often threaten the birds especially during the breeding season. Efforts in Texas and Oklahoma are underway to trap and remove cowbirds and restrict human activities from areas where black-capped vireos have been most hurt.   ■

Rufous-browed peppershrike (*Cyclarhis gujanensis*)

Resident

RUFOUS-BROWED PEPPERSHRIKE
Cyclarhis gujanensis

Physical characteristics: Rufous-browed peppershrikes have a somewhat heavy body, large head, and heavy bill. The back is dark olive-green, chest and flanks are yellow, the belly is white, and the top of head is gray with a broad rufous (reddish) stripe over the eyes. Males and females look alike. They are 5.5 to 6.0 inches (14 to 15 centimeters) long.

Rufous-browed peppershrikes stay in the thicker parts of the foliage, and so they are easier to hear than see. Their song is a repeated, musical phrase, and each individual's is a bit different. (Illustration by Michelle Meneghini. Reproduced by permission.)

Geographic range: They are widely found in Central America from southeastern Mexico to Panama, and in parts of South America as far south as central Argentina (but are not found around most of the area affected by the Amazon River).

Habitat: Their habitat consists of both dry and moist evergreen forest borders, scrublands, gallery and secondary forests, and clearings with trees. The birds are found at altitudes up to 9,200 feet (2,800 meters).

Diet: The birds feed on insects, caterpillars, and other invertebrates found on foliage, flowers, and tree limbs. They also eat small fruits.

Behavior and reproduction: Rufous-browed peppershrikes move about in trees with sluggish movements. They usually stay in the thicker parts of the foliage, so are more often heard, rather than seen. The birds do not migrate, but do defend their breeding territory. Their song is a repeated, musical phrase that is sung year-long. The type of song differs depending on individual birds, and where they are located in their range.

The birds stay together throughout the year. They build cup-shaped, thin-walled nests from grasses, which hang from a fork of a high tree branch. Both the male and female incubate the eggs and feed the young.

Rufous-browed peppershrikes and people: There is no known significant relationship between people and rufous-browed peppershrikes.

Conservation status: Rufous-browed peppershrikes are not threatened. ■

FOR MORE INFORMATION

Books:

Alsop, Fred J. III. *Birds of North America.* New York: Dorling Kindersley, 2001.

Baughman, Mel M., ed. *Reference Atlas to the Birds of North America.* Washington, DC: National Geographic, 2003.

del Hoyo, Josep, Andrew Elliott, Jordi Sargatal, Jose Cabot, et al., eds. *Handbook of the Birds of the World.* Barcelona: Lynx Edicions, 1992.

Field Guide to the Birds of North America, 4th ed. Washington, DC: National Geographic Society, 2002.

Forshaw, Joseph, ed. *Encyclopedia of Birds,* 2nd ed. San Diego, CA: Academic Press, 1998.

Harrison, Colin James Oliver. *Birds of the World.* London and New York: Dorling Kindersley, 1993.

Kaufman, Kenn, with collaboration of Rick and Nora Bowers and Lynn Hassler Kaufman. *Birds of North America.* New York: Houghton Mifflin, 2000.

Sibley, David. *The Sibley Guide to Birds.* New York: Alfred A. Knopf, 2000.

Terres, John K. *The Audubon Society Encyclopedia of North American Birds.* New York: Knopf, 1980.

NEW WORLD FINCHES
Emberizidae

Class: Aves

Order: Passeriformes

Family: Emberizidae

Number of species: 291 species

phylum

class

subclass

order

monotypic order

suborder

▲ **family**

PHYSICAL CHARACTERISTICS

New World finches consist of buntings and New World sparrows. They are small- to medium-sized birds, with a short, conical bill, medium-sized legs, rather large feet, and a short- to medium-length tail. The bill's upper and lower parts can be moved sideways in some species. Most species have dull black, brown, olive, gray, or beige plumage (feathers), but some species are brightly colored in rich chestnut or pale buffy browns with white or black areas. All have wings with nine main feathers, although a short tenth may be present. Faces contain patterns of black, white, and buff, sometimes with yellow or buffy orange stripes. Males are generally larger than females. Sexes look alike in plumage in most species but are very different in others. New World finches are 4.0 to 9.5 inches (10 to 24 centimeters) long and weigh between 0.3 and 2.6 ounces (8 and 75 grams).

GEOGRAPHIC RANGE

New World finches range throughout the world, except for the interior of Greenland, far Southeast Asia, New Guinea, Australia, and Madagascar. They have been introduced in New Zealand.

HABITAT

New World finches live in open and semi-open bushy or grassland areas, forest edges, tundra, prairies and meadows, deserts, hilly meadows, salt and freshwater marshes, and oak and pine woods.

DIET

Diet consists mostly of seeds, berries, fruits, and other vegetation, but often switches to protein-rich insects when birds are feeding their young. Many birds feed near the ground, scratching away leaf litter to find food. Its conical bill is adapted to pick up seed shells and take out seeds.

BEHAVIOR AND REPRODUCTION

New World finches are diurnal (active during the day) birds; although some species sing at night during breeding. While singing, males sit where they will be easily seen, and throw back their head and ruffle their crown (top of head) or rump feathers. The birds sing mostly songs of simple notes. Species of tundra or prairie regions sing while in flight. The birds are territorial, with males defending with the use of songs, chases, and fights. Territories are used for nesting and foraging, but may leave the territory to look for food. New World finches usually migrate in small, loose flocks of numerous species. Some species form large flocks.

They are for the most part monogamous (muh-NAH-guh-mus) birds (that is, during a breeding season, one male is associated with one female). Exceptions occur in some species, probably due to differences in territory quality. Males sing to attract a mate, followed by chasing and shaking her, and then tumbling together on the ground. In some cases, birds mate with several individuals. The nest that is built is usually cup-shaped, and neatly made from grasses, weeds, roots, and other fibers. It is lined with mosses, hair, feathers, or wool. Nests are usually built on the ground or low in a bush. Females lay four to six off-white (usually light brown or light blue with reddish, brownish, or blackish marks) eggs. In all cases, only the female incubates (sitting before hatching) her eggs, usually for ten to fourteen days. When a breeding pair is present, both members will help to feed and care for young. The fledgling period (time necessary for young bird to grow feathers necessary to fly) is ten to fifteen days.

NEW WORLD FINCHES AND PEOPLE

People often keep New World finches as pets in order to enjoy their beautiful songs. They are beneficial in agricultural communities because they eat many insects.

CONSERVATION STATUS

Six species of emberizids are listed as Critically Endangered, facing an extremely high risk of extinction; seven species are listed as Endangered, facing a very high risk of extinction; nine species are listed as Vulnerable, facing a high risk of extinction; and two species are listed as Near Threatened, in danger of becoming threatened with extinction.

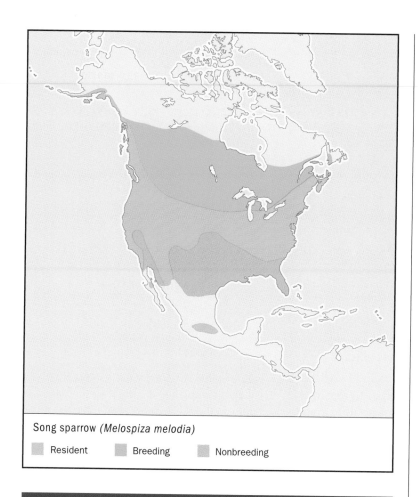

Song sparrow (*Melospiza melodia*)

Resident   Breeding   Nonbreeding

SONG SPARROW
Melospiza melodia

Physical characteristics: Song sparrows are medium- to large-sized sparrows that vary greatly in physical characteristics due to its large geographical range. They have streaked plumage (feathers), a long tail with a rounded tail tip, a brown to light rusty rounded head with a paler median crown stripe, a broad, grayish stripe above the eyes and very visible brown cheek stripes. They also have a whitish throat, stout bill, a brownish, grayish, or brownish gray patchy back, a heavily streaked breast with a dark central spot, whitish under parts, and pinkish legs and feet. Males and females look alike. Young song sparrows have brown crowns, heavily streaked under parts, and are more buff colored than adults. Adults are 5.75 to 7.50 inches (14.6 to

Song sparrows live in a variety of habitats throughout North America. (Bob & Clara Calhoun/ Bruce Coleman Inc. Reproduced by permission.)

19.1 centimeters) long, with a wingspan of 8.25 to 12.5 inches (21.0 to 31.8 centimeters) and a weight of about 0.7 ounces (20 grams).

Geographic range: They live along the western coast of Alaska, Canada, central Mexico, Baja California, and the western coast of the United States and throughout most of the northern, west-central and east-central parts of the United States. They breed from the Aleutian Island, along the southern coast of Alaska, east across southern Nunavut, northern Ontario, and central Quebec to southwest New-foundland, and south to Georgia, Missouri, Nebraska, New Mexico, Arizona, and California. Most of the northern breeding birds migrate in the fall to southern Florida, the Gulf Coast, northern Mexico, and southern Baja California.

Habitat: Song sparrows are located in open brushy and shrubby ar-eas, thickets, riparian (along the riverbank) scrublands, weedy fields, and grassy areas; often near ponds, streams, marshes, and seacoasts, especially where thickets occur. In winter, they are found in brush lands and woodland edges.

Diet: Song sparrows feed mostly on insects (and their larvae [LAR-vee]) and other invertebrates in the summer, but switch to mostly seeds in the winter. They also eat grains, berries, and some fruits, mostly from the ground or by picking food off of trees, bushes, and other vegetation. Coastal species catch small mollusks and crustaceans (hard-shelled creatures).

Behavior and reproduction: Song sparrows prefer to stay in low vegetation. When on the ground, they hop or run. When singing, they perch in a tree, bush, or on top of a weed where they are easily seen. They sing loud, pleasant, musical phrases; usually whistling two to three clear notes, followed by a trill. There is much song variation with the typical song being three or four short clear notes followed by a buzzy "tow-wee," then a trill. Their hollow call is a "chimp" or "what." When alarmed, they give a high, hard "tik." When flying, they pump their tail up and down and give out a thin "seeet." Territories are defended with chases and fights. In winter, they form into loose flocks that contain many sparrow species.

They prefer living alone and in pairs, but may be found in small loose flocks in winter, often with other sparrow species. They are generally monogamous birds, but can be polygynous (puh-LIJ-uh-nus; having more than one mate). Males aggressively defend their territory, often fighting with other males. Their bulky cup-shaped nests are made of leaves, bark strips, grasses, stems, and other plants; and lined with fine materials. Song sparrows usually place nests on the ground, among grasses, or in a low-lying bush or thicket. Nests are usually near a stream. Females lay three to six eggs that are greenish white with reddish brown markings. Nesting is done from late February to August. The incubation period is ten to fourteen days, and the fledgling period is seven to fourteen days. The pair feeds and takes care of the young. Two to three broods are possible each year, with four broods possible in southern areas.

Song sparrows and people: There is no known significant relationship between song sparrows and people.

Conservation status: Song sparrows are not threatened. They are often hurt by parasitism from the brown-headed cowbird, which lays its eggs in the song sparrows' nests so that the song sparrow takes care of the cowbird's young, neglecting its own chicks. ■

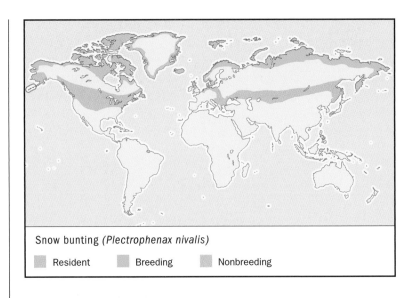

Snow bunting (*Plectrophenax nivalis*)

■ Resident   ■ Breeding   ■ Nonbreeding

SNOW BUNTING
Plectrophenax nivalis

Physical characteristics: Snow buntings show differences between males and females, but all have a rounded head, stocky body, and white outer tail feathers. Generally, females are browner in color, with less white on the plumage. Males (in summer) have a white head, black back that sometimes has brown patches, a black rump patched with white, white outer tail feathers partially tipped with black, and white under parts. The white areas, in winter, are thinly coated with pale rusty brown. Females (in summer) look like breeding males, but have a crown that is dusky and black areas are paler, often brownish. In winter, females look like winter males. Juveniles are grayish with a pale abdomen and buffy eye rings. They are 6.0 to 7.5 inches (15 to 19 centimeters) long, and weigh about 1.5 ounces (42 grams).

Geographic range: In the autumn, they migrate to the British Isles, the coast of northern France, Denmark, Poland, Germany, southern Russia, Manchuria, Kuril Islands, Korea, and Hokkaido (the northernmost Japanese island); and in North America to western and southern Alaska and from central and southern Canada south along the Pacific coast to northern California, the central Plains, and coastal North Carolina. In the spring, they move north to Iceland, northern Scotland, the mountains of Sweden and Norway, Spitzbergen, Franz

Snow buntings eat insects and other invertebrates during the summer, but switch mostly to seeds and grains in the winter. (Hans Reinhard/Bruce Coleman Inc. Reproduced by permission.)

Joseph Land, north Kola Peninsula, Novaya Zemlya, northern Russia and northern Siberia east to Wrangel Island, the Bering Strait, and south to east Kamchatka, northern Alaska and mountains of Alaska, northern Canada north to Labrador, and the coast of Greenland.

Habitat: During breeding season, they are found in sparse, dry, rocky tundra areas such as seashores, mountain slopes, and cliffs. During times of migration and nonbreeding season, they are found in fields, pastures, roadsides, and at beaches.

Diet: Snow buntings eat insects and other invertebrates during the summer, but switch mostly to seeds and grains in the winter.

Behavior and reproduction: They are migratory birds, with males arriving at breeding areas before females. At this time, males find a territory and begin to defend it by chasing away other birds, singing while in flight to make their presence known, and fighting when necessary. They run while on the ground, generally staying on the ground when not flying. Their song, sung during breeding, is a loud, high-pitched musical warbling. Their calls include a sharp, whistled "tew," a short buzz, and a musical rattle or twitter.

Snow buntings are for the most part monogamous birds, but sometimes males or females will have two mates. Nesting occurs from late May through July. Nests are made with dried grassy plants, lichens, and grasses, and look like a large, thick-walled bulky cup. They are constructed on the ground, frequently in rock crevices. Sometimes they build nests in birdhouses and other artificial structures. Females lay between three to nine eggs, but usually from four to seven. The incubation period is from ten to fifteen days, and the fledgling period is from ten to seventeen days after hatching. Both in the breeding pair feed and take care of young.

Snow buntings and people: There is no known significant relationship between people and snow buntings.

Conservation status: Snow buntings are not threatened. ■

Blue-black grassquit *(Volatinia jacarina)*

   Resident

BLUE-BLACK GRASSQUIT
Volatinia jacarina

Physical characteristics: Blue-black grassquit males and females portray different characteristics. Males are blue-black all over, while females are brown with paler under parts and a dark-streaked chest. Juveniles look like adult females. They are 4.0 to 4.3 inches (10.2 to 10.9 centimeters) long, and weigh about 0.34 ounces (9.7 grams).

Blue-black grassquits almost always eat grass seeds, although they do sometimes eat insects and berries. (© J. Dunning/VIREO. Reproduced by permission.)

Geographic range: They range from central Mexico south to northern Chile, east to the eastern coast of Brazil, and south to central Argentina. They are also found on Grenada.

Habitat: Blue-black grassquits like low, seasonally wet grasslands, arid lowland scrublands, farmlands, riverside thickets, and weedy fields. The birds are found from sea level to 3,600 feet (1,100 meters) in altitude.

Diet: Their diet is almost always grass seeds, although they do sometimes eat insects and berries. They pick seeds from grass seed heads and from grit and seeds left on roads.

Behavior and reproduction: Males sing from perches that make them very visible. The also jump upward with a flick of their wings. In winter, they join flocks of a few hundred seed-eating birds. They are monogamous birds. Nests are built low to the ground, usually not more than 10 feet (3 meters) off the ground. From May through October, females lay two to three eggs. Incubation and fledgling periods are not known.

Blue-black grassquits and people: People and blue-black grassquits have no known significance between them.

Conservation status: Blue-black grassquits are not threatened. They are abundant in many areas. ∎

Savanna sparrow (*Passerculus sandwichensis*)

■ Resident ■ Breeding ■ Nonbreeding

SAVANNA SPARROW
Passerculus sandwichensis

Physical characteristics: Savanna sparrows are very variable in color. But, they are generally brown or dark brown streaked on the back and breast. They have a whitish yellow stripe above the eyes, a pale or whitish median crown stripe, a rather short, notched tail, buff to white under parts with brown streaking, and pinkish legs and feet. Males and females are alike in color. Birds differ in physical characteristics due to where they are located. They are about 5.5 inches (14 centimeters) long, with a wingspan of about 6.75 inches (17 centimeters) and a weight of about 0.7 ounces (20 grams).

Geographic range: They live along the west coast from southern British Columbia south to southern Baja California, along the west coast of Mexico, south to central Sinaloa, and in the highlands of central Mexico. During the winter, they migrate to the east coast of the United States, west through the central Plains, and south to northern Central America. They breed from northern Alaska, northern Canada (except for the arctic islands), south to northern Georgia, the central Great Plains, and south in the mountains to Guatemala.

Savanna sparrows are found alone, in pairs, and in small family groups during the summer, but during migration and winter they are found in larger loose flocks. (Robert J. Huffman/Field Mark Publications. Reproduced by permission.)

Habitat: Savanna sparrows live in open areas, such as grassy and wet meadows, farm fields, pastures, roadsides, bogs, the edge of salt marshes, and tundra.

Diet: They eat insects, spiders, and a number of other invertebrates, seeds, and fruits in the summer, but forage mostly on seeds in the winter. They forage on the ground, low in bushes and weeds, and on beaches along the tide line and in piles of seaweed, terrestrial plants, and animal remains that wash ashore.

Behavior and reproduction: They are found alone, in pairs, and in small family groups during the summer, but during migration and winter they are found in loose flocks. The birds spend most of their time on the ground, usually hopping or running about. When disturbed, they scurry through grasses, only flying off a short distance as a last resort. At night, savanna sparrows roost on the ground in small huddled groups. Males are very territorial, and can be found singing from an exposed perch to warn intruders. They are strong fliers, usually flying in direct routes. Their song begins with two to three "chip" notes, followed by two buzzy insect-like trills "tip-tip-seeeee-saaaay." Their general call is a thin "seep," while their flight call is a high "tsiw."

Savanna sparrows are usually monogamous, but males are sometimes bigamists (having two mates). Some marsh-dwelling species are polygynous. Nests are woven into the shape of a cup; made with grasses and other vegetation. Nests are made on the ground or in a slight depression that is partly covered by grasses or other vegetation. From February to August, females lay one to two clutches of two to six eggs. The incubation period is ten to thirteen days and the fledgling period is seven to fourteen days. Both parents share in feeding and caring of young.

Savannah sparrow and people: There is no known significant relationship between people and savanna sparrows.

Conservation status: Savanna sparrows are common throughout most of their range, but are declining in eastern North America as their natural habitats are degraded or lost. The marsh-dwelling birds are Vulnerable because flooding, draining, and filling of marshes can rapidly change the environment. Pollution is particularly hurtful to the birds in agricultural lands. ■

FOR MORE INFORMATION

Books:

Alsop, Fred J. III. *Birds of North America.* New York: Dorling Kindersley, 2001.

Baughman, Mel M., ed. *Reference Atlas to the Birds of North America.* Washington, DC: National Geographic, 2003.

del Hoyo, Josep, Andrew Elliott, Jordi Sargatal, Jose Cabot, et al., eds. *Handbook of the Birds of the World.* Barcelona: Lynx Edicions, 1992.

Field Guide to the Birds of North America, 4th ed. Washington, DC: National Geographic Society, 2002.

Forshaw, Joseph, ed. *Encyclopedia of Birds,* 2nd ed. San Diego, CA: Academic Press, 1998.

Harrison, Colin James Oliver. *Birds of the World.* London and New York: Dorling Kindersley, 1993.

Kaufman, Kenn, with collaboration of Rick and Nora Bowers and Lynn Hassler Kaufman. *Birds of North America.* New York: Houghton Mifflin, 2000.

Sibley, David. *The Sibley Guide to Birds.* New York: Alfred A. Knopf, 2000.

Terres, John K. *The Audubon Society Encyclopedia of North American Birds.* New York: Knopf, 1980.

NEW WORLD WARBLERS
Parulidae

Class: Aves
Order: Passeriformes
Family: Parulidae
Number of species: 126 species

family
C H A P T E R

phylum
class
subclass
order
monotypic order
suborder
▲ family

PHYSICAL CHARACTERISTICS

New World warblers are relatively small birds ranging from 4 to 7.5 inches (10 to 19 centimeters) long, although most are 4 to 5.5 inches (10 to 14 centimeters). They stand on thin, delicate-looking legs, typically have short and pointy beaks that are either slender or flat, but a few have heavier-appearing bills. Unlike all other songbirds, New World warblers have only nine primary feathers rather than ten. Many are colorful or boldly patterned, but the females' duller colors make them appear quite drab next to their striking male counterparts. The juveniles usually look much like the adult females, and males of some of the cooler-climate species also switch to a female-like, dull coloration in the fall and winter.

GEOGRAPHIC RANGE

New World warblers live in North America, South America, Central America, and the West Indies.

HABITAT

Primarily forest birds, different species of New World warblers, also known as wood warblers, may be found in everything from thick and dark forests to dry and open woods. Some have more unusual habits, and will live either in deserts or swamps.

DIET

These smallish birds spend much of their days on the move and looking for insect meals. Using their slender beaks, the birds are skillful at plucking small insects and spiders from even very tiny cracks and crevices in tree bark, between leaves, and from other hideaways. A few species add berries and seeds to their diets, and some even rely on those food sources to survive snowy winters. Most New World warblers scrounge for food on the ground or on plants or trees.

BEHAVIOR AND REPRODUCTION

Perhaps the most characteristic behavior, and the most frustrating for birders who are trying to spy one of the birds through their binoculars, is the nearly constant motion of New World warblers. No sooner do they land on a tree branch than they are off again to new destination. For this reason, plus the sometimes-dense woods that hide them from view, most birders in the field recognize different species of warblers not by sight but by their songs. Only the males sing, except in a few species when the females also join the chorus. Many species have lovely, bright songs, but others are merely loud, and some have quite quiet, scratchy voices that sound more like insects than birds. Each song, however, is characteristic to a particular species. By learning their songs, birders can walk into the woods and know which species are there without ever seeing a single bird. As in other birds, both males and females also communicate through various quick cheeps and chips, some of which may also be very distinctive to a particular species.

Most of the species that summer in North America migrate far south for the winter, sometimes flying 3,000 miles (4,800 kilometers) or more to a warm, sunny location. Usually, the birds leave their northern haunts in the fall, long before bitter temperatures settle in. Fall migration flocks can number in the thousands and include many different species of birds. The flocks travel from sunset to sunup. On a night with a full moon, a careful observer can sometimes spot the flocks as silhouettes against the surface of the moon. The birds return the following spring.

THE THREAT FROM COWBIRDS

Warbler numbers are declining in many areas due to the much larger brown-headed cowbird. Unlike a predator that directly attacks and kills warblers or eats their eggs, the cowbird's threat comes from its breeding habits. Instead of laying eggs in its own nest and raising its own young, the cowbird lays its eggs in other birds' nests and leaves the parenting to the adoptive parents. Unfortunately for the warbler, the small birds do not recognize the foreign egg and raise it as their own. Cowbird eggs are larger and typically hatch a bit earlier, which gives the young cowbird a distinct advantage over its smaller nest mates. Sometimes, the cowbird pushes the others out of the nest and to their death, but even the baby warblers that remain often miss out on feedings from their mother as the larger cowbird can push its beak to the front for meals. As a result, young warblers starve to death. The behavior of the cowbird is known as brood parasitism, because it actually becomes a parasite on the mother warbler's family, or brood.

The male warblers usually arrive in the spring shortly before the females. The head start allows the males to set up their breeding territories. As the females arrive, the males begin singing to entice a mate. Once a pair forms, the warblers go about making a nest and preparing for egg laying. Some species make their typically cup-shaped nests on the ground, others in shrubs, and some high in the trees. A typical clutch is three or four eggs, which are usually white with irregular spots. The female sits on the eggs while the male dashes about finding food and bringing it back to her. When the eggs hatch nearly two weeks later, the mother helps the father find and deliver food to the babies. The young grow quickly, and are nearly adult weight by the time they are ten days old. At that point, they test their wings and leave the nest, but they don't go far. The parents continue to feed them, but since the young are no longer together in the nest, the mother generally takes care half the offspring, and the male feeds the other half. After a few weeks, the parents stop their care and the young birds are on their own.

NEW WORLD WARBLERS AND PEOPLE

Warblers have a special place in the hearts of birders and anyone else who enjoys a lilting song or a glimpse of color while walking outdoors. Some North American communities even have festivals to herald the return of the small birds each spring.

CONSERVATION STATUS

According to the Red List of the World Conservation Union (IUCN), three species are Critically Endangered, facing an extremely high risk of extinction; five are Endangered, facing a very high risk of extinction; seven are Vulnerable, facing a high risk of extinction; and eight are Near Threatened, in danger of becoming threatened with extinction. The U.S. Fish and Wildlife Service lists five endangered species: Bachman's warbler, Barbados yellow warbler, golden-cheeked warbler, Kirtland's warbler, and Semper's warbler. For the most part, a small breeding range and shrinking habitat are the primary threats to these species. When people undertake habitat-preservation efforts, however, the species generally respond favorably.

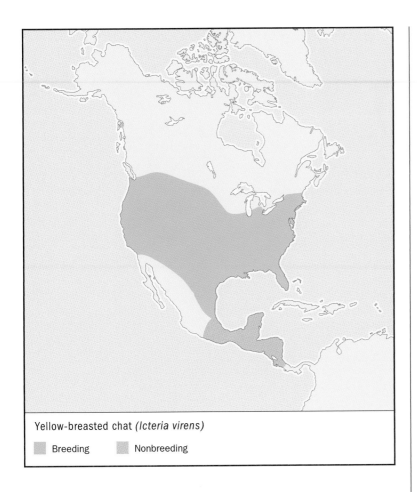

Yellow-breasted chat (*Icteria virens*)

◾ Breeding ◾ Nonbreeding

YELLOW-BREASTED CHAT
Icteria virens

Physical characteristics: The largest of the New World warblers, both male and female yellow-breasted chats have an olive-colored back, yellow throat and breast, and white belly. Eyes are ringed in white, and the blackish face has white stripes. The beak is larger and appears heavier than most other warblers. The bird reaches about 7.5 inches (19 centimeters) long.

Geographic range: Its breeding grounds are in southern Canada, the United States, and northern and eastern Mexico, and its wintering grounds in Central America.

The yellow-breasted chat is usually found near water, where it typically remains hidden from sight in thick brush. (Barth Schorre/Bruce Coleman Inc. Reproduced by permission.)

Habitat: Usually found near water, where it typically remains hidden from sight in thick brush.

Diet: It mostly eats insects, but also snacks on berries on occasion.

Behavior and reproduction: This bird can often be heard flying and otherwise pushing its way through brambles and thickets. In addition to its typical daytime activities, this warbler also sometimes sings at night. The song is a mixture of caws, gobbles, and a few singsong phrases. Unlike other nesting pairs of warblers that are quite territorial, several chat pairs will sometimes share a single nesting site. Their cup-shaped nests are tucked in thick brush. Eggs, which typically number up to six, are speckled with brown and purple.

Yellow-breasted chats and people: Seldom seen, but often heard, chats add to nature's outdoor symphony.

Conservation status: This species is not threatened. ■

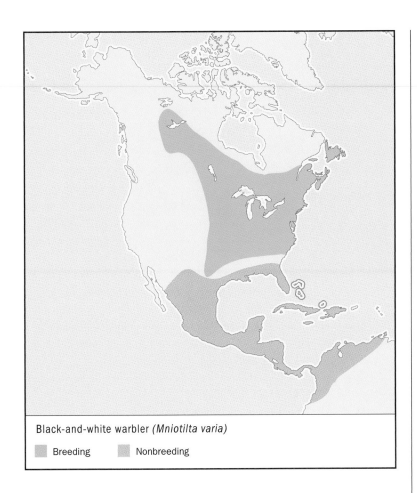

Black-and-white warbler *(Mniotilta varia)*

■ Breeding   ■ Nonbreeding

BLACK-AND-WHITE WARBLER
Mniotilta varia

Physical characteristics: An appropriately named bird, this warbler has black and white stripes over much of its body. A male has a black patch on his throat, and a female has a grayish white patch on hers. Size ranges from about 4.5 to 5.5 inches (11.4 to 14 centimeters), and the bird weighs 0.3 to 0.5 ounces (9 to 15 grams).

Geographic range: The black-and-white warbler spends the warmer months in Canada and the eastern half of the United States, then migrates for the winter months to southern U.S., Mexico, West Indies, Central America, and northeastern South America.

Black-and-white warblers spend much of their time creeping up tree trunks in search of small insects and other creatures in the little openings and cracks in the bark. (© G. Bailey/VIREO. Reproduced by permission.)

Habitat: They tend to live in areas with numerous large trees, as well as a tall, thick understory. The trees provide a place for finding food, and the thickets provide a place to hide.

Diet: These birds eat caterpillars, flies, beetles, and other insects; and spiders.

Behavior and reproduction: It spends much of its time creeping up tree trunks in search of small insects and other creatures in the little openings and cracks in the bark. Its song is a quiet and short peeping phrase. These warblers migrate north a bit earlier than most other warblers, and soon begin breeding. They usually build their nests on the ground, although a few construct theirs in a hidden spot just up the side of a tree trunk, and then use some carefully placed leaves to camouflage the nest. Each pair has four or five eggs that hatch in ten days. Predation on the ground nests by dogs, cats, raccoons, and other animals is common.

Black-and-white warblers and people: As with most warblers, its primary benefit to people is its beauty.

Conservation status: This bird is not threatened. ■

Kirtland's warbler (*Dendroica kirtlandii*)

▢ Breeding ▢ Nonbreeding

KIRTLAND'S WARBLER
Dendroica kirtlandii

Physical characteristics: This bird reaches about 6 inches (15.3 centimeters) and 0.5 ounces (15 grams). It has a dark, bluish gray back and head, white eye ring, and a gray-specked, yellow throat and belly. Males are slightly more vividly colored than females, and have a blackish stripe on the face.

Geographic range: This bird summers in Michigan, and winters in the Bahamas.

Habitat: Its summertime home is primarily forests of jack pine trees, usually preferring forests with many young trees whose branches dip

Kirtland's warbler is listed as Endangered by the IUCN and the U.S. Fish and Wildlife Service. It spends the summer in Michigan and the winter in the Bahamas. (Richard Baetson. U. S. Fish and Wildlife Service. Reproduced by permission.)

close to the ground and provide cover for their ground nests.

Diet: Kirtland's warblers eat insects, and occasionally berries, or pine needles.

Behavior and reproduction: Although the warbler is quite rare, a birder who knows where to look can readily see them flying between pine trees and nabbing insects in midair. In late spring to early summer, Kirtland's warblers build small cup-shaped nests on the ground under low-lying pine branches. Broods typically number four or five eggs. The eggs hatch in about two weeks, and the young birds leave the nest about a week and a half later. One of greatest dangers to the birds comes not from direct predation, but from the wily brown-headed cowbird, which lays its eggs in the warbler's nest. The warbler cares for the cowbird young, often neglecting its own chicks.

Kirtland's warblers and people: People from around the world come to Michigan in the spring and summer to spot this bi-colored bird. Kirtland Community College, located in the breeding area, holds an annual festival in the bird's honor.

Conservation status: The need for the Kirtland's warbler to breed in young jack pine stands in northern Michigan has contributed to its low numbers. In response, efforts to improve its habitat have occurred, and the number of breeding pairs is increasing. The U.S. Fish and Wildlife Service currently defines this species as endangered, but its ranking on the Red List has improved from Endangered in 1994 to Vulnerable in 2000. ■

FOR MORE INFORMATION

Bent, Arthur C. *Life Histories of North American Wood Warblers.* New York: Dover Publications, Inc., 1963.

Cassidy, James, ed. *Book of North American Birds.* New York: The Reader's Digest Association, Inc., 1990.

Dock Jr., George. "Yellow-Breasted Chat." In *Audubon's Birds of America.* New York: Harry N. Abrams, Inc., 1979.

Ehrlich, Paul R., David S. Dobkin, and Darryl Wheye. *The Birder's Handbook.* New York: Simon and Schuster, Inc. (Fireside Books), 1988.

Garrett, Kimball L., and John B. Dunning Jr. "Wood-Warblers." In *The Sibley Guide to Bird Life and Behavior,* edited by Chris Elphick, John B. Dunning Jr., and David Allen Sibley. New York: Alfred A. Knopf, 2001.

Peterson, Roger Tory. *A Field Guide to the Birds of Eastern and Central North America.* Boston: Houghton Mifflin Co., 1980.

Periodicals:

Berger, Cynthia. "Exposed: Secret Lives of Warblers." *National Wildlife* 23 (2000): 46–52.

Lichtenstein, G., and S. G. Sealy. "Nestling Competition, Rather than Supernormal Stimulus, Explains the Success of Parasitic Brown-headed Cowbird Chicks in Yellow Warbler Nests." *Proceedings of the Royal Society of London* 265, no. 1392 (2000): 249–254.

Price, T., H.L. Gibbs, L. de Sousa, and A. D. Richman. "Different Timing of the Adaptive Radiations of North American and Asian Warblers." *Proceedings of the Royal Society of London* 265 (1998): 1969–1975.

Weidensaul, Scott. "Jewels in the Treetops." *Country Journal* 23 (1996): 58–61.

Web sites:

Endangered Species Program, U.S. Fish & Wildlife Service. http://endangered.fws.gov/ (accessed on May 5, 2004).

IUCN Red List of Threatened Species—Species information. http://www.redlist.org (accessed on May 29, 2004).

NEW WORLD BLACKBIRDS AND ORIOLES

Icteridae

Class: Aves

Order: Passeriformes

Family: Icteridae

Number of species: 103 species

family

CHAPTER

phylum

class

subclass

order

monotypic order

suborder

▲ **family**

PHYSICAL CHARACTERISTICS

New World blackbirds and orioles (called "icterids" as a group) are physically diverse in coloring, size, and shape. Common colorings are black, dark purple, yellow, brown, and orange. Bill size and shape is also variable—some species like the great-tailed grackle and the meadowlarks have long, curved beaks while others have shorter conical, or cone-shaped, ones. All blackbirds have a unique jaw structure that enables them to force their jaw and bill open, a practice known as gaping that lets them forage, or search for food, more effectively.

GEOGRAPHIC RANGE

As their name implies, New World blackbirds are found throughout North and South America, as are orioles. Some species are also found in the Caribbean.

HABITAT

Grasslands and marshes are popular breeding grounds for icterids, but this diverse family of birds can be found in a number of different biomes.

DIET

Birds in the Icteridae family have a diverse diet, feeding on insects, seeds, fruits, and grains.

BEHAVIOR AND REPRODUCTION

Blackbirds build their bowl-shaped nests in shrubs, trees, and reeds, with the exception of a few species that live in vegetation-free areas that build nests in rock crevices. Orioles build orb-shaped nests constructed of grasses that hang down from a tree branch. One species of Icteridae, the baybird, takes over abandoned nests of other birds. Others are parasitic, meaning that they lay their eggs in another bird's nests for the nest-owner to hatch and fledge, when the young bird is ready to fly on its own.

Depending on the species, male blackbirds have anywhere from one to up to fifteen female mates. Often those male birds that are polygynous (puh-LIJ-uh-nus; have more than one mate) live with a bird population that is mostly female.

BLACKBIRDS, ORIOLES, AND PEOPLE

Because of their large and loud flock sizes and their feeding on agricultural crops such as rice, sunflowers, and corn, many people consider blackbirds and orioles pests.

CONSERVATION STATUS

One species—the slender-billed grackle—is extinct, or has died out. Three more species of Icteridae are Critically Endangered, facing an extremely high risk of extinction in the wild; and four are considered Endangered, facing a very high risk of extinction.

STRENGTH IN NUMBERS

As the breeding season ends, red-winged blackbirds take to the skies in enormous flocks that can contain tens to hundreds of thousands of birds. They share the skies with other species of blackbirds and starlings, and forage for food together. The size of these flocks helps protect them from predators, animals that hunt them for food, and keeps them protected from the elements. Roosting flocks can be even larger than foraging flocks, and may number over a million birds.

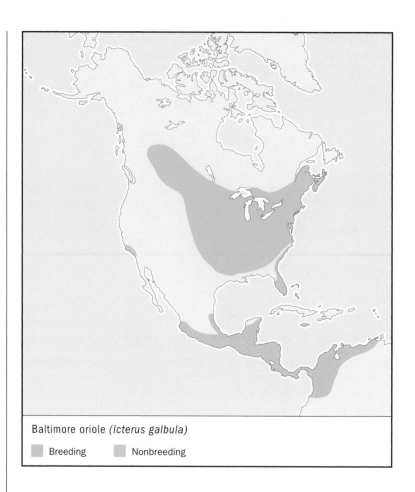

Baltimore oriole (*Icterus galbula*)

■ Breeding   ■ Nonbreeding

BALTIMORE ORIOLE
Icterus galbula

Physical characteristics: The Baltimore oriole has a black back, head, and throat and a yellow to orange belly, rump, and shoulders. Wings are black with white-edged feather tips, and the tail has yellow or orange markings. The species is sexually dimorphic in color, meaning that males and females have different color patterns; males are bright orange and jet black, while females are yellow and brown. The female also has two white wingbars, as opposed to one on the male. Average length is 8.75 inches (22.23 centimeters) with a wingspan of 11.5 inches (29.21 centimeters) and a weight of 1.2 ounces (33 grams).

Geographic range: In the summer breeding months the Baltimore oriole can be found in eastern North America, from Alberta to Newfoundland in Canada and from the Dakotas to Maine in the United States. Their range runs south to Texas, Louisiana, and Georgia. Some birds winter in the U.S. in parts of Florida, California, and the Carribean; the rest migrate to Mexico, Central America, and northern South America.

Habitat: Baltimore orioles prefer wooded areas, and build their nests high from the ground. In the fall they migrate south to tropical climates.

Diet: Eats insects (especially caterpillars), berries, and fruit. They also will feed on human-provided foods such as suet, jams and jellies, and sugar-water in hummingbird feeders.

Female Baltimore orioles weave basket-like nests of grass and plant and human-made fibers that hang from tree branches. (© Gregory K. Scott/Photo Researchers, Inc. Reproduced by permission.)

Behavior and reproduction: Baltimore orioles breed in monogamous (muh-NAH-guh-mus) pairs, with one male and one female. The male attracts a mate by singing, chasing, and showing off his plumage. Females weave basket-like nests of grass and plant and human-made fibers that hang from tree branches. They lay eggs in average clutches of four to five eggs, which hatch in approximately two weeks. Both mother and father feed the hatchlings until they leave the nest after two weeks.

Baltimore orioles and people: Because of their bright plumage and loud, clear song, Baltimore orioles are considered desirable neighbors to many people. The birds also help control the population of insects that are destructive to vegetation, like gypsy moth caterpillars and grasshoppers.

Conservation status: Baltimore orioles are not threatened. ■

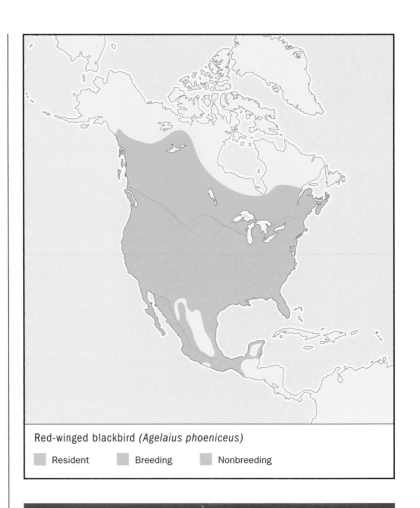

Red-winged blackbird (*Agelaius phoeniceus*)

■ Resident   ■ Breeding   ■ Nonbreeding

RED-WINGED BLACKBIRD
Agelaius phoeniceus

Physical characteristics: The male red-winged blackbird can be identified by the yellow-bordered red patches on the shoulder portion of the wing. While the adult male is a glossy black with black bill and feet, the adult female is streaked or striped with shades of brown and white. She is marked with a white stripe across her eye, a buff colored throat, and a faint orange patch on her shoulder. Birds don't attain their full adult coloring until they are three years old. Average size is 8.75 inches (22.23 centimeters) in length with a wingspan of 13 inches (33.02 centimeters) and a weight of 1.8 ounces (52 grams).

The male red-winged blackbird can be identified by the yellow-bordered red patches on the shoulder portion of the wing. The adult female is streaked or striped with shades of brown and white. (George J. Sanker/ Bruce Coleman Inc. Reproduced by permission.)

Geographic range: Like other New World blackbirds, the red-winged blackbird has an extensive North and South American range. The birds breed throughout Canada, the entire contiguous United States, and in southeastern Alaska all the way southward through Central America. They spend their winters as far north as southern Canada and south through Costa Rica. Some southern subspecies, population groups, are non-migratory.

Habitat: During breeding season red-winged blackbirds favor areas with tall vegetation such as marshes or grassland. They weave their nests into reeds or other vegetation to prevent access by predators. Wetlands also provide ample insects for feeding. In nonbreeding season, they descend on agricultural crops in large flocks.

Diet: Insects are the red-winged blackbird's staple during the summer months, but after breeding season they forage for grains and seeds.

Behavior and reproduction: Red-winged blackbird males mate with multiple females. Males are very territorial and will vigorously defend their space. Females select their mates based on the quality of the territory they have secured for nesting. Behaviors such as chasing, singing, and a "song spread" (in which the male sings loudly, spreads his wings, and puffs out his brightly colored epaulets, or shoulder feathers) are used by male birds to attract a mate. Interestingly, these same behaviors are also used to defend breeding territory from other males once it has been established.

The species travels and roosts with other types of blackbirds and starlings when they are not breeding, in flocks that can sometimes number in the hundreds of thousands.

Red-winged blackbirds and people: Because of their love of grains, rice, and seeds, the red-winged blackbird is considered a nuisance to many farmers. Crops for human and livestock consumption are frequently scavenged by large flocks of blackbirds. The United States Department of Agriculture estimates that sunflower growers in both North and South Dakota lose an estimated $4 to 7 million annually to blackbird damage to their crops. The USDA has used several pilot programs to try and reduce crop damage in recent years, including avicide (bird poisoning) programs, herbicide destruction of desirable red-winged blackbird habitat (such as cattail stands), and use of protective aerial lines over crops.

Conservation status: Despite concerted efforts to reduce their population, the red-winged blackbird continues to thrive in abundance.   ■

Baywing (*Agelaioides badius*)

Resident

BAYWING
Agelaioides badius

Physical characteristics: The baywing, sometimes called the bay-winged cowbird, is a small olive-gray bird. Wings are chestnut with black markings, and the bill, feet, and tail are black as well. Average size is about 7 inches (18 centimeters) in length and 1.4 to 1.8 ounces (41 to 50 grams).

Geographic range: A year-round resident of South America, the baywing is found in parts of Bolivia and Argentina, northeastern Brazil, Paraguay, and Uruguay.

Baywings typically take over abandoned nests of other birds instead of building their own nests. (© T. J. Ulrich/VIREO. Reproduced by permission.)

Habitat: Baywings are found at higher altitudes, up to 9,500 feet (2,880 meters), and favor scrub or wooded terrain.

Diet: Baywings eat primarily insects.

Behavior and reproduction: Instead of building their own nests, baywings typically take over abandoned nests of other birds (although some will either build their own cup-shaped nests or dwell in woodpecker holes). They are frequent victims of screaming cowbirds, a brood parasite species that lays their eggs in other birds' nests for incubation and fledging. It is thought that baywings lay clutches of four to five eggs.

Baywings and people: Baywings are not considered agricultural pests and enjoy a harmonious relationship with people.

Conservation status: Baywings are not a threatened species. ■

FOR MORE INFORMATION

Books:

George, Phillip Brandt. "Blackbirds, Orioles." In *Reference Atlas to the Birds of North America,* edited by Mel Baughman. Washington, DC: National Geographic Press, 2003.

Jaramillo, Alvaro, and Peter Burke. *New World Blackbirds: The Icterids.* Princeton, NJ: Princeton University Press, 1999.

Sibley, David Allen. *National Audubon Society: The Sibley Guide to Birds.* New York: Alfred A. Knopf, 2000.

Periodicals:

Harrison, George. "The Lord and Master: The Flashy Red-winged Blackbird is a Joyful Songster, a Master Weaver, and One of Our Most Easily Recognized Birds." *Birder's World* (February 2003): 42–5.

Web sites:

Cornell Lab of Ornithology. "Baltimore Oriole." All About Birds. http://birds.cornell.edu/programs/AllAboutBirds/BirdGuide/Baltimore_Orile_tl.html (accessed on May 28, 2004).

Cornell Lab of Ornithology. "Red-winged Blackbird." All About Birds. http://birds.cornell.edu/programs/AllAboutBirds/BirdGuide/Red-winged_Blackbird.html (accessed on May 28, 2004).

United States Department of Agriculture, Animal and Plant Health Inspection Service, Wildlife Services. "Development and Evaluation of Management Techniques for Reducing Blackbird Damage to Ripening Sunflower Crops and to Feedlots." National Wildlife Research Center. http://www.aphis.usda.gov/ws/nwrc/research/sunflowers/ (accessed on May 29, 2004).

FINCHES
Fringillidae

Class: Aves
Order: Passeriformes
Family: Fringillidae
Number of species: 137 species

family
CHAPTER

phylum
class
subclass
order
monotypic order
suborder
▲ family

PHYSICAL CHARACTERISTICS

The family Fringillidae consists of "true" finches that are small-to moderately large-sized birds with a compact body, a short, conical-shaped bill, strong skull, and a peaked head with large jaw muscles. They have easily seen shoulder patches, a short neck, plumage (feathers) that vary from dull to colorful, nine small outer primary feathers on their wings that are hidden by wing coverts (small feather around quill base), and a long tail with twelve feathers. Finches are 3 to 10 inches (7.6 to 25.4 centimeters) long and weigh between 0.3 and 2.1 ounces (8 and 60 grams).

GEOGRAPHIC RANGE

Finches range throughout the Americas, Europe, Asia, and Africa.

HABITAT

They prefer forests, shrubby areas, savannas (flat grasslands), grasslands, agricultural areas, parks, and gardens.

DIET

Finches eat seeds, grains, and other vegetable matter. They also eat insects and other small invertebrates (animals without a backbone). Many species forage on the ground, while others feed in trees.

BEHAVIOR AND REPRODUCTION

Finches are strong fliers, and able to hop and run over short distances. Some species migrate long distances to warmer climates, while others wander constantly in search for food. Finches are mostly quiet birds, but do have short, sharp calls that are used to communicate and to warn of predators. Males use unique songs to defend a large breeding territory and to attract a mate. Because finches are spread out throughout the world, songs vary widely.

Female finches build cup-shaped nests of grasses and other plant fibers. Nests are constructed in trees, shrubs, or rocky crevices. Most species breed as a mating pair, but others form small family groups. Once the male and female bonds, they are monogamous (muh-NAH-guh-mus; one mate) for the breeding season. Females lay two to six eggs, which vary with respect to species as to color and markings. The eggs are incubated (kept warm for hatching) usually by the female, but sometimes by both parents, which also take care of young.

BILLS FOR SHELLING SEEDS

Finches have a bill suited for shelling seeds. Each seed is wedged in a special groove on the side of the palate (roof of the mouth) and crushed by raising its lower jaw onto it. The shell husk is then peeled off with the tongue, releasing the kernel. The bird throws away the husk, and the kernel is taken off with its tongue and swallowed.

FINCHES AND PEOPLE

Many species have been captured and bred as cage-birds or pets because people like their beautiful songs, attractive plumage, and habits.

CONSERVATION STATUS

One species is listed as Critically Endangered, facing an extremely high risk of extinction; five species are Endangered, facing a very high risk of extinction; three species are Vulnerable, facing a high risk of extinction; four species are Near Threatened, in danger of becoming threatened with extinction; and one species is Extinct, died out.

Chaffinch (*Fringilla coelebs*)

▨ Resident

CHAFFINCH
Fringilla coelebs

Physical characteristics: Chaffinches have a white shoulder patch, a white wing-bar, and white tail markings. Males are patterned with a blue-gray back and front of head, a pink-to-rust face, throat, breast, and sides, a gray-green rump, a white belly, flanks, and undertail coverts, and a gray-blue tail. Females are duller with a yellow-brown overall color, a paler colored belly, a brown eye line, and light olive-brown upperparts. Color variations and streaking patterns occur because of wide geographical range. Adults are about 6 inches (15.2 centimeters) long, with a wingspan of about 9.5 inches (24.1 centimeters).

Geographic range: Chaffinches are widely spread throughout most of Europe, across the Middle East, through the Ukraine and western Russia to Afghanistan, and in North Africa, the Canary Islands, and the Azores.

Habitat: They are found in a variety of woodlands and open forests, urban and suburban parks and gardens, and fields with hedgerows.

Diet: Their diet consists of seeds (including pine) and fruits. Young chaffinches are fed insect larvae (LAR-vee), caterpillars, butterflies, moths, and other invertebrates, which are brought up from the stomachs of parents as partially digested food. They feed from trees and bushes.

Behavior and reproduction: Chaffinches are found alone or in pairs during the nesting season, and in groups and small flocks after breeding. They are migratory birds and females prefer to migrate farther south than males. Their song is a bold warbling such as "fyeet, fyeet, lya-lya-vee, chee-yew-keak." Their call is a "pink-pink" and their flight call is "cheup." Chaffinches build well-hidden, cup-shaped nests of grasses and lichens. Nests are neatly constructed in trees or shrubs that are near to trunks or large branches. The incubation period (time sitting on eggs) is ten to sixteen days, only done by the female. One to two broods (young born and raised together) are raised each year by the pair (mostly by female).

Chaffinches and people: People enjoy chaffinches for their beauty and song both in residential and agricultural areas. They have been kept as pets for their beautiful singing.

Conservation status: Chaffinches are not threatened. They are widespread and abundant throughout their habitat. In fact, they have grown in numbers as their native habitats of forests have been turned into urbanized and agricultural lands, but only when such areas contain trees, shrubs, and hedgerows. ■

Chaffinches are found in a variety of woodlands and open forests, urban and suburban parks and gardens, and fields with hedgerows. (Illustration by Barbara Duperron. Reproduced by permission.)

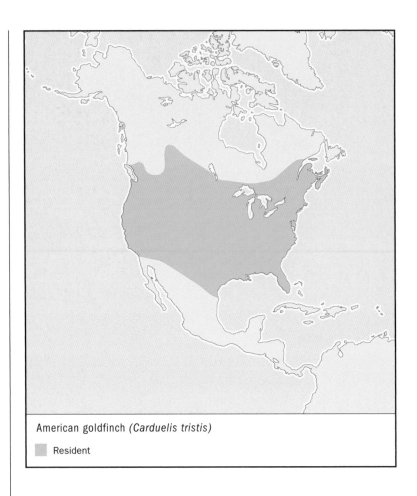

American goldfinch (*Carduelis tristis*)

Resident

AMERICAN GOLDFINCH
Carduelis tristis

Physical characteristics: Male American goldfinches are colored an overall bright canary yellow, with black wings marked in double white bars and white edging, a black tail, and a black face cap. Males are not as brightly colored in the winter. Females are a dull grayish-yellow, with dark wings and tails, pale yellow under parts without a black cap, and olive upper parts. Juveniles are olive-yellow, with darker wings. Adults are 4.3 to 5.0 inches (10.9 to 12.7 centimeters) long and weigh about 0.5 ounces (14 grams). Their wingspan is 8.8 to 9.0 inches (22.4 to 22.9 centimeters) long.

Male and female American goldfinches feed their young after they've hatched. (© Anthony Mercieca/Photo Researchers, Inc. Reproduced by permission.)

Geographic range: American goldfinches breed throughout most of southern Canada and the northern half of the United States. It winters in extreme southern Canada, through most of the United States, and northern Mexico.

Habitat: American goldfinch is one of the most common birds in the United States, usually seen in parks, farms, and suburban gardens. They inhabit open, mixed-species forests, and shrubby areas. They winter in shrubby habitats, old fields, and parks and gardens.

Diet: Their diet consists of small seeds and grains, especially liking plants in the aster family, including sunflower, lettuce, and thistles. They also eat insects.

Behavior and reproduction: American goldfinches fly with a very unique bounding flight. They are migratory birds, and social during the nonbreeding season when they are often found in large flocks, usually with other finches. The birds breed in loose colonies (bird groups that live together and are dependent on each other). Their courtship rituals include daring maneuvers and singing by males. Males court when their bright plumage appears. Their song is a series of musical warbles and trills, often with a long "baybeee" note. When flying, they sing songs like "per-chick-oree" or "po-tato-chips."

Monogamous American goldfinches begin to breed around the middle of June in their northern habitat, while in southern climates, they breed as early as March and continue through July. They defend a nesting territory. Most mating pairs raise only one brood each year. They build small cup-shaped nests that are woven with grasses and other plant fibers. Nests are placed in large thistles, other tall weeds, shrubs, or trees. Females lay four to six pale bluish white eggs. The incubation period is ten to twelve days, performed only by females. Both mates feed their young with a fledgling period lasting eleven to seventeen days. Young spend the fall following their parents. One to two broods occur each year.

American goldfinches and people: People find American goldfinches to be very popular birds to watch. It is the state bird of Iowa, New Jersey, and Washington.

Conservation status: American goldfinches are not threatened. They are widespread throughout their geographical range. However, their numbers have been decreasing during recent decades mostly due to habitat loss through developing their native lands for urban and agricultural uses. ■

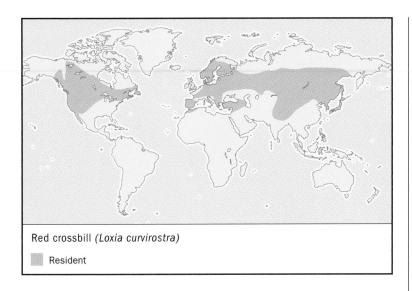

Red crossbill *(Loxia curvirostra)*

▨ Resident

RED CROSSBILL
Loxia curvirostra

Physical characteristics: Red crossbills show much geographic variation in body size, and in bill size and shape, but not in color. They have a fairly heavy body (about the size of sparrows), a short forked tail, and a stout bill where the tips of the upper and lower mandibles (parts of bill) cross over. Males are colored an overall dusky brick red with dusky wings that have reddish edging, and a dusky black tail that is short and notched. The undertail coverts are dark with whitish edging, while the belly is whitish gray. Females are gray tinged with dull green, brightest on rump, with darker (dusky black) wings. Juveniles have weakly crossed mandibles, gray-olive upperparts, whitish under parts that are streaked with dark brown and washed with yellow, and a buff-yellow rump. Adults are 5.3 to 6.5 inches (14.0 to 16.5 centimeters) long and weigh about 1.4 ounces (40 grams). Their wingspan is 10.0 to 10.8 inches (25.4 to 27.4 centimeters) long.

Geographic range: Red crossbills range through the boreal and montane forest regions of both North America and Eurasia. They are found from coast to coast on both continents, breeding from southern Alaska, Manitoba, Quebec, and Newfoundland, south in west to northern Nicaragua, in eastern United States to Wisconsin and North Carolina.

The red crossbill can remove conifer seeds from pine cones with its crossed bills and flexible tongue. (© S. Holt/VIREO. Reproduced by permission.)

Habitat: Red crossbills are mostly found in pine-containing conifer forests.

Diet: Their diet consists of conifer seeds mostly from the tree but sometimes off the ground, especially liking pine seeds. They remove seeds with its crossed bills and flexible tongue. The birds also eat insects and caterpillars.

Behavior and reproduction: Red crossbills are very social birds, especially during their nonbreeding season when they are found in large flocks. They sing a series of two-note phrases followed by a trilled warble, such as "jitt, jitt, jitt, jiiaa-jiia-jiiaaaa," "chipa-chipa-chipa," and "kip-kip-kip." The birds defend their territory with a repeated series of simple chirps as they fly around. During courtship, males fly above a female while vibrating wings and singing. Breeding pairs are monogamous. Females build saucer-shaped nests of twigs, grass, bark strips, and rootlets. Nests are lined with finer grasses, fur, feathers, hair, and moss, located near the end of conifer branches, and 6.6 to 40.0 feet (2 to 12 meters) off the ground. Females lay three to four light green-blue eggs that are spotted with brown and lilac. The incubation period is twelve to eighteen days. Only females incubate. The helpless newborns are brooded by the female and fed by both parents. The fledgling period is fifteen to twenty days. One to two broods occur each year.

Red crossbills and people: There is no known significant relationship between people and red crossbills.

Conservation status: Red crossbills are not threatened. They are abundant throughout their range, but some species are declining in numbers due to human activities such as logging operations. ■

FOR MORE INFORMATION

Books:

Alsop, Fred J. III. *Birds of North America.* New York: Dorling Kindersley, 2001.

Baughman, Mel M., ed. *Reference Atlas to the Birds of North America.* Washington, DC: National Geographic, 2003.

del Hoyo, Josep, Andrew Elliott, Jordi Sargatal, Jose Cabot, et al., eds. *Handbook of the Birds of the World.* Barcelona: Lynx Edicions, 1992.

Dickinson, Edward C., ed. *The Howard and Moore Complete Checklist of the Birds of the World,* 3rd ed. Princeton, NJ and Oxford, U.K.: Princeton University Press, 2003.

Field Guide to the Birds of North America, 4th ed. Washington, DC: National Geographic Society, 2002.

Forshaw, Joseph, ed. *Encyclopedia of Birds,* 2nd ed. San Diego, CA: Academic Press, 1998.

Harrison, Colin James Oliver. *Birds of the World.* London and New York: Dorling Kindersley, 1993.

Kaufman, Kenn, with collaboration of Rick and Nora Bowers and Lynn Hassler Kaufman. *Birds of North America.* New York: Houghton Mifflin, 2000.

Sibley, David. *The Sibley Guide to Birds.* New York: Alfred A. Knopf, 2000.

Terres, John K. *The Audubon Society Encyclopedia of North American Birds.* New York: Knopf, 1980.

Web sites:

Adkisson, Curtis S. "Red Crossbill." The Birds of North America, No. 256, 1996 (Cornell University). http://birds.cornell.edu/birdsofna/excerpts/crossbill.html.

HAWAIIAN HONEYCREEPERS
Drepanididae

Class: Aves

Order: Passeriformes

Family: Drepanididae

Number of species: 51 species

phylum

class

subclass

order

monotypic order

suborder

▲ family

PHYSICAL CHARACTERISTICS

Hawaiian honeycreepers are a group of birds with very unique appearances. The Drepanididae family is divided into three groups: Hawaiian finches, seed-eaters with thick finch-like bills and songs similar to the cardueline finches; Hawaiian creepers and relatives, including nukupuu, generally green-plumaged (feathered) birds with thin bills that feed on nectar and insects; and mamos, iiwis, and relatives, red plumaged birds that feed on nectar and sing songs of squeaks and whistles.

Hawaiian honeycreepers are small- to medium-sized birds that are often mistaken for finches. They have a compact body and a relatively straight to greatly curved bill, with the wide variation of bill sizes and shapes due to the type of food eaten (some have finch-like bills adapted to feeding on seed pods, while many others have pointed or curved bills in order to forage (search for food) for insects and nectar). They have nine large primary feathers on each wing (with a tenth primary feather that no longer functions and has mostly disappeared), and a tube-like tongue (in most species) with a fringed tip that is adapted to nectar feeding. Plumage comes in a wide variety of colors from dull olive green to brilliant yellow, crimson, and multi-colors. Male Hawaiian honeycreepers are often more brightly colored than females.

GEOGRAPHIC RANGE

Hawaiian honeycreepers are found only on the Hawaiian Islands. They are believed to have descended from a single species of cardueline finch that came to the Hawaiian Islands (it is believed) about three to four million years ago.

HABITAT

Most Hawaiian honeycreepers live in forests, which range from mostly dry to very wet (tropical and semi-tropical) climates. A few species live on small, treeless islets (small islands).

DIET

Hawaiian honeycreepers eat almost anything that is edible. They commonly eat nectar, insects, spiders, slugs, land snails, fruits, seeds and seed pods, tree sap, seabird eggs, and carrion (decaying animals). The flowers of the native plant *Metrosideros polymorpha* are especially liked by a number of nectar-eating Hawaiian honeycreepers.

BEHAVIOR AND REPRODUCTION

All Hawaiian honeycreepers are diurnal (active during the day). They forage mostly alone and in family groups, but some species feed in mixed flocks. Breeding pairs form strong bonds, and such pairings result in monogamous (having one mate) behaviors for most species. They have a wide range of calls and songs, sometimes described as canary-like. Songs and calls vary sometimes even within a species. Territories for nesting and feeding are often defended aggressively by some species. Other species tolerate visitors into their area. Territories are 1.0 to 1.5 acres (0.4 to 1.0 hectare) in area. Breeding takes place usually from May through July but can go from January to August. The mating pair builds a simple, open cup-shaped nest of grasses, twigs, lichens, rootlets, and other plant materials that is lined with fine fibers and found usually on tree branches. Hatchlings (newborn birds) are born naked, blind, and helpless. Only the female incubates (sits on) the young, but the male feeds the brooding female (mother-bird that gives birth and raises her young) and the young.

HAWAIIAN HONEYCREEPERS AND PEOPLE

Hawaiian honeycreepers pollinate (fertilize) native plants and keep the insect population under control, much to the

HUNTING RED FEATHERS OF APAPANES

Apapanes were captured by early Hawaiian natives in order to pluck some of their feathers for use in various cultural purposes. Expert hunters mixed a sticky paste made from the sap of the breadfruit tree, applied it on tree limbs, and then caught the stuck birds (who were attracted to the sap) with nooses, fiber nets, or their bare hands. Only a feather or two was taken, so the birds were often released if the bird was too small to eat. The feathers would eventually grow back.

benefit of people. They also attract tourists to Hawaii who enjoy watching the colorful birds.

CONSERVATION STATUS

Seven species are listed as Critically Endangered, facing an extremely high risk of extinction; five are Endangered, facing a very high risk of extinction; and three are Vulnerable, facing a high risk of extinction. Sixteen species of Hawaiian honeycreeper have become extinct in the recent past, mostly since the arrival of the Polynesians who introduced rats, and later other species of rodents and the mongoose. All species have been hurt, and continue to be hurt, by various degrees with respect to loss of habitat, introduction of diseases, and invasion of introduced predators, animals that hunt them for food. Many conservation programs are currently under way to protect most of the species.

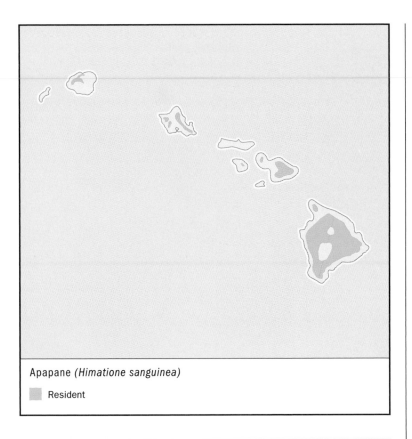

Apapane (*Himatione sanguinea*)

☐ Resident

APAPANE
Himatione sanguinea

Physical characteristics: Apapanes have bright crimson plumage, along with black wings and tails, a white undertail and abdomen, and a long, down-curved bill. They are about 5.25 inches (13.3 centimeters) long and weigh between 0.50 and 0.56 ounces (14 and 16 grams).

Geographic range: Apapanes are found in ohia lehua rainforests (forests that contain ohia lehua trees) of Hawaii. They commonly range in forested areas over 3,300 feet (1,000 meters) in elevation on Hawaii, Oahu, and Kauai. They are vary rare or extinct on Lanai and Molokai.

Habitat: They inhabit forests over 3,300 feet (1,000 meters) in elevation.

Apapanes feed mainly on nectar, and eat some insects that are on the flowers. (© P. La Tourrette/ VIREO. Reproduced by permission.)

Diet: Nectar makes up the main part of the diet of the apapane species, which is found on the flowering ohia trees. They also feed on insects that are found close to these flowering trees. The birds fly between forest patches of the trees, finding ones that are blooming. Apapanes feed in large flocks of the species, numbering as many as 3,000 individuals per 0.4 square miles (1 square meters) of area.

Behavior and reproduction: The social birds gather in large flocks and fly about forests in search of blooming ohia trees. Their calls include whistles, squeaks, raspings, clickings, and trillings. Their blunt wing tips make loud and distinctive noises while flying. They breed throughout the year, but primarily from February to June, which is the months where ohia nectar is most available.

Apapanes and people: There is no known significant relationship between people and apapanes. Early Hawaiian natives used the red feathers of the apapanes for their feather capes, kahilis (works of art), and helmets.

Conservation status: Apapane are not threatened. They are the most abundant species of Hawaiian honeycreeper. ■

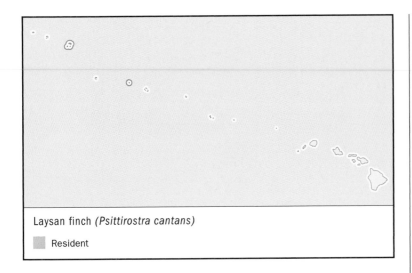

Laysan finch (*Psittirostra cantans*)

Resident

LAYSAN FINCH
Psittirostra cantans

Physical characteristics: Laysan finches have a large parrot-like (heavy, hooked) bill with the tip of the upper mandible (top part of a bird's bill) forming a tiny downward hook. Adult males have a bright yellow head, throat, and breast, and a gray collar around the neck. They have a grayish brown lower back and rump, and a whitish abdomen. Females are less colorful, with dark streaks in a yellowish crown, a gray collar, a yellowish throat and breast, some streaking on the flanks, and dark brown spots along the back. They are 6.0 to 6.5 inches (15 to 18 centimeters) long.

Geographic range: They are found on Laysan Island in the northwestern Hawaiian Island chain. A small population, which was introduced, exists on Pearl and Hermes Reef (a coral atoll). Both locations are part of a long series of islets northwest of the main Hawaiian Islands.

Habitat: Laysan is a low-lying, sandy island about 1,000 acres (405 hectares) in area that contains no trees but plenty of shrubbery and grasses. Pearl and Hermes Reef is a coral atoll containing several small islands.

Diet: Laysan finches are omnivorous (eating both animals and plants), eating such foods as carrion (decaying animals), various

The Laysan finch punctures seabird eggs with its bill to eat the food inside. (© M.J. Rauzon/ VIREO. Reproduced by permission.)

invertebrates (animals without a backbone) such as insects, roots, sprouts, soft parts of plants and seeds, and seabird eggs (including the interiors of tern eggs). With respect to tern eggs, Laysan finches puncture their eggshells with its bill in order to get to the food inside.

Behavior and reproduction: Laysan finches are lively and sociable birds. They are very curious and have no fear of humans, often even letting people to feed them from their hands. Males gather at the start of the breeding season in order to make courting displays toward females. Their song is a complex, canary-like warbling. They make cup-shaped nests from grasses and twigs and place them in clumps of grass or in small bushes.

Laysan finches and people: Wildlife biologists have made strong efforts to preserve the species, and to study the evolution of the species.

Conservation status: Laysan finches are listed as Endangered by the U.S. Fish and Wildlife Service (USFWS) and the State of Hawaii, and as Vulnerable by the World Conservation Union (IUCN). They are often injured or killed by violent storms and the increasing numbers of introduced species of animals that compete with them on their limited habitat. ■

FOR MORE INFORMATION

Books:

Alsop, Fred J. III. *Birds of North America.* New York: Dorling Kindersley, 2001.

Baughman, Mel M., ed. *Reference Atlas to the Birds of North America.* Washington, DC: National Geographic, 2003.

del Hoyo, Josep, Andrew Elliott, Jordi Sargatal, Jose Cabot, et al., eds. *Handbook of the Birds of the World.* Barcelona: Lynx Edicions, 1992.

Dickinson, Edward C., ed.*The Howard and Moore Complete Checklist of the Birds of the World,* 3rd ed. Princeton, NJ and Oxford, U.K.: Princeton University Press, 2003.

Field Guide to the Birds of North America, 4th ed. Washington, DC: National Geographic Society, 2002.

Forshaw, Joseph, ed. *Encyclopedia of Birds,* 2nd ed. San Diego, CA: Academic Press, 1998.

Harrison, Colin James Oliver. *Birds of the World.* London and New York: Dorling Kindersley, 1993.

Kaufman, Kenn, with collaboration of Rick and Nora Bowers and Lynn Hassler Kaufman. *Birds of North America.* New York: Houghton Mifflin, 2000.

Sibley, David. *The Sibley Guide to Birds.* New York: Alfred A. Knopf, 2000.

Terres, John K. *The Audubon Society Encyclopedia of North American Birds.* New York: Knopf, 1980.

Web sites:

"Hawaiian Honeycreepers: Family Drepanididae." Southwestern Adventist University, Department of Biology, Keene, Texas. http://biology.swau.edu/faculty/petr/ftphotos/hawaii/postcards/birds/ (accessed on July 20, 2004).

WAXBILLS AND GRASSFINCHES
Estrildidae

Class: Aves
Order: Passeriformes
Family: Estrildidae
Number of species: 129 species

phylum

class

subclass

order

monotypic order

suborder

▲ **family**

PHYSICAL CHARACTERISTICS

Waxbills and grassfinches, commonly called weaverfinches, are relatively small, often brightly colored birds with large, cone-shaped bills. Projections (or swellings) of thick connective tissue, which are located at the edges of the bill and at the gape (width of the open mouth), are one of the weaverfinches most interesting features. The projections are colored a bright white, blue, or yellow, and often edged with black. Their plumage (feathers) often blends in with their environment, but can still be quite colorful. Adults are 3.5 to 6.7 inches (9 to 17 centimeters) long, with a wingspan of about 6 inches (15 centimeters).

GEOGRAPHIC RANGE

They are found in sub-Saharan Africa, southeastern Asia, Australia, and South Pacific islands. Various small populations have been introduced throughout other parts of the world.

HABITAT

Weaverfinches are found in savannas (flat grasslands), forests, and semi-deserts, preferring forest edges.

DIET

Their diet consists of small half-ripe and fully ripe grass seeds, and during the breeding season they also eat arthropods (invertebrate animals with jointed limbs). Ants and termites are eaten at the beginning of the rainy season. They often dash out from a perch to grab an insect and then return to the same perch.

BEHAVIOR AND REPRODUCTION

Weaverfinches are highly social birds that maintain strong bonds between the mating pair and among members of small flocks. They often perch in close contact with each other, often preening each other (grooming feathers with the bill). Males do a dance for females where they sing and either hop toward the female, or perform bows or stretching movements while hopping about in front of the female. If interested, females will cower on a branch and tremble her tail (that is, shake it slightly while keeping the wings still).

The song of weaverfinches is usually soft. Weaverfinches do not use songs to defend their territory or show aggression. The short song often sounds unpleasant, and is usually heard only by a nearby female as part of the courtship ritual. Songs are learned while in the fledgling period (time necessary for young bird to grow feathers necessary to fly).

Nests of weaverfinches are often roofed over, and shaped like a sphere (ball) with a diameter of 4 to 8 inches (10 to 20 centimeters). Many species attach a long tube to the nest that is used as an entrance. Males gather the nesting materials that consist of fresh or dry grass stalks, coconut fibers, animal hair, and feathers (for the nest itself) and feathers and other soft materials (for the lining). Females weave very complex nests, which is often also used for roosting during the nonbreeding season. Nests are usually placed in bushes or low trees, but can be found on the ground, hanging between reeds or grass stalks, or in tree holes.

Females lay four to six eggs, but once in awhile can lay up to nine eggs. Both sexes incubate (sit on and warm) eggs and brood (raise) young. During the day they switch sitting on the eggs around every one and one half hours, but at night both parents sit on the eggs together. Males often give brooding females a bit of grass or feather. The incubation period (time that it takes to sit on and warm the eggs before they hatch) is twelve to sixteen days. The young eat half-ripe seeds that are regurgitated (food brought up from the stomach) by the parents into their open mouth. The nestling period (time necessary to take care of young birds unable to leave nest) lasts about twenty-one days. Even after the young leave the nest, parents will direct the young birds back into the nest for sleeping and eating. They still take food from the parents from one to two weeks after fledging (first time that young are able to fly away from the nest). Many weaverfinches reach breeding age before their first birthday, sometimes even before they molt from their juvenal (present while a juvenile, young) plumage.

WEAVERFINCHES AND PEOPLE

Weaverfinches are often kept in aviaries (large cages) where a mixed group of different species and colored birds are kept in the same environment. Many species such as the Java sparrow, the zebra finch, and the gouldian finch are domesticated species.

CONSERVATION STATUS

Two species of weaverfinches are listed as Endangered, facing a veryhigh risk of extinction; eight species as Vulnerable, facing a high risk of extinction; and six species as Near Threatened, in danger of becoming threatened with extinction.

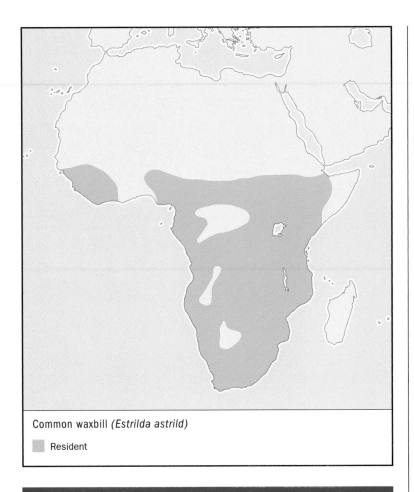

Common waxbill (*Estrilda astrild*)

Resident

COMMON WAXBILL
Estrilda astrild

Physical characteristics: Common waxbills are mostly fawn in color, with upperparts that are darker than lower parts, a striped body, red bill, and a red stripe from the bill across the eye to the ear. Males and females look alike, having the same colors. Juveniles look paler than adults and with fainter barring. Adults are 4.3 to 5.1 inches (11 to 13 centimeters) long.

Geographic range: They are found generally in southern Africa, specifically in southern Senegal, east to Ethiopia, south to South Africa, and generally throughout most of sub-Saharan Africa. They have been introduced in Portugal, Brazil, and many islands throughout the world,

Common waxbills live in areas with tall grasses such as marshes, reed beds, gardens, farms, and plantations. (© P. Craig-Cooper/ VIREO. Reproduced by permission.)

including Hawaii, Amirantes, Tahiti, Rodriques, Reunion, Mauritius, St. Helena, the Seychelles, Puerto Rico, and Bermuda.

Habitat: Common waxbills live in areas with tall grasses such as marshes, reed beds, abandoned cultivated areas, gardens, grassy paths and clearings, and farms and plantations.

Diet: They eat small seeds (such as grass seeds) taken from plants and off the ground. Termites and other insects are also sometimes eaten.

Behavior and reproduction: Common waxbills are very social birds, often found in small flocks during the breeding season and larger flocks (sometimes numbering in the thousands) at other times. Their calls include such sounds as "chip," "tchic," and "pit" while their song is often described as a "tcher-tcher-preee," although other varieties are often heard. They build a pear-shaped nest of grass stems that is located at or near the ground. Females lay four to six white eggs. The incubation period is eleven to thirteen days, and the fledgling period is about twenty days.

Common waxbills and people: People often keep common waxbills in cages, and have been bred in aviaries.

Conservation status: These birds are not threatened, but their trade (importing and exporting them) is regulated. ∎

Zebra finch *(Taeniopygia guttata)*

□ Resident

ZEBRA FINCH
Taeniopygia guttata

Physical characteristics: Adult males have an orange cheek patch, chestnut ear patches, black barring at the throat, red eyes, white-spotted chestnut flanks, black and white bars on the tail, a gray head and back, orange legs, and a red bill. Adult females lack most of the colors of the males, but do have an orange bill. Juveniles look similar to females but have a dark bill. Adults are 3.9 to 4.3 inches (10 to 11 centimeters) long and weigh about 0.4 ounces (12 grams).

Geographic range: They are found throughout most of the interior of Australia (being absent from the north, east, and south coasts) and

Male (left) and female (right) zebra finches have different coloring, but both have a brightly colored bill. (Illustration by Joseph E. Trumpey. Reproduced by permission.)

in Timor (an island in Southeast Asia) and the surrounding Indonesian islands.

Habitat: Zebra finches inhabit a wide variety of habitats but prefer open areas such as plains, woodlands, savannas (flat grasslands), mulga scrubs (acacia [uh-KAY-shuh] trees that grow in arid regions of Australia), grasslands, salt marshes, orchards, cultivated areas and farmlands, and inhabited areas and gardens.

Diet: These birds feed on a variety of grass seeds and shoots, mostly from the ground, but also eat insects. They are able to live up to about 500 days without drinking water.

Behavior and reproduction: Zebra finches are very social birds that are found in pairs but more often found in large flocks. Their call is a "tya" or "tchee." Males courting females give out a mixture of trills and nasal notes. They build flask-shaped nests of many types of materials but mostly of grasses that is lined with feathers and wool. An entrance tunnel is built on the side. Sometimes other bird nests or roosts are used, often redone to suit their own needs. Females lay three to eight white eggs. The incubation period is eleven to sixteen days, and the fledgling period is fifteen to twenty-two days.

Zebra finches and people: People often keep zebra finches as pets. They are often bred, studied, and sometimes domesticated.

Conservation status: Zebra finches are not threatened. ∎

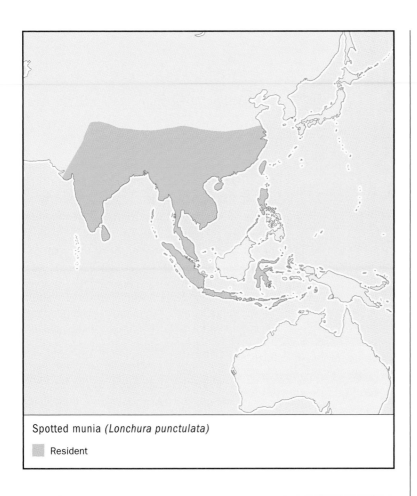

Spotted munia (*Lonchura punctulata*)

▨ Resident

SPOTTED MUNIA
Lonchura punctulata

Physical characteristics: Spotted munias look alike with respect to males and females. They have big heads and large, conical bills, brown, scale-patterned feathers on a white breast and flanks, and a dusky brown face and throat. They also have plain brown upperparts and small grayish traces on rump. Juveniles have brown upperparts and buffy under parts, but do not have the scaled pattern on their under parts. Adults are 3.9 to 4.7 inches (10 to 12 centimeters) long.

Geographic range: They range from India, southern China, and Southeast Asia including parts of Malaysia and Indonesia. They have

been introduced in Australia, Puerto Rico, Hawaii, Japan, and the Seychelles.

Habitat: Spotted munias inhabit open or semi-open habitats including cultivated and inhabited areas, parks and gardens, rice fields, grasslands, and forest edges.

Diet: The birds eat grass seeds, especially rice, from off of the ground and on live plants. They also eat small berries. Sometimes, they eat dead animals along roadsides. When human trash dumps are available, they are seen removing scraps of food, such as bread, from the area.

Behavior and reproduction: Spotted munias are often found in large flocks of birds of various species. Their call is a series of repeated "kitty-kitty-kitty." Their wide variety of calls is used for keeping in contact with other birds or to express alarm. The soft song is a "klik-klik-klik" followed by a series of whistles and ending with a "weeee." The song has many variations. A breeding colony is often built consisting of hundreds of round nests of grass and tree bark. Females lay three to seven white eggs. The incubation period is about fourteen days.

Spotted munias are often found in large flocks of birds with their own and other species. (Illustration by Joseph E. Trumpey. Reproduced by permission.)

Spotted munias and people: People often keep and breed spotted munias. Many are caught for eventual sale into the pet business.

Conservation status: Spotted munias are not threatened. There is no noticeable impact on its numbers with respect to many of its numbers being caught as pets, except for those in Vietnam and Southeast Asia, where they are also caught for human consumption and as part of religious ceremonies. ■

FOR MORE INFORMATION

Books:

del Hoyo, Josep, Andrew Elliott, Jordi Sargatal, Jose Cabot, et al., eds. *Handbook of the Birds of the World.* Barcelona: Lynx Edicions, 1992.

Dickinson, Edward C., ed. *The Howard and Moore Complete Checklist of the Birds of the World,* 3rd ed. Princeton, NJ and Oxford, U.K.: Princeton University Press, 2003.

Forshaw, Joseph, ed. *Encyclopedia of Birds,* 2nd ed. San Diego, CA: Academic Press, 1998.

Harrison, Colin James Oliver. *Birds of the World.* London and New York: Dorling Kindersley, 1993.

Perrins, Christopher M., and Alex L. A. Middleton, eds. *The Encyclopedia of Birds.* New York: Facts on File, 1985.

WEAVERS
Ploceidae

Class: Aves
Order: Passeriformes
Family: Ploceidae
Number of species: 117 species

phylum
class
subclass
order
monotypic order
suborder
▲ family

PHYSICAL CHARACTERISTICS

Weavers are small, finch-like birds, 4.3 to 10 inches (11 to 25 centimeters) in body length. Weavers are closely related to finches (family Fringillidae) and are sometimes referred to as "weaver finches." Other common names for various genera within the family include queleas, fodies (in Madagascar), bishops, malimbes, mynas, and widowbirds. They are called "weavers" because of the complex, elaborate nests that various species build.

The weaver's beak is short, sturdy, massive, and conical, like a typical finch's beak. The legs are short and resemble those of passerines, except that in some species the feet are larger. The tail is usually long, occasionally as long as the head and body, or even longer, as in the widowbirds.

Weavers could be described as finch-like birds in tropical dress. A few are dull in color, while many others are brilliant and unique, the brightest and most widely seen colors being yellow, orange, and red. Males tend to be more colorful than females. The grosbeak weaver is mainly dark gray with white patches on its forehead and outer edges of the wings. Widowbird species have long, loose, elaborate black tails.

Males of most Ploceidae species change colors during the breeding season, from duller to more vivid, changing back to the duller coat when the breeding season over. The dull phase plumage of the male looks very similar to that of the female, which does not change color. A male red-collared widowbird, in the nonbreeding seasons, is colored light brown on its sides, under parts and head, with dark gray wings, a yellow streak over each eye and yellowish on the cheeks, but the breeding plumage is shiny black with a bright red-orange collar across the throat, extending upwards in two broad red bands near the back of the head, and forming a red cap on the crown.

GEOGRAPHIC RANGE

Weavers live mainly in tropical Africa, as well as Madagascar, southern Asia, and as far east as Borneo and Java. Some species have been introduced into non-native habitats, where they have quickly adapted and flourished.

HABITAT

Habitat preferences among weaver species vary as much as their appearance and behavior. Most prefer open spaces, like grassland with or without scattered trees. The red-billed buffalo-weaver prefers savanna with acacia or baobab trees in east Africa, but is even more partial to areas disturbed by natural forces, such as wild animal herds, or human activities. Some species prefer living close to villages, probably for protection from predators that naturally fear humankind. If the people of the village abandon it, the weavers will desert their nest.

Many weaver species change habitats in the breeding season. The thick-billed weaver, during its breeding season, lives in spreads of grasses, reeds, and papyrus in marshes and rivers. During nonbreeding periods of the year, the species returns to tropical forest.

DIET

The staple food for most weaver species is seeds of various wild grasses, supplemented with insects, spiders, freshwater snails, and fruits. They also help themselves to discarded scraps of human food.

BEHAVIOR AND REPRODUCTION

Weavers are energetic and noisy, especially when gathered together in flocks, which is a large majority of the time for some species and most of the time for a few. Individuals of some weaver species may live alone, but even they periodically form social groups of up to a thousand birds.

Weavers forage in groups, and feed by picking grass seeds, insects, and spiders off the ground, or perching on stalks of grass and yanking seeds from the stalk, crushing all but the hardest seeds with their powerful beaks. Some snag insects in mid-flight. Some weaver species stay more or less in one place, others migrate to greater or lesser degrees.

Weaver voices and songs are long-winded, complex, and vary with circumstances, including displays of aggression, mating, and warning. The song of the red-headed weaver has been transcribed as "chu-tsee-tsi, chu-tsi, tsee-tsi, tswi-tsi-tswee, tzirrrr," morphing into "tchu-thi-tseee-iiiiii-i, swizzzzzzz" or "sizzi-sizzi-sizzi-sizzi."

Reproduction types vary among species and reflect the sort of nest-building used by each. One species, the cuckoo finch, is a brood parasite, similar to cuckoos, cowbirds, and honeyguides. The cuckoo finch lays her eggs in other birds' nests. Consequently, her eggs are treated as family by the receiving birds, allowing the cuckoo to reproduce without caring for her own young. A few weaver species have individual, isolated nests for breeding couples, but most species build colonial nests, either individual nests in one tree, or a giant common nest. Entrances are on the bottom or sides. The communal nest of the social weaver can hold up to three hundred breeding pairs and may reach 10 feet (3 meters) in height and 15 feet (5 meters) in width.

Weavers living in colonies may be polygamous (puh-LIH-guh-mus; one dominant male, several breeding females), polygynous (puh-LIJ-uh-nus; one dominant female, several breeding males), cooperative (two or more males mate with all females, males help care for the young), or monogamous (muh-NAH-guh-mus; one breeding pair), but monogamous pairs may inhabit communal nests. More than one of these systems may be used even within one species. In communities with several breeding pairs, a dominant male mates with the largest number of females possible.

Weavers build nests in large, isolated trees and on power line support towers and windmills. In most species, the male builds the nest or adds onto a communal nest, then invites and entices females to mate with him and move into the nest to raise the young. Large birds of prey may build nests on top of communal weaver nests, partially camouflaging the raptor nest and lending some protection to the weavers. The birds finish the entire structure with a roof of intertwined leaves on twigs, for repelling rain.

The red-billed buffalo-weaver shows both polygamous and cooperative breeding behaviors. In polygamous systems, one male rules and defends up to eight chambers, each with a female and young, in a single large, communal nest. In the co-operative method, two males build and defend nests, and feed the young.

Weavers aggressively defend their nests, not only from predators but also from other members of their own species. The defenders can distinguish nest-family members from strangers of the same species, threatening and driving them off. One or more males are the principal defenders and if they are away from the nest, a female may take over the task of defense.

Female weavers lay two to eight eggs per clutch. The eggs hatch in about fourteen days. In monogamous species, both parents raise the chicks, while in polygamous and polygynous species, adults other than the parents may help care for the young.

WEAVERS AND PEOPLE

It has been suggested that in prehistory, weaver birds may have inspired humans to try their own hand at weaving baskets and cloth. Since most weaver species eat grass seeds, including those of cultivated grasses like rice, wheat, and millet, some of these species have become pests, raiding grain crops. The most pestiferous (pest-like) of all weaver species, is the red-billed quelea. Other weaver species that are more or less sedentary can still cause major local losses of grain crops. These species include the red-headed quelea, the red bishop, and the yellow crowned bishop.

CONSERVATION STATUS

The World Conservation Union (IUCN) lists six species of Ploceidae as Endangered, facing a very high risk of extinction, and seven as Vulnerable, facing a high risk of extinction. The main factor in declining populations of these species is habitat loss by humanity to agriculture and forestry.

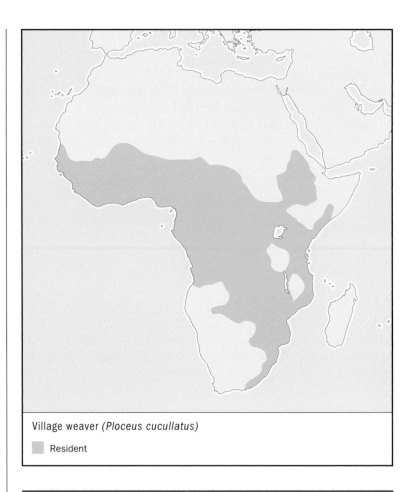

Village weaver (*Ploceus cucullatus*)

███ Resident

VILLAGE WEAVER
Ploceus cucullatus

Physical characteristics: Also called the spotted-back weaver and black-headed weaver, the adult body length runs 6 to 7 inches (15 to 17 centimeters), males being larger than females.

During the breeding season, the male is a combination of brilliant yellow on the under parts, and back of the neck and crown, as well as shiny black on the face and bib. The posterior belly may be bright orange-red. The folded wings show alternating streaks and spots of yellow and black, hence the common name, spotted-back weaver. The eyes are orange-red, the beak is black and the legs and feet are brown. The female is less garish, her upper parts olive with dark brown stripes

Village weavers have adapted well to changes that humans make in their environment. They often nest in or near villages. (Illustration by Amanda Humphrey. Reproduced by permission.)

paralleling the body length. The sides are yellow-brown, and the abdomen is whitish with some yellow. Outside the breeding season, the male plumage closely resembles that of the female, whose colors never change.

Geographic range: Africa, western through central to southern and southeastern.

Habitat: Open woods, forest edges, savanna, along rivers and streams, often close to or within villages.

Diet: The village weaver's diet consists of seeds, green vegetation, fruit, ant eggs, and mealworms.

Behavior and reproduction: Mating is at first monogamous, later changing to polygamous, meaning that the birds begin with one mate each and the male eventually finds other females to mate with. After the male has built one nest and attracted and mated with a female, he builds another nest and tries to entice another female to move in. One male may support up to five females in five nests.

Females usually lay two eggs per clutch, which hatch in about fourteen days. The male builds the nest, which holds one female and young, out of grass blades or other vegetation.

Village weavers derive that common name from their frequent habit of nesting near villages in Africa, probably for protection from predators that naturally fear people. Village weavers are well-known for their skills in adapting to new environments, often ones much different from the original and far from home, including the New World, where they were brought by humans. The species has been living on various Caribbean islands for two hundred years. On Hispaniola, village weavers have adapted to near-desert conditions by eating the fruits of the *Stenocereus hystrix* cactus and depending on them for water.

Village weavers might be frequent hosts for parasitic eggs of the dideric cuckoo. However, village weaver eggs frequently and constantly change color among individual females. Part of the ploy of brood parasites is ensuring the intruder egg closely resembles the host eggs, especially in color. Otherwise, the host mother may spot the intruder egg and pitch it from the nest. Village weavers keep ahead of the game by constantly changing egg colors to keep the parasitic weavers confused.

Village weavers and people: Village weavers may make minor nuisances of themselves by raiding grain crops for the seeds.

Conservation status: These weavers are not threatened, but are numerous, widespread, and adaptable. ■

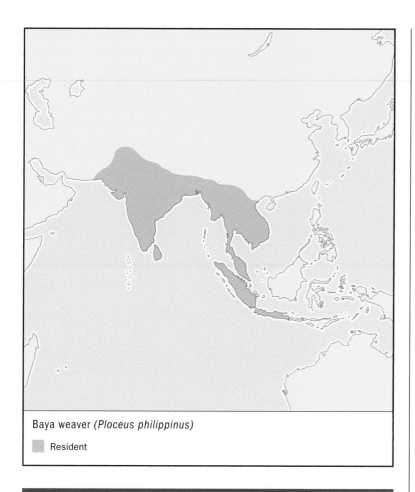

Baya weaver *(Ploceus philippinus)*

▨ Resident

BAYA WEAVER
Ploceus philippinus

Physical characteristics: Adult body length is 5.9 inches (15 centimeters). Outside the breeding season, the male and female are similarly colored, yellow-brown with dark streaks on the upper body, off-white below. During the breeding season, the male has a yellow crown and breast, the upper body dark brown with yellow streaks, and off-white under parts.

Geographic range: India and Sri Lanka through southwestern China, Singapore, Sumatra, and Java.

Habitat: Baya weavers live in grassland, scrub, secondary forest, farmed areas, usually near fresh or brackish water.

Male baya weavers have brighter colors during the breeding season, and build nests to help attract females. (Illustration by Amanda Humphrey. Reproduced by permission.)

Diet: These weavers eat mainly seeds of guinea grass, *Panicum maximum*.

Behavior and reproduction: Males change to brighter plumage during the mating season and start building nests to attract females. Nests, one per breeding female, are built in trees, sometimes alongside hornet nests or aggressive, stinging red ants. In these cases, each species lives in peace with one another, and both gain protection from predators specific to each species.

Each nest is shaped more or less like a vase, constricted in the middle and with an entrance at the bottom. It may hang by a long rope from a tree branch or be directly attached to the branch. The baya weavers build their nests out of sectioned blades of guinea grass, the seeds of which are their main food staple.

The male usually assembles several partially built nests that look like domes with hanging straps, then sings and displays on the unfinished nests to attract females. An interested female will inspect one of these nests carefully. If it suits her, she displays approval and mates, after which either the male or female completes the nest. As soon as the female is busy tending the eggs, the male starts singing and displaying for females on another half-built nest, eventually taking in and mating with as many as three females. A female lays three or four eggs and must care for the chicks alone.

Baya weavers and people: Baya weavers have earned reputations as pests by raiding rice fields. Consequently, the birds often end up as food for humans.

Conservation status: Baya weavers are not threatened. ■

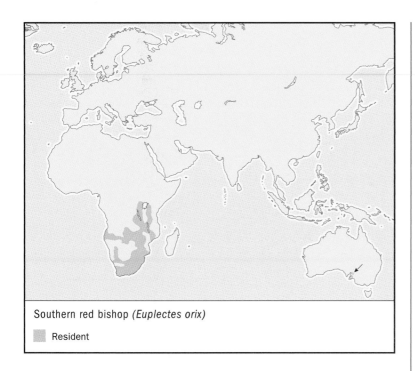

Southern red bishop *(Euplectes orix)*

Resident

SOUTHERN RED BISHOP
Euplectes orix

Physical characteristics: The southern red bishop is also called the grenadier weaver because of the bright colorings of the male in the breeding season. The adult body length is 4 inches (12.5 centimeters). During the breeding season, the neck, tail and wings of the male become brilliant red-orange, while the breast, underside, and the top of the head and face become a lustrous black. Even the beak changes to black. Out of season, the male's coloring reverts to dull shades of brown. The females look similar to out-of-season males and do not change color during the breeding season.

Geographic range: All of Africa south of the Sahara, except part of southwest, and horn of Africa (northeast).

Habitat: Grasslands with tall grass, near water sources.

Diet: Green or ripe seeds of wild grasses and shrubs, young leaves and flowers, and insects.

Although most weavers are vocal with their calls, the red bishop is not especially. It will screech if alarmed, and uses a small number of other calls, but nothing drawn out and elaborate as in most other weavers. (© R. Drummond/VIREO. Reproduced by permission.)

Behavior and reproduction: The red bishop forages in tall grasses, plucking seeds from grass stalks, often perching on grass stalks to reach the seeds, and on shrub seeds, leaves, flowers and occasional insects.

The red bishop is polygynous, one male mating with several females who settle in nests made by the male. At the start of a breeding season, groups of males will settle in one large area, among treetops, each male building one or more nests, then singing and posing to attract females.

Oddly enough among weavers, the red bishop is not especially vocal. It will screech if alarmed, and uses a small number of other calls, but nothing drawn out and elaborate as in most other weavers.

Red bishops and people: Red bishops can be serious pests, flocks of them descending on grain fields and helping themselves to the seeds.

Conservation status: The red bishop is not considered threatened.   ■

FOR MORE INFORMATION

Books:

Goodman, Steven M., and Jonathan P. Benstead. *The Natural History of Madagascar.* Chicago: University of Chicago Press, 2003.

Kavanagh, James. *African Birds.* Chandler, AZ: Waterford Press, 2001.

Morris, P., and F. Hawkins. *Birds of Madagascar: A Photographic Guide.* New Haven, CT: Yale University Press, 1998.

Strange, Morten. *Birds of Southeast Asia: A Photographic Guide to the Birds of Thailand, Malaysia, Singapore, the Philippines and Indonesia.* London: New Holland, 1998.

Strange, Morten. *A Photographic Guide to Birds of Malaysia and Singapore: Including Southeast Asia, the Philippines and Borneo.* Singapore: Periplus, 2000.

Periodicals:

Collias, E. C. "Inheritance of Egg-color Polymorphism in the Village Weaver (*Ploceus cucullatus*)." *Auk* 110, no. 4 (1993): 983–692.

Keng, Wang Luan. "Nature's Nest Architects at Sungei Buloh." *Wetlands* 3, no. 1 (1996). Online at http://www.sbwr.org.sg/wetlands/text/96-3-1-1.htm (accessed on July 12, 2004).

Lahti, David C. "Cactus Fruits May Facilitate Village Weaver (*Ploceus cucullatus*) Breeding in Atypical Habitat on Hispaniola." *The Wilson Bulletin* 115, no. 4 (2003): 487–489.

Lawes, Michael J., and Steven Kirkman. "Egg Recognition and Interspecific Brood Parasitism Rates in Red Bishops (Aves: Ploceidae)." *Animal Behaviour* 52, no. 3 (1996): 553–563

Victoria, J. K. "Clutch Characteristics and Egg Discriminative Ability of the African Village Weaverbird, *Ploceus cucullatus.*" *Ibis* 114 (1972): 367–376.

Williams, J. G., and G. S. Keith. "A Contribution to Our Knowledge of the Parasitic Weaver *Anomalospiza imberbis.*" *Bulletin of the British Ornithological Club* 82 (1962): 141–142.

Web sites:

Percy FitzPatrick Institute of African Ornithology: Roberts VII Project. http://web.uct.ac.za/depts/fitzpatrick/docs/listlink.html (accessed on July 12, 2004).

SPARROWS
Passeridae

Class: Aves
Order: Passeriformes
Family: Passeridae
Number of species: 39 species

phylum

class

subclass

order

monotypic order

suborder

▲ family

PHYSICAL CHARACTERISTICS

Sparrows are small plumpish birds with short, powerful bills and short tails. They have different shades of brown and gray on their upperparts that is sometimes streaked lightly to heavily, and white or buff under parts that are streaked with black or brown. Adults are 4.5 to 7.0 inches (12.0 to 17.5 centimeters) long and weigh in the approximate range of 0.4 to 1.9 ounces (10 to 55 grams).

GEOGRAPHIC RANGE

They are found worldwide except for Antarctica, north and west Australia, and the most northern parts of Eurasia.

HABITAT

Sparrows are found in open habitats with scattered trees such as arid steppes (treeless plains that is often semiarid and grass-covered) and woodlands.

DIET

Sparrows eat seeds of small plants including weeds, seeds from cultivated cereals, tree seeds, small berries, invertebrates such as insects (mostly for the young), food left out for animals and livestock, and human food wastes. Sparrows that forage in flocks often alternate feeding and resting, probably in order to digest hard seeds.

BEHAVIOR AND REPRODUCTION

Sparrows are very social birds. They often are found in large flocks while searching for food and while roosting. Sparrows regularly dust themselves off in dirt and bathe in water, oftentimes with other sparrows. While roosting, the birds usually remain close together and keep in contact with each other through soft calls. Sparrows are not migratory birds, but do wander during the nonbreeding season in search of food. A few species that live in cold, high-latitude and high-altitude climates regularly migrate to milder climates in the winter.

Males usually call out to females at nest sites. Their territory is only the nearby area around a nest. The usually monogamous (muh-NAH-guh-mus; having one mate) breeding pair builds a domed-over nest with a side entrance. Nests are sometimes built close to other nests but others are more scattered about, with space between each depending on the number of good nesting sites. Nests are made with grasses and rootlets lined with fine grasses and long hair, often on the ground. Females lay four to six eggs that vary in color and shape. Several broods (young birds that are born and raised together) are possible each year for most species. Both parents take part in incubating (sitting on and warming) the eggs and taking care of the young. Young are born with down, but feathers develop quickly. The fledgling period (time necessary for young bird to grow feathers necessary to fly) is twelve to twenty days. The breeding pair keeps the nest throughout the year.

SPARROWS AND PEOPLE

People sometimes consider sparrows as pests when seeds of cultivated grains are eaten by the birds in large amounts. Otherwise, sparrows and people do not have a significant relationship.

CONSERVATION STATUS

Sparrows are not under any threat, however the house sparrow in western Europe has declined in large numbers.

BROOKLYN, NEW YORK: BIRTHPLACE OF U.S. HOUSE SPARROW

About one hundred house sparrows were introduced into Brooklyn, New York, from Europe from the autumn of 1851 into the spring of 1852. The species quickly moved throughout the eastern United States and Canada.

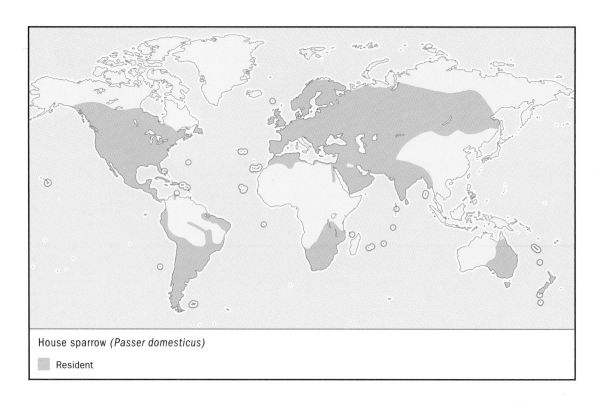

House sparrow *(Passer domesticus)*

Resident

SPECIES ACCOUNTS

HOUSE SPARROW
Passer domesticus

Physical characteristics: House sparrows are short and stocky birds with very short legs and thick bills. Male house sparrows have a gray crown (top part of head) and cheeks edged with chestnut, a chestnut nape (back part of neck), a black bill, and a usually small (but sometimes larger) black bib (area under bill, just above the breast) with a white moustache-like area below. They also have a white wing-bar, buff-brown back and black-streaked wings, pale gray under parts, and a gray rump and tail. Females are colored a drab brown overall with a dusky stripe below buff-colored eye brows, blackish streaked buff-brown upperparts, a dusky bill with a yellowish base that reaches to the lower mandible (lower part of bill), a white wing bar, and brownish gray under parts. Juveniles are similar to females but have browner upperparts, buffier under parts, and a pinkish bill. Adults are 5.5 to 6.3 inches (14 to 16 centimeters) long and weigh between 0.7 and 1.4 ounces (20 and 40 grams). Their wingspan is 9.5 to 10.0 inches (24.1 to 25.4 centimeters) long.

Geographic range: House sparrows are found in north Africa and Eurasia, excluding the most northern regions and the area from Japan west to Thailand. Beginning in the mid-nineteenth century, they were introduced to most of the rest of the human-inhabited world.

Habitat: House sparrows inhabit all areas throughout the world that are inhabited by humans. They often breed and winter in towns, cities, and farmlands. The bird is not usually found in woodlands and forests that have dense foliage.

Diet: They eat seeds (especially weed seeds), household scraps, insects, caterpillars, grains, and fruits, mostly from the ground around trees and shrubs. Most of their food comes from livestock feed. Young are fed small invertebrates (animals without a backbone).

House sparrows live throughout the world, wherever humans live. (Richard Galosy/Bruce Coleman Inc. Reproduced by permission.)

Behavior and reproduction: House sparrows are aggressive and noisy birds. They generally do not migrate, but stay in one area throughout the year in small colonies (groups of birds that live together and are dependent on each other). They prefer to live around humans. Their song is a twittering series of cheeps or chirrups. The birds sing year-round, although less often on the hottest, coldest, and rainiest days. Females sing most frequently when they are without a mate. During breeding season, they join in pairs, but otherwise are found in family groups and flocks. They like to build nests in holes within buildings and trees, but also will build free-standing domed nests on tree branches. Sometimes they take nests away from other bird species. Females may lay up to five clutches (group of eggs hatched together) of eggs each year, but two to three are average. One clutch is two to five eggs. The incubation period (time to sit on eggs before they hatch) is ten to fourteen days, and the fledgling period is fourteen to sixteen days. Both sexes are involved in breeding activities, but females do more of the brooding. Both parents fed regurgitated (partially digested) food to the young.

House sparrows and people: People sometimes consider house sparrows pests when they feed too much on cereal grains being raised by farmers.

Conservation status: House sparrows are not threatened, but have seen major decreases in their numbers in western Europe at the end of the twentieth century and into the twenty-first century. ■

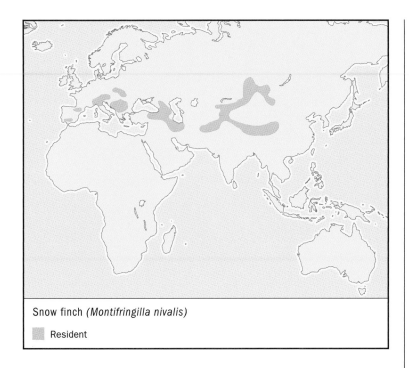

Snow finch (*Montifringilla nivalis*)

▨ Resident

SNOW FINCH
Montifringilla nivalis

Physical characteristics: Snow finches are large, plumpish finch-like birds with a blue-gray head, brownish body, and white colorings that are visible while flying (on wings nearest the body and on tail except for dark brown bar that goes down the middle and dark brown spots across the ends). Males and females look similar, with females being paler and less white on the wings. Adults are 6.7 to 6.9 inches (17.0 to 17.5 centimeters) long and weigh between 28 and 54 centimeters).

Geographic range: They are found only on mountains over 6,600 feet (2,000 meters) in Europe and Asia.

Habitat: They are found in areas of barren, rocky ground and mountains at elevations from 6,600 to 11,500 feet (2,000 to 3,500 meters). They are sometimes found near buildings that are located within these mountainous areas.

Diet: Their diet consists of grains during the winter, but will eat invertebrates during other seasons. Often, snow finches feed on seeds

Snow finches are found only on mountains over 6,600 feet (2,000 meters) in Europe and Asia. (Illustration by Amanda Humphrey. Reproduced by permission.)

blown onto high snowfields. They also eat on scraps tossed out from human settlements. Young are fed only animal food.

Behavior and reproduction: Snow finches are very social birds, often forming wandering groups and large flocks outside the breeding season. They spend most of their time on the ground hopping around with their wings folded. During the breeding season, they form loose colonies of up to six pairs. They build nests in rock crevices or holes in buildings. Nests are often built where trees are no longer found. They fill the crevice or hole with grasses and moss and line it with feathers. Females lay three to four eggs. The incubation period is thirteen to fourteen days, and the fledgling period is twenty to twenty-one days. Two clutches are possible each year. Both parents help to fed and take care of the young.

Snow finches and people: There is no known significant relationship between people and snow finches.

Conservation status: Snow finches are considered common. ∎

FOR MORE INFORMATION

Books:

del Hoyo, Josep, Andrew Elliott, Jordi Sargatal, Jose Cabot, et al., eds. *Handbook of the Birds of the World.* Barcelona: Lynx Edicions, 1992.

Dickinson, Edward C., ed. *The Howard and Moore Complete Checklist of the Birds of the World,* 3rd ed. Princeton, NJ and Oxford, U.K.: Princeton University Press, 2003.

Forshaw, Joseph, ed. *Encyclopedia of Birds,* 2nd ed. San Diego, CA: Academic Press, 1998.

Harrison, Colin James Oliver. *Birds of the World.* London and New York: Dorling Kindersley, 1993.

Perrins, Christopher M., and Alex L. A. Middleton, eds. *The Encyclopedia of Birds.* New York: Facts on File, 1985.

Web sites:

"House Sparrow. *Passer domesticus.*" U.S. Geological Survey, Department of the Interior. http://www.mbr-pwrc.usgs.gov/id/framlst/i6882id.html (accessed on July 20, 2004).

STARLINGS AND MYNAS
Sturnidae

Class: Aves
Order: Passeriformes
Family: Sturnidae
Number of species: 104 to 118
species

family

phylum
class
subclass
order
monotypic order
suborder
▲ **family**

PHYSICAL CHARACTERISTICS

Starlings and mynas (MYE-nahz), also called sturnids, are stocky, small- to medium-sized birds with strong, straight bills (either thin and pointed or somewhat blunt, depending on the species), short wings that are rounded (in forest and resident species) and somewhat longer (in open country and migrant species), a short squared-off tail, and strong legs. Many species have plumage (feathers) that is black or dark, while others are white or other colors, and still others are iridescent (brilliant colors). Many species have colorful bare facial skin or wattles (skin that hangs from throat). They often have long, narrow feathers on the neck, with those of the males being most noticeable.

Mynas have a dark brown body, black head and tail, bright yellow bill and legs, and often display white wing patches on the primary feathers. Starlings are mainly glossy green and purple with large buffy-white spots at the tips of feathers. Bills are dark brown in winter, but turn yellow in spring. Starlings molt (lose, then re-grow, feathers) once a year, following breeding, but seasonal differences are found in some species. Adult starlings and mynas are 7 to 17 inches (18 to 43 centimeters) long and weigh between 1.0 and 3.8 ounces (30 and 105 grams).

GEOGRAPHIC RANGE

Starlings and mynas range through Africa (except for northern regions), Eurasia (except for northern areas), the South Pacific, and southeastern Australia. The birds have been introduced onto all continents except for South America and Antarctica, and on many oceanic islands.

HABITAT

These birds are located in barren semi-deserts, temperate (mild) grasslands, tropical savannas (flat grasslands), tropical rain-forests, dry to moist evergreen and deciduous forest, and agricultural and urban areas.

DIET

They eat mostly insects, but also fruits, berries, grains, dead fish, garbage, and nectar. The birds often eat different foods depending on the time of year and availability of certain foods. They probe for food by opening its bill into materials, pushing loose particles apart, and creating an open area in which to look for food.

BEHAVIOR AND REPRODUCTION

Most starlings and mynas are fairly social birds. Some live in trees, but most spend much time on the ground. They often nest in loose colonies (birds that live together and are dependent on each other). Some species are aggressive, while others are shy and quiet, generally staying by themselves or in small groups. Their songs and calls are loud, varied, sometimes unpleasant and mechanical sounding, and rarely with any melody. Many species can imitate other birds. Starlings and mynas fly swiftly and can easily maneuver, even twisting and turning together in flocks. Species that nest in temperate climates often migrate to warmer climates during winters.

Most sturnids use the nests of other birds, often barbets and woodpeckers, many times taking away a bird's nest with its aggressive behavior. Other sturnids use crevices and holes in rocks, nest boxes, or recesses in building and other structures. They construct a large nest of grasses, leaves, fine twigs, and other available materials. Both sexes work together to make the nest, and nests are often reused.

Starling eggs are often pale blue, but also white to cream-colored or have dark spots on them. In some cases, only females incubate (sit on) eggs, while in other cases both parents incubate. The incubation period (time to sit on eggs before hatching) is

SHAKESPEARE'S STARLINGS

All of the 200 million or so European starlings that are found today in North America came from approximately 100 birds that were released in New York City's Central Park in the early 1890s. An American society dedicated to introducing all birds mentioned in Shakespeare's works set these birds free. The migrating birds reached northern Florida by the winter of 1918, and breeding birds were found by the 1920s in Ontario and Maine. By the 1940s, European starlings reached the west coast and, in the 1970s, the birds were seen in Alaska.

usually less than fourteen days. Hatchlings (newly born birds) are pink with some patches of down on top of head and back. They are blind for the first few days of life. Both parents feed young and, in some cases, helpers (from earlier offspring) assist in the feeding and care. The fledgling period (time for young to grow feathers necessary to fly) is usually no longer than twenty-one days. Many species produce one to three broods (young birds that are born and raised together) each year.

STARLINGS, MYNAS, AND PEOPLE

Many species are considered agricultural pests. Some occur in such great numbers in urban areas that their acidic droppings damage buildings and monuments and cause health risks. Many species are considered beneficial because they help control insect pests. Others help to scatter seeds around. Starlings and mynas are often captured for food.

CONSERVATION STATUS

Five species of starlings and mynas are listed as Extinct (died out within historic times); two species as Critically Endangered, facing an extremely high risk of extinction; two species as Endangered, facing a very high risk of extinction; five species as Vulnerable, facing a high risk of extinction; and eight species as Near Threatened, in danger of becoming threatened with extinction.

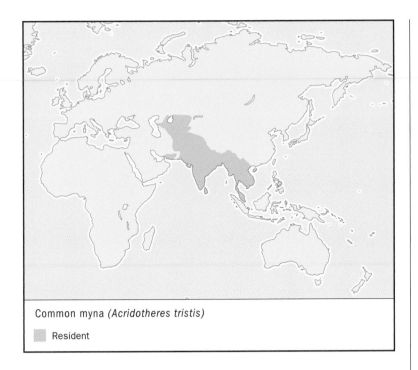

Common myna (*Acridotheres tristis*)

Resident

COMMON MYNA
Acridotheres tristis

Physical characteristics: Common mynas are stocky, brown birds with a glossy black head and throat; yellow bill; bare yellow skin behind the eyes; and yellow legs. Females and males are familiar in appearance, while juveniles are duller in colors. Adults are 9.1 to 9.8 inches (23 to 25 centimeters) long and weigh between 2.9 and 5.0 ounces (82 and 143 grams).

Geographic range: They are found in lowlands and to elevations of 4,500 feet (1,370 meters) in southern Asia from southeastern Iran though Afghanistan, Pakistan, India, Sri Lanka, southern China, and Vietnam. They have been introduced in Arabia (the peninsula in far southwestern Asia), South Africa, Madagascar, Australia, New Zealand, Fiji, Cook Islands, Society Islands, Hivaoa in the Marquesas Islands, and Hawaii.

Habitat: Common mynas inhabit open habitats such as farmlands and cities.

Common mynas are usually seen in pairs or small flocks.
(© A. Morris/VIREO. Reproduced by permission.)

Diet: Their diet consists of insects, small vertebrates (animals with backbone), carrion (decaying animals), fruits, grains, and occasionally on eggs and the nestlings (young bird unable to leave nest) of other birds. They feed mostly on the ground.

Behavior and reproduction: Common mynas are tame, bold, and noisy birds; usually seen in pairs or small flocks. They build bulky nests in tree cavities, pockets in buildings, and in heavy vegetation. Females lay four to five glossy, pale blue eggs. The incubation period is thirteen to eighteen days. Both parents incubate the eggs. The nestlings may leave the nest at around twenty-two days or longer, but may still not be able to fly for another seven days or so.

Common mynas and people: Common mynas are considered a pest in Australia where thousands of noisy birds roost near populated areas. They are also considered a pest when they eat grain or fruit from agricultural lands.

Conservation status: Common mynas are not threatened. ■

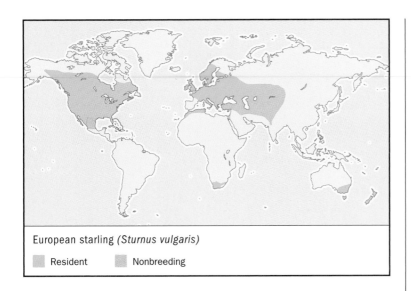

European starling (*Sturnus vulgaris*)

▨ Resident   ▨ Nonbreeding

EUROPEAN STARLING
Sturnus vulgaris

Physical characteristics: European starlings are a purple-green iridescent, short-tailed black bird with a long thin bill that changes seasonally from black in winter to yellow during the nesting period, and buffy-to-white tips and edging on feathers. Following the fall molt, the birds are very spotted with white as a result of white-tipped body feathers. As winter continues, the white tips wear off and the birds show mostly the iridescent black with little spotting. Males have longer, narrower neck feathers and, during nesting season, a blue base to the bill. Females have a pink base to the bill. Juveniles are gray-brown with a streaked breast and dark bill. Adults are about 8.5 inches (21.6 centimeters) long, with a wingspan of about 15.5 inches (39.4 centimeters).

Geographic range: The birds range throughout most of temperate Eurasia from Iceland east. They have been introduced in South Africa, Polynesia, (Fiji and Tonga), Australia, New Zealand, Bermuda, North America (across both coasts, Pacific and Atlantic, and southern Alaska into Mexico), Puerto Rico, and Jamaica.

Habitat: European starlings are found in open country, open woods, and urban and suburban areas.

European starling females incubate their eggs alone, but both males and females help feed the young once they've hatched. (B. and C. Calhoun/ Bruce Coleman Inc. Reproduced by permission.)

Diet:　The birds eat many types of insects, other arthropods, grains, and fruits. They usually feed off the ground, and often in large flocks.

Behavior and reproduction:　European starlings are aggressive birds that often fight with woodpeckers who have built nests or who are already using nests. They roost in flocks that may number in the millions. Their songs include melodies, clear whistles, clatters, and twitters, and they sometimes imitate other bird species, and even human voices. They build nests either alone or in loose colonies, mostly from

March to May in the Northern Hemisphere, and September to December in South Africa. Females lay three to six pale blue eggs, and incubate them alone. The incubation period is eleven to fifteen days. Both parents feed the young. The fledgling period is eighteen to twenty-one days, and two to three broods are produced each year.

European starlings and people: European starlings eat many insect pests and weed seeds so are seen as beneficial in that respect. They are considered a pest in North America because of huge numbers within flocks, building messy nests on buildings, taking grains and fruits from agricultural lands, and competing with songbirds and woodpeckers for nest sites.

Conservation status: European starlings are not threatened. ■

Red-billed oxpecker (*Buphagus erythrorhynchus*)

▮ Resident

RED-BILLED OXPECKER
Buphagus erythrorhynchus

Physical characteristics: Red-billed oxpeckers have olive-brown or gray-brown upperparts, a red short, thick bill, red eyes with very noticeable yellow circles of flesh around the eyes; light gray-brown wings and tail; tan or pale yellow rump and breast, and gray legs and feet. Juveniles have a dark bill and eyes, and brown area around the eyes. Adults are 7.5 to 8.7 inches (19 to 22 centimeters) long and weigh between 1.5 and 2.1 ounces (42 and 59 grams).

Geographic range: They range widely in east and southeast Africa with a scattered distribution from western Central African Republic, Sudan, Ethiopia, and Somalia, south in Uganda, Kenya, Tanzania,

Red-billed oxpeckers feed on ticks, fleas, and other biting flies taken from animals such as rhinoceros, elephants, giraffes, and cape buffaloes. (Kim Taylor/ Bruce Coleman Inc. Reproduced by permission.)

eastern and southern Democratic Republic of the Congo to northern and eastern South Africa.

Habitat: Red-billed oxpeckers live in open savannas, bushlands, and forests (up to elevations of 9,000 feet (2,745 meters) that contain large mammals including domestic livestock.

Diet: The birds feed on parasites (organism living on another) such as ticks, fleas, and other biting flies taken from host mammals and on host blood and dead tissues and skin. They can eat hundreds of these parasites each day.

Behavior and reproduction: Red-billed oxpeckers remain in the same area and do not migrate. They live alongside large mammals and are often found perching (sitting) on the heads and necks of rhinoceros, elephants, giraffes, and cape buffaloes. Courtship often takes place on the backs of these host mammals. Breeding occurs at different times in different areas, often at the beginning of the rainy season but has been reported in all months. They build nests in natural tree cavities made of grasses lined with hair and dung. Females lay one to five creamy white eggs with brown to lilac speckles. The incubation period is twelve to thirteen days, and is done by both parents. Both parents and helpers feed the young. The fledgling period is about thirty days, but remain dependent on the parents for another thirty days.

Red-billed oxpeckers and people: People often consider red-billed oxpeckers as pests, especially around livestock. Extermination programs have been carried out in various agricultural areas to kill off the birds.

Conservation status: Red-billed oxpeckers are listed as Not Threatened. Their numbers have declined in areas that use pesticides to control the birds around livestock. ■

FOR MORE INFORMATION

Books:

Alsop, Fred J. III. *Birds of North America.* New York: Dorling Kindersley, 2001.

Baughman, Mel M., ed. *Reference Atlas to the Birds of North America.* Washington, DC: National Geographic, 2003.

del Hoyo, Josep, Andrew Elliott, Jordi Sargatal, Jose Cabot, et al., eds. *Handbook of the Birds of the World.* Barcelona: Lynx Edicions, 1992.

Dickinson, Edward C., ed. *The Howard and Moore Complete Checklist of the Birds of the World,* 3rd ed. Princeton, NJ and Oxford, U.K.: Princeton University Press, 2003.

Field Guide to the Birds of North America, 4th ed. Washington, DC: National Geographic Society, 2002.

Forshaw, Joseph, ed. *Encyclopedia of Birds,* 2nd ed. San Diego, CA: Academic Press, 1998.

Harrison, Colin James Oliver. *Birds of the World.* London and New York: Dorling Kindersley, 1993.

Kaufman, Kenn, with collaboration of Rick and Nora Bowers and Lynn Hassler Kaufman. *Birds of North America.* New York: Houghton Mifflin, 2000.

Sibley, David. *The Sibley Guide to Birds.* New York: Alfred A. Knopf, 2000.

Terres, John K. *The Audubon Society Encyclopedia of North American Birds.* New York: Knopf, 1980.

OLD WORLD ORIOLES
AND FIGBIRDS

Oriolidae

Class: Aves

Order: Passeriformes

Family: Oriolidae

Number of species: 29 to 30
species

phylum

class

subclass

order

monotypic order

suborder

▲ **family**

PHYSICAL CHARACTERISTICS

Orioles and figbirds are thrush-like birds in size and shape. Adults have patterns of brilliant yellows and blacks, while juveniles (and some adults) are streaked near the abdomen. They have long rounded wings and square-tipped, twelve-feathered tail. The tenth primary feather is well developed, while the number of secondary feathers is usually eleven in orioles and ten in figbirds. Bills are straight, stout, and notched at the tip of the upper mandible (top part of a bird's bill). On the sides of the bill are bristles and narrow nostrils that are partly protected by a membrane. Their feet are stout, but shorter than the longest toe. Adults are 7.0 to 11.5 inches (20 to 28 centimeters) long and weigh between 2 and 5 ounces (50 and 135 grams).

Orioles have brightly colored yellow and black plumage (feathers), a brick red bill, and slate gray feet. Male orioles are more brightly plumaged that females and have a bare patch of red skin around the eyes. Juveniles have brown-olive backs with dull bill, eyes, and feet, and a white abdomen with dusky streaks.

Figbirds (and some orioles) have black or slate-colored bill, sometimes pale eyes, and flesh-colored or black feet. Males have a black crown (top of head) and bill, an olive back, and yellow, white, olive, or gray breasts, while females and juveniles are plumaged like juvenile orioles.

GEOGRAPHIC RANGE

Orioles and figbirds are located throughout the far northwest Africa and the sub-Saharan, temperate Eurasia (except its central deserts), south and east to India, Southeast Asia, and Indonesian archipelagos as far as New Guinea, and north and east Australia.

HABITAT

Orioles and figbirds are found in medium to tall woodlands and forests, including rainforests. They prefer to live in the upper dense foliage and crowns of broadleaf trees within forests and woodlands, generally in temperate (mild) regions but also in rainforests in the topics.

DIET

These birds eat fruits and insects.

BEHAVIOR AND REPRODUCTION

Figbirds usually live in communities of twenty to forty birds during the nonbreeding season and in larger colonies during the breeding season, while orioles are usually solitary birds. Figbirds like to perch on high bare branches. They give one- or two-note whistled songs all year round in order to maintain contact with other figbirds. Orioles sing a short rolling warble that is repeated many times during breeding and is heard for nearly 0.5 mile (0.8 kilometers) in order to show they are defending a territory. The grouping and pitch of notes vary among species, but the basic sound is the same. Both orioles and figbirds use short, harsh squawks when they are nervous or angry. They fly in direct and wavy flights, from tree to tree, but orioles are faster and swoop up just before perching. Orioles and figbirds are quiet and motionless while in tree crowns, often sun-bathing or rain-bathing there. About two to ten breeding pairs are found per 0.6 square miles (1 square kilometer), with the exact number determined by their surroundings.

Breeding occurs from time-to-time all year-round in the tropics, but is from spring to early summer in temperate regions. Orioles and figbirds are basically monogamous (muh-NAH-guh-mus; having one mate). Oriole males find and hold a small territory while females build the nest (sometimes more than one) and incubate (sit on) the eggs with some help from her mate. Orioles build thick, deep basket-shaped nests of dry plant fiber tied together with animal wool, moss, and lichen. The nest is hung from a horizontal fork in the outer branches of trees usually high off the ground. Strips are moistened with their saliva to hold the nest together. Figbirds build a rough cup of twigs and tendrils in small outer branches. Figbird and oriole females lay two to four eggs (usually three in figbirds) that are pale gray olive in figbirds and pinkish white to pale cream buff in orioles. Both eggs can be spotted and speckled with black to reddish browns. The incubation period (time to sit on and warm the eggs before they hatch) is sixteen to eighteen days. Young have yellow down and are fed by regurgitated food (food brought up from stomach) from their parents. Sometimes male helpers also help out. Usually only one brood (young birds born and raised together) occurs each year.

ORIOLES, FIGBIRDS, AND PEOPLE

There is very little significance between orioles and figbirds and people.

CONSERVATION STATUS

One species of orioles and figbirds are listed as Endangered, facing a very high risk of extinction; two species as Vulnerable, facing a high risk of extinction; and three species as Near Threatened, in danger of becoming threatened with extinction.

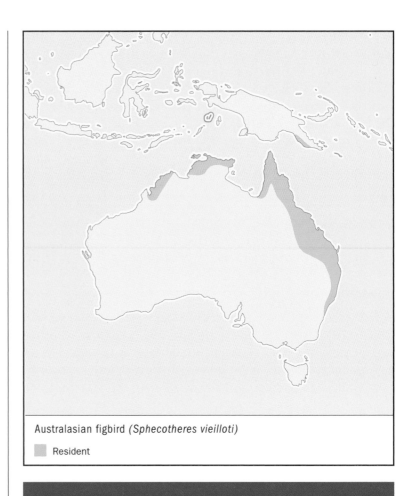

Australasian figbird *(Sphecotheres vieilloti)*

■ Resident

AUSTRALASIAN FIGBIRD
Sphecotheres vieilloti

Physical characteristics: Australasian figbirds are stout, fairly short-tailed figbirds with olive-green upperparts, a gray throat, buff-red bare eye skin, and a black head. They also have black primary feathers and tails. Adults are 10.0 to 11.5 inches (25 to 29 centimeters) long and weigh between 4.0 and 4.5 ounces (110 and 130 grams).

Geographic range: They are located on the coastal northern and eastern Australia (Kimberley Division to Illawarra district), southeast New Guinea, and Kai Islands (in the Banda Sea).

Habitat: Australasian figbirds are found at the edges of rainforests, gallery vine forests, mangroves, and gardens.

Diet: Australasian figbirds feed on small, soft fruit such as figs, native cherries, and ink weed and tobacco bushes. They also eat guavas, bananas, and mulberries. They usually feed in tree crowns.

Behavior and reproduction: Australasian figbirds live in communities of loose, noisy, locally nomadic (wandering) flocks of up to thirty to fifty birds in the tree canopy. They often perch high on bare branches and power lines. Their calls are loud, single- or double-note whistles. They are monogamous birds, usually breeding in small groups that defend a small territory during a breeding season from spring to summer (October to February). Nests are shallow, fragile, and saucer-like, and are built of plant fiber and tendrils. Females usually lay three eggs. Both parents share all nesting activities, while other birds may help out.

Australasian figbirds and people: There is no known significant relationship between people and Australasian figbirds.

Conservation status: Australasian figbirds have been able to adapt quickly to habitats that have been altered by people. They are common and under no threat of diminished populations. ■

Australasian figbirds are seasonally nomadic birds, they move around as fruit ripens on trees in different areas.
(© Wayne Lawler/Photo Researchers, Inc. Reproduced by permission.)

Eurasian golden oriole (*Oriolus oriolus*)

▮ Breeding   ▮ Nonbreeding

EURASIAN GOLDEN ORIOLE
Oriolus oriolus

Physical characteristics: Eurasian golden orioles are covered with a golden color except for black wings, tails, and a stripe through the eyes. Females are duller than males with a greenish back.

Geographic range: They range in Europe and far northwest Africa east to Asia Minor, the Caspian Sea, western Siberia, and, in winter, sub-Saharan Africa; Central Asia, from western Siberia south in winter to Afghanistan and Himalayas, peninsular India, and north Sri Lanka.

Habitat: Eurasian golden orioles prefer woodlands and open forests of mostly broadleaf and deciduous mature trees.

Diet: Their diet consists of a variety of insects including hairy caterpillars and a range of small fruits, some seeds, buds, small reptiles, nestling birds, and eggs. They feed from foliage at the tree crowns but also hover near the ground in search of food and perch on branches and fly to food when found.

Male and female golden orioles feed their chicks. They are sometimes assisted by "helper" birds, young birds without their own nest of chicks. (© H.D. Brandl/OKAPIA/Photo Researchers, Inc. Reproduced by permission.)

Behavior and reproduction: Eurasian golden orioles are solitary birds. They stay in the upper areas of trees. Songs that are sung all year round, but more often by males than females, is a loud, warbled whistle of three or four syllables that is repeated and sung in different ways. When anxious, they give out a grating, drawn-out squalling.

The birds are monogamous. Females produce one brood each year. Males defend territories. The nest is built in the shape of a shallow cup, using plant fiber and stems. It is hung over a thin horizontal fork in high foliage. Females build it, with some early help by her mate, usually in six to twelve days. Females lay three to four creamy or pink-white eggs that are scattered with dark brown and blackish spots. The incubation period is fifteen to eighteen days, and is performed by the female with assistance from the male. Both parents feed the young and sometimes helpers feed them, too. The fledgling period is sixteen to twenty days.

Eurasian golden orioles and people: People in northern Europe like to predict the coming of spring with the arrival of Eurasian golden orioles. They also like the golden plumage and fluted song of the birds.

Conservation status: Eurasian golden orioles do not appear to be threatened in any way. Species in central and eastern Europe seem to be declining, but populations in western Europe seem to be increasing. ■

FOR MORE INFORMATION

Books:

del Hoyo, Josep, Andrew Elliott, Jordi Sargatal, Jose Cabot, et al., eds. *Handbook of the Birds of the World.* Barcelona: Lynx Edicions, 1992.

Dickinson, Edward C., ed. *The Howard and Moore Complete Checklist of the Birds of the World,* 3rd ed. Princeton, NJ and Oxford, U.K.: Princeton University Press, 2003.

Forshaw, Joseph, ed. *Encyclopedia of Birds,* 2nd ed. San Diego, CA: Academic Press, 1998.

Harrison, Colin James Oliver. *Birds of the World.* London and New York: Dorling Kindersley, 1993.

Perrins, Christopher M., and Alex L. A. Middleton, eds. *The Encyclopedia of Birds.* New York: Facts on File, 1985.

Web sites:

"Eurasian Golden Oriole." Haryana, India, haryana-online.com. http://www.haryanaonline.com/Fauna/Birds/eurasian_golden_oriole.htm (accessed on July 20, 2004).

DRONGOS

Dicruridae

Class: Aves

Order: Passeriformes

Family: Dicruridae

Number of species: 27 species

family

CHAPTER

PHYSICAL CHARACTERISTICS

Drongos are small to medium sized, crow-like birds, usually very dark gray to black all over, a few species being light gray. Black plumage (feathers) shimmers with iridescent green, deep blue, or purple, or the plumage may show spangles, or colored, iridescent spots. The eyes are vivid red or orange, usually a giveaway that the bird is a drongo and not some unrelated black bird. The tail is typically long, often forked, with a complex, ornate shape. The head in most species bears some sort of crest. Body length in drongos ranges from 7 to 15 inches (18 to 38 centimeters) among species.

The beak resembles that of jays, being robust, hooked, notched behind the hooked end, and black in most species. There are long bristles, or retrices (REH-truh-suhz), around the base of the beak. The wings are long and rounded or pointed. The legs, black in most species, are short, with strong feet and toes. Males are slightly larger than females, but both sexes are identical, or show slight variation, in coloration.

GEOGRAPHIC RANGE

Tropical Africa, Madagascar, Asia, Australia, New Guinea, Java, Taiwan, Solomon Islands.

HABITAT

Tropical rain forest, mixed open forest and grassland.

DIET

Drongos eat mainly insects, but sometimes spiders, small birds, and nectar.

BEHAVIOR AND REPRODUCTION

Drongos are notorious for aggressive behavior. They will fiercely defend their nests, and attack or harass predators like birds of prey, hornbills, crows, snakes, and humans. Drongos are accomplished, acrobatic flyers. In one recorded instance, a drongo individual escaped the clutches of a little sparrowhawk, which was chasing it in mid-air, by aerial acrobatics, out-maneuvering the predator.

Drongos forage, search for food, alone, in pairs, or in groups. The birds catch insects in mid-flight, often following larger animals such as deer, cattle, or monkeys in order to catch insects flushed out by the larger animals' motions. They may even follow grass fires, snagging insects escaping the flames. Drongos also glean (pluck) insects from foliage and probe under bark for insects and related creatures. They may also forage in mixed-species flocks of one or more other bird species. Some drongo species just share in the abundance of insects driven out of hiding by the mixed-species flocks. Other species, especially during lean times, join mixed-species flocks but engage in kleptoparasitism, stealing food from other birds. They rob either directly, or, as in the forktailed drongos, by distracting another bird with alarm calls as it sees and closes in on an insect, then zooming in and snagging the insect.

When feeding on insects in mid-flight, drongos use long, wire-like bristles at the base of the beak, to guide insects into the beak. The bristles are modified feathers.

Drongos have an incredibly varied repertoire of voice sounds, even within a species, and often imitate the calls of other bird species. Some species imitate calls of birds of prey, if disturbed at nesting sites, to scare off intruders. One call of the spangled drongo sounds metallic, resembling the plucking of a taut wire.

Drongos form monogamous (muh-NAH-guh-mus) mating pairs. Male and female contribute in building the nest, incubating the eggs (keeping them warm for hatching), and caring for the young. Nests are cup-shaped, and built with a hammock-style support, hanging from horizontal tree branches or forks. Monogamous pairs fiercely defend their territory, nest, and young. Other than those few facts, very little is known about other details of breeding behavior among drongos.

DRONGOS AND PEOPLE

There is little interaction between drongos and humans.

CONSERVATION STATUS

The World Conservation Union (IUCN) lists two drongo species as Endangered, facing a very high risk of extinction, and four as Near Threatened, in danger of becoming threatened with extinction. Five of the six listed species live on small islands—Aldabra, Andamans, Comoros, Principe, and Mayotte—the sixth on a much larger island, Sumatra. The small islands have lost most of their original habitat, while Sumatra has lost half of its original habitat.

Square-tailed drongo *(Dicrurus ludwigii)*

▨ Resident

SPECIES ACCOUNTS

SQUARE-TAILED DRONGO
Dicrurus ludwigii

Physical characteristics: The body length is 7.5 inches (19 centimeters). No weights are recorded. The plumage of males is mostly black with a deep blue sheen, the tail has a small notch, the underwing bears white-tipped feathers. The bill is black, the eyes an intense red, black legs and feet. The female is colored similarly but the overall coloring is duller.

Geographic range: Square-tailed drongos live in Africa south of the Sahara.

Habitat: These birds are found in lowland and mountain tropical rainforest.

Diet: Square-tailed drongos eat mainly insects, also nectar.

Behavior and reproduction: Individuals forage alone, in pairs, and in association with other bird species that forage in flocks. It is often kleptoparasitic on other foraging birds. When foraging alone, a square-tailed drongo sits on a branch, waiting for an insect to fly within striking distance. When it does, the bird flies off the branch and snags the insect in mid-flight.

Square-tailed drongos have loud voices with many variations of sounds produced, generally a jumbled string of tweets, whistlings, and twangings. Like most drongo species, the square-tailed drongo can imitate the voices of other bird species.

Square-tailed drongos form monagamous breeding pairs, and both parents incubate the eggs and care for the young. The female lays two or three eggs. The nest is a small cuplike structure made of leaves, small twigs, plant fibers, spider webs and lichens. The nest is hung like a hammock from a tree branch.

Square-tailed drongos and people: There is little interaction between square-tailed drongos and people.

Conservation status: These birds are not threatened. ◼

When foraging alone, a square-tailed drongo sits on a branch, waiting for an insect to fly within striking distance. When it does, the bird flies off the branch and snags the insect in mid-flight. (Illustration by Brian Cressman. Reproduced by permission.)

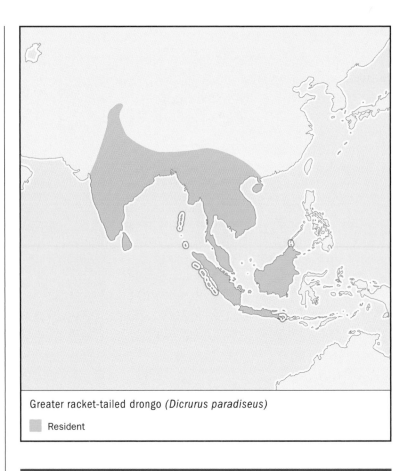

Greater racket-tailed drongo (*Dicrurus paradiseus*)

▨ Resident

GREATER RACKET-TAILED DRONGO
Dicrurus paradiseus

Physical characteristics: The body length is 13 inches (33 centimeters). The plumage is black all over with iridescent shades of blue on the upper wings. The head bears a crest of feathers that begins at the upper base of the beak. The eyes are bright red. The bill is gray. The tail is as long as the body, forked into two narrow, almost wirelike feathers, each of which flares into a rounded shape at the tip, thus the "racket-tail."

Geographic range: Greater racket-tailed drongos live in all of India, Sri Lanka, Andaman and Nicobar Islands, into Southeast Asia, including southwestern China, Hainan Island, Sumatra, Java, and Borneo.

Habitat: These drongos are found in tropical rainforest.

Diet: These birds eat insects, including moths, termites and dragonflies. Also lizards, small birds and nectar.

Behavior and reproduction: There is limited information. The species forms monogamous pairs, female and male sharing in incubating the clutch of up to three eggs, and feeding the young. The parents savagely defend the nest and young. The nest is cup-shaped and built in at the fork of a tree branch.

Greater racket-tailed drongos and people: There is no significant interaction between greater racket-tailed drongos and people.

Conservation status: These birds are not threatened. ■

FOR MORE INFORMATION

The greater racket-tailed drongo gets its name from its long tail, which is forked into two narrow, almost wirelike feathers, each of which flares into a rounded shape at the tip—the "racket-tail." (© R. & N. Bowers/VIREO. Reproduced by permission.)

Books:

Goodman, Steven M., and Jonathan P. Benstead. *The Natural History of Madagascar.* Chicago: University of Chicago Press, 2003.

Kavanagh, James. *African Birds.* Chandler, AZ: Waterford Press, 2001.

Morris, P., and F. Hawkins. *Birds of Madagascar: A Photographic Guide.* New Haven, CT: Yale University Press, 1998.

Pizzey, G., and F. Knight. *Field Guide to the Birds of Australia.* Sydney, Australia: Angus and Robertson, 1997.

Strange, Morten. *Birds of Southeast Asia: A Photographic Guide to the Birds of Thailand, Malaysia, Singapore, the Philippines and Indonesia.* London: New Holland, 1998.

Strange, Morten. *A Photographic Guide to Birds of Malaysia and Singapore: Including Southeast Asia, the Philippines and Borneo.* Singapore: Periplus, 2000.

Periodicals:

Duckworth, J. W. "Mobbing of a Drongo Cuckoo *Surniculus lugubris.*" *Ibis* 139, no. 1 (1997): 190–192.

Herremans, M., and T. D. Herremans. "Social Foraging of the Forktailed

Drongo *Dicrurus adsimilis*: Beater Effect of Kleptoparasitism?" *Bird Behavior* 12, nos. 1–2 (1997): 41–45.

Khacher, L. "Mimicry by Grey Drongo *Dicrurus leucophaeus*." *Journal of the Bombay Natural History Society* 94, no. 3 (1997): 569.

Manson, A. J. "Unusual Behaviour of Square-tailed Drongo." *Honeyguide* 114/115, no. 54 (1983).

Nair, M. V. "An Instance of Play Behaviour in Black Drongo *Dicrurus adsimilis* (Bechstein)." *Journal of the Bombay Natural History Society* 92, no. 2 (1995): 266.

Vernon, C. J. "Vocal Imitation by Southern African Birds." *Ostrich* 44, no. 1 (1973): 23–30

Web sites:

"MAGPIE-LARKS Grallinidae." CREAGRUS@Monterey Bay. http://www.montereybay.com/creagrus/magpie-larks.html (accessed on July 20, 2004).

NEW ZEALAND WATTLEBIRDS

Callaeidae

Class: Aves

Order: Passeriformes

Family: Callaeidae

Number of species: 2 species

phylum

class

subclass

order

monotypic order

suborder

▲ **family**

PHYSICAL CHARACTERISTICS

The New Zealand wattlebirds' common name is based on their "wattles," little, drooping flaps of brightly colored skin that decorate their faces just behind the beaks, in pairs, on either side of the throat. Plumage (feathers) in adult wattlebirds is medium blue-gray in the kokako and near-black with red-brown areas in the saddleback. Both sexes within a species have similar colorings, and all species have brightly colored wattles. The wings are short and rounded, and all species are poor flyers, able only to glide downward from a perch, although all can run, hop and jump along the ground or tree branches and all are good tree climbers. Adult length in both sexes, from beak tip to tail tip, runs 10 to 19 inches (25 to 48 centimeters). Weight is 2.5 to 10 ounces (70 to 380 grams).

GEOGRAPHIC RANGE

Wattlebirds live on both main islands (North and South Islands) of New Zealand and many offshore islands. Wattlebirds are New Zealand endemics, meaning that they are found only there and nowhere else in the world.

HABITAT

Wattlebirds inhabit native temperate forests of New Zealand, which are made up of a mix of hardwoods and podocarps (Southern Hemisphere conifers).

DIET

Wattlebirds eat mostly insects, including insect larvae (LAR-vee), wetas (giant New Zealand crickets), fruits of native trees,

WETAS: BIG, FAT CRICKETS

Among the more exotic food items that New Zealand wattlebirds prey upon is a sort of creature as unique to New Zealand as the wattlebirds. They are wetas, giant crickets that can grow larger than mice. Most weta species are omnivorous, just as are most mice species, eating mostly plant material with some insect prey, but a few species have become more or less completely carnivorous. They are no sort of threat to human beings.

fern fronds, and leaves. On Cuvier Island, a small bird, the fantail, has taken to following foraging saddlebacks, snagging various flying insects escaping from the disturbances made by the saddlebacks. Since the saddlebacks eat noisily while producing a small rain of shredded bark and leaves, and occasionally call out during feeding, they are easy to find.

BEHAVIOR AND REPRODUCTION

Wattlebirds spend their days foraging mainly for insect food in forest trees and in the leaf litter on forest floors. They are poor fliers but quick, efficient ground runners and tree climbers. Since they had little to fear in the way of ground predators before the arrival of humankind, flight became less of a necessity for the wattlebirds' ancestors in New Zealand, so that they were freed from having to consume the enormous amounts of energy needed for flying.

Saddlebacks breed from October into January. The female builds a nest of twigs and grasses in a rock crevice or a hollow in a tree, then lays two light gray or whitish eggs, which the female incubates for twenty days. The male feeds the female while she is nesting, and both parents feed the chicks. The chicks fledge at twenty-one days of age. Kokako pairs breed from November through February and raise up to three clutches of chicks over the course of one year.

Wattlebirds sing to attract mates and establish and keep territory. Their singing has been described as similar to organ music, haunting, melodious, and complex.

NEW ZEALAND WATTLEBIRDS AND PEOPLE

One species, the huia, went extinct, died out, in the early twentieth century. Maori chiefs and nobles wore huia feathers as symbols of office and kept them in specially carved boxes. These same feathers eventually became fashionable as hat decorations in Europe. Traders offered bounties to native people to hunt, kill, and bring back huia feathers for export. The last sighting of huias is generally listed as having been in 1907, but

William Cobeldick, a forest ranger, claimed to have spotted a huia pair in Urewera National Park in 1924.

CONSERVATION STATUS

The huia and the South Island subspecies of kokako are extinct. The North Island subspecies of the kokako and the saddleback looked likely to follow until work on the part of the government of New Zealand brought about an increase in their populations since the 1960s. According to the World Conservation Union (IUCN), the kokako is listed as Endangered, facing a very high risk of extinction, and the saddleback is Near Threatened, in danger of becoming threatened with extinction.

Once inhabiting large stretches of forest on the mainlands and some islands, saddlebacks are no longer found on the mainland. Of the South Island subspecies, only 650 individuals were still alive in the early 1960s, and confined to Big South Cape, Pukeweka, and Solomon Islands. The North Island subspecies lived only on Hen Island.

In 1964, the New Zealand Wildlife Service (NZWS) captured a number of North Island saddlebacks on Hen Island, then released them on nearby Whatapuke Island, where any introduced predators had been exterminated. The new colony proved successful. Rats had gained a foothold on Big South Cape Island, so, during the same year, the NZWS transferred thirty-six saddlebacks from Big South Cape Island to other, pest-free islands. That modest number has since increased its population to over 700. The North Island saddleback now inhabits nine large islands. The South Island saddleback lives on eleven smaller islands.

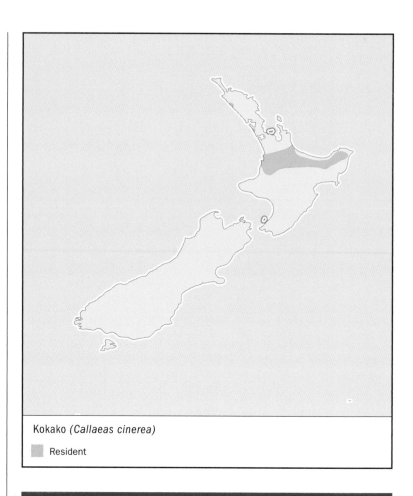

Kokako (*Callaeas cinerea*)

Resident

KOKAKO
Callaeas cinerea

Physical characteristics: Also commonly called the blue wattled crow, the cinerous wattled bird, and the organbird, the kokako still hangs on in the face of habitat loss and introduced predators. There are two subspecies, populations, the North Island kokako and the South Island kokako. The South Island kokako has not been seen since 1967 and is presumed to be extinct.

The adult head-and-body length of the kokako is 15 inches (38 centimeters) and the adult weight is around 8 ounces (230 grams). The body and head plumage is medium blue-gray, and a black bandit-mask marking surrounds the eyes. The beak and legs are black. The North Island subspecies has blue wattles, while the wattles of the South Is-

land subspecies were orange. The young have pink wattles that assume their proper hues by the time they fledge.

Geographic range: Kokakos live on North Island, New Zealand.

Habitat: These birds are found in native temperate forests of New Zealand, made up of a mix of hardwoods and podocarps (Southern Hemisphere conifers).

Diet: Food eaten in the wild includes fruits, insects and other invertebrates, animals without a backbone, buds, flowers, and nectar. Food choices and amounts consumed vary according to season. Fruit makes up about half the amount of food consumed during three-fourths of the year.

Behavior and reproduction: Kokakos forage during the day among forest trees from the highest reaches to about 9 feet (2.7 meters) from the ground.

Single kokakos and kokako male and female mated pairs begin their territorial songs at dawn, from treetops and tops of ridges. After fanning wings and tail, they warm up with some preliminary buzzing and meowing sounds, then explode into fantastically complex organ-like music. Soon, other kokakos answer, their music partly repeating that

The female kokako incubates the eggs and feeds the young, and the male brings her food while she is sitting on the nest. (Frank Lane Agency/G.M./Bruce Coleman Inc. Reproduced by permission.)

of the first singers but with some improvisations of their own. People privileged to hear this rare natural music have often described it in almost supernatural terms as an unforgettable experience.

Kokako pairs breed from November through February, although in years of unusual food abundance that period may begin in October and extend until May. Pairs have been known to raise up to three clutches of chicks in a year's time. The female does most of the nest building, in a tree, up to 100 feet (30 meters) above the ground. The male helps by occasionally bringing in building materials. The nest is well hidden and complex. The female begins with a twig framework, over which she builds a main mass of intertwined moss, lichen, ferns, and orchids, finally ending the construction by lining the bowl with tree fern scales. The female lays up to three pinkish gray eggs, which hatch after an incubation period of eighteen days. The chicks take thirty to forty-five days to fledge, grow their flying feathers, but may remain in the nest, still being fed by the parents, for up to a year. Only the female incubates eggs and cares for the young, although the male feeds the female while she is incubating and feeds the chicks.

Because of the long time spent in the nest by kokako mothers and chicks, they are particularly vulnerable to being killed by introduced mammalian predators. By 1990, at least two-thirds of the population of kokako females had been killed, leaving a surplus of males.

Kokako males sometimes form pairs with other males and a pair will go on and build nests. This behavior may have arisen recently, since throughout the last century, males far outnumbered females, many of which were killed while brooding, and the frustrated male mating urge found this new outlet.

Individual kokakos have been known to live up to twenty years.

Kokakos and people: In addition to being well known for their singing, kokakos are a symbol for conservation in New Zealand and even appear on some of their paper currency. Feathers of the kokako were used to adorn certain Maori garments. In Maori myth, a kokako aided the warrior Maui by transporting water to him in its wattles.

Conservation status: In 1990, the total population of kokakos on North Island was estimated at 1,160, of which only 396 were females, scattered about the island in isolated populations. Through an intensive program of breeding and habitat protection and regeneration, New Zealand's Department of Conservation has enabled the species to increase its numbers and recolonize abandoned habitat on North

Island. By 2003, the population had added about 500 individuals. Thriving colonies have also been established on several satellite islands. ■

FOR MORE INFORMATION

Books:

Birdlife International. *Threatened Birds of the World.* Barcelona and Cambridge, U.K.: Lynx Edicions, 2000.

Field, L. H., ed. *The Biology of Wetas, King Crickets, and Their Allies.* Wallingford, U.K.: CABI Publishing, 2001.

Heather, Barrie, and Hugh Robertson. *Field Guide to the Birds of New Zealand,* rev ed. New York: Oxford University Press, 2001.

Moon, Geoff. *Photographic Guide to the Birds of New Zealand.* London: New Holland Publishers, 2002.

Phillipps, W. J. *The Book of the Huia.* Christchurch, New Zealand: Whitcombe & Tombs, 1963.

Periodicals:

Hooson, S., and G. Jamieson. "Variation in Breeding Success Among Reintroduced Island Populations of South Island Saddlebacks, *Philesturnus carunculatus carunculatus.*" *Ibis* 146, no. 3 (July 2004): 417.

McLean, Ian G. "Feeding Association Between Fantails and Saddlebacks." *Journal of Ecology* 7 (1984): 165–168.

Web sites:

The Moa Pages. http://www.duke.edu/mrd6/moa (accessed on July 8, 2004).

Royal Forest and Bird Protection Society of New Zealand. http://www.forest-bird.org.nz (accessed on July 8, 2004).

MUDNEST BUILDERS
Grallinidae

Class: Aves
Order: Passeriformes
Family: Grallinidae
Number of species: 4 species

family

CHAPTER

phylum

class

subclass

order

monotypic order

suborder

▲ **family**

PHYSICAL CHARACTERISTICS

Members of the Grallinidae family are various colorations of black, white, gray, and brown. The average length of an adult is 8 to 18 inches (20 to 45 centimeters).

GEOGRAPHIC RANGE

Mudnest builders are found in Australia, New Guinea, Timor, and Lord Howe Island.

HABITAT

All but one species of Grallinidae dwell in open space with trees for nesting. The torrent-lark prefers wooded areas near rivers and streams, where it forages for food.

DIET

Mudnest builders eat insects and other invertebrates, animals without a backbone, such as snails and worms. The apostlebird also feeds on seeds.

BEHAVIOR AND REPRODUCTION

Members of the Grallinidae family are monogamous (muh-NAH-guh-mus), and the majority pair with a single mate for their lifespan. Both males and females feed their offspring, and in some species, other group members (usually juveniles) will also feed nestlings.

While paired Australian magpie-larks like to travel with their mates, both apostlebirds and white-winged choughs (CHUFFS) prefer to flock in small groups of up to twenty birds.

MUDNEST BUILDERS AND PEOPLE

Mudnest builders and humans coexist peacefully.

CONSERVATION STATUS

None of the Grallinidae species are currently endangered.

DEFENSIVE DUETS

Pairs of male and female Australian magpie-larks defend their nest and territory with a song and wing display known as an antiphonal (an-TIFF-uh-nul) duet. They perch out in the open together, and alternate their distinctive "pee-wee" call. While one calls and the other answers, they both raise their wings high in a display of power to show would-be intruders who's in charge.

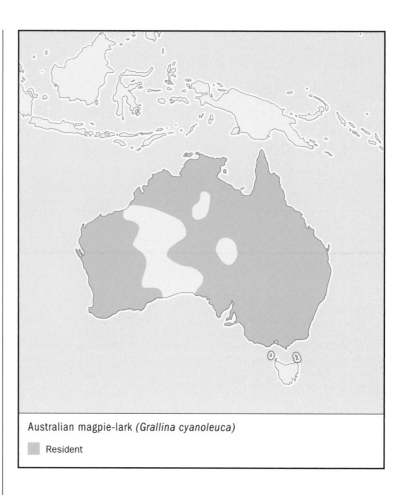

Australian magpie-lark (*Grallina cyanoleuca*)

Resident

SPECIES ACCOUNT

AUSTRALIAN MAGPIE-LARK
Grallina cyanoleuca

Physical characteristics: The Australian magpie-lark has a black and white body. The male has a black back, chest, and face, with a white stripe above the eye. The female's face is all white. Both have white markings on their predominantly black wings. The birds' legs are exceptionally long, and adults have white eyes and beaks. Juveniles of the species have plumage coloring similar to adults, but their eyes and bills are white. Adult magpie-larks are 10 to 12 inches (25 to 30 centimeters) in length and weigh an average of 3 to 4 ounces (80 to 115 grams).

Australian magpie-lark males and females take part in nest building, egg incubation, and in feeding their nestlings. (Jen and Des Bartlett/Bruce Coleman Inc. Reproduced by permission.)

Geographic range: The Australian magpie-lark is found throughout Australia (except in desert areas) and in southern New Guinea, Timor, and Lord Howe Island.

Habitat: Australian magpie-larks are highly adaptable birds, and make their home in a wide variety of habitats both near and far from people, including urban, agricultural, and residential areas. When they dwell in forests, it is usually near the edge or in a clearing where there is open space to forage. They choose nest-building locations where there is access to water and therefore mud.

Diet: Magpie-larks forage at ground level for insects, insect larvae, earthworms, and freshwater snails. They will also eat at backyard feeders.

Behavior and reproduction: Like other members of the family, the Australian magpie-lark builds a cup-shaped mud nest lined with soft grasses and feathers. Male and female magpie-larks are monogamous, and usually stay together throughout their lifespan, breeding each season as a pair. If a male leaves a female after mating for any reason, the female will abandon the nest.

Australian magpie-larks are biparental, meaning that both male and female take part in nest building, egg incubation, and in feeding their nestlings. The female lays a clutch of three to five oval-shaped white-to-pink eggs speckled with brown.

Studies of Australian magpie-lark breeding behavior have found that those pairs of birds who have bred together successfully in previous seasons will raise more fledglings in subsequent seasons than other newly-mated pairs. Researchers attribute this to the fact that established magpie-lark "couples" start breeding earlier in the season, allowing them to fledge multiple broods.

Magpie-larks aggressively defend their nest and surrounding territory, and have been known to attack other birds, animals, humans, and even images of themselves in mirrors or other reflective surfaces when they felt their nest was threatened. Human attacks are rare.

Incubation of eggs takes up to eighteen days, and the young birds fledge about three weeks after hatching. Young birds, and those adults who aren't paired with a mate, travel in large flocks that move northward in fall and winter and south in spring and summer.

Australian magpie-larks and people: The Australian magpie-lark, called the peewee by many Australians because of their "pee-o-wit" call, are not considered agricultural or residential pests. In agricultural areas their presence is often encouraged, as they feed on disease-carrying freshwater snails that can infect sheep and cattle.

Conservation status: Australian magpie-larks are plentiful and not considered threatened. ■

FOR MORE INFORMATION

Books:

Simpson, Ken, Nicolas Day, and Peter Trusler. *Birds of Australia* Princeton, NJ: Princeton University Press, 2000.

Simpson, Ken, and Nicolas Day. *Field Guide to the Birds of Australia,* 4th ed. Ringwood, Australia: Viking O'Neil, 1993.

Periodicals:

Davidson, Steve. "For These Birds, Fidelity's a Lark." *Ecos* (April–June 2000): 36.

Web sites:

"Magpie-Lark." Australian Museum. http://www.amonline.net.au/factsheets/magpie_lark.htm (accessed on June 14, 2004).

WOODSWALLOWS
Artamidae

Class: Aves
Order: Passeriformes
Family: Artamidae
Number of species: 11 species

phylum

class

subclass

order

monotypic order

suborder

▲ family

PHYSICAL CHARACTERISTICS

Woodswallows are small, robust, mostly nomadic (wandering) birds. They have a stout body, soft plumage (feathers), brush-tipped tongue, short neck, short legs, weak-grasping feet, short toes, and a short, stumpy tail that is sometimes white-tipped. The bill is blue-gray, long, slightly curved, and sharply pointed with a bluish black tip. Wings are long, strong, and pointed (such that when flying they look like a common starling).

Their generally dullish looking colors consist of mostly grays, with mixtures of white, black, or reddish on the upper parts of the body, and white below, with several species having also russet colors. Woodswallows also have patches of powder down feathers. Unlike other feathers, powder down feathers crumble at the tips into a soft powder that the birds use for grooming. Males and females look alike in appearance. Adults are 4.7 to 7.9 inches (13 to 20 centimeters) long and weigh between 0.5 and 1.6 ounces (13 and 46 grams).

GEOGRAPHIC RANGE

Woodswallows are found in Australia and Tasmania, throughout the islands of the South Pacific region, Southeast Asia, and across south China to India and Sri Lanka.

HABITAT

This family lives in a wide variety of habitats including open forests, woodlands, scrublands, mangroves (groups of tropical evergreen trees located near tidal coasts), edges of forests, orchards, urban areas, and clearings. In fact, they prefer any habitat that contains plenty of insects.

DIET

Woodswallows eat flying insects, caterpillars, grasshoppers, nectar (sweet liquid that flowering plants produce), and pollen (powdery substance produced by flowering plants that contains reproductive cells). The birds fly to areas that have plentiful insects to eat. They forage primarily by flying high and sweeping up flying insects but, also at times, by dropping from tree limbs to capture prey on the ground. Their brush-like tongue enables them to lap up nectar and pollen when it is available within its environment (in a style similar to honeyeaters).

BEHAVIOR AND REPRODUCTION

Woodswallows are highly social and swiftly flying birds. When not foraging, they often are seen preening (grooming feathers with bill) each other and perching together, clustered together in large numbers on visible tree branches, wires, utility poles, and other such objects. Although clusters of more than 100 have been recorded, most numbers are in the range of fifteen to twenty. Most species remain in the same area all year-round, but at least three species are widely nomadic; that is, they like to wander in (sometimes) mixed species flocks of 100 or more, often traveling from tropical to temperate (mild) environments at different times of the year. Sometimes, at night, they roost as a community, with dozens of birds huddled together, often on the trunk of a tree or in a hollow. In winter, they often join mixed species flocks in order to forage. They have no true song, but do communicate with a soft twittering call that is sounded almost all of the time while foraging for insects. When predators are nearby, woodswallows often mob about them, frequently attacking them, while making harsh calls in the attempt to drive them away.

Woodswallows are monogamous (muh-NAH-guh-mus; having one mate) birds, becoming less social while in their breeding periods. Their courtship, which is usually begun at the start of rainfall in arid, dry, regions, may involve one bird presenting the other one with a piece of food. Later, one of the pair will start to flutter its partly opened wings and to rotate its spread-out tail. The other partner will respond with similar actions for up to a minute or so. The male will then fly to the female in order to mate. They nest in loose colonies (large groups of birds that live together and are dependent on each other) during the rainy season. Nests are usually clumsily made, shallow, bowl-like structures made of plant fibers such as rootlets, fine twigs, and grasses, lined with thin green plant stems, and placed in trees, shrubs, stumps, fence posts, and rocky crevices (bird-watchers can often see woodswallow eggs through the bottom of the frail nest).

Woodswallows are opportunistic breeders; that is, they take advantage of unpredictable environmental conditions when re-producing. In fact, in arid regions, nests may be built within six days of rainfall and eggs laid within twelve days, which is much shorter in time than the normal nest-building period. Both parents build the nest. Females lay two to four white eggs that are spotted or blotched with a variety of colors, but often reddish. The incubation period (time that it takes to sit on eggs before hatching) is twelve to sixteen days, with both parents helping to incubate (sit on eggs). The fledgling period (time necessary for young bird to grow feathers necessary to fly) is fourteen to twenty days. Both parents, and sometimes one or two helpers, feed and take care of their young, continuing of-ten a month after they can first leave the nest.

WOODSWALLOWS AND PEOPLE

People like to watch the highly visible but soft and modest colorations and daring aerial displays of woodswallows.

CONSERVATION STATUS

Woodswallows are not considered to be threatened. How-ever, species with small habitats are sometimes hurt by adverse changes in their environment and by human development and activities within their habitats.

Dusky woodswallow *(Artamus cyanopterus)*

■ Breeding ■ Nonbreeding

DUSKY WOODSWALLOW
Artamus cyanopterus

Physical characteristics: Dusky woodswallows are medium-sized, swallow-like birds that have a smoky blue to smoky brown body; small patch of black in the front of the eyes; dark gray to blackish wings with a white leading edge; dark gray to blackish tail with distinctive white spots at the end; and silvery underwings. The bill is short and pale blue with a black tip. Adults are 6.7 to 7.1 inches (17 to 18 centimeters) long and weigh between 1.1 and 1.6 ounces (31 and 46 grams).

Geographic range: Dusky woodswallows are found in Australia, specifically the eastern and southern portions of the country. They migrate northward for the winter.

Dusky woodswallows are often found in small communal flocks of ten to thirty birds. (© R. Drummond/VIREO. Reproduced by permission.)

Habitat: Dusky woodswallows inhabit open eucalyptus (yoo-kah-LIP-tus) forests (those consisting of tall, aromatic trees) and woodlands, along water courses, and over natural clearings. They especially like rural areas and wet climates.

Diet: Their diet consists of insects, foliage, and nectar. They usually catch flying insects, but will also take prey off the ground.

Behavior and reproduction: Dusky woodswallows are often found in small communal flocks of ten to thirty birds. They are social birds, often roosting in a tight group within a tree hollow or fork. Dusky woodswallows rest during the day, usually perching closely together as a group. They communicate with each other with a chattering call, and will display anxiety when predators or intruders are close by giving out a harsh mobbing call.

Males and females build a small, flimsy, cup-like nest made of plant fibers. The nest, made from August to January, is constructed within a colony of other dusky woodswallows, often within a tree trunk or other similar structure. A small territory surrounding the nest is defended by the mated pair. Parents may use helpers to take care of their young. Females lay three to four blotched white eggs. The incubation period is around sixteen days. The fledgling period is sixteen to twenty days.

Dusky woodswallows and people: There is no known significance between people and dusky woodswallows.

Conservation status: Dusky woodswallows are not considered to be threatened. ■

FOR MORE INFORMATION

Books:

del Hoyo, Josep, A. Elliott, J. Sargatal, J. Cabot, et al., eds. *Handbook of the Birds of the World.* Barcelona: Lynx Edicions, 1992.

Dickinson, Edward C., ed. *The Howard and Moore Complete Checklist of the Birds of the World,* 3rd ed. Princeton, NJ and Oxford, U.K.: Princeton University Press, 2003.

Forshaw, Joseph, ed. *Encyclopedia of Birds,* 2nd ed. San Diego, CA: Academic Press, 1998.

Harrison, Colin James Oliver. *Birds of the World.* London and New York: Dorling Kindersley, 1993.

Perrins, Christopher M., and Alex L. A. Middleton, eds. *The Encyclopedia of Birds.* New York: Facts on File, 1985.

MAGPIE-SHRIKES
Cracticidae

Class: Aves

Order: Passeriformes

Family: Cracticidae

Number of species: 14 species

phylum

class

subclass

order

monotypic order

suborder

▲ family

PHYSICAL CHARACTERISTICS

Magpie-shrikes are members of the family Cracticidae, which is divided into five groups: peltopses, bristleheads, currawongs, Australian magpies, and butcherbirds. All are black-and-white or blackish birds with strong black feet and booted or scaled legs. The bill is straight, strong, has a tip ranging from hooked and notched to pick-shaped, lacks bristles, is swollen at the upper jaw base, and has nostrils that are deep within bony slits.

Peltopses have a black body with large white patches on face and back; a black bill; a red rump, lower belly, and undertail; and a long tail. Bristleheads have a red head, a black bill, and a dusky-gray short tail. Currawongs are big but slender birds with a black bill, bright yellow eyes, dark gray to blackish plumage (feathers) with white patches in the wings, a long, white-tipped tail, and rounded wings. Australian magpies have black-and-white plumage; black-and-white upperparts, black underparts, pointed wings, short tail, and long legs. Butcherbirds may be all-black to black-hooded with white patches, or all-white with black, gray, and white patterning. These birds have a two-colored bill with a blackish tip and whitish or pale bluish gray base.

Juveniles have similar plumage to adults, although duller and grayer. Fledglings (young birds with recently grown flight feathers), depending on species, may be rusty-brown, washed olive-yellow, or lack clear head patterns. Adults are 6.5 to 22 inches (17 to 55 centimeters) long and weigh between 1.1 and 17.6 ounces (30 and 500 grams).

GEOGRAPHIC RANGE

Magpie-shrikes are found in Australia and New Guinea, along with one species in Borneo.

HABITAT

Magpie-shrikes inhabit wooded regions that include rainforests, savannas (grasslands), and pastures with trees. Peltopses live on the edge of canopies (uppermost vegetation layer of forest) in both mature and re-growth rainforests; bristleheads occupy the mid-strata of mature, lowland alluvial (river and lake systems) and swamp rainforests; currawongs range from dense, tall, wet forests to open, low, eucalyptus-dominated (yoo-kah-LIP-tus; tall, aromatic tree) woodlands; Australian magpies occupy open habitats such as savannas and pastures; and butcherbirds live in the middle and upper strata of forests and woodlands.

DIET

Their diet consists of various small vertebrates and invertebrates (animals with backbones and without backbones), such as insects, grubs, and worms. Magpie-shrikes also eat eggs, nestlings (young birds unable to leave the nest), and berries.

BEHAVIOR AND REPRODUCTION

All five groups make loud flutings, gargles, and bell-like whistles, except for peltopses that make "tick" or "tinckle" sounds. Magpie-shrikes roost in medium-height tree foliage. Australian magpies sing together in groups, and currawongs call out and answer back while in flocks. Australian magpies and currawongs roost in loose groups.

Butcherbirds, bristleheads, and peltopses live in trees, perching for long time periods while looking for prey, and fly rapidly and directly between trees. They pounce on prey, coming to the ground only to catch food. These birds remain in one large foraging territory throughout the year and are solitary birds, rarely gathering in groups larger than families. Australian magpies feed mostly from the ground. They are social birds with complex social organizations that include senior pairs or small breeding groups in permanent desirable territories, while larger groups of juveniles and other non-breeders live in less desirable territories. Australian magpies walk quietly on the ground and fly swiftly and directly. Currawongs are sometimes social throughout the year in some species, but in other species only gather in large wandering groups when not breeding. They live in all forest levels, fly in easy, wavy movements, and hop and run on the ground.

Breeding for all groups occurs irregularly throughout the year in tropical areas but only from early spring to summer (August to January) in temperate and subtropical regions. More than one brood (young birds born and raised together) can be raised in a year, but usually only one. Most species are monogamous (muh-NAH-guh-mus; having one mate), except for the polygynous (puh-LIJ-uh-nus; having several mates) Australian magpies. They are territorial birds. Only females build nests, which are rough cups of twigs and rootlets lined with finer fibers. The female does all of the incubating (sitting on eggs) while the male takes care of his nesting mate. Clutches (eggs hatched together) are one to five eggs that are cream or pinkish buff to pale green, lined or spotted with red-browns and gray-blacks.

MAGPIE-SHRIKES AND PEOPLE

There is little significance between people and magpie-shrikes other than with Australian magpies, which are known for their aggressiveness and caroling songs.

CONSERVATION STATUS

One species of magpie-shrike, the Bornean bristlehead, is listed as Near Threatened, in danger of becoming threatened with extinction.

Bornean bristlehead (*Pityriasis gymnocephala*)

◼ Resident

BORNEAN BRISTLEHEAD
Pityriasis gymnocephala

Physical characteristics: Bornean bristleheads are thick-bodied, dusky to mostly black colored birds. They have a massively hooked bill; a red, mostly bare head with a patch of orange-yellow stubble (small projection-like bare feather shafts that give its name "bristle-head") on the crown; an edge of scarlet feathering on upper back and breast; a lower breast covered in bristle-like brown and red feathers; a very short tail; and black wings, tail, and bill. Females have chest-nut eyes, a red patch on the flanks, and yellow feet. Adults are 10 to 11 inches (26 to 28 centimeters) long.

Geographic range: They are found in Borneo, except for its north-central areas, at elevations below 3,900 feet (1,200 meters).

Bornean bristleheads forage in the forest in groups of six to ten. (Illustration by Dan Erickson. Reproduced by permission.)

Habitat: Bornean bristleheads are found in lowland swamps and rainforests.

Diet: Their diet consists primarily of large insects such as arboreal (living in trees) beetles, grasshoppers, cockroaches, bugs, and larvae (LAR-vee). They take prey mostly from branches and trunks in the middle parts of forests, but will also go to recently cleared areas to find exposed food. Small olive- to plum-sized fruits are occasionally eaten.

Behavior and reproduction: Bornean bristleheads forage through the forest's mid-strata in noisy groups of about six to ten birds. They are very active while foraging, moving with sideward hops while calling loudly, and bending and looking closely for prey. They make direct flights on fast, shallow wings and make noisy calls of whines, honks, and chortles to maintain contacts, which often turn into loud, mixed choruses of various calls.

Bornean bristleheads and people: There is no known significance between people and Bornean bristleheads.

Conservation status: Bornean bristleheads are listed as Near Threatened because of deforestation. ■

Gray butcherbird (*Cracticus torquatus*)

Resident

GRAY BUTCHERBIRD
Cracticus torquatus

Physical characteristics: Gray butcherbirds are medium-sized, bull-headed birds with a tapered body; patterned plumage of blacks, grays, and whites; black head with white spot (between eyes and upper bill) and collar; dark brown eyes; gray-and-black bill; gray back; white rump; black tail (with white tips) and wings (with white stripes); grayish white underparts; and dark gray legs and feet. Females are smaller than males, generally have more gray on their breast, and have a shorter bill. Juveniles look like adults but have a dull-gray bill without a hook, are patterned with dusky-olive and speckled upperparts, and have buff to yellowish underparts. Adults

Young gray butcherbirds leave the nest after about twenty-eight days, but remain in the breeding territory for about one year to help parents raise future broods. (Illustration by Dan Erickson. Reproduced by permission.)

are 10 to 12 inches (25 to 30 centimeters) long and weigh between 2.8 and 4 ounces (80 and 110 grams).

Geographic range: Gray butcherbirds are found in much of southern and inland Australia from mid-eastern Queensland through southern Australia to northern Western Australia. They are also found in the northernmost parts of the Northern Territory, and in Tasmania.

Habitat: Gray butcherbirds inhabit closed woodlands and open forests of eucalyptus and acacias (uh-KAY-shuhz; flowering trees). They are not found in treeless deserts.

Diet: Their diet consists of mostly insects but also small birds, nestlings, reptiles (such as lizards), mice, fruits, and seeds. They sit on open perches at 6.5 to 40 feet (2 to 12 meters) while searching for prey. Once sighted, they aggressively pounce, mostly from the ground but sometimes while in flight. Feeding is done alone, in pairs, or in small family groups.

Behavior and reproduction: Monogamous mating pairs defend the same breeding territory (20 to 99 acres, or 8 to 40 hectares) all year-round, but have a larger home range. The pair sings back-and-forth with songs of fluted whistles and ringing caws, which are also heard when alarmed or to show aggression. Gray butcherbirds breed from July to August and December to January. They construct (in about four weeks) tight, bowl-shaped nests that are made with sticks and twigs and lined with grasses and other soft fibers. Nests are usually located about 33 feet (10 meters) or less from the ground, within upright forks in outer foliage. Females lay three to five brownish green eggs that are spotted in red-browns and are incubated by the female while the male defends the area. The incubation period (time to sit on eggs before hatching) is twenty-two to twenty-five days. The young are fed by both parents and leave the nest after about twenty-eight days, but remain in the breeding territory for about one year to help parents raise future broods.

Gray butcherbirds and people: Gray butcherbirds feed on food scraps thrown out by people.

Conservation status: Gray butcherbirds are not considered to be threatened. However, many populations are declining because of habitat clearance. ■

FOR MORE INFORMATION

Books:

del Hoyo, Josep, A. Elliott, J. Sargatal, J. Cabot, et al., eds. *Handbook of the Birds of the World.* Barcelona: Lynx Edicions, 1992.

Dickinson, Edward C., ed. *The Howard and Moore Complete Checklist of the Birds of the World,* 3rd ed. Princeton, NJ and Oxford, U.K.: Princeton University Press, 2003.

Forshaw, Joseph, ed. *Encyclopedia of Birds,* 2nd ed. San Diego, CA: Academic Press, 1998.

Harrison, Colin James Oliver. *Birds of the World.* London and New York: Dorling Kindersley, 1993.

Perrins, Christopher M., and Alex L. A. Middleton, eds. *The Encyclopedia of Birds.* New York: Facts on File, 1985.

BOWERBIRDS
Ptilonorhynchidae

Class: Aves

Order: Passeriformes

Family: Ptilonorhynchidae

Number of species: 20 species

PHYSICAL CHARACTERISTICS

Bowerbirds are small- to medium-sized, stocky birds that are related to birds of paradise. They are known for the bower-building activities of males within some species. The bower is a shady, leafy, elaborate shelter that the male builds for courtship to females. Bowerbirds show a range of colors in their plumage (feathers) including bold patterns of yellow, orange, green, and lavender with gray or black in many species; plain brown or gray in other species; and a few species that are spotted. In the brightly colored species, males are brighter than females; while in the duller colored species, males and females look alike. There are about fifty to sixty plumage variations within bowerbirds. Some species have only one primary color that blends into their environment, while others have two primary colors, with adult males showing colorful plumages and females being drab. Nestlings (young birds unable to leave the nest) have pinkish, orange-pink, or pale flesh-colored skin. Plumages of juveniles and immature males are similar to those of adult females. Males take five to seven years to fully acquire adult plumage.

Bowerbirds have a stout, powerful bill, except for the thinner, longer bill of regent bowerbirds and the falcon-like mandibles (upper and lower parts of bill) of tooth-billed bowerbirds. The bill is dark brown to black but can be pale; slightly hooked at tip in all species; and can be slightly downcurved, straight, thin and weak, or heavy. Bowerbirds have a black, pale yellow, or orange-yellow mouth; strong legs and feet that are usually dark brown, olive-brown, olive, blue-gray, or black; and toes with hard scales.

Some species have a crest (growth on top of head) of elongated feathers, often brilliantly colored. In other species, the crest forms a complicated mane that hangs over the upper back. Adults are 8.7 to 14.6 inches (22 to 37 centimeters) long and weigh between 0.18 and 0.64 pounds (80 and 290 grams).

GEOGRAPHIC RANGE

Bowerbirds are found primarily on the mainland of New Guinea, but also in Australia and the offshore islands of both countries.

HABITAT

They inhabit rainforests, rainforest edges, moss forests, woodlands, open riverine (located near river) forests, borders between forests and grasslands, open woodlands, savannas (flat grasslands), and semi-deserts.

DIET

Their diet consists of fruits from trees and bushes along with arthropods (invertebrate animals with jointed limbs) and other animals such as insects, spiders, small snakes, worms, frogs, birds, and skinks (small insect-eating lizards). They also eat flowers, leaves, seeds, and sap.

BEHAVIOR AND REPRODUCTION

Depending on species, bowerbirds can be monogamous (muh-NAH-guh-mus; having one mate) or polygynous (puh-LIJ-uh-nus). Monogamous pairs defend a territory, while males do not help with nest building, incubation (process of sitting on eggs), or the raising of young, though they do help with feeding. Males of polygynous species defend only the nearby area of their bowers. They court and mate with many females, being able to supply many females and their young with large amounts of food in territories with plenty of fruits. Unlike any other bird families, a polygynous male clears a courting area where he builds a bower, a complex symmetrical structure of sticks, grasses, and other vegetation, and decorates it with various colorful objects.

The three types of nesting structures made by bowerbirds are: courts (cleared and decorated with leaves); maypole bowers (constructed of branches, sticks, saplings, and orchid stems along with an elaborate and decorated mat underneath it); and avenue bowers (made of two parallel, vertical walls of sticks or grass stems placed onto a foundation that is set on a ground court that may extend past one or both ends of the bower, making a platform). Courts and bowers are decorated with flowers, leaves, lichens (LYE-kenz), fruits, beetle wing cases, insect skeletons, snail shells, tree resin, bones, river-worn pebbles and stones, and tail feathers of parrots and plumes of adult males of certain birds of paradise. The incubation period (time to sit on eggs before hatching) is twenty-one to twenty-seven days. The nestling period (time necessary to take care of young unable to leave nest) lasts seventeen to thirty days. They live longer than most birds, many twenty to thirty years.

BOWERBIRDS AND PEOPLE

A few groups of native New Guinean and Australian aborigines have used the crests of some male species as clothing decorations, while some natives believe that male bowerbirds use the same techniques as male humans to find a mate; still other natives believe that some species steal human bones for their own ceremonial purposes. Eight species have been bred in aviaries (large enclosures or cages for birds).

CONSERVATION STATUS

One species of bowerbird is considered Vulnerable, facing a high risk of extinction, and one species is listed as Near Threatened, close to becoming threatened with extinction.

Satin bowerbird (*Ptilonorhynchus violaceus*)

▨ Resident

SATIN BOWERBIRD
Ptilonorhynchus violaceus

Physical characteristics: Male satin bowerbirds have iridescent (lustrous appearance) black plumage, bright lavender eyes, pale yellow bill, and light legs. Females are slightly smaller than males, with green, gray-green, brown, and buff colorings that help to camouflage them (blend into the environment). Adults are about 13 inches (33 centimeters) long, with females weighing between 0.38 and 0.57 pounds (170 and 258 grams) and males weighing between 0.38 and 0.64 pounds (173 and 290 grams).

Geographic range: They are found in eastern and southeastern Australia.

Habitat: Satin bowerbirds inhabit rainforests and eucalypt forests, clearly preferring forest edges and nearby woodlands with dense sapling understories. During winter months, they like more open habitats such as pastures and urban and suburban areas.

A female satin bowerbird visits a male's bower, which he has built and decorated to attract her to mate with him. (© Tom McHugh, National Audubon Society Collection/Photo Researchers, Inc. Reproduced by permission.)

Diet: Their diet consists mostly of fruits but also some insects. They also eat flowers, leaves, herbs, nectar, seeds, and animals including cicadas, beetles, and other arthropods. Satin bowerbirds forage from the forest canopy during summer, but eat from the ground in winter.

Behavior and reproduction: Males clear off a circular area on the rainforest floor and build avenue bowers to attract females. They are usually built about 990 feet (300 meters) apart when along rainforest edges, but are spaced further apart in rainforest patches and woodlands. Decorative bluish and greenish yellow objects such as flowers, fruits, parrot feathers, snakeskins, snail shells, and human-made objects (such as pen caps) are often used. Bowers are used from late August/September through December (peaking in October). Adult males make their presence known with a clearly-whistled "quoo-eeew," various harsh and scratchy hisses (called "skraa" calls), and vocal mimicry, often sung within the understory above his bower.

Satin bowerbirds are polygynous. Breeding begins in August/September and continues through February (peaking in November/December). Nests are usually open cup-shaped structures built in trees or bushes, but sometimes in vines and mistletoe, normally at

7 to 130 feet (2 to 40 meters) off the ground. Nests are made with sticks and twigs and lined with green and dry leaves. Females lay one to three colored and blotched eggs. The incubation period is twenty-one to twenty-two days. The nestling period is seventeen to twenty-one days.

Satin bowerbirds and people: Male satin bowerbirds often remove people's jewelry, keys, and other items in order to decorate bowers.

Conservation status: Satin bowerbirds are not threatened. They are commonly to reasonably abundant birds in their current habitats, but have lost much territory to human land use.   ■

Spotted bowerbird *(Chlamydera maculata)*

▨ Resident

SPOTTED BOWERBIRD
Chlamydera maculata

Physical characteristics: Spotted bowerbirds look similar to song thrushes, being relatively plain in appearance. They are mottled brown with a lilac to pink bar across the back of the neck. This vivid bar, which easily recognizes them, is erected into a crest-like peak during times of anxiety or excitement. Adults are 10.6 to 12.2 inches (27 to 31 centimeters) long, with females weighing between 0.27 and 0.36 pounds (124 and 162 grams) and males weighing between 0.28 and 0.33 pounds (125 and 150 grams).

Geographic range: Spotted bowerbirds are found in the interior of Queensland south of 20 degrees south latitude, except the far west and southwest; interior of west and central New South Wales, except the far western border country; and extends a short way into the northwest corner of Victoria and just into South Australia along the Murray River system. They are found from sea level to about 1,640 feet (500 meters).

Habitat: Spotted bowerbirds are found among brigalow (Australian acacia tree that grows in semiarid regions) and open eucalyptus woodlands, with a preference for riverine woodlands.

Diet: They eat fruits, flowers, leaves, seeds, and arthropods. Nestlings are fed mostly grasshoppers.

Behavior and reproduction: Spotted bowerbirds build avenue bowers beneath low bushes or shrubs. The nests are made from grasses and are often 3,300 to 6,600 feet (1,000 to 2,000 meters) apart from each other. The walls are about 7.8 to 19.7 inches (20 to 50 centimeters) high. Up to 1,000 or more decorations such as berries, seedpods, pebbles and stones, bones, snail shells, and glass are attached to the bowers. Adult males occasionally make loud, harsh churrings and other notes (including vocal mimicry) in order to make themselves known.

Spotted bowerbirds are polygynous. Breeding occurs during July through March (peaking from September to February). Males make a sparse open cup-like nest in trees and bushes, often 10 to 40 feet (3 to 12 meters) off the ground. The loose bulky foundation for nests

Spotted bowerbirds build avenue bowers with walls as tall as 7.8 to 19.7 inches (20 to 50 centimeters) high. The male adds up to 1,000 or more decorations to his bower. (Frithfoto/Bruce Coleman Inc. Reproduced by permission.)

are made of dead twigs and sticks, with fine twiglets and (sometimes) dried grass stalks used for the nest. Males spend much time watching and tending to their bowers. Two to three eggs are laid. The incubation and nestling periods are unknown.

Spotted bowerbirds and people: People often cage spotted bowerbirds within avaries. The birds frequently steal items from homes, camps, and vehicles for decorating their bowers. People often kill them when they become pests within gardens and orchards.

Conservation status: Spotted bowerbirds are not considered to be threatened. They have declined in some areas because of illegal hunting and killing of the birds by humans, domesticated and feral cats, and foxes, and the widespread clearing and/or modification of habitat. Populations are listed as endangered, however, within the state of Victoria.   ■

FOR MORE INFORMATION

Books:

del Hoyo, Josep, A. Elliott, J. Sargatal, J. Cabot, et al., eds. *Handbook of the Birds of the World.* Barcelona: Lynx Edicions, 1992.

Dickinson, Edward C., ed. *The Howard and Moore Complete Checklist of the Birds of the World,* 3rd ed. Princeton, NJ and Oxford, U.K.: Princeton University Press, 2003.

Forshaw, Joseph, ed. *Encyclopedia of Birds,* 2nd ed. San Diego, CA: Academic Press, 1998.

Harrison, Colin James Oliver. *Birds of the World.* London and New York: Dorling Kindersley, 1993.

Perrins, Christopher M., and Alex L. A. Middleton, eds. *The Encyclopedia of Birds.* New York: Facts on File, 1985.

BIRDS OF PARADISE
Paradisaeidae

Class: Aves
Order: Passeriformes
Family: Paradisaeidae
Number of species: 42 species

family
CHAPTER

PHYSICAL CHARACTERISTICS

Birds of paradise are known for their bright and beautiful plumage and unique ornamental tail and head feathers. Males are almost universally more colorful than their female counterparts. Most species have a hooked bill that they use to extract insects from dead wood and tree bark. Sizes range from 6.3 to 43.3 inches (16 to 110 centimeters) in length and 0.11 to 1 pound (50 to 450 grams) in weight.

GEOGRAPHIC RANGE

Eastern Australia, Indonesia, and New Guinea and surrounding islands.

HABITAT

The majority of Paradisaeidae species live in the rainforest, ranging from high altitude sub-alpine to lowland; however, one species, the glossy-mantled manucodes, inhabits savanna (or tropical grassland) woodlands as well as rainforest.

DIET

Birds of paradise eat fruits and insects.

BEHAVIOR AND REPRODUCTION

Although a few species of the Paradisaeidae family are monogamous (muh-NAH-guh-mus; having only one mate), the majority are polygynous (puh-LIJ-uh-nus; one male mates with several females). Males choose a display site from which to attract females, either by themselves or in a group of other males

phylum

class

subclass

order

monotypic order

suborder

▲ **family**

SNAKESKIN NESTS

Some female riflebirds decorate the outside rim of their woven plant and stick cup-shaped nests with cast-off snake skins. Researchers are unsure as to exactly why they do so, but one theory is that the snake skin is a decoy of sorts to keep predators away from the riflebird eggs.

known as a lek. Their display behavior consists of a combination of song and a variety of maneuvers that show off his plumage. Some species spread their wings wide, while others hang upside down. Females approach the solitary or lekking male to mate, then raise and feed their hatchlings on their own.

BIRDS OF PARADISE AND PEOPLE

Many people seek out members of the Paradisaeidae family to witness their elaborate courtship rituals and enjoy their beautiful plumage. Some native New Guinea tribes wear the highly prized feathers of some of the more colorful species.

CONSERVATION STATUS

Four species of the Paradisaeidae family are considered Vulnerable, facing a high risk of extinction, including the blue bird of paradise, Wahnes's parotia, MacGregor's bird of paradise, and the black sicklebill. Eight additional species are listed as Near Threatened, in danger of becoming threatened with extinction: ribbon-tailed bird of paradise, Wilson's bird of paradise, pale-billed sicklebill, yellow-breasted bird of paradise, long-tailed paradigalla, Goldie's bird of paradise, emperor bird of paradise, and the red bird of paradise.

Some species, such as the blue bird of paradise and the black sicklebill, are hunted for their beautiful, bright plumage and/or skins; others are hunted for food. The other major reason for dwindling numbers of certain species is habitat loss due to forest clearing for agriculture and logging.

Ribbon-tailed astrapia *(Astrapia mayeri)*

▨ Resident

RIBBON-TAILED ASTRAPIA
Astrapia mayeri

Physical characteristics: As is typical with most birds of paradise, the male of the ribbon-tailed astrapia species is both larger and more colorful than the female. Males average 12.6 to 13.8 inches (32 to 35 centimeters) in body length, and 0.30 to 0.36 pounds (134 to 164 grams) in weight. Their plumage is primarily iridescent green, blue, and olive, with a bright green bib and cap and a band of red across the chest. A dark green tuft sits at the top of the beak.

The male ribbon-tailed astrapia's most striking feature is his long, white tail feathers, which extend an additional 8 to 15 inches (20 to 38 centimeters) past his body and are tipped with black at the bottom. Females lack the long tail feathers, and are brown in color.

Geographic range: The ribbon-tailed astrapia lives in the tropical and subtropical rainforests of central Papua New Guinea.

Female ribbon-tailed astrapias are solely responsible for both building the nest and feeding the hatchlings. (Frithfoto/ Olympus/Bruce Coleman Inc. Reproduced by permission.)

Habitat: The ribbon-tailed astrapia lives in upper montane (mountainous) and subalpine forests and forest edges.

Diet: These birds use their bill to dig insects out of the ground and trees. About half of their daily diet is comprised of fruit.

Behavior and reproduction: Males are polygynous, meaning that they breed with multiple females. They attract mates through a courtship ritual known as lekking, in which they gather together with other male astrapias and sing together, hop from perch to perch, and display their plumage to draw female mates.

Breeding season takes place for the greater part of the year (May through March). Female ribbon-tailed astrapias lay a single egg at a time, which incubates for about three weeks. The females are solely responsible for both building their nest (which is deep and cup-shaped) and feeding their hatchlings.

Ribbon-tailed astrapias and people: Ribbon-tailed astrapias have little contact with humans. However, males are sometimes hunted by native populations for their colorful tail feathers and skins.

Conservation status: These birds are listed as Near Threatened due to habitat destruction and hunting. ∎

Victoria's riflebird (*Ptiloris victoriae*)

    Resident

VICTORIA'S RIFLEBIRD
Ptiloris victoriae

Physical characteristics: The male Victoria's riflebird has a curved bill; a bright green cap, throat, and belly; and a black back and breast band. It also sports short, iridescent blue-green tail feathers. The female of the species has a brown back and head, a spotty buff belly and throat, and a buff stripe above the eye. Average length for both is 9.5 inches (24 centimeters).

Geographic range: The species is found in northeast Queensland, Australia between Townsville and Cooktown.

Habitat: The Victoria's riflebird lives in what is known as the wet tropics region of Queensland. It lives in low-lying rainforest and coastal mangroves.

The Victoria's riflebird uses its hooked bill to dig insects out of tree bark. It also eats some fruit. (Illustration by Emily Damstra. Reproduced by permission.)

Diet: Like many other birds of paradise, the Victoria's riflebird uses its hooked bill to dig insects (such as insect larvae [LAR-vee], cockroaches, spiders, wood lice, and centipedes) out of tree bark. This species also eats fruit.

Behavior and reproduction: Breeding season typically lasts from August through January. Male Victoria's riflebirds have multiple female mates. They perform an elaborate courtship "dance" of sorts by perching alone on a tree stump, outstretching their wings, bobbing their head from side to side, and calling loudly to potential mates.

The female builds and tends the nest alone, and lays a clutch of one or two eggs, which incubate for up to eighteen days. She also feeds the nestlings alone until they leave the nest about fifteen days after hatching.

Aside from the loud vocalizations of the Victoria's riflebird, the bird's wings also make a unique rustling sound both in flight and when extending and flapping its wings during its display, which helps birdwatchers track the species.

Victoria's riflebird and people: The Victoria's riflebird has a fairly harmonious relationship with people. Although a good deal of the species' rainforest habitat has been cleared for sugar cane plantations and logging over the past century, the majority of the wet tropics area of Queensland is now protected against logging and habitat destruction by the Wet Tropics World Heritage Area Conservation Act and Protection and Management Act.

Conservation status: The Victoria's riflebird is not considered to be threatened. ■

King bird of paradise (*Cicinnurus regius*)

Resident

KING BIRD OF PARADISE
Cicinnurus regius

Physical characteristics: The male king bird of paradise can be spotted by his brilliant red coloring and two long, wire-like ornamental tail feather shafts, which are tipped at the bottom with a circular swirl of bright green feathers. His underside is white, with a green band across the chest. The male also has a black spot over each eye. Both male and female have blue legs and feet; the female's coloring is much more subdued with an olive-brown back, head, and throat and a variegated buff chest. Both are about 6.3 to 7.25 inches (16 to 19 centimeters) in length, not counting the added length of the male's tail, which may be as long as the body.

Geographic range: The species is found on the New Guinea mainland and on surrounding islands, including Aru, Missol, Salawati, and Yapen.

The female (left) and male king birds of paradise show the sexual dimorphism typical of this family. (© W. Peckover/VIREO. Reproduced by permission.)

Habitat: King birds of paradise live in lowland rainforests, forest edges, and secondary forests. The female builds her nest in cavities of lower trees, and the male selects short, shrubby trees to perform his display (or courtship ritual) upon.

Diet: The species eats both fruit and insects.

Behavior and reproduction: Males perform their courtship ritual of persistent calling and displaying of plumage in solitude rather than in a lek (or cluster of other male birds of the species). During the display, they pose with their tail wires extended so that the green disks they are tipped with are over their heads. They may also hang upside down from a tree branch.

Male king birds of paradise are polygynous, and once they mate they move on to attracting the next female, while the female goes on to lay her eggs and incubate and feed her chicks by herself.

King bird of paradise and people: The bright feathers and skins of the male king birds of paradise are sometimes sought after by native men of New Guinea, but for the most part the bird enjoys a harmonious relationship with people.

Conservation status: King birds of paradise are abundant and not considered to be threatened. ■

FOR MORE INFORMATION

Books:

Dickinson, Edward C., ed. *The Howard and Moore Complete Checklist of the Birds of the World,* 3rd ed. Princeton, NJ and Oxford, U.K.: Princeton University Press, 2003.

Frith, Clifford B., and Bruce Beehler. *The Birds of Paradise.* Oxford, U.K.: Oxford University Press, 1998.

Harrison, Colin James Oliver. *Birds of the World.* London and New York: Dorling Kindersley, 1993.

Simpson, Ken and Nicolas Day. *Field Guide to the Birds of Australia,* 4th ed. Ringwood, Australia: Viking O'Neil, 1993.

Periodicals:

Clode, Danielle. "Kicked Out of Paradise." *Nature Australia* 26, no. 12 (Autumn 2001): 15.

Smith, Dwight G. "On Heaven's Wings." *World & I* 12, no. 11 (November 1997): 184.

Web sites:

"2003 BirdLife's Online World Bird Database." BirdLife International. http://www.birdlife.org (accessed on June 14, 2004).

"Animals of New Guinea: Birds of Paradise." World Wildlife Foundation. http://www.worldwildlife.org/expeditions/newguinea/spec_bop.cfm (accessed on June 14, 2004).

CROWS AND JAYS
Corvidae

Class: Aves
Order: Passeriformes
Family: Corvidae
Number of species: 123 species

family

CHAPTER

phylum

class

subclass

order

monotypic order

suborder

▲ family

PHYSICAL CHARACTERISTICS

Corvids, members of the Corvidae family, range in length from 7.4 inches (19 centimeters) in Hume's ground jay to the northern raven, which is 22.62 to 26.91 inches (58 to 69 centimeters) long. Hume's ground jays weigh 1.47 to 1.61 ounces (42 to 46 grams). Northern ravens range from 2.02 to 3.43 pounds (.92 to 1.6 kilograms).

The *Corvus* genus of crows includes the crow, raven, jackdaw, and rook. These birds have shiny black plumage, feathers, and harsh calls. Jays are the colorful members of this family. The Eurasian jay and blue jay have blue and white feathers. Magpies are related to jays and plumage (feather) color is often described in the names of these birds, like the green magpie.

Corvids have strong bills. Most birds have black or dark bills, and feathers or whisker-like bristles cover the nostrils of many birds. Members of this family have large feet with strong toes. Birds use their toes to hold onto prey, the food that they hunt.

Corvids have long tails and rounded wings. Wing length varies with the amount of flying a bird does. Long wings are found on birds that migrate, travel long distances from one place to another.

Corvids belong to the Passeriformes, song bird or perching bird, order. While other birds in this order sing sweetly, the corvids' loud, harsh calls are described as screeching or croaking sounds.

GEOGRAPHIC RANGE

Corvids are located throughout most of the world. They are found on all continents except Antarctica.

HABITAT

Members of this large family live in habitats ranging from treeless tundras where land is flat to mountain forests. Birds live in deciduous forests, where trees shed their leaves, and coniferous forests, with cone-bearing evergreen trees. Corvids range in deserts, grassland steppes where there are few trees, and on the edge of rainforests, where heavy rain produces much growth. In addition, corvids live in cities and small villages.

DIET

Corvids mainly eat seeds and nuts. However, they are omnivores, eat animals and plants. These birds are scavengers and take food from places like garbage dumps. Another corvid habit is hoarding food. Birds hide food, often burying it. They stockpile food for times like winter when there is a shortage of seeds and nuts.

BEHAVIOR AND REPRODUCTION

Corvids are family-oriented. Many species travel in a flock, a group of birds. Birds in this group are monogamous (muh-NAH-guh-mus), with a single male mating with a single female. The female corvid lays from two to seven eggs. Females incubate the clutch of eggs, sitting on them to keep them warm.

Older offspring act as cooperative breeders, helping the parents protect and rear young. The male and the older offspring feed the female. They also protect the female from predators like cats, hawks, and people. A mob, usually a group of crows or jays, will fly after hawks and owls. The corvids yell loudly, scolding the birds as they chase them away.

Corvid eggs do not all hatch at the same time. The young birds stay in the nest from five weeks to three months.

CROWS, JAYS, AND PEOPLE

People have mixed feelings about corvids. Birds can imitate human words and have been kept as pets. However,

CLEVER CROWS FIND FOOD

A prime example of crows' intelligence is how birds solve the problem of getting food. Hooded crows in Finland know that lines left in the water by fishermen lead to food. The birds use their bills and feet to pull up the line and get fish. And in New Zealand, New Caledonian crows make tools out of leaves. Bird use the hooked tools to get hard-to-reach insects.

people have also killed corvids to prevent damage to crops and cattle.

Corvid names have long been used to describe negative traits in humans. For example, to crow means to brag, and to rook is to cheat. The little-used verb raven means hunt for prey, and ravenous means extremely hungry. A jay is a foolish person, and a magpie is someone who chatters or collects many things.

CONSERVATION STATUS

According to the World Conservation Union (IUCN), the Hawaiian crow is Critically Endangered, facing an extremely high risk of extinction; four species are Endangered, facing a very high risk of extinction; eight species are Vulnerable, facing a high risk of extinction; and eleven species are Near Threatened, in danger of becoming threatened with extinction. The primary cause is the destruction of habitat as trees are cut down.

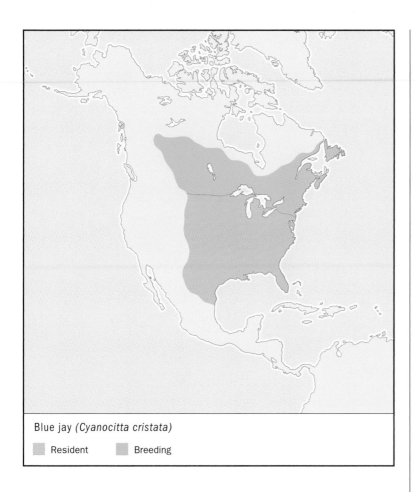

Blue jay *(Cyanocitta cristata)*

▨ Resident ▨ Breeding

BLUE JAY
Cyanocitta cristata

Physical characteristics: Blue jays are colorful members of the crow family. They have a crest of blue feathers that tops their head. Their rounded wings and fan-shaped tails are dark blue with black and white markings. Blue jays have pale gray faces and bodies. There's a "necklace" of black feathers around the throat. The bird has a long black bill, long legs and black feet.

Adult blue jays range in length from 9.36 to 11.7 inches (24 to 30 centimeters). Birds weigh from 2.27 to 3.8 ounces (65 to 109 grams). The wingspan is 16 inches (40.54 centimeters).

Blue jays typically hatch four to five young at a time. (© Gregory K. Scott/Photo Researchers, Inc. Reproduced by permission.)

Geographic range: Blue jays are found east of the Rocky Mountains in the United States and Canada.

Habitat: Blue jays live in woods, parks, and suburbs.

Diet: Blue jays eat insects, nuts, and seeds. During the summer, they steal other birds' eggs. They add acorns to their diet in winter. Blue jays bury some acorns to eat in the future.

Behavior and reproduction: Blue jays frequently travel in small groups. They live in trees and build nests of twigs, feathers, and roots.

Birds are monogamous, and the female lays eggs during the months of March through June. The clutch of four of five eggs hatches in sixteen to eighteen days. Younger birds are grayer than adults.

Blue jays and people: People admire the blue jay's beauty, and Toronto, Canada, named its baseball team the Blue Jays.

Conservation status: Blue jays are not in danger of extinction, dying out. ∎

Western scrub-jay *(Aphelocoma californica)*

Resident

WESTERN SCRUB-JAY
Aphelocoma californica

Physical characteristics: Western scrub-jays look somewhat like blue jays. Both species have dark blue heads, wings, and tails. The scrub-jays do not have feathered crests on their heads. Scrub-jays have white chests, and white coloring on the face that resembles an eyebrow. The throat is white with a blue necklace. There is a blue band on the chest, and the lower body coloring is white, tan, and gray.

The length of western scrub-jays ranges from 10.53 to 12.09 inches (27 to 31 centimeters). They weigh about 3 ounces (85 grams).

Geographic range: Western scrub-jays live in the western United States and northwestern Mexico.

Habitat: Western scrub-jays live in desert areas.

Diet: Western scrub-jays are omnivores. They eat acorns, pine seeds, invertebrates, animals without backbones, like insects, reptiles, eggs and nestlings, mammals, and amphibians, animals able to live on land and in the water.

Behavior and reproduction: Western scrub-jays are solitary breeders. The male and female are not helped by other birds. The female lays two to six eggs from March through May. Females incubate the eggs, which hatch after sixteen to nineteen days. Birds fledge, grow feathers, in approximately eighteen days.

Western scrub-jays and people: Seeds hidden by western scrub-jays grow into trees.

Conservation status: Western scrub-jays are not in danger of extinction. ■

Western scrub-jays are solitary breeders—the male and female are not helped by other birds. (© H. P. Smith, Jr/VIREO. Reproduced by permission.)

Green magpie (*Cissa chinensis*)

■ Resident

GREEN MAGPIE
Cissa chinensis

Physical characteristics: Green magpies have bright green heads and reddish brown wings. Their bodies are a lighter green, and their long, tapered tails have white tips. Black coloring on the face resembles a mask. Flesh around the eyes is red, and their bills, legs, and feet are also bright red. Green magpies range in length from 14.43 to 15.21 inches (37 to 39 centimeters). They weigh from 4.55 to 4.65 ounces (120 to 124 grams).

Geographic range: Green magpies live on the continent of Asia and are found in India, China, Malaysia, Borneo, and Sumatra.

Habitat: Green magpies live in forests and build nests in vines and in bamboo, which are woody, evergreen trees. Evergreens are coniferous trees that do not undergo seasonal changes.

Diet: Green magpies hunt for food on the ground and in trees. The magpies eat insects, small reptiles, young birds, eggs, amphibians, berries, and fruit. Magpies also eat the flesh of recently killed animals.

Behavior and reproduction: Green magpies are solitary breeders. The male and female birds do not receive help, such as protection, from their older offspring. The magpie nest resembles a platform. The female magpie lays three to seven eggs during the months of January through April. Green magpies remain hidden during this time, and it is not known how long it takes for eggs to hatch. Within their habitat, groups of green magpies fly around with other groups of birds.

Green magpies hunt for food—insects, small reptiles, young birds, eggs, amphibians, berries, and fruit—on the ground and in trees. (Illustration by Gillian Harris. Reproduced by permission.)

Green magpies and people: Green magpies, which are also known as cissas, are captured and sold as cage birds.

Conservation status: Green magpies are not in danger of extinction. ■

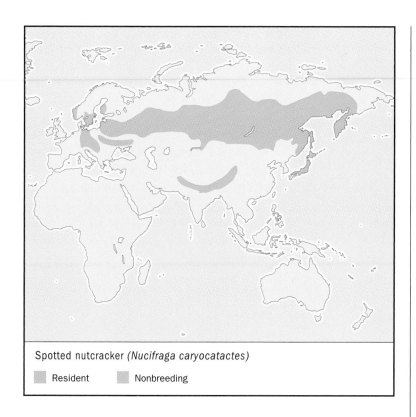

Spotted nutcracker *(Nucifraga caryocatactes)*

▨ Resident   ▨ Nonbreeding

SPOTTED NUTCRACKER
Nucifraga caryocatactes

Physical characteristics: Spotted nutcrackers are named for their appearance and the way they use their large bills to take the shells off of nuts. There are white spots and streaks in their feathers. The spotted nutcracker's brown body plumage is the color of chocolate. The lower part of the body is white. The wing and tail feathers are a shiny black. There are white tips at the ends of the wings and feathers. The spotted nutcracker's bill, legs, and feet are black.

The length of nutcrackers ranges from 12.48 to 13.26 inches (32 to 34 centimeters). Birds weigh from 4.3 to 7 ounces (124 to 200 grams).

Geographic range: Spotted nutcrackers live in Europe and are found in nations including Switzerland, England, Netherlands, and Scandinavian countries. The birds also range in Japan, China, and other Asian countries.

Spotted nutcrackers have thick bills that they use to open nuts, their main food. (Illustration by Gillian Harris. Reproduced by permission.)

Habitat: Spotted nutcrackers live in coniferous forests, where trees such as pines do not shed their leaves.

Diet: Spotted nutcrackers eat conifer seeds, or nuts, of trees in the pine and spruce families. Larger birds eat the hard-shelled hazel nuts. Spotted nutcrackers get the edible meat inside the shell by hitting the shell with their bill.

Spotted nutcrackers have thick bills that they use to open nuts. They place the nut between their feet and then begin pecking on the shell. Nutcrackers use their beaks to hit the nut until the shell cracks.

Like other corvids, nutcrackers store food. They bury nuts and seeds to eat at a later time. If no seeds or nuts can be found, nutcrackers eat insects and berries.

Behavior and reproduction: Spotted nutcrackers are solitary breeders. The female lays two to four eggs during March through May. The female incubates the eggs that hatch in eighteen days. Both parents feed the chicks. The young birds fledge after about three weeks. The nestlings remain with their parents throughout the summer or longer.

Spotted nutcrackers and people: Seeds hidden by spotted nutcrackers sometimes sprout into saplings that grow into trees. The spotted nutcracker's habit of hiding food caused the growth of new Swiss pine trees in areas of the European Alps where people had cut down all the trees.

Conservation status: Spotted nutcrackers are not in danger of extinction. ∎

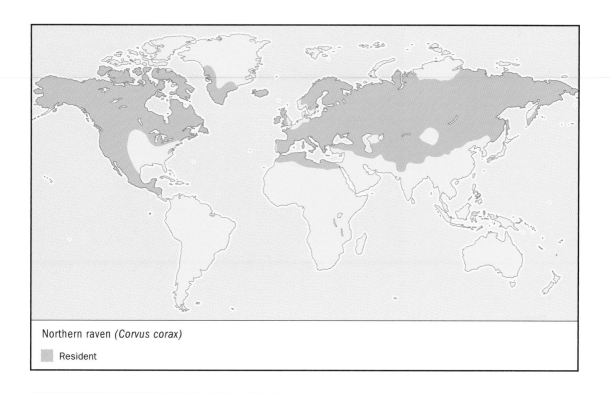

Northern raven *(Corvus corax)*

Resident

NORTHERN RAVEN
Corvus corax

Physical characteristics: Northern ravens have shiny black plumage, black bills, and black legs and feet. These birds have long bills. There are long, pointed feathers around the neck. The length of northern ravens ranges from 22.62 to 26.91 inches (58 to 69 centimeters). Birds weigh from 2.02 to 3.43 pounds (92 to 156 grams).

Geographic range: Northern ravens are found throughout the Northern Hemisphere. In North America they range from Alaska to Greenland, south through Canada, and into the United States and Mexico. In the United States they are typically found west of the Rocky Mountains and along the east coast from Canada to Georgia. Birds also range throughout Europe.

Habitat: Northern ravens live in many different habitats, including the treeless tundra. They choose locations away from people.

Northern ravens live in many different habitats in North America and Europe. They choose locations away from people. (Joe McDonald/Bruce Coleman Inc. Reproduced by permission.)

Diet: Northern ravens eat carrion, the decaying bodies of dead animals. They use their strong bills to rip into dead animals or kill live prey. Ravens also eat plants and berries.

Behavior and reproduction: Northern ravens have long-term mating partners. The female raven lays from three to seven eggs in the spring. Eggs hatch in eighteen to twenty-one days. Birds grow feathers five to six weeks later.

Northern ravens and people: People killed northern ravens because they wrongly blamed ravens for the death of cattle. The raven is a symbol of death and the bird's ability to say words is the subject of Edgar Allen Poe's poem, "The Raven."

Conservation status: Northern ravens are not threatened. ■

FOR MORE INFORMATION

Books:

Stuart, Chris and Tilde. *Birds of Africa From Seabirds to Seed Eaters.* Cambridge, MA: The MIT Press, 1999.

Wade, Nicholas, ed. *The New York Times Book of Birds.* New York: The Lyons Press, 2001.

Periodicals:

Youth, Howard. "The Revered, Reviled Crow Clan." *ZooGoer* 30, no. 3 (2001). Online at http://nationalzoo.si.edu/publications/zoogoer/2001/3/reviledcrowclan.cfm (accessed on July 20, 2004).

Species List by Biome

CONIFEROUS FOREST

African broadbill
African pitta
American cliff swallow
American goldfinch
American robin
Anna's hummingbird
Barn swallow
Barred eagle-owl
Belted kingfisher
Black-and-red broadbill
Black-and-white warbler
Black-capped chickadee
Black-capped vireo
Black-crowned barwing
Blue-gray gnatcatcher
Bornean bristlehead
Brown creeper
Brown kiwi
Cedar waxwing
Chaffinch
Chimney swift
Crag martin
Cuban tody
Dollarbird
Dunnock
Dusky woodswallow
Eastern bluebird
Eastern screech-owl
Emu

Fan-tailed berrypecker
Fiery minivet
Fire-breasted flowerpecker
Gray butcherbird
Gray nightjar
Gray parrot
Gray potoo
Green magpie
House sparrow
House wren
Ivory-billed woodpecker
Japanese white-eye
Kirtland's warbler
Kokako
Laughing kookaburra
Little slaty flycatcher
Malaysian honeyguide
Northern bobwhite quail
Northern wryneck
Nuthatch
Oilbird
Orange-breasted trogon
Osprey
Palmchat
Peregrine falcon
Red crossbill
Red-breasted nuthatch
Red-cockaded woodpecker
Resplendent quetzal
Rifleman

Rose-throated becard
Rufous treecreeper
Rufous-browed peppershrike
Rufous-capped nunlet
Rufous-tailed jacamar
Satyr tragopan
Scarlet macaw
Sparkling violet-ear
Spotted nutcracker
Striated pardalote
Whip-poor-will
White-necked puffbird
White-throated fantail
Winter wren
Wrentit
Yellow-bellied sapsucker
Yellow-breasted chat

CONTINENTAL MARGIN

Blue-footed booby
Brown pelican
Great cormorant
Northern gannet

DECIDUOUS FOREST

African broadbill
African pitta
American cliff swallow
American goldfinch

American robin
Anna's hummingbird
Arctic warbler
Asian fairy-bluebird
Australian magpie-lark
Baltimore oriole
Bar-breasted mousebird
Barn owl
Barn swallow
Baywing
Black bulbul
Black guan
Black-and-white warbler
Black-capped chickadee
Black-capped vireo
Blue jay
Blue-crowned motmot
Blue-gray gnatcatcher
Brown creeper
Brown kiwi
Bushtit
Cedar waxwing
Chaffinch
Chimney swift
Coppersmith barbet
Crag martin
Crested tree swift
Cuban tody
Dollarbird
Dunnock
Dusky woodswallow
Eastern bluebird
Eastern screech-owl
Emu
Eurasian golden oriole
European bee-eater
European roller
Fire-breasted flowerpecker
Gray catbird
Gray nightjar
Gray-crowned babbler
Great tit
House sparrow
House wren
Ivory-billed woodpecker
Jacky winter

Japanese white-eye
Leaf-love
Northern wryneck
Nuthatch
Orange-breasted trogon
Osprey
Painted buttonquail
Peregrine falcon
Peruvian plantcutter
Plain chachalaca
Red-breasted nuthatch
Red-cockaded woodpecker
Rifleman
Rose-ringed parakeet
Rufous scrub-bird
Rufous vanga
Rufous-capped nunlet
Rufous-tailed jacamar
Satyr tragopan
Scarlet macaw
Southern scrub robin
Spotted flycatcher
Striated pardalote
Tawny frogmouth
Toucan barbet
Whip-poor-will
White-breasted mesite
White-helmet shrike
White-necked puffbird
Wild turkey
Willie wagtail
Willow ptarmigan
Winter wren
Wood duck
Yellow-bellied sapsucker
Yellow-breasted chat
Yellow-fronted tinkerbird
Yellowhead
Yellow-rumped thornbill

DESERT

American cliff swallow
American mourning dove
Barn swallow
Cactus wren

California condor
Collared pratincole
Crab plover
Crested caracara
Crimson chat
Egyptian vulture
Emu
Gray catbird
Gray hypocolius
Greater hoopoe-lark
Greater roadrunner
Harris's hawk
House sparrow
Malleefowl
Namaqua sandgrouse
Northern lapwing
Ostrich
Pallas's sandgrouse
Peregrine falcon
Peruvian plantcutter
Rock pigeon
Snow finch
Splendid fairy-wren
Striated grasswren
Verdin
Western scrub-jay
Willie wagtail

GRASSLAND

African broadbill
African palm swift
African paradise-flycatcher
American cliff swallow
American mourning dove
American robin
Anna's hummingbird
Arctic skua
Australasian lark
Australian magpie-lark
Australian pratincole
Bar-breasted mousebird
Barn owl
Barn swallow
Baya weaver
Baywing

Black rail
Black-capped chickadee
Black-capped vireo
Black-crowned barwing
Black-faced sheathbill
Blue bustard
Blue jay
Blue-black grassquit
California condor
Cape sugarbird
Cattle egret
Cedar waxwing
Collared pratincole
Common cuckoo
Common myna
Common waxbill
Corncrake
Crag martin
Crested caracara
Crimson chat
Dollarbird
Eastern phoebe
Eclectus parrot
Egyptian vulture
Emu
Eurasian bittern
European bee-eater
European roller
European starling
European white stork
Fan-tailed berrypecker
Golden-winged sunbird
Gray go-away-bird
Gray hypocolius
Gray potoo
Gray woodpecker
Gray-crowned crane
Great blue heron
Great bustard
Great kiskadee
Green woodhoopoe
Gyrfalcon
Harris's hawk
Helmeted guineafowl
Hoopoe

Horned lark
House sparrow
Jacky winter
Killdeer
King vulture
Laysan finch
Lesser rhea
Loggerhead shrike
Long-billed curlew
Malleefowl
Northern bobwhite quail
Northern lapwing
Northern raven
Northern wryneck
Ostrich
Painted buttonquail
Pallas's sandgrouse
Palmchat
Peregrine falcon
Peruvian plantcutter
Purple sunbird
Rainbow lorikeet
Red-billed oxpecker
Red-legged seriema
Red-winged blackbird
Rock pigeon
Roseate spoonbill
Rose-ringed parakeet
Rosy-breasted longclaw
Rufous-capped nunlet
Sacred ibis
Sandhill crane
Savanna sparrow
Secretary bird
Shoebill
Small buttonquail
Snowy owl
Song sparrow
Southern ground-hornbill
Southern red bishop
Southern scrub robin
Spotted munia
Sprague's pipit
Stonechat
Tawny frogmouth
Village weaver

White-helmet shrike
White-necked puffbird
Wild turkey
Wrentit
Yellow-fronted tinkerbird
Yellow-rumped thornbill
Zebra finch

LAKE AND POND
African jacana
American anhinga
American cliff swallow
American white pelican
Australian magpie-lark
Barn swallow
Baya weaver
Belted kingfisher
Black tern
Black-and-red broadbill
Black-capped donacobius
Canada goose
Chaffinch
Common iora
Common loon
Crag martin
Eurasian bittern
Gray wagtail
Great blue heron
Great cormorant
Great crested grebe
Greater flamingo
Greater thornbird
Hammerhead
Hoatzin
Mallard
Mute swan
Northern wryneck
Osprey
Peregrine falcon
Pheasant-tailed jacana
Red-throated loon
Roseate spoonbill
Rosy-breasted longclaw
Rufous hornero
Sacred ibis

Shoebill
Song sparrow
Sunbittern
Sungrebe
Village weaver
Western grebe
Wood duck
Yellow-breasted chat
Zebra finch

OCEAN
Arctic skua
Blue-footed booby
Chatham mollymawk
Common diving-petrel
Common iora
Common loon
Common murre
Emperor penguin
Great auk
King eider
Laysan albatross
Laysan finch
Macaroni penguin
Magellanic penguin
Magnificent frigatebird
Manx shearwater
Northern fulmar
Northern gannet
Puffin
Red-throated loon
White-tailed tropicbird
Wilson's storm-petrel

RAINFOREST
African paradise-flycatcher
African pitta
Albert's lyrebird
Amazonian umbrellabird
American cliff swallow
Apapane
Arctic warbler
Asian fairy-bluebird
Australasian figbird
Baltimore oriole

Barn owl
Barn swallow
Barred antshrike
Bishop's oo
Black-naped monarch
Blue-crowned motmot
Bornean bristlehead
Buff-spotted flufftail
Cape batis
Common bulbul
Common cuckoo
Common iora
Common sunbird-asity
Common trumpeter
Coppery-chested jacamar
Crag martin
Cuban tody
Dodo
Eclectus parrot
Fan-tailed berrypecker
Feline owlet-nightjar
Fiery minivet
Golden whistler
Golden-winged sunbird
Gray antbird
Gray nightjar
Gray potoo
Gray-breasted mountain-
  toucan
Gray-necked picathartes
Great blue turaco
Greater racket-tailed drongo
Greater thornbird
Guianan cock-of-the-rock
Hairy hermit
Helmeted hornbill
Highland tinamou
Hooded pitta
House sparrow
Kagu
King bird of paradise
King vulture
Kokako
Little slaty flycatcher
Long-tailed manakin
Luzon bleeding heart

Lyre-tailed honeyguide
Malaysian honeyguide
Maleo
Mauritius cuckoo-shrike
Osprey
Peregrine falcon
Purple sunbird
Purple-bearded bee-eater
Rainbow lorikeet
Red-billed scythebill
Ribbon-tailed astrapia
Roseate spoonbill
Rose-ringed parakeet
Ruby-cheeked sunbird
Rufous scrub-bird
Rufous vanga
Rufous-collared kingfisher
Rusty-belted tapaculo
Satin bowerbird
Sharpbill
Southern cassowary
Southern logrunner
Spangled cotinga
Spotted quail-thrush
Square-tailed drongo
Striated pardalote
Stripe-headed rhabdornis
Sulawesi red-knobbed
  hornbill
Sunbittern
Toco toucan
Toucan barbet
Variable pitohui
Victoria's riflebird
Wattled curassow
White-breasted mesite
Willie wagtail
Wire-tailed manakin

RIVER AND STREAM
African broadbill
African pitta
American anhinga
American cliff swallow
American dipper
American white pelican

Australian magpie-lark
Baltimore oriole
Barn swallow
Baya weaver
Black-and-red broadbill
Black-capped donacobius
Canada goose
Cedar waxwing
Chaffinch
Common loon
Crag martin
Crested caracara
Cuban tody
Dusky woodswallow
Eurasian dipper
European bee-eater
European roller
Gray catbird
Gray hypocolius
Gray wagtail
Gray woodpecker
Great blue heron
Great cormorant
Great crested grebe
Green woodhoopoe
Gyrfalcon
Hoatzin
Mute swan
Northern wryneck
Peregrine falcon
Red-breasted nuthatch
Red-throated loon
Roseate spoonbill
Rosy-breasted longclaw
Rufous-capped nunlet
Rufous hornero
Rufous-tailed jacamar
Sacred ibis
Shoebill
Snow bunting
Song sparrow
Southern red bishop
Spotted bowerbird
Striped honeyeater
Sunbittern
Sungrebe

Village weaver
Wood duck
Yellow-breasted chat
Yellow-fronted tinkerbird

SEASHORE
American cliff swallow
American white pelican
Arctic warbler
Australian magpie-lark
Barn swallow
Beach thick-knee
Belted kingfisher
Black tern
Black-faced sheathbill
Blue-footed booby
Brown pelican
Cactus wren
California condor
Collared pratincole
Common iora
Common murre
Crab plover
Crag martin
Cuban tody
Fiery minivet
Golden whistler
Gray wagtail
Great auk
Great blue heron
Great cormorant
Greater flamingo
Gyrfalcon
Hood mockingbird
Horned lark
Magnificent frigatebird
Northern gannet
Osprey
Peregrine falcon
Puffin
Roseate spoonbill
Ruddy turnstone
Sacred ibis
Saunder's gull
Snow bunting

Song sparrow
Splendid fairy-wren
Stonechat
Variable oystercatcher
Victoria's riflebird
White-tailed tropicbird

TUNDRA
American robin
Arctic skua
Arctic warbler
Canada goose
Common loon
Gyrfalcon
Horned lark
Northern raven
Peregrine falcon
Red-throated loon
Ruddy turnstone
Savanna sparrow
Snow bunting
Snowy owl
Willow ptarmigan

WETLAND
African jacana
African snipe
American anhinga
American avocet
American cliff swallow
American white pelican
Australasian lark
Australian magpie-lark
Baltimore oriole
Barn swallow
Black rail
Black tern
Black-faced sheathbill
Black-winged stilt
Canada goose
Cattle egret
Common bulbul
Common iora
Crag martin
Crested caracara

Eurasian bittern
European white stork
Gray wagtail
Gray-crowned crane
Great blue heron
Great cormorant
Greater flamingo
Greater painted snipe
Hairy hermit
Hammerhead
Harris's hawk
Horned screamer
House sparrow
Killdeer

King eider
Leaf-love
Limpkin
Long-billed curlew
Mallard
Mute swan
Northern lapwing
Osprey
Peregrine falcon
Pheasant-tailed jacana
Red-crowned crane
Red-winged blackbird
Roseate spoonbill
Rosy-breasted longclaw

Ruddy turnstone
Rufous-bellied seedsnipe
Sacred ibis
Sandhill crane
Saunder's gull
Shoebill
Sunbittern
Village weaver
Wood duck
Wood stork
Yellow-breasted chat
Zebra finch
Zitting cisticola

Species List by Geographic Range

AFGHANISTAN
Barn swallow
Chaffinch
Common myna
Crag martin
Egyptian vulture
Eurasian golden oriole
European bee-eater
European roller
European starling
Gray hypocolius
Great cormorant
Great crested grebe
Great tit
Greater hoopoe-lark
Hoopoe
House sparrow
Mute swan
Northern lapwing
Northern raven
Peregrine falcon
Rock pigeon
Snow finch
Spotted flycatcher
Spotted nutcracker
Winter wren

ALBANIA
Barn swallow
Chaffinch
Common cuckoo
Corncrake
Crag martin
Dunnock
Egyptian vulture
Eurasian dipper
Eurasian golden oriole
European bee-eater
European roller
European starling
Gray wagtail
Great cormorant
Great crested grebe
Great tit
Hoopoe
Horned lark
House sparrow
Mallard
Northern gannet
Northern lapwing
Northern raven
Northern wryneck
Nuthatch
Peregrine falcon
Red crossbill
Rock pigmeon
Snow bunting
Spotted flycatcher
Stonechat
Winter wren

Zitting cisticola

ALGERIA
Barn swallow
Black-winged stilt
Chaffinch
Common bulbul
Common cuckoo
Common murre
Corncrake
Crag martin
Dunnock
Egyptian vulture
Eurasian bittern
Eurasian golden oriole
European bee-eater
European roller
European starling
Gray wagtail
Great cormorant
Great crested grebe
Greater hoopoe-lark
Hoopoe
House sparrow
Mallard
Northern gannet
Northern lapwing
Northern raven
Northern wryneck
Peregrine falcon

Rock pigeon
Ruddy turnstone
Small buttonquail
Spotted flycatcher
Stonechat
Winter wren
Zitting cisticola

ANDORRA
Great cormorant
Peregrine falcon

ANGOLA
African jacana
African palm swift
African paradise-flycatcher
African snipe
Bar-breasted mousebird
Barn swallow
Black tern
Black-winged stilt
Buff-spotted flufftail
Cattle egret
Collared pratincole
Common bulbul
Common cuckoo
Common waxbill
Eurasian golden oriole
European bee-eater
European roller
European white stork
Gray go-away-bird
Great cormorant
Greater painted snipe
Green woodhoopoe
Hammerhead
Helmeted guineafowl
Hoopoe
House sparrow
Lyre-tailed honeyguide
Namaqua sandgrouse
Osprey
Ostrich
Peregrine falcon
Red-billed oxpecker

Rock pigeon
Rosy-breasted longclaw
Ruddy turnstone
Sacred ibis
Secretary bird
Small buttonquail
Southern ground-hornbill
Southern red bishop
Spotted flycatcher
Square-tailed drongo
Stonechat
Village weaver
White-helmet shrike
Wilson's storm-petrel
Yellow-fronted tinkerbird
Zitting cisticola

ANTARCTICA
Black-faced sheathbill
Emperor penguin
Macaroni penguin
Wilson's storm-petrel

ARGENTINA
American anhinga
American cliff swallow
Arctic skua
Barn owl
Barn swallow
Barred antshrike
Baywing
Black rail
Black-capped donacobius
Black-winged stilt
Blue-black grassquit
Cattle egret
Common diving-petrel
Crested caracara
Emperor penguin
Gray potoo
Great kiskadee
Greater thornbird
Harris's hawk
House sparrow
King vulture
Lesser rhea

Limpkin
Macaroni penguin
Magellanic penguin
Manx shearwater
Peregrine falcon
Red-billed scythebill
Red-legged seriema
Rock pigeon
Roseate spoonbill
Ruddy turnstone
Rufous hornero
Rufous-bellied seedsnipe
Rufous-browed peppershrike
Rufous-tailed jacamar
Sharpbill
Sparkling violet-ear
Sungrebe
Toco toucan
Wilson's storm-petrel
Wood stork

ARMENIA
Barn swallow
Chaffinch
Common cuckoo
Dunnock
Egyptian vulture
Eurasian dipper
Eurasian golden oriole
European bee-eater
European roller
European starling
Great cormorant
Great crested grebe
Great tit
Hoopoe
Horned lark
House sparrow
Northern lapwing
Northern raven
Nuthatch
Peregrine falcon
Red crossbill
Rock pigeon
Snow finch
Stonechat

Winter wren

ASCENSION
White-tailed tropicbird

AUSTRALIA
Albert's lyrebird
Arctic skua
Australasian figbird
Australasian lark
Australian magpie-lark
Australian pratincole
Beach thick-knee
Black-winged stilt
Cattle egret
Common diving-petrel
Crimson chat
Dollarbird
Dusky woodswallow
Eclectus parrot
Emu
European starling
Golden whistler
Gray butcherbird
Gray-crowned babbler
Great cormorant
Great crested grebe
Greater painted snipe
House sparrow
Jacky winter
Laughing kookaburra
Mallard
Malleefowl
Mute swan
Osprey
Painted buttonquail
Peregrine falcon
Rainbow lorikeet
Rock pigeon
Ruddy turnstone
Rufous scrub-bird
Rufous treecreeper
Satin bowerbird
Southern cassowary
Southern logrunner
Southern scrub robin

Splendid fairy-wren
Spotted bowerbird
Spotted quail-thrush
Striated grasswren
Striated pardalote
Striped honeyeater
Tawny frogmouth
Victoria's riflebird
Willie wagtail
Wilson's storm-petrel
Yellow-rumped thornbill
Zebra finch
Zitting cisticola

AUSTRIA
Barn swallow
Black tern
Chaffinch
Collared pratincole
Common cuckoo
Corncrake
Crag martin
Dunnock
Eurasian golden oriole
European bee-eater
European roller
European starling
European white stork
Gray wagtail
Great cormorant
Great crested grebe
Great tit
Hoopoe
House sparrow
Mallard
Mute swan
Northern lapwing
Northern raven
Northern wryneck
Nuthatch
Peregrine falcon
Red crossbill
Rock pigeon
Snow bunting
Snow finch
Spotted flycatcher

Spotted nutcracker
Stonechat
Winter wren

AZERBAIJAN
Barn swallow
Cattle egret
Chaffinch
Common cuckoo
Dunnock
Egyptian vulture
Eurasian dipper
Eurasian golden oriole
European bee-eater
European roller
European starling
European white stork
Great cormorant
Great crested grebe
Great tit
Hoopoe
Horned lark
House sparrow
Mallard
Northern lapwing
Northern raven
Nuthatch
Peregrine falcon
Red crossbill
Red-throated loon
Rock pigeon
Snow finch
Spotted flycatcher
Winter wren

BAHAMAS
American avocet
American mourning dove
American robin
Barn owl
Belted kingfisher
Black-and-white warbler
Black-winged stilt
Blue-gray gnatcatcher
Brown pelican
Cattle egret

Crested caracara
European starling
Gray catbird
House sparrow
Killdeer
Kirtland's warbler
Osprey
Peregrine falcon
Rock pigeon
Ruddy turnstone
White-tailed tropicbird
Wood stork
Yellow-bellied sapsucker

BANGLADESH
Barn swallow
Baya weaver
Black bulbul
Black-naped monarch
Black-winged stilt
Cattle egret
Common cuckoo
Common iora
Common myna
Coppersmith barbet
Crested tree swift
Dollarbird
Eurasian bittern
European white stork
Gray nightjar
Gray wagtail
Great cormorant
Great crested grebe
Great tit
Greater painted snipe
Greater racket-tailed drongo
Green magpie
Hooded pitta
Hoopoe
House sparrow
Mallard
Northern wryneck
Osprey
Peregrine falcon
Pheasant-tailed jacana
Purple sunbird

Rock pigeon
Rose-ringed parakeet
Ruby-cheeked sunbird
Ruddy turnstone
Small buttonquail
Spotted munia
Stonechat
White-throated fantail
Zitting cisticola

BELARUS
Barn swallow
Black tern
Chaffinch
Common cuckoo
Corncrake
Dunnock
Eurasian bittern
Eurasian golden oriole
European roller
European starling
European white stork
Great cormorant
Great crested grebe
Great tit
Hoopoe
House sparrow
Mallard
Northern lapwing
Northern raven
Northern wryneck
Nuthatch
Peregrine falcon
Red crossbill
Rock pigeon
Spotted flycatcher
Spotted nutcracker
Winter wren

BELGIUM
Barn swallow
Black tern
Chaffinch
Common cuckoo
Common murre
Corncrake

Dunnock
Eurasian golden oriole
European roller
European starling
European white stork
Gray wagtail
Great auk
Great cormorant
Great crested grebe
Great tit
Hoopoe
House sparrow
Mallard
Manx shearwater
Mute swan
Northern fulmar
Northern gannet
Northern lapwing
Northern wryneck
Nuthatch
Peregrine falcon
Puffin
Red-throated loon
Rock pigeon
Ruddy turnstone
Spotted flycatcher
Stonechat
Winter wren

BELIZE
American anhinga
American mourning dove
Baltimore oriole
Barn owl
Barred antshrike
Belted kingfisher
Black rail
Black-and-white warbler
Black-winged stilt
Blue-black grassquit
Blue-crowned motmot
Blue-gray gnatcatcher
Brown pelican
Cattle egret
Cedar waxwing
Crested caracara

Gray catbird
Great blue heron
Great kiskadee
Harris's hawk
House sparrow
Killdeer
King vulture
Limpkin
Magnificent frigatebird
Northern raven
Osprey
Peregrine falcon
Plain chachalaca
Rock pigeon
Rose-throated becard
Ruddy turnstone
Rufous-browed peppershrike
Rufous-tailed jacamar
Savanna sparrow
Scarlet macaw
Sungrebe
Whip-poor-will
White-necked puffbird
Wood stork
Yellow-bellied sapsucker
Yellow-breasted chat

BENIN
African jacana
African palm swift
African paradise-flycatcher
Barn swallow
Black tern
Black-winged stilt
Cattle egret
Collared pratincole
Common bulbul
Eurasian bittern
European bee-eater
European roller
Gray parrot
Gray woodpecker
Great blue turaco
Greater painted snipe
Green woodhoopoe
Hammerhead

Helmeted guineafowl
Hoopoe
Leaf-love
Northern wryneck
Osprey
Peregrine falcon
Rose-ringed parakeet
Ruddy turnstone
Sacred ibis
Secretary bird
Small buttonquail
Spotted flycatcher
Square-tailed drongo
Village weaver
White-helmet shrike
Wilson's storm-petrel
Yellow-fronted tinkerbird
Zitting cisticola

BERMUDA
European starling
Gray catbird
House sparrow
White-tailed tropicbird

BHUTAN
Asian fairy-bluebird
Barn swallow
Black-naped monarch
Cattle egret
Common cuckoo
Coppersmith barbet
Crested tree swift
Dollarbird
Eurasian bittern
European white stork
Fire-breasted flowerpecker
Gray nightjar
Great cormorant
Great crested grebe
Greater painted snipe
Hooded pitta
Hoopoe
House sparrow
Northern wryneck
Osprey

Pheasant-tailed jacana
Purple sunbird
Rock pigeon
Rose-ringed parakeet
Satyr tragopan
Small buttonquail
Snow finch
Spotted munia
Spotted nutcracker
Stonechat
White-throated fantail
Zitting cisticola

BOLIVIA
Amazonian umbrellabird
American anhinga
Barn owl
Barn swallow
Barred antshrike
Baywing
Black-capped donacobius
Black-winged stilt
Blue-black grassquit
Blue-crowned motmot
Cattle egret
Chimney swift
Crested caracara
Gray antbird
Gray potoo
Great kiskadee
Greater thornbird
Hairy hermit
Harris's hawk
Horned screamer
House sparrow
Killdeer
King vulture
Lesser rhea
Limpkin
Oilbird
Peregrine falcon
Red-billed scythebill
Red-legged seriema
Roseate spoonbill
Rufous hornero
Rufous-bellied seedsnipe

Rufous-browed peppershrike
Rufous-capped nunlet
Rufous-tailed jacamar
Scarlet macaw
Sharpbill
Spangled cotinga
Sparkling violet-ear
Sunbittern
Sungrebe
Toco toucan
Wattled curassow
White-necked puffbird
Wood stork

BOSNIA AND HERZEGOVINA
Barn swallow
Chaffinch
Common cuckoo
Corncrake
Dunnock
Eurasian dipper
Eurasian golden oriole
European bee-eater
European roller
European starling
European white stork
Gray wagtail
Great cormorant
Great crested grebe
Great tit
Hoopoe
House sparrow
Mallard
Northern lapwing
Northern raven
Northern wryneck
Nuthatch
Peregrine falcon
Red crossbill
Rock pigeon
Snow bunting
Snow finch
Spotted flycatcher
Stonechat
Winter wren

Zitting cisticola

BOTSWANA
African jacana
African palm swift
African paradise-flycatcher
African snipe
Bar-breasted mousebird
Barn swallow
Black-winged stilt
Cattle egret
Common bulbul
Common waxbill
Corncrake
Eurasian golden oriole
European roller
European white stork
Gray go-away-bird
Great cormorant
Greater painted snipe
Green woodhoopoe
Hammerhead
Helmeted guineafowl
Hoopoe
House sparrow
Namaqua sandgrouse
Osprey
Ostrich
Peregrine falcon
Red-billed oxpecker
Rock pigeon
Rosy-breasted longclaw
Sacred ibis
Secretary bird
Small buttonquail
Southern ground-hornbill
Southern red bishop
Spotted flycatcher
Stonechat
Village weaver
White-helmet shrike
Yellow-fronted tinkerbird
Zitting cisticola

BRAZIL
Amazonian umbrellabird

American anhinga
American cliff swallow
Barn owl
Barn swallow
Barred antshrike
Baywing
Black-capped donacobius
Black-winged stilt
Blue-black grassquit
Blue-crowned motmot
Brown pelican
Cattle egret
Chimney swift
Common trumpeter
Coppery-chested jacamar
Crested caracara
Gray antbird
Gray potoo
Great kiskadee
Greater thornbird
Guianan cock-of-the-rock
Hairy hermit
Harris's hawk
Hoatzin
Horned screamer
House sparrow
King vulture
Limpkin
Magellanic penguin
Magnificent frigatebird
Manx shearwater
Oilbird
Osprey
Peregrine falcon
Red-billed scythebill
Red-legged seriema
Rock pigeon
Roseate spoonbill
Ruddy turnstone
Rufous hornero
Rufous-browed peppershrike
Rufous-capped nunlet
Rufous-tailed jacamar
Rusty-belted tapaculo
Scarlet macaw

Sharpbill
Spangled cotinga
Sparkling violet-ear
Sunbittern
Sungrebe
Toco toucan
Wattled curassow
White-necked puffbird
Wilson's storm-petrel
Wire-tailed manakin
Wood stork

BULGARIA
Barn swallow
Black-winged stilt
Chaffinch
Common cuckoo
Corncrake
Dunnock
Egyptian vulture
Eurasian bittern
Eurasian golden oriole
European bee-eater
European roller
European starling
European white stork
Gray wagtail
Great cormorant
Great crested grebe
Great tit
Hoopoe
House sparrow
Mallard
Mute swan
Northern lapwing
Northern raven
Northern wryneck
Nuthatch
Peregrine falcon
Red crossbill
Red-throated loon
Rock pigeon
Snow bunting
Spotted flycatcher
Stonechat
Winter wren

Zitting cisticola

BURKINA FASO
African jacana
African palm swift
Barn swallow
Black-winged stilt
Cattle egret
Collared pratincole
Common bulbul
Egyptian vulture
Eurasian bittern
European bee-eater
European roller
European white stork
Gray woodpecker
Greater painted snipe
Green woodhoopoe
Hammerhead
Helmeted guineafowl
Hoopoe
Northern wryneck
Osprey
Peregrine falcon
Rose-ringed parakeet
Sacred ibis
Secretary bird
Small buttonquail
Village weaver
White-helmet shrike
Yellow-fronted tinkerbird

BURUNDI
African jacana
African palm swift
African paradise-flycatcher
African pitta
African snipe
Bar-breasted mousebird
Barn swallow
Black-winged stilt
Buff-spotted flufftail
Cattle egret
Collared pratincole
Common bulbul
Common cuckoo

Common waxbill
Corncrake
Eurasian golden oriole
European bee-eater
European roller
European white stork
Gray parrot
Gray-crowned crane
Great blue turaco
Great cormorant
Great crested grebe
Green woodhoopoe
Hammerhead
Helmeted guineafowl
Hoopoe
Osprey
Ostrich
Peregrine falcon
Red-billed oxpecker
Sacred ibis
Small buttonquail
Southern ground-hornbill
Southern red bishop
Spotted flycatcher
Stonechat
Village weaver
Yellow-fronted tinkerbird
Zitting cisticola

CAMBODIA
Arctic warbler
Asian fairy-bluebird
Australasian lark
Barn swallow
Baya weaver
Black-naped monarch
Black-winged stilt
Cattle egret
Common cuckoo
Common iora
Common myna
Coppersmith barbet
Crested tree swift
Dollarbird
Fire-breasted flowerpecker
Gray nightjar

Gray wagtail
Great cormorant
Great tit
Greater painted snipe
Greater racket-tailed drongo
Green magpie
Hoopoe
Northern wryneck
Orange-breasted trogon
Osprey
Peregrine falcon
Pheasant-tailed jacana
Purple sunbird
Rock pigeon
Ruby-cheeked sunbird
Ruddy turnstone
Small buttonquail
Spotted munia
Stonechat
White-throated fantail
Zitting cisticola

CAMEROON
African broadbill
African jacana
African palm swift
African paradise-flycatcher
African pitta
Bar-breasted mousebird
Barn swallow
Black tern
Black-winged stilt
Buff-spotted flufftail
Cattle egret
Collared pratincole
Common bulbul
Common waxbill
Eurasian bittern
Eurasian golden oriole
European roller
European white stork
Gray parrot
Gray woodpecker
Gray-necked picathartes
Great blue turaco
Great cormorant

Green woodhoopoe
Hammerhead
Helmeted guineafowl
Hoopoe
Leaf-love
Lyre-tailed honeyguide
Northern wryneck
Osprey
Peregrine falcon
Rose-ringed parakeet
Ruddy turnstone
Sacred ibis
Secretary bird
Small buttonquail
Spotted flycatcher
Square-tailed drongo
Stonechat
Village weaver
White-helmet shrike
Wilson's storm-petrel
Yellow-fronted tinkerbird
Zitting cisticola

CANADA
American cliff swallow
American dipper
American goldfinch
American mourning dove
American robin
American white pelican
Anna's hummingbird
Arctic skua
Baltimore oriole
Barn owl
Barn swallow
Belted kingfisher
Black tern
Black-and-white warbler
Black-capped chickadee
Blue jay
Brown creeper
Bushtit
Canada goose
Cattle egret
Cedar waxwing
Chimney swift

Common loon
Common murre
Eastern bluebird
Eastern phoebe
Eastern screech-owl
European starling
Gray catbird
Great auk
Great blue heron
Great cormorant
Gyrfalcon
Horned lark
House sparrow
House wren
Killdeer
King eider
Loggerhead shrike
Long-billed curlew
Mallard
Manx shearwater
Northern fulmar
Northern gannet
Northern raven
Osprey
Peregrine falcon
Puffin
Red crossbill
Red-breasted nuthatch
Red-throated loon
Red-winged blackbird
Rock pigeon
Ruddy turnstone
Sandhill crane
Savanna sparrow
Snow bunting
Snowy owl
Song sparrow
Sprague's pipit
Western grebe
Whip-poor-will
Willow ptarmigan
Wilson's storm-petrel
Winter wren
Wood duck
Yellow-bellied sapsucker
Yellow-breasted chat

CENTRAL AFRICAN REPUBLIC

African broadbill
African jacana
African palm swift
African paradise-flycatcher
Bar-breasted mousebird
Barn swallow
Black-winged stilt
Buff-spotted flufftail
Cattle egret
Collared pratincole
Common bulbul
Common waxbill
Eurasian bittern
Eurasian golden oriole
European white stork
Gray parrot
Gray woodpecker
Great blue turaco
Great cormorant
Green woodhoopoe
Hammerhead
Helmeted guineafowl
Hoopoe
Leaf-love
Lyre-tailed honeyguide
Northern wryneck
Osprey
Ostrich
Peregrine falcon
Red-billed oxpecker
Rose-ringed parakeet
Sacred ibis
Secretary bird
Shoebill
Small buttonquail
Spotted flycatcher
Square-tailed drongo
Village weaver
White-helmet shrike
Yellow-fronted tinkerbird

CHAD

African jacana
African palm swift
African paradise-flycatcher
Barn swallow
Black-winged stilt
Cattle egret
Collared pratincole
Common bulbul
Egyptian vulture
Eurasian bittern
European white stork
Gray woodpecker
Great cormorant
Green woodhoopoe
Hammerhead
Helmeted guineafowl
Hoopoe
Northern wryneck
Osprey
Ostrich
Peregrine falcon
Rock pigeon
Rose-ringed parakeet
Sacred ibis
Secretary bird
Small buttonquail
Square-tailed drongo
Village weaver
White-helmet shrike
Yellow-fronted tinkerbird

CHILE

Arctic skua
Barn owl
Barn swallow
Black rail
Black-winged stilt
Blue-black grassquit
Brown pelican
Cattle egret
Chimney swift
Common diving-petrel
Crested caracara
Emperor penguin
Harris's hawk
House sparrow
Killdeer
Lesser rhea
Macaroni penguin
Magellanic penguin
Osprey
Peregrine falcon
Rock pigeon
Ruddy turnstone
Rufous-bellied seedsnipe
Sparkling violet-ear
Wilson's storm-petrel

CHINA

Arctic warbler
Asian fairy-bluebird
Barn swallow
Baya weaver
Black bulbul
Black tern
Black-naped monarch
Black-winged stilt
Cattle egret
Chaffinch
Common cuckoo
Common iora
Common murre
Common myna
Coppersmith barbet
Crag martin
Crested tree swift
Dollarbird
Eurasian bittern
Eurasian dipper
Eurasian golden oriole
European roller
European starling
Fire-breasted flowerpecker
Gray nightjar
Gray wagtail
Great bustard
Great cormorant
Great crested grebe
Great tit
Greater painted snipe
Greater racket-tailed drongo
Green magpie

Hooded pitta
Hoopoe
Horned lark
House sparrow
Japanese white-eye
Mallard
Mute swan
Northern lapwing
Northern raven
Northern wryneck
Nuthatch
Orange-breasted trogon
Osprey
Pallas's sandgrouse
Peregrine falcon
Pheasant-tailed jacana
Purple sunbird
Red crossbill
Red-crowned crane
Red-throated loon
Rock pigeon
Rose-ringed parakeet
Ruby-cheeked sunbird
Ruddy turnstone
Satyr tragopan
Saunder's gull
Small buttonquail
Snow bunting
Snow finch
Spotted flycatcher
Spotted munia
Spotted nutcracker
Stonechat
White-throated fantail
Willow ptarmigan
Winter wren
Zitting cisticola

COLOMBIA
Amazonian umbrellabird
American anhinga
Baltimore oriole
Barn owl
Barn swallow
Barred antshrike

Belted kingfisher
Black tern
Black-and-white warbler
Black-capped donacobius
Black-winged stilt
Blue-black grassquit
Blue-crowned motmot
Blue-footed booby
Brown pelican
Cattle egret
Common trumpeter
Coppery-chested jacamar
Crested caracara
Gray antbird
Gray potoo
Gray-breasted mountain-
  toucan
Great blue heron
Great kiskadee
Greater flamingo
Guianan cock-of-the-rock
Hairy hermit
Harris's hawk
Highland tinamou
Hoatzin
Horned lark
Horned screamer
House sparrow
Killdeer
King vulture
Limpkin
Magnificent frigatebird
Oilbird
Osprey
Peregrine falcon
Red-billed scythebill
Roseate spoonbill
Ruddy turnstone
Rufous-browed peppershrike
Rufous-tailed jacamar
Rusty-belted tapaculo
Scarlet macaw
Spangled cotinga
Sparkling violet-ear
Sunbittern
Sungrebe

Toucan barbet
Wattled curassow
White-necked puffbird
Wilson's storm-petrel
Wire-tailed manakin
Wood stork

COMOROS
White-tailed tropicbird

CONGO
African jacana
African palm swift
African paradise-flycatcher
African pitta
Bar-breasted mousebird
Barn swallow
Black tern
Black-winged stilt
Buff-spotted flufftail
Cattle egret
Collared pratincole
Common bulbul
Common cuckoo
Common waxbill
Eurasian golden oriole
Gray parrot
Great blue turaco
Great cormorant
Greater painted snipe
Hammerhead
Helmeted guineafowl
Hoopoe
Leaf-love
Lyre-tailed honeyguide
Osprey
Peregrine falcon
Ruddy turnstone
Sacred ibis
Small buttonquail
Spotted flycatcher
Square-tailed drongo
Stonechat
Village weaver
Zitting cisticola

COSTA RICA

American anhinga
American dipper
American mourning dove
Baltimore oriole
Barn owl
Barn swallow
Barred antshrike
Belted kingfisher
Black guan
Black rail
Black tern
Black-and-white warbler
Black-winged stilt
Blue-black grassquit
Blue-crowned motmot
Blue-footed booby
Brown pelican
Cattle egret
Cedar waxwing
Crested caracara
Gray catbird
Gray potoo
Great blue heron
Great kiskadee
Harris's hawk
Highland tinamou
House sparrow
Killdeer
King vulture
Limpkin
Long-tailed manakin
Magnificent frigatebird
Oilbird
Osprey
Peregrine falcon
Plain chachalaca
Resplendent quetzal
Rock pigeon
Roseate spoonbill
Rose-throated becard
Ruddy turnstone
Rufous-browed peppershrike
Rufous-tailed jacamar
Scarlet macaw
Sharpbill
Sunbittern
Sungrebe
White-necked puffbird
Wood stork
Yellow-bellied sapsucker
Yellow-breasted chat

CROATIA

Barn swallow
Chaffinch
Collared pratincole
Common cuckoo
Corncrake
Dunnock
Eurasian bittern
Eurasian dipper
Eurasian golden oriole
European bee-eater
European roller
European starling
European white stork
Gray wagtail
Great cormorant
Great crested grebe
Great tit
Hoopoe
House sparrow
Mallard
Northern lapwing
Northern raven
Northern wryneck
Nuthatch
Peregrine falcon
Red crossbill
Red-throated loon
Rock pigeon
Snow bunting
Snow finch
Spotted flycatcher
Stonechat
Winter wren
Zitting cisticola

CUBA

American avocet
American mourning dove
Barn owl
Belted kingfisher
Black rail
Black-and-white warbler
Black-winged stilt
Blue-gray gnatcatcher
Brown pelican
Crested caracara
Cuban tody
Gray catbird
Greater flamingo
House sparrow
Ivory-billed woodpecker
Killdeer
Limpkin
Magnificent frigatebird
Northern bobwhite quail
Osprey
Peregrine falcon
Rock pigeon
Roseate spoonbill
Ruddy turnstone
Whip-poor-will
White-tailed tropicbird
Wood duck
Wood stork
Yellow-bellied sapsucker

CYPRUS

European roller
Great cormorant
Northern gannet
Peregrine falcon
Zitting cisticola

CZECH REPUBLIC

Barn swallow
Black tern
Chaffinch
Common cuckoo
Corncrake
Dunnock
Eurasian dipper
Eurasian golden oriole
European roller
European starling

European white stork
Gray wagtail
Great cormorant
Great crested grebe
Great tit
Hoopoe
House sparrow
Mallard
Mute swan
Northern lapwing
Northern raven
Northern wryneck
Nuthatch
Peregrine falcon
Red crossbill
Rock pigeon
Snow bunting
Spotted flycatcher
Spotted nutcracker
Stonechat
Winter wren

DEMOCRATIC REPUBLIC OF THE CONGO

African broadbill
African jacana
African palm swift
African paradise-flycatcher
African pitta
African snipe
Barn swallow
Black tern
Black-winged stilt
Buff-spotted flufftail
Cattle egret
Collared pratincole
Common bulbul
Common cuckoo
Common waxbill
Corncrake
Egyptian vulture
Eurasian bittern
Eurasian golden oriole
European bee-eater
European roller

European white stork
Golden-winged sunbird
Gray go-away-bird
Gray parrot
Gray woodpecker
Gray-crowned crane
Great blue turaco
Great cormorant
Great crested grebe
Greater painted snipe
Green woodhoopoe
Hammerhead
Helmeted guineafowl
Hoopoe
House sparrow
Leaf-love
Lyre-tailed honeyguide
Northern wryneck
Osprey
Peregrine falcon
Red-billed oxpecker
Ruddy turnstone
Sacred ibis
Secretary bird
Shoebill
Small buttonquail
Southern ground-hornbill
Southern red bishop
Spotted flycatcher
Square-tailed drongo
Stonechat
Village weaver
White-helmet shrike
Yellow-fronted tinkerbird
Zitting cisticola

DENMARK

Barn swallow
Canada goose
Chaffinch
Common cuckoo
Common murre
Corncrake
Dunnock
Eurasian bittern
European roller

European starling
Great auk
Great cormorant
Great crested grebe
Great tit
House sparrow
Mallard
Manx shearwater
Mute swan
Northern fulmar
Northern gannet
Northern lapwing
Northern wryneck
Nuthatch
Peregrine falcon
Puffin
Red crossbill
Red-throated loon
Rock pigeon
Snow bunting
Spotted flycatcher
Stonechat
Winter wren

DJIBOUTI

African paradise-flycatcher
African snipe
Bar-breasted mousebird
Cattle egret
Collared pratincole
Common bulbul
Corncrake
Crab plovers
Egyptian vulture
European roller
Great cormorant
Greater flamingo
Greater hoopoe-lark
Green woodhoopoe
Hammerhead
Hoopoe
Osprey
Ostrich
Peregrine falcon
Red-billed oxpecker
Ruddy turnstone

Sacred ibis
Secretary bird
Small buttonquail
Stonechat
Wilson's storm-petrel

DOMINICAN REPUBLIC
American mourning dove
Barn owl
Belted kingfisher
Black rail
Black-and-white warbler
Black-winged stilt
Brown pelican
Cattle egret
Crested caracara
Greater flamingo
House sparrow
Killdeer
Limpkin
Magnificent frigatebird
Osprey
Palmchat
Peregrine falcon
Rock pigeon
Roseate spoonbill
Ruddy turnstone
White-tailed tropicbird
Wilson's storm-petrel
Wood stork
Yellow-bellied sapsucker

ECUADOR
Amazonian umbrellabird
American anhinga
Barn owl
Barn swallow
Barred antshrike
Black tern
Black-winged stilt
Blue-black grassquit
Blue-crowned motmot
Blue-footed booby
Brown pelican
Cattle egret
Chimney swift

Common trumpeter
Coppery-chested jacamar
Crested caracara
Gray antbird
Gray potoo
Gray-breasted mountain-
  toucan
Great kiskadee
Greater flamingo
Harris's hawk
Highland tinamou
Hood mockingbird
Horned screamer
House sparrow
Killdeer
King vulture
Limpkin
Magnificent frigatebird
Oilbird
Osprey
Peregrine falcon
Red-billed scythebill
Roseate spoonbill
Ruddy turnstone
Rufous-bellied seedsnipe
Rufous-browed peppershrike
Rufous-tailed jacamar
Rusty-belted tapaculo
Scarlet macaw
Sharpbill
Spangled cotinga
Sparkling violet-ear
Sunbittern
Sungrebe
Toucan barbet
White-necked puffbird
Wilson's storm-petrel
Wire-tailed manakin

EGYPT
Barn swallow
Black tern
Black-winged stilt
Cattle egret
Common bulbul
Corncrake

Egyptian vulture
Eurasian bittern
European roller
Gray wagtail
Great cormorant
Great crested grebe
Greater flamingo
Greater hoopoe-lark
Greater painted snipe
Hoopoe
House sparrow
Mallard
Northern gannet
Northern lapwing
Northern raven
Osprey
Peregrine falcon
Rock pigeon
Ruddy turnstone
Stonechat
Zitting cisticola

EL SALVADOR
American anhinga
American mourning dove
Baltimore oriole
Barn owl
Barred antshrike
Belted kingfisher
Black rail
Black tern
Black-and-white warbler
Black-winged stilt
Blue-black grassquit
Blue-crowned motmot
Blue-footed booby
Blue-gray gnatcatcher
Brown creeper
Brown pelican
Cattle egret
Cedar waxwing
Crested caracara
Great blue heron
Great kiskadee
Harris's hawk
House sparrow

Killdeer
King vulture
Limpkin
Long-tailed manakin
Magnificent frigatebird
Northern raven
Osprey
Peregrine falcon
Rock pigeon
Roseate spoonbill
Rose-throated becard
Ruddy turnstone
Rufous-browed peppershrike
Rufous-tailed jacamar
Sunbittern
Sungrebe
Whip-poor-will
White-necked puffbird
Wood stork
Yellow-bellied sapsucker
Yellow-breasted chat

EQUATORIAL GUINEA
African jacana
African palm swift
African paradise-flycatcher
African pitta
Barn swallow
Black tern
Black-winged stilt
Cattle egret
Collared pratincole
Common bulbul
Common waxbill
Gray parrot
Gray-necked picathartes
Great blue turaco
Great cormorant
Great crested grebe
Hammerhead
Helmeted guineafowl
Leaf-love
Lyre-tailed honeyguide
Osprey
Peregrine falcon
Ruddy turnstone

Sacred ibis
Spotted flycatcher
Village weaver
Wilson's storm-petrel
Zitting cisticola

ERITREA
African paradise-flycatcher
African snipe
Bar-breasted mousebird
Cattle egret
Collared pratincole
Common bulbul
Corncrake
Crab plovers
Egyptian vulture
Eurasian bittern
European roller
European white stork
Gray woodpecker
Greater flamingo
Greater hoopoe-lark
Greater painted snipe
Green woodhoopoe
Hammerhead
Helmeted guineafowl
Hoopoe
Osprey
Ostrich
Peregrine falcon
Red-billed oxpecker
Rock pigeon
Rose-ringed parakeet
Ruddy turnstone
Sacred ibis
Secretary bird
Small buttonquail
Stonechat
White-helmet shrike
Wilson's storm-petrel
Zitting cisticola

ESTONIA
Barn swallow
Black tern
Chaffinch

Common cuckoo
Common murre
Corncrake
Dunnock
Eurasian bittern
Eurasian dipper
Eurasian golden oriole
European roller
European starling
European white stork
Great cormorant
Great crested grebe
Great tit
Hoopoe
House sparrow
Mallard
Northern fulmar
Northern gannet
Northern lapwing
Northern raven
Northern wryneck
Nuthatch
Osprey
Red crossbill
Rock pigeon
Spotted flycatcher
Willow ptarmigan
Winter wren

ETHIOPIA
African jacana
African palm swift
African paradise-flycatcher
African snipe
Bar-breasted mousebird
Barn swallow
Black-winged stilt
Buff-spotted flufftail
Cattle egret
Collared pratincole
Common bulbul
Common waxbill
Corncrake
Egyptian vulture
Eurasian bittern
European roller

European white stork
Gray wagtail
Gray woodpecker
Great cormorant
Great crested grebe
Greater painted snipe
Green woodhoopoe
Hammerhead
Helmeted guineafowl
Hoopoe
Northern wryneck
Osprey
Ostrich
Peregrine falcon
Red-billed oxpecker
Rose-ringed parakeet
Sacred ibis
Secretary bird
Small buttonquail
Stonechat
Village weaver
White-helmet shrike
Yellow-fronted tinkerbird
Zitting cisticola

FALKLAND ISLANDS
Arctic skua
Crested caracara
Emperor penguin
House sparrow
Macaroni penguin
Magellanic penguin
Peregrine falcon

FIJI
European starling
Golden whistler
White-tailed tropicbird

FINLAND
Arctic warbler
Barn swallow
Chaffinch
Common cuckoo
Common murre

Corncrake
Dunnock
Eurasian bittern
Eurasian dipper
European roller
European starling
Gray wagtail
Great cormorant
Great crested grebe
Great tit
Gyrfalcon
Horned lark
House sparrow
Mute swan
Northern fulmar
Northern gannet
Northern lapwing
Northern raven
Northern wryneck
Osprey
Peregrine falcon
Puffin
Red crossbill
Red-throated loon
Rock pigeon
Ruddy turnstone
Spotted flycatcher
Spotted nutcracker
Willow ptarmigan
Winter wren

FRANCE
Barn swallow
Black tern
Black-winged stilt
Cattle egret
Chaffinch
Common cuckoo
Common loon
Common murre
Corncrake
Dunnock
Eurasian bittern
Eurasian dipper
Eurasian golden oriole
European bee-eater

European roller
European starling
European white stork
Gray wagtail
Great auk
Great cormorant
Great crested grebe
Great tit
Greater flamingo
Hoopoe
House sparrow
Mallard
Manx shearwater
Mute swan
Northern fulmar
Northern gannet
Northern lapwing
Northern raven
Northern wryneck
Nuthatch
Osprey
Peregrine falcon
Puffin
Red crossbill
Red-throated loon
Rock pigeon
Ruddy turnstone
Snow finch
Spotted flycatcher
Stonechat
Wilson's storm-petrel
Winter wren
Zitting cisticola

FRENCH GUIANA
American anhinga
Barn owl
Barn swallow
Barred antshrike
Black tern
Black-capped donacobius
Black-winged stilt
Blue-black grassquit
Blue-crowned motmot
Brown pelican
Cattle egret

Common trumpeter
Crested caracara
Gray antbird
Gray potoo
Great kiskadee
Guianan cock-of-the-rock
Hairy hermit
Hoatzin
King vulture
Limpkin
Magnificent frigatebird
Osprey
Peregrine falcon
Roseate spoonbill
Ruddy turnstone
Rufous-browed peppershrike
Rufous-tailed jacamar
Scarlet macaw
Spangled cotinga
Sunbittern
Sungrebe
White-necked puffbird
Wilson's storm-petrel
Wood stork

GABON

African broadbill
African jacana
African palm swift
African paradise-flycatcher
African pitta
Bar-breasted mousebird
Barn swallow
Black tern
Black-winged stilt
Buff-spotted flufftail
Cattle egret
Collared pratincole
Common bulbul
Common cuckoo
Common waxbill
Eurasian golden oriole
Gray parrot
Gray-necked picathartes
Great blue turaco
Great cormorant

Greater painted snipe
Hammerhead
Helmeted guineafowl
Hoopoe
Leaf-love
Lyre-tailed honeyguide
Osprey
Peregrine falcon
Ruddy turnstone
Sacred ibis
Small buttonquail
Spotted flycatcher
Square-tailed drongo
Stonechat
Village weaver
Wilson's storm-petrel
Zitting cisticola

GAMBIA

African palm swift
African paradise-flycatcher
Black tern
Black-winged stilt
Cattle egret
Collared pratincole
Common bulbul
Egyptian vulture
Eurasian bittern
Gray woodpecker
Greater flamingo
Green woodhoopoe
Hammerhead
Helmeted guineafowl
Hoopoe
Leaf-love
Magnificent frigatebird
Northern wryneck
Osprey
Peregrine falcon
Rose-ringed parakeet
Ruddy turnstone
Sacred ibis
Secretary bird
Small buttonquail
Village weaver
White-helmet shrike

Wilson's storm-petrel
Yellow-fronted tinkerbird

GEORGIA

Barn swallow
Chaffinch
Common cuckoo
Corncrake
Dunnock
Egyptian vulture
Eurasian dipper
Eurasian golden oriole
European bee-eater
European roller
European starling
Gray wagtail
Great cormorant
Great crested grebe
Great tit
Hoopoe
Horned lark
House sparrow
Northern raven
Northern wryneck
Nuthatch
Peregrine falcon
Red crossbill
Rock pigeon
Snow finch
Spotted flycatcher
Stonechat
Winter wren

GERMANY

Barn swallow
Black tern
Canada goose
Chaffinch
Common cuckoo
Common murre
Corncrake
Dunnock
Eurasian bittern
Eurasian dipper
Eurasian golden oriole

European roller
European starling
European white stork
Gray wagtail
Great auk
Great bustard
Great cormorant
Great crested grebe
Great tit
Hoopoe
House sparrow
Mallard
Manx shearwater
Mute swan
Northern fulmar
Northern gannet
Northern lapwing
Northern raven
Northern wryneck
Nuthatch
Peregrine falcon
Puffin
Red crossbill
Red-throated loon
Rock pigeon
Ruddy turnstone
Snow bunting
Snow finch
Spotted flycatcher
Spotted nutcracker
Stonechat
Winter wren

GHANA
African broadbill
African jacana
African palm swift
African paradise-flycatcher
African pitta
Barn swallow
Black tern
Black-winged stilt
Cattle egret
Collared pratincole
Common bulbul
Eurasian bittern

European bee-eater
European roller
Gray parrot
Gray woodpecker
Great blue turaco
Greater painted snipe
Green woodhoopoe
Hammerhead
Helmeted guineafowl
Hoopoe
Leaf-love
Northern wryneck
Osprey
Peregrine falcon
Rose-ringed parakeet
Ruddy turnstone
Sacred ibis
Secretary bird
Small buttonquail
Spotted flycatcher
Square-tailed drongo
Village weaver
White-helmet shrike
Wilson's storm-petrel
Yellow-fronted tinkerbird
Zitting cisticola

GREECE
Barn swallow
Chaffinch
Common cuckoo
Corncrake
Crag martin
Dunnock
Egyptian vulture
Eurasian bittern
Eurasian dipper
Eurasian golden oriole
European bee-eater
European roller
European starling
Gray wagtail
Great cormorant
Great crested grebe
Great tit
Hoopoe

Horned lark
House sparrow
Mallard
Mute swan
Northern gannet
Northern lapwing
Northern raven
Northern wryneck
Peregrine falcon
Red crossbill
Rock pigeon
Spotted flycatcher
Stonechat
Winter wren
Zitting cisticola

GREENLAND
Arctic skua
Common loon
Common murre
Great auk
Great cormorant
Gyrfalcon
King eider
Mallard
Manx shearwater
Northern fulmar
Northern gannet
Northern raven
Peregrine falcon
Puffin
Red-throated loon
Ruddy turnstone
Snow bunting
Snowy owl

GUATEMALA
American anhinga
American dipper
American mourning dove
American robin
Baltimore oriole
Barn owl
Barred antshrike
Belted kingfisher
Black rail

Black tern
Black-and-white warbler
Black-capped vireo
Black-winged stilt
Blue-black grassquit
Blue-crowned motmot
Blue-footed booby
Blue-gray gnatcatcher
Brown creeper
Brown pelican
Cattle egret
Cedar waxwing
Crested caracara
Gray catbird
Great blue heron
Great kiskadee
Harris's hawk
House sparrow
Killdeer
King vulture
Limpkin
Long-tailed manakin
Magnificent frigatebird
Northern raven
Osprey
Peregrine falcon
Plain chachalaca
Resplendent quetzal
Rock pigeon
Roseate spoonbill
Rose-throated becard
Ruddy turnstone
Rufous-browed peppershrike
Rufous-tailed jacamar
Savanna sparrow
Scarlet macaw
Sunbittern
Sungrebe
Whip-poor-will
White-necked puffbird
Wood stork
Yellow-bellied sapsucker
Yellow-breasted chat

GUINEA
African palm swift

African paradise-flycatcher
Barn swallow
Black tern
Black-winged stilt
Buff-spotted flufftail
Cattle egret
Collared pratincole
Common bulbul
Common waxbill
Eurasian bittern
European bee-eater
European roller
Gray parrot
Gray woodpecker
Great blue turaco
Green woodhoopoe
Hammerhead
Helmeted guineafowl
Hoopoe
Leaf-love
Northern wryneck
Osprey
Peregrine falcon
Rock pigeon
Rose-ringed parakeet
Ruddy turnstone
Sacred ibis
Small buttonquail
Square-tailed drongo
Stonechat
Village weaver
White-helmet shrike
Wilson's storm-petrel
Yellow-fronted tinkerbird

GUINEA-BISSAU
African palm swift
African paradise-flycatcher
Barn swallow
Black tern
Black-winged stilt
Cattle egret
Collared pratincole
Common bulbul
Common waxbill
Egyptian vulture

Eurasian bittern
Gray parrot
Gray woodpecker
Green woodhoopoe
Hammerhead
Helmeted guineafowl
Hoopoe
Leaf-love
Magnificent frigatebird
Northern wryneck
Osprey
Peregrine falcon
Rose-ringed parakeet
Ruddy turnstone
Sacred ibis
Small buttonquail
Square-tailed drongo
Village weaver
Wilson's storm-petrel

GUYANA
American anhinga
Barn owl
Barn swallow
Barred antshrike
Belted kingfisher
Black tern
Black-capped donacobius
Black-winged stilt
Blue-black grassquit
Blue-crowned motmot
Brown pelican
Cattle egret
Common trumpeter
Crested caracara
Gray antbird
Gray potoo
Great kiskadee
Greater flamingo
Guianan cock-of-the-rock
Hairy hermit
Hoatzin
King vulture
Limpkin
Magnificent frigatebird
Oilbird

Osprey
Peregrine falcon
Roseate spoonbill
Ruddy turnstone
Rufous-browed peppershrike
Rufous-tailed jacamar
Scarlet macaw
Sharpbill
Spangled cotinga
Sparkling violet-ear
Sunbittern
Sungrebe
White-necked puffbird
Wilson's storm-petrel
Wood stork

HAITI
American mourning dove
Barn owl
Belted kingfisher
Black-and-white warbler
Black-winged stilt
Brown pelican
Cattle egret
Crested caracara
Greater flamingo
House sparrow
Killdeer
Limpkin
Magnificent frigatebird
Osprey
Palmchat
Peregrine falcon
Rock pigeon
Roseate spoonbill
Ruddy turnstone
White-tailed tropicbird
Wood stork
Yellow-bellied sapsucker

HONDURAS
American anhinga
American mourning dove
Baltimore oriole
Barn owl
Barred antshrike

Belted kingfisher
Black tern
Black-and-white warbler
Black-winged stilt
Blue-black grassquit
Blue-crowned motmot
Blue-footed booby
Blue-gray gnatcatcher
Brown creeper
Brown pelican
Cattle egret
Cedar waxwing
Crested caracara
Gray catbird
Great blue heron
Great kiskadee
Harris's hawk
House sparrow
Killdeer
King vulture
Limpkin
Long-tailed manakin
Magnificent frigatebird
Northern raven
Osprey
Peregrine falcon
Plain chachalaca
Resplendent quetzal
Rock pigeon
Roseate spoonbill
Rose-throated becard
Ruddy turnstone
Rufous-browed peppershrike
Rufous-tailed jacamar
Scarlet macaw
Sunbittern
Sungrebe
Whip-poor-will
White-necked puffbird
Wood stork
Yellow-bellied sapsucker
Yellow-breasted chat

HUNGARY
Barn swallow
Black tern

Chaffinch
Collared pratincole
Common cuckoo
Corncrake
Dunnock
Eurasian golden oriole
European bee-eater
European roller
European starling
European white stork
Gray wagtail
Great bustard
Great cormorant
Great crested grebe
Great tit
Hoopoe
House sparrow
Mallard
Northern lapwing
Northern raven
Northern wryneck
Nuthatch
Peregrine falcon
Red crossbill
Rock pigeon
Snow bunting
Spotted flycatcher
Stonechat
Winter wren

ICELAND
Arctic skua
Common loon
Common murre
European starling
Great auk
Great cormorant
Gyrfalcon
King eider
Mallard
Manx shearwater
Northern fulmar
Northern gannet
Northern raven
Puffin
Red-throated loon

Snow bunting

INDIA
Asian fairy-bluebird
Barn swallow
Baya weaver
Black bulbul
Black-naped monarch
Black-winged stilt
Cattle egret
Chaffinch
Collared pratincole
Common cuckoo
Common iora
Common myna
Coppersmith barbet
Crab plovers
Crag martin
Crested tree swift
Dollarbird
Egyptian vulture
Eurasian bittern
Eurasian golden oriole
European bee-eater
European roller
European starling
European white stork
Fire-breasted flowerpecker
Gray hypocolius
Gray nightjar
Gray wagtail
Great cormorant
Great crested grebe
Great tit
Greater flamingo
Greater painted snipe
Greater racket-tailed drongo
Green magpie
Hooded pitta
Hoopoe
House sparrow
Mallard
Northern lapwing
Northern raven
Northern wryneck
Osprey

Peregrine falcon
Pheasant-tailed jacana
Purple sunbird
Rock pigeon
Rose-ringed parakeet
Ruby-cheeked sunbird
Ruddy turnstone
Satyr tragopan
Small buttonquail
Spotted munia
Spotted nutcracker
Stonechat
White-throated fantail
Wilson's storm-petrel
Zitting cisticola

INDONESIA
Arctic warbler
Asian fairy-bluebird
Australasian figbird
Australasian lark
Australian magpie-lark
Australian pratincole
Barn swallow
Barred eagle-owl
Baya weaver
Beach thick-knee
Black-and-red broadbill
Black-naped monarch
Black-winged stilt
Bornean bristlehead
Cattle egret
Common iora
Coppersmith barbet
Dollarbird
Eclectus parrot
Fan-tailed berrypecker
Feline owlet-nightjar
Fiery minivet
Fire-breasted flowerpecker
Golden whistler
Gray nightjar
Gray wagtail
Gray-crowned babbler
Great cormorant
Great tit

Greater painted snipe
Greater racket-tailed drongo
Green magpie
Helmeted hornbill
Hooded pitta
King bird of paradise
Malaysian honeyguide
Maleo
Orange-breasted trogon
Osprey
Peregrine falcon
Pheasant-tailed jacana
Purple-bearded bee-eater
Rainbow lorikeet
Rock pigeon
Ruby-cheeked sunbird
Ruddy turnstone
Rufous-collared kingfisher
Small buttonquail
Southern cassowary
Spotted munia
Sulawesi red-knobbed
  hornbill
Variable pitohui
White-throated fantail
Willie wagtail
Wilson's storm-petrel
Zebra finch
Zitting cisticola

IRAN
Barn swallow
Black-winged stilt
Cattle egret
Chaffinch
Common cuckoo
Common myna
Corncrake
Crab plovers
Crag martin
Dunnock
Egyptian vulture
Eurasian dipper
Eurasian golden oriole
European bee-eater
European roller

European starling
European white stork
Gray hypocolius
Gray wagtail
Great bustard
Great cormorant
Great crested grebe
Great tit
Greater flamingo
Greater hoopoe-lark
Hoopoe
Horned lark
House sparrow
Mallard
Mute swan
Northern lapwing
Northern raven
Nuthatch
Osprey
Peregrine falcon
Purple sunbird
Red-throated loon
Rock pigeon
Ruddy turnstone
Snow finch
Spotted flycatcher
Stonechat
Wilson's storm-petrel
Winter wren

IRAQ
Black-winged stilt
Cattle egret
Chaffinch
Collared pratincole
Corncrake
Dunnock
Egyptian vulture
Eurasian bittern
European bee-eater
European roller
European starling
Gray hypocolius
Gray wagtail
Great cormorant
Great crested grebe

Greater hoopoe-lark
Hoopoe
House sparrow
Mallard
Northern lapwing
Nuthatch
Osprey
Peregrine falcon
Rock pigeon
Spotted flycatcher
Stonechat

IRELAND
Barn owl
Barn swallow
Canada goose
Chaffinch
Common cuckoo
Common loon
Common murre
Corncrake
Dunnock
Eurasian dipper
European starling
Gray wagtail
Great auk
Great cormorant
Great crested grebe
Great tit
House sparrow
Mallard
Manx shearwater
Mute swan
Northern gannet
Northern lapwing
Northern raven
Peregrine falcon
Puffin
Red-throated loon
Rock pigeon
Ruddy turnstone
Spotted flycatcher
Stonechat
Willow ptarmigan
Winter wren

ISRAEL
Black-winged stilt
Cattle egret
Collared pratincole
Common cuckoo
Egyptian vulture
European bee-eater
European roller
Great cormorant
Greater flamingo
Hoopoe
Horned lark
House sparrow
Mallard
Northern gannet
Northern lapwing
Peregrine falcon
Rock pigeon
Stonechat
Winter wren
Zitting cisticola

ITALY
Barn swallow
Black tern
Black-winged stilt
Cattle egret
Chaffinch
Common cuckoo
Corncrake
Crag martin
Dunnock
Egyptian vulture
Eurasian dipper
Eurasian golden oriole
European bee-eater
European roller
European starling
Gray wagtail
Great cormorant
Great crested grebe
Great tit
Greater flamingo
Hoopoe
House sparrow
Mallard

Mute swan
Northern gannet
Northern lapwing
Northern raven
Northern wryneck
Nuthatch
Peregrine falcon
Red crossbill
Rock pigeon
Snow finch
Spotted flycatcher
Stonechat
Winter wren
Zitting cisticola

IVORY COAST
African broadbill
African jacana
African palm swift
African paradise-flycatcher
African pitta
Barn swallow
Black tern
Black-winged stilt
Cattle egret
Collared pratincole
Common bulbul
Common waxbill
Eurasian bittern
European bee-eater
European roller
Gray parrot
Gray woodpecker
Great blue turaco
Green woodhoopoe
Hammerhead
Hoopoe
Leaf-love
Lyre-tailed honeyguide
Northern wryneck
Osprey
Peregrine falcon
Rose-ringed parakeet
Ruddy turnstone
Sacred ibis
Small buttonquail

Spotted flycatcher
Square-tailed drongo
Village weaver
White-helmet shrike
Wilson's storm-petrel
Yellow-fronted tinkerbird
Zitting cisticola

JAMAICA
American mourning dove
Barn owl
Belted kingfisher
Black rail
Black-and-white warbler
Brown pelican
Cattle egret
Crested caracara
European starling
Gray catbird
House sparrow
Killdeer
Magnificent frigatebird
Osprey
Peregrine falcon
Rock pigeon
Ruddy turnstone
White-tailed tropicbird
Wood stork

JAPAN
Arctic warbler
Barn swallow
Cattle egret
Common murre
Dollarbird
Eurasian bittern
Gray nightjar
Gray wagtail
Great cormorant
Great tit
Greater painted snipe
Hoopoe
Japanese white-eye
Laysan albatross
Mallard
Mute swan

Northern fulmar
Northern lapwing
Northern raven
Nuthatch
Osprey
Peregrine falcon
Red crossbill
Red-crowned crane
Red-throated loon
Rock pigeon
Saunder's gull
Spotted nutcracker
Stonechat
Willow ptarmigan
Winter wren

JORDAN
Black-winged stilt
Cattle egret
Collared pratincole
Common bulbul
Egyptian vulture
European bee-eater
European roller
Gray wagtail
Great cormorant
Hoopoe
House sparrow
Northern gannet
Northern lapwing
Peregrine falcon
Rock pigeon
Stonechat
Winter wren

KAZAKHSTAN
Barn swallow
Black tern
Black-winged stilt
Chaffinch
Collared pratincole
Common cuckoo
Common myna
Corncrake
Egyptian vulture
Eurasian bittern

Eurasian golden oriole
European bee-eater
European roller
European starling
European white stork
Great cormorant
Great crested grebe
Great tit
Greater flamingo
Hoopoe
Horned lark
House sparrow
Mallard
Mute swan
Northern raven
Pallas's sandgrouse
Peregrine falcon
Red crossbill
Red-throated loon
Rock pigeon
Snow bunting
Spotted flycatcher
Spotted nutcracker
Stonechat
Willow ptarmigan
Winter wren

KENYA

African broadbill
African jacana
African palm swift
African paradise-flycatcher
African snipe
Bar-breasted mousebird
Barn swallow
Black-winged stilt
Buff-spotted flufftail
Cattle egret
Collared pratincole
Common bulbul
Common cuckoo
Common waxbill
Corncrake
Crab plovers
Egyptian vulture
Eurasian golden oriole

European bee-eater
European roller
European white stork
Golden-winged sunbird
Gray parrot
Gray wagtail
Gray woodpecker
Gray-crowned crane
Great blue turaco
Great cormorant
Great crested grebe
Greater flamingo
Greater painted snipe
Green woodhoopoe
Hammerhead
Helmeted guineafowl
Hoopoe
Northern wryneck
Osprey
Ostrich
Peregrine falcon
Red-billed oxpecker
Rock pigeon
Rosy-breasted longclaw
Ruddy turnstone
Sacred ibis
Secretary bird
Shoebill
Small buttonquail
Southern ground-hornbill
Southern red bishop
Spotted flycatcher
Square-tailed drongo
Stonechat
Village weaver
White-helmet shrike
Wilson's storm-petrel
Zitting cisticola

KUWAIT

Black-winged stilt
Cattle egret
Chaffinch
Collared pratincole
Crab plovers
Eurasian bittern

European roller
Gray wagtail
Great cormorant
Great crested grebe
Greater hoopoe-lark
House sparrow
Mallard
Northern lapwing
Nuthatch
Osprey
Peregrine falcon
Rock pigeon
Ruddy turnstone
Spotted flycatcher
Wilson's storm-petrel
Zitting cisticola

KYRGYZSTAN

Barn swallow
Chaffinch
Common cuckoo
Crag martin
Egyptian vulture
Eurasian bittern
Eurasian golden oriole
European roller
European starling
Gray wagtail
Great cormorant
Great crested grebe
Great tit
Hoopoe
House sparrow
Mallard
Northern raven
Pallas's sandgrouse
Peregrine falcon
Rock pigeon
Snow finch
Spotted flycatcher
Stonechat
Winter wren

LAOS

Asian fairy-bluebird
Australasian lark

Barn swallow
Baya weaver
Black bulbul
Black-and-red broadbill
Black-crowned barwing
Black-naped monarch
Black-winged stilt
Cattle egret
Common cuckoo
Common iora
Common myna
Coppersmith barbet
Crested tree swift
Dollarbird
Eurasian bittern
Fire-breasted flowerpecker
Gray nightjar
Gray wagtail
Great cormorant
Greater painted snipe
Greater racket-tailed drongo
Green magpie
Hoopoe
Northern wryneck
Orange-breasted trogon
Peregrine falcon
Pheasant-tailed jacana
Purple sunbird
Rock pigeon
Ruby-cheeked sunbird
Small buttonquail
Spotted munia
Stonechat
White-throated fantail
Zitting cisticola

LATVIA
Barn swallow
Black tern
Chaffinch
Common cuckoo
Common murre
Corncrake
Dunnock
Eurasian bittern
Eurasian dipper

Eurasian golden oriole
European roller
European starling
European white stork
Great cormorant
Great crested grebe
Great tit
Hoopoe
House sparrow
Mallard
Northern fulmar
Northern gannet
Northern lapwing
Northern raven
Northern wryneck
Nuthatch
Red crossbill
Rock pigeon
Spotted flycatcher
Spotted nutcracker
Willow ptarmigan
Winter wren

LEBANON
Black-winged stilt
Cattle egret
Collared pratincole
Common bulbul
Common cuckoo
Dunnock
Egyptian vulture
European bee-eater
European roller
Great cormorant
Greater flamingo
Hoopoe
Horned lark
House sparrow
Mallard
Northern gannet
Northern lapwing
Nuthatch
Peregrine falcon
Rock pigeon
Spotted flycatcher
Stonechat

Winter wren

LESOTHO
African jacana
African snipe
Barn swallow
Black-winged stilt
Blue bustard
Cattle egret
Common cuckoo
Common waxbill
Corncrake
European roller
European white stork
Great cormorant
Great crested grebe
Greater painted snipe
Green woodhoopoe
Hammerhead
Helmeted guineafowl
Hoopoe
House sparrow
Osprey
Peregrine falcon
Sacred ibis
Secretary bird
Small buttonquail
Southern red bishop
Spotted flycatcher
Stonechat
Village weaver
Zitting cisticola

LESSER ANTILLES
Barn owl
Belted kingfisher
Brown pelican
Cattle egret
Crested caracara
Greater flamingo
House sparrow
Killdeer
Magnificent frigatebird
Osprey
Peregrine falcon
Rock pigeon

Ruddy turnstone
White-tailed tropicbird
Wood stork

LIBERIA
African broadbill
African palm swift
African paradise-flycatcher
African pitta
Barn swallow
Black tern
Black-winged stilt
Buff-spotted flufftail
Cattle egret
Collared pratincole
Common bulbul
Common waxbill
Eurasian bittern
Gray parrot
Gray woodpecker
Great blue turaco
Hammerhead
Leaf-love
Lyre-tailed honeyguide
Northern wryneck
Osprey
Peregrine falcon
Ruddy turnstone
Sacred ibis
Small buttonquail
Spotted flycatcher
Village weaver
Wilson's storm-petrel

LIBYA
Barn swallow
Black-winged stilt
Common bulbul
Crag martin
Egyptian vulture
Eurasian bittern
Gray wagtail
Greater hoopoe-lark
House sparrow
Mallard
Northern gannet

Northern lapwing
Northern raven
Peregrine falcon
Rock pigeon
Ruddy turnstone
Stonechat
Winter wren

LIECHTENSTEIN
Barn swallow
Black tern
Chaffinch
Common cuckoo
Corncrake
Dunnock
Eurasian golden oriole
European roller
European starling
Gray wagtail
Great cormorant
Great crested grebe
Great tit
Hoopoe
House sparrow
Mallard
Mute swan
Northern lapwing
Northern raven
Northern wryneck
Nuthatch
Peregrine falcon
Red crossbill
Rock pigeon
Snow finch
Spotted flycatcher
Stonechat
Winter wren

LITHUANIA
Barn swallow
Black tern
Chaffinch
Common cuckoo
Common murre
Corncrake
Dunnock

Eurasian bittern
Eurasian dipper
Eurasian golden oriole
European roller
European starling
European white stork
Great cormorant
Great crested grebe
Great tit
Hoopoe
House sparrow
Mallard
Northern fulmar
Northern gannet
Northern lapwing
Northern raven
Northern wryneck
Nuthatch
Red crossbill
Rock pigeon
Spotted flycatcher
Spotted nutcracker
Winter wren

LUXEMBOURG
Barn swallow
Black tern
Chaffinch
Common cuckoo
Corncrake
Dunnock
Eurasian golden oriole
European roller
European starling
European white stork
Gray wagtail
Great cormorant
Great crested grebe
Great tit
Hoopoe
House sparrow
Mallard
Mute swan
Northern lapwing
Northern raven
Northern wryneck

Nuthatch
Peregrine falcon
Red crossbill
Rock pigeon
Spotted flycatcher
Stonechat
Winter wren

MACEDONIA
Barn swallow
Chaffinch
Common cuckoo
Corncrake
Crag martin
Dunnock
Egyptian vulture
Eurasian dipper
Eurasian golden oriole
European bee-eater
European roller
European starling
European white stork
Gray wagtail
Great cormorant
Great crested grebe
Great tit
Hoopoe
Horned lark
House sparrow
Mallard
Northern lapwing
Northern raven
Northern wryneck
Nuthatch
Peregrine falcon
Red crossbill
Rock pigeon
Snow bunting
Spotted flycatcher
Stonechat
Winter wren

MADAGASCAR
African palm swift
Black-winged stilt
Cattle egret

Common sunbird-asity
Crab plovers
Greater flamingo
Greater painted snipe
Hammerhead
Hoopoe
Peregrine falcon
Ruddy turnstone
Rufous vanga
Sacred ibis
Stonechat
White-breasted mesite
Wilson's storm-petrel

MALAWI
African broadbill
African jacana
African palm swift
African paradise-flycatcher
African pitta
African snipe
Bar-breasted mousebird
Barn swallow
Black-winged stilt
Buff-spotted flufftail
Cape batis
Cattle egret
Collared pratincole
Common bulbul
Common cuckoo
Common waxbill
Corncrake
Eurasian golden oriole
European bee-eater
European roller
European white stork
Gray go-away-bird
Gray-crowned crane
Great cormorant
Greater painted snipe
Green woodhoopoe
Hammerhead
Helmeted guineafowl
Hoopoe
House sparrow
Osprey

Peregrine falcon
Red-billed oxpecker
Rock pigeon
Sacred ibis
Secretary bird
Small buttonquail
Southern ground-hornbill
Southern red bishop
Spotted flycatcher
Square-tailed drongo
Stonechat
Village weaver
White-helmet shrike
Yellow-fronted tinkerbird
Zitting cisticola

MALAYSIA
Arctic warbler
Asian fairy-bluebird
Barn swallow
Barred eagle-owl
Baya weaver
Black-and-red broadbill
Black-naped monarch
Black-winged stilt
Common iora
Common myna
Coppersmith barbet
Dollarbird
Fiery minivet
Fire-breasted flowerpecker
Gray nightjar
Gray wagtail
Great cormorant
Greater painted snipe
Greater racket-tailed drongo
Green magpie
Helmeted hornbill
Hooded pitta
Malaysian honeyguide
Orange-breasted trogon
Osprey
Peregrine falcon
Pheasant-tailed jacana
Rock pigeon
Ruby-cheeked sunbird

Ruddy turnstone
Rufous-collared kingfisher
Spotted munia
White-throated fantail
Zitting cisticola

MALI
African jacana
African palm swift
African paradise-flycatcher
Barn swallow
Black-winged stilt
Cattle egret
Collared pratincole
Common bulbul
Egyptian vulture
Eurasian bittern
European bee-eater
European roller
European white stork
Gray wagtail
Gray woodpecker
Greater hoopoe-lark
Greater painted snipe
Green woodhoopoe
Hammerhead
Helmeted guineafowl
Hoopoe
Leaf-love
Northern wryneck
Osprey
Ostrich
Peregrine falcon
Rock pigeon
Rose-ringed parakeet
Sacred ibis
Secretary bird
Small buttonquail
Stonechat
Village weaver
White-helmet shrike
Yellow-fronted tinkerbird
Zitting cisticola

MAURITANIA
Barn swallow

Black-winged stilt
Cattle egret
Collared pratincole
Common bulbul
Crag martin
Egyptian vulture
Eurasian bittern
European roller
European white stork
Gray woodpecker
Greater flamingo
Greater hoopoe-lark
Greater painted snipe
Green woodhoopoe
Hammerhead
Helmeted guineafowl
Hoopoe
Magnificent frigatebird
Manx shearwater
Northern gannet
Osprey
Ostrich
Peregrine falcon
Rock pigeon
Rose-ringed parakeet
Ruddy turnstone
Secretary bird
Small buttonquail
Wilson's storm-petrel
Zitting cisticola

MAURITIUS
Dodo
Mauritius cuckoo-shrike

MEXICO
American anhinga
American avocet
American cliff swallow
American dipper
American goldfinch
American mourning dove
American robin
American white pelican
Anna's hummingbird
Baltimore oriole

Barn owl
Barn swallow
Barred antshrike
Belted kingfisher
Black rail
Black tern
Black-and-white warbler
Black-capped vireo
Black-winged stilt
Blue jay
Blue-black grassquit
Blue-crowned motmot
Blue-footed booby
Blue-gray gnatcatcher
Brown creeper
Brown pelican
Bushtit
Cactus wren
Canada goose
Cattle egret
Cedar waxwing
Common loon
Crested caracara
Eastern bluebird
Eastern phoebe
Eastern screech-owl
European starling
Gray catbird
Great blue heron
Great kiskadee
Greater roadrunner
Harris's hawk
Horned lark
House sparrow
House wren
Killdeer
King vulture
Limpkin
Loggerhead shrike
Long-billed curlew
Long-tailed manakin
Magnificent frigatebird
Mallard
Northern bobwhite quail
Northern gannet
Northern raven

Osprey
Peregrine falcon
Plain chachalaca
Red-throated loon
Red-winged blackbird
Resplendent quetzal
Rock pigeon
Roseate spoonbill
Rose-throated becard
Ruddy turnstone
Rufous-browed peppershrike
Rufous-tailed jacamar
Sandhill crane
Savanna sparrow
Scarlet macaw
Song sparrow
Sprague's pipit
Sungrebe
Verdin
Western grebe
Western scrub-jay
Whip-poor-will
White-necked puffbird
Wild turkey
Wilson's storm-petrel
Winter wren
Wood duck
Wood stork
Wrentit
Yellow-bellied sapsucker
Yellow-breasted chat

MOLDOVA

Barn swallow
Black tern
Chaffinch
Collared pratincole
Common cuckoo
Corncrake
Dunnock
Eurasian bittern
Eurasian golden oriole
European bee-eater
European roller
European starling
European white stork

Great cormorant
Great crested grebe
Great tit
Hoopoe
House sparrow
Mallard
Northern lapwing
Northern raven
Northern wryneck
Nuthatch
Peregrine falcon
Rock pigeon
Snow bunting
Spotted flycatcher
Stonechat
Winter wren

MONACO

Greater flamingo
Northern gannet

MONGOLIA

Barn swallow
Black tern
Black-winged stilt
Common cuckoo
Crag martin
Eurasian bittern
Gray wagtail
Great bustard
Great cormorant
Great crested grebe
Hoopoe
Horned lark
House sparrow
Mallard
Mute swan
Northern raven
Northern wryneck
Nuthatch
Pallas's sandgrouse
Peregrine falcon
Red crossbill
Rock pigeon
Snow bunting
Snow finch

Spotted flycatcher
Spotted nutcracker
Stonechat

MOROCCO

Barn swallow
Black-winged stilt
Cattle egret
Chaffinch
Collared pratincole
Common bulbul
Common cuckoo
Common murre
Corncrake
Crag martin
Dunnock
Egyptian vulture
Eurasian dipper
Eurasian golden oriole
European bee-eater
European roller
European starling
Gray wagtail
Great bustard
Great cormorant
Great crested grebe
Greater flamingo
Greater hoopoe-lark
Hoopoe
Horned lark
House sparrow
Magnificent frigatebird
Mallard
Manx shearwater
Northern gannet
Northern raven
Ostrich
Peregrine falcon
Rock pigeon
Ruddy turnstone
Small buttonquail
Spotted flycatcher
Stonechat
Wilson's storm-petrel
Winter wren
Zitting cisticola

MOZAMBIQUE

African broadbill
African jacana
African palm swift
African paradise-flycatcher
African pitta
African snipe
Bar-breasted mousebird
Barn swallow
Black-winged stilt
Buff-spotted flufftail
Cape batis
Cattle egret
Collared pratincole
Common bulbul
Common cuckoo
Common waxbill
Corncrake
Crab plovers
Eurasian golden oriole
European bee-eater
European roller
European white stork
Gray go-away-bird
Gray-crowned crane
Great cormorant
Greater painted snipe
Green woodhoopoe
Hammerhead
Helmeted guineafowl
Hoopoe
House sparrow
Osprey
Ostrich
Peregrine falcon
Rock pigeon
Rosy-breasted longclaw
Ruddy turnstone
Sacred ibis
Secretary bird
Small buttonquail
Southern ground-hornbill
Southern red bishop
Spotted flycatcher
Square-tailed drongo
Stonechat

Village weaver
White-helmet shrike
Wilson's storm-petrel
Yellow-fronted tinkerbird
Zitting cisticola

MYANMAR

Asian fairy-bluebird
Australasian lark
Barn swallow
Barred eagle-owl
Baya weaver
Black bulbul
Black-and-red broadbill
Black-naped monarch
Black-winged stilt
Cattle egret
Common cuckoo
Common iora
Common myna
Coppersmith barbet
Crested tree swift
Dollarbird
Fiery minivet
Fire-breasted flowerpecker
Gray nightjar
Gray wagtail
Great cormorant
Great crested grebe
Great tit
Greater painted snipe
Greater racket-tailed drongo
Green magpie
Helmeted hornbill
Hooded pitta
Hoopoe
House sparrow
Mallard
Northern wryneck
Orange-breasted trogon
Osprey
Peregrine falcon
Pheasant-tailed jacana
Purple sunbird
Rock pigeon
Rose-ringed parakeet

Rose-ringed parakeet
Ruby-cheeked sunbird
Ruddy turnstone
Rufous-collared kingfisher
Small buttonquail
Spotted munia
Stonechat
White-throated fantail
Winter wren
Zitting cisticola

NAMIBIA

African jacana
African palm swift
African paradise-flycatcher
Arctic skua
Barn swallow
Black tern
Black-winged stilt
Cattle egret
Common cuckoo
Common waxbill
Egyptian vulture
Eurasian golden oriole
European roller
European white stork
Gray go-away-bird
Great cormorant
Great crested grebe
Greater painted snipe
Green woodhoopoe
Hammerhead
Helmeted guineafowl
Hoopoe
House sparrow
Namaqua sandgrouse
Osprey
Ostrich
Peregrine falcon
Rock pigeon
Ruddy turnstone
Sacred ibis
Secretary bird
Small buttonquail
Southern ground-hornbill
Southern red bishop

Spotted flycatcher
White-helmet shrike
Wilson's storm-petrel
Yellow-fronted tinkerbird
Zitting cisticola

NEPAL
Asian fairy-bluebird
Barn swallow
Black-naped monarch
Cattle egret
Common cuckoo
Coppersmith barbet
Crested tree swift
Dollarbird
Egyptian vulture
Eurasian bittern
Eurasian golden oriole
European roller
European white stork
Fire-breasted flowerpecker
Gray nightjar
Gray wagtail
Great cormorant
Great crested grebe
Greater painted snipe
Hooded pitta
Hoopoe
House sparrow
Northern wryneck
Osprey
Peregrine falcon
Pheasant-tailed jacana
Purple sunbird
Rock pigeon
Rose-ringed parakeet
Ruby-cheeked sunbird
Satyr tragopan
Small buttonquail
Snow finch
Spotted munia
Spotted nutcracker
Stonechat
White-throated fantail
Winter wren

Zitting cisticola

NETHERLANDS
Barn swallow
Black tern
Chaffinch
Common cuckoo
Common murre
Corncrake
Dunnock
Eurasian golden oriole
European roller
European starling
European white stork
Great auk
Great cormorant
Great crested grebe
Great tit
House sparrow
Mallard
Manx shearwater
Mute swan
Northern fulmar
Northern gannet
Northern lapwing
Northern wryneck
Nuthatch
Peregrine falcon
Puffin
Red-throated loon
Rock pigeon
Ruddy turnstone
Spotted flycatcher
Stonechat
Winter wren

NEW CALEDONIA
Beach thick-knee
Black-winged stilt
House sparrow
Kagu
Osprey
Painted buttonquail
Peregrine falcon
Rainbow lorikeet

White-tailed tropicbird

NEW ZEALAND
Arctic skua
Black-winged stilt
Brown kiwi
Canada goose
Cattle egret
Chatham mollymawk
Common diving-petrel
Emperor penguin
European starling
Great cormorant
Great crested grebe
House sparrow
Kokako
Laughing kookaburra
Mallard
Mute swan
Rifleman
Rock pigeon
Ruddy turnstone
Variable oystercatcher
Wilson's storm-petrel
Yellowhead

NICARAGUA
American anhinga
American dipper
American mourning dove
Baltimore oriole
Barn owl
Barred antshrike
Belted kingfisher
Black tern
Black-and-white warbler
Black-winged stilt
Blue-black grassquit
Blue-crowned motmot
Blue-footed booby
Brown creeper
Brown pelican
Cattle egret
Cedar waxwing
Crested caracara

Gray catbird
Gray potoo
Great blue heron
Great kiskadee
Harris's hawk
House sparrow
Killdeer
King vulture
Limpkin
Long-tailed manakin
Magnificent frigatebird
Northern raven
Osprey
Peregrine falcon
Plain chachalaca
Resplendent quetzal
Rock pigeon
Roseate spoonbill
Rose-throated becard
Ruddy turnstone
Rufous-browed peppershrike
Rufous-tailed jacamar
Scarlet macaw
Sunbittern
Sungrebe
White-necked puffbird
Wood stork
Yellow-bellied sapsucker
Yellow-breasted chat

NIGER
African jacana
African palm swift
African paradise-flycatcher
Barn swallow
Black-winged stilt
Cattle egret
Collared pratincole
Common bulbul
Egyptian vulture
Eurasian bittern
European white stork
Gray woodpecker
Greater hoopoe-lark
Greater painted snipe
Green woodhoopoe

Hammerhead
Helmeted guineafowl
Hoopoe
Northern wryneck
Osprey
Ostrich
Peregrine falcon
Rock pigeon
Rose-ringed parakeet
Sacred ibis
Secretary bird
Small buttonquail
Village weaver
Yellow-fronted tinkerbird
Zitting cisticola

NIGERIA
African jacana
African palm swift
African paradise-flycatcher
African pitta
Bar-breasted mousebird
Barn swallow
Black tern
Black-winged stilt
Buff-spotted flufftail
Cattle egret
Collared pratincole
Common bulbul
Common waxbill
Eurasian bittern
European roller
European white stork
Gray parrot
Gray woodpecker
Gray-necked picathartes
Great blue turaco
Greater painted snipe
Green woodhoopoe
Hammerhead
Helmeted guineafowl
Hoopoe
Leaf-love
Lyre-tailed honeyguide
Northern wryneck
Osprey

Peregrine falcon
Rose-ringed parakeet
Ruddy turnstone
Sacred ibis
Secretary bird
Small buttonquail
Spotted flycatcher
Square-tailed drongo
White-helmet shrike
Wilson's storm-petrel
Yellow-fronted tinkerbird
Zitting cisticola

NORTH KOREA
Arctic warbler
Barn swallow
Common cuckoo
Common murre
Dollarbird
Eurasian bittern
Gray nightjar
Gray wagtail
Great bustard
Great cormorant
Great tit
Greater painted snipe
Hoopoe
Mute swan
Nuthatch
Red crossbill
Red-crowned crane
Red-throated loon
Rock pigeon
Saunder's gull
Stonechat
Winter wren

NORWAY
Arctic skua
Arctic warbler
Barn swallow
Chaffinch
Common cuckoo
Common loon
Common murre

Corncrake
Dunnock
Eurasian dipper
European starling
Gray wagtail
Great auk
Great cormorant
Great crested grebe
Great tit
Gyrfalcon
Horned lark
House sparrow
King eider
Manx shearwater
Northern fulmar
Northern gannet
Northern lapwing
Northern raven
Northern wryneck
Nuthatch
Osprey
Peregrine falcon
Puffin
Red crossbill
Red-throated loon
Rock pigeon
Ruddy turnstone
Snow bunting
Snowy owl
Spotted flycatcher
Spotted nutcracker
Willow ptarmigan
Winter wren

OMAN
Crab plovers
Egyptian vulture
European roller
Gray wagtail
Greater hoopoe-lark
Hoopoe
House sparrow
Osprey
Peregrine falcon
Purple sunbird
Rock pigeon

Ruddy turnstone
Wilson's storm-petrel

PAKISTAN
Barn swallow
Baya weaver
Black bulbul
Black-winged stilt
Cattle egret
Chaffinch
Collared pratincole
Common cuckoo
Common myna
Coppersmith barbet
Crab plovers
Crag martin
Egyptian vulture
Eurasian bittern
Eurasian golden oriole
European bee-eater
European roller
European starling
European white stork
Gray hypocolius
Gray wagtail
Great cormorant
Great crested grebe
Great tit
Greater flamingo
Greater hoopoe-lark
Greater painted snipe
Hoopoe
House sparrow
Mallard
Mute swan
Northern lapwing
Northern raven
Osprey
Peregrine falcon
Pheasant-tailed jacana
Purple sunbird
Rock pigeon
Rose-ringed parakeet
Ruddy turnstone
Small buttonquail
Snow finch

Spotted flycatcher
Spotted nutcracker
Stonechat
White-throated fantail
Wilson's storm-petrel

PANAMA
American anhinga
American dipper
American mourning dove
Baltimore oriole
Barn owl
Barn swallow
Barred antshrike
Belted kingfisher
Black guan
Black rail
Black tern
Black-and-white warbler
Black-capped donacobius
Black-winged stilt
Blue-black grassquit
Blue-crowned motmot
Blue-footed booby
Brown pelican
Cattle egret
Crested caracara
Gray catbird
Gray potoo
Great blue heron
Great kiskadee
Hairy hermit
Harris's hawk
Highland tinamou
House sparrow
Killdeer
King vulture
Limpkin
Magnificent frigatebird
Oilbird
Osprey
Peregrine falcon
Red-billed scythebill
Resplendent quetzal
Rock pigeon
Roseate spoonbill

Rose-throated becard
Ruddy turnstone
Rufous-browed peppershrike
Rufous-tailed jacamar
Scarlet macaw
Sharpbill
Sunbittern
Sungrebe
White-necked puffbird
Wood stork
Yellow-bellied sapsucker

PAPUA NEW GUINEA
Australasian figbird
Australasian lark
Australian magpie-lark
Australian pratincole
Barn swallow
Beach thick-knee
Black-winged stilt
Cattle egret
Dollarbird
Eclectus parrot
Fan-tailed berrypecker
Feline owlet-nightjar
Golden whistler
Gray wagtail
Gray-crowned babbler
Hooded pitta
Jacky winter
King bird of paradise
Osprey
Peregrine falcon
Rainbow lorikeet
Ribbon-tailed astrapia
Ruddy turnstone
Southern cassowary
Variable pitohui
White-tailed tropicbird
Willie wagtail
Wilson's storm-petrel
Zitting cisticola

PARAGUAY
American anhinga
American cliff swallow

Barn owl
Barn swallow
Barred antshrike
Baywing
Black-capped donacobius
Black-winged stilt
Blue-black grassquit
Blue-crowned motmot
Cattle egret
Crested caracara
Gray potoo
Great kiskadee
Greater thornbird
Hairy hermit
Harris's hawk
House sparrow
King vulture
Limpkin
Peregrine falcon
Red-billed scythebill
Red-legged seriema
Roseate spoonbill
Rufous hornero
Rufous-browed peppershrike
Rufous-tailed jacamar
Sharpbill
Sungrebe
Toco toucan
Wood stork

PERU
Amazonian umbrellabird
American anhinga
Arctic skua
Barn owl
Barn swallow
Barred antshrike
Black rail
Black tern
Black-capped donacobius
Black-winged stilt
Blue-black grassquit
Blue-crowned motmot
Blue-footed booby
Brown pelican
Cattle egret

Chimney swift
Common trumpeter
Coppery-chested jacamar
Crested caracara
Gray antbird
Gray potoo
Gray-breasted mountain-
  toucan
Great kiskadee
Hairy hermit
Harris's hawk
Highland tinamou
Hoatzin
Horned screamer
House sparrow
Killdeer
King vulture
Lesser rhea
Limpkin
Magellanic penguin
Oilbird
Osprey
Peregrine falcon
Peruvian plantcutter
Red-billed scythebill
Rock pigeon
Roseate spoonbill
Ruddy turnstone
Rufous-bellied seedsnipe
Rufous-browed peppershrike
Rufous-capped nunlet
Rufous-tailed jacamar
Rusty-belted tapaculo
Scarlet macaw
Sharpbill
Spangled cotinga
Sparkling violet-ear
Sunbittern
Sungrebe
Wattled curassow
White-necked puffbird
Wilson's storm-petrel
Wire-tailed manakin
Wood stork

PHILIPPINES
Arctic warbler

Asian fairy-bluebird
Australasian lark
Barn swallow
Beach thick-knee
Black-naped monarch
Black-winged stilt
Cattle egret
Coppersmith barbet
Dollarbird
Fiery minivet
Fire-breasted flowerpecker
Gray nightjar
Gray wagtail
Greater painted snipe
Hooded pitta
Japanese white-eye
Little slaty flycatcher
Luzon bleeding heart
Osprey
Peregrine falcon
Pheasant-tailed jacana
Rock pigeon
Ruddy turnstone
Small buttonquail
Spotted munia
Stripe-headed rhabdornis
Zitting cisticola

POLAND
Barn swallow
Black tern
Chaffinch
Common cuckoo
Common murre
Corncrake
Dunnock
Eurasian bittern
Eurasian dipper
Eurasian golden oriole
European roller
European starling
European white stork
Gray wagtail
Great cormorant
Great crested grebe
Great tit

Hoopoe
House sparrow
Mallard
Northern fulmar
Northern gannet
Northern lapwing
Northern raven
Northern wryneck
Nuthatch
Osprey
Peregrine falcon
Puffin
Red crossbill
Rock pigeon
Snow bunting
Snow finch
Spotted flycatcher
Spotted nutcracker
Winter wren

PORTUGAL
Barn swallow
Black-winged stilt
Chaffinch
Collared pratincole
Common cuckoo
Common loon
Common murre
Crag martin
Dunnock
Egyptian vulture
Eurasian dipper
Eurasian golden oriole
European bee-eater
European roller
European white stork
Gray wagtail
Great bustard
Great cormorant
Great crested grebe
Great tit
Hoopoe
House sparrow
Mallard
Manx shearwater
Northern gannet

Northern lapwing
Northern raven
Northern wryneck
Nuthatch
Osprey
Peregrine falcon
Red crossbill
Red-throated loon
Rock pigeon
Ruddy turnstone
Spotted flycatcher
Stonechat
Wilson's storm-petrel
Winter wren
Zitting cisticola

PUERTO RICO
American mourning dove
Barn owl
Belted kingfisher
Brown pelican
Cattle egret
Crested caracara
European starling
Greater flamingo
House sparrow
Killdeer
Magnificent frigatebird
Osprey
Peregrine falcon
Rock pigeon
Ruddy turnstone
White-tailed tropicbird
Wood stork
Yellow-bellied sapsucker

QATAR
European roller
Greater hoopoe-lark
Hoopoe
House sparrow
Stonechat

ROMANIA
Barn swallow

Black tern
Black-winged stilt
Chaffinch
Collared pratincole
Common cuckoo
Corncrake
Dunnock
Egyptian vulture
Eurasian bittern
Eurasian dipper
Eurasian golden oriole
European bee-eater
European roller
European starling
European white stork
Gray wagtail
Great cormorant
Great crested grebe
Great tit
Hoopoe
House sparrow
Mallard
Northern lapwing
Northern raven
Northern wryneck
Nuthatch
Peregrine falcon
Red crossbill
Red-throated loon
Rock pigeon
Snow bunting
Spotted flycatcher
Stonechat
Winter wren

RUSSIA
Arctic skua
Arctic warbler
Barn swallow
Black tern
Black-winged stilt
Cattle egret
Chaffinch
Collared pratincole
Common cuckoo

Common murre
Corncrake
Crag martin
Dollarbird
Dunnock
Eurasian bittern
Eurasian dipper
Eurasian golden oriole
European bee-eater
European starling
European white stork
Gray nightjar
Gray wagtail
Great bustard
Great cormorant
Great crested grebe
Great tit
Greater painted snipe
Gyrfalcon
Hoopoe
Horned lark
House sparrow
King eider
Mallard
Mute swan
Northern fulmar
Northern gannet
Northern lapwing
Northern raven
Northern wryneck
Nuthatch
Osprey
Pallas's sandgrouse
Peregrine falcon
Puffin
Red crossbill
Red-crowned crane
Red-throated loon
Rock pigeon
Ruddy turnstone
Sandhill crane
Snow bunting
Snow finch
Snowy owl
Spotted flycatcher
Spotted nutcracker

Stonechat
Willow ptarmigan
Winter wren

RWANDA
African jacana
African palm swift
African paradise-flycatcher
African pitta
African snipe
Bar-breasted mousebird
Barn swallow
Black-winged stilt
Buff-spotted flufftail
Cattle egret
Collared pratincole
Common bulbul
Common cuckoo
Common waxbill
Corncrake
Eurasian golden oriole
European bee-eater
European roller
European white stork
Gray parrot
Gray woodpecker
Gray-crowned crane
Great blue turaco
Great cormorant
Great crested grebe
Green woodhoopoe
Hammerhead
Helmeted guineafowl
Hoopoe
Osprey
Ostrich
Peregrine falcon
Red-billed oxpecker
Sacred ibis
Shoebill
Small buttonquail
Southern red bishop
Spotted flycatcher
Stonechat
Village weaver

Yellow-fronted tinkerbird
Zitting cisticola

SÃO TOMÉ AND PRÍNCIPE
White-tailed tropicbird

SAUDI ARABIA
African palm swift
Black-winged stilt
Cattle egret
Crab plovers
Crag martin
Egyptian vulture
European roller
Gray hypocolius
Gray wagtail
Great cormorant
Greater hoopoe-lark
Hammerhead
Hoopoe
House sparrow
Mallard
Northern lapwing
Osprey
Peregrine falcon
Rock pigeon
Ruddy turnstone
Stonechat
Wilson's storm-petrel

SENEGAL
African palm swift
African paradise-flycatcher
Black tern
Black-winged stilt
Cattle egret
Collared pratincole
Common bulbul
Common waxbill
Egyptian vulture
Eurasian bittern
European roller
European white stork
Gray wagtail

Gray woodpecker
Greater flamingo
Greater hoopoe-lark
Greater painted snipe
Green woodhoopoe
Hammerhead
Helmeted guineafowl
Hoopoe
Leaf-love
Magnificent frigatebird
Northern wryneck
Osprey
Peregrine falcon
Rose-ringed parakeet
Ruddy turnstone
Sacred ibis
Secretary bird
Small buttonquail
Village weaver
White-helmet shrike
Wilson's storm-petrel
Yellow-fronted tinkerbird
Zitting cisticola

SEYCHELLES
White-tailed tropicbird

SIERRA LEONE
African broadbill
African palm swift
African paradise-flycatcher
African pitta
Barn swallow
Black tern
Black-winged stilt
Buff-spotted flufftail
Cattle egret
Collared pratincole
Common bulbul
Common waxbill
Eurasian bittern
Gray parrot
Gray woodpecker
Great blue turaco
Hammerhead
Leaf-love

Lyre-tailed honeyguide
Northern wryneck
Osprey
Peregrine falcon
Rose-ringed parakeet
Ruddy turnstone
Sacred ibis
Small buttonquail
Spotted flycatcher
Square-tailed drongo
Village weaver
Wilson's storm-petrel

SINGAPORE
Baya weaver

SLOVAKIA
Barn swallow
Black tern
Chaffinch
Collared pratincole
Common cuckoo
Corncrake
Dunnock
Eurasian golden oriole
European bee-eater
European roller
European starling
European white stork
Gray wagtail
Great cormorant
Great crested grebe
Great tit
Hoopoe
House sparrow
Mallard
Northern lapwing
Northern raven
Northern wryneck
Nuthatch
Peregrine falcon
Red crossbill
Rock pigeon
Snow bunting
Snow finch
Spotted flycatcher

Stonechat
Winter wren

SLOVENIA
Barn swallow
Black tern
Chaffinch
Collared pratincole
Common cuckoo
Corncrake
Dunnock
Eurasian dipper
Eurasian golden oriole
European bee-eater
European roller
European starling
Gray wagtail
Great cormorant
Great crested grebe
Great tit
Hoopoe
House sparrow
Mallard
Northern lapwing
Northern raven
Northern wryneck
Nuthatch
Peregrine falcon
Rock pigeon
Snow bunting
Snow finch
Spotted flycatcher
Stonechat
Winter wren
Zitting cisticola

SOMALIA
African jacana
African palm swift
African paradise-flycatcher
Bar-breasted mousebird
Barn swallow
Black-winged stilt
Cattle egret
Collared pratincole
Common bulbul

Corncrake
Crab plovers
Egyptian vulture
European roller
European white stork
Gray wagtail
Great cormorant
Greater hoopoe-lark
Green woodhoopoe
Hammerhead
Hoopoe
Ostrich
Peregrine falcon
Red-billed oxpecker
Rose-ringed parakeet
Ruddy turnstone
Sacred ibis
Small buttonquail
Spotted flycatcher
Square-tailed drongo
Stonechat
White-helmet shrike
Wilson's storm-petrel

SOUTH AFRICA
African jacana
African palm swift
African paradise-flycatcher
African snipe
Arctic skua
Bar-breasted mousebird
Barn swallow
Black tern
Black-winged stilt
Blue bustard
Buff-spotted flufftail
Cape batis
Cape sugarbird
Cattle egret
Collared pratincole
Common bulbul
Common cuckoo
Common waxbill
Corncrake
Crab plovers
Eurasian golden oriole

European bee-eater
European roller
European starling
European white stork
Gray-crowned crane
Great cormorant
Great crested grebe
Greater flamingo
Greater painted snipe
Green woodhoopoe
Hammerhead
Helmeted guineafowl
Hoopoe
House sparrow
Manx shearwater
Mute swan
Namaqua sandgrouse
Osprey
Ostrich
Peregrine falcon
Red-billed oxpecker
Rock pigeon
Rosy-breasted longclaw
Ruddy turnstone
Sacred ibis
Secretary bird
Small buttonquail
Southern ground-hornbill
Southern red bishop
Spotted flycatcher
Square-tailed drongo
Stonechat
Village weaver
White-helmet shrike
Wilson's storm-petrel
Yellow-fronted tinkerbird
Zitting cisticola

SOUTH KOREA
Arctic warbler
Barn swallow
Cattle egret
Common cuckoo
Common murre
Dollarbird
Eurasian bittern

Gray nightjar
Gray wagtail
Great cormorant
Great tit
Greater painted snipe
Japanese white-eye
Mallard
Mute swan
Northern lapwing
Nuthatch
Red crossbill
Red-throated loon
Rock pigeon
Saunder's gull
Stonechat
Winter wren

SPAIN

Barn swallow
Black-winged stilt
Chaffinch
Collared pratincole
Common cuckoo
Common loon
Common murre
Corncrake
Crag martin
Dunnock
Egyptian vulture
Eurasian bittern
Eurasian dipper
Eurasian golden oriole
European bee-eater
European roller
European white stork
Gray wagtail
Great auk
Great bustard
Great cormorant
Great crested grebe
Great tit
Greater flamingo
Hoopoe
House sparrow
Mallard
Manx shearwater

Northern fulmar
Northern gannet
Northern lapwing
Northern raven
Northern wryneck
Nuthatch
Peregrine falcon
Red crossbill
Red-throated loon
Rock pigeon
Ruddy turnstone
Small buttonquail
Snow finch
Spotted flycatcher
Stonechat
Wilson's storm-petrel
Winter wren
Zitting cisticola

SRI LANKA

Baya weaver
Black bulbul
Common iora
Common myna
Coppersmith barbet
Crested tree swift
Dollarbird
Eurasian golden oriole
Gray nightjar
Great tit
Greater racket-tailed drongo
House sparrow
Pheasant-tailed jacana
Purple sunbird
Rose-ringed parakeet
Spotted munia
White-throated fantail
Wilson's storm-petrel

SUDAN

African jacana
African palm swift
African paradise-flycatcher
Bar-breasted mousebird
Barn swallow

Black tern
Black-winged stilt
Buff-spotted flufftail
Cattle egret
Collared pratincole
Common bulbul
Common waxbill
Corncrake
Crab plovers
Crag martin
Egyptian vulture
Eurasian bittern
European roller
European white stork
Gray wagtail
Gray woodpecker
Great blue turaco
Great cormorant
Greater flamingo
Greater hoopoe-lark
Greater painted snipe
Green woodhoopoe
Hammerhead
Helmeted guineafowl
Hoopoe
Leaf-love
Northern wryneck
Osprey
Ostrich
Peregrine falcon
Red-billed oxpecker
Rock pigeon
Rose-ringed parakeet
Ruddy turnstone
Sacred ibis
Secretary bird
Shoebill
Small buttonquail
Spotted flycatcher
Square-tailed drongo
Stonechat
Village weaver
White-helmet shrike
Wilson's storm-petrel
Yellow-fronted tinkerbird
Zitting cisticola

SURINAME

American anhinga
Barn owl
Barn swallow
Barred antshrike
Black tern
Black-capped donacobius
Black-winged stilt
Blue-black grassquit
Blue-crowned motmot
Brown pelican
Cattle egret
Common trumpeter
Crested caracara
Gray antbird
Gray potoo
Great kiskadee
Guianan cock-of-the-rock
Hairy hermit
Hoatzin
King vulture
Limpkin
Magnificent frigatebird
Osprey
Peregrine falcon
Roseate spoonbill
Ruddy turnstone
Rufous-browed peppershrike
Scarlet macaw
Sharpbill
Spangled cotinga
Sunbittern
Sungrebe
White-necked puffbird
Wilson's storm-petrel
Wood stork

SWAZILAND

African jacana
African palm swift
African paradise-flycatcher
African snipe
Barn swallow
Black-winged stilt
Buff-spotted flufftail
Cape batis

Cattle egret
Collared pratincole
Common bulbul
Common cuckoo
Common waxbill
Corncrake
European bee-eater
European roller
European white stork
Great cormorant
Greater painted snipe
Green woodhoopoe
Hammerhead
Helmeted guineafowl
Hoopoe
House sparrow
Osprey
Peregrine falcon
Sacred ibis
Secretary bird
Small buttonquail
Southern ground-hornbill
Southern red bishop
Spotted flycatcher
Stonechat
Village weaver
White-helmet shrike
Zitting cisticola

SWEDEN

Barn swallow
Chaffinch
Common cuckoo
Common murre
Corncrake
Dunnock
Eurasian bittern
Eurasian dipper
European roller
European starling
Gray wagtail
Great auk
Great cormorant
Great crested grebe
Great tit
Gyrfalcon

Hoopoe
Horned lark
House sparrow
Mute swan
Northern fulmar
Northern gannet
Northern lapwing
Northern raven
Northern wryneck
Nuthatch
Osprey
Peregrine falcon
Puffin
Red crossbill
Red-throated loon
Rock pigeon
Ruddy turnstone
Snow bunting
Spotted flycatcher
Spotted nutcracker
Willow ptarmigan
Winter wren

SWITZERLAND

Barn swallow
Black tern
Chaffinch
Common cuckoo
Corncrake
Dunnock
Eurasian dipper
Eurasian golden oriole
European roller
European starling
European white stork
Gray wagtail
Great cormorant
Great crested grebe
Great tit
Hoopoe
House sparrow
Mallard
Mute swan
Northern lapwing
Northern raven
Northern wryneck

Nuthatch
Peregrine falcon
Red crossbill
Rock pigeon
Snow finch
Spotted flycatcher
Spotted nutcracker
Stonechat
Winter wren

SYRIA

Black-winged stilt
Cattle egret
Chaffinch
Collared pratincole
Common bulbul
Common cuckoo
Corncrake
Crag martin
Dunnock
Egyptian vulture
European bee-eater
European roller
European starling
Great bustard
Great cormorant
Greater flamingo
Hoopoe
House sparrow
Mallard
Northern gannet
Northern lapwing
Nuthatch
Peregrine falcon
Red crossbill
Rock pigeon
Spotted flycatcher
Stonechat
Winter wren

TAJIKISTAN

Barn swallow
Chaffinch
Common cuckoo
Crag martin
Egyptian vulture

Eurasian golden oriole
European roller
European starling
Great bustard
Great cormorant
Great crested grebe
Great tit
Hoopoe
House sparrow
Mallard
Northern raven
Peregrine falcon
Rock pigeon
Snow finch
Spotted flycatcher
Stonechat
Winter wren

TANZANIA

African broadbill
African jacana
African palm swift
African paradise-flycatcher
African pitta
African snipe
Bar-breasted mousebird
Barn swallow
Black-winged stilt
Buff-spotted flufftail
Cattle egret
Collared pratincole
Common bulbul
Common waxbill
Corncrake
Crab plovers
Eurasian golden oriole
European bee-eater
European roller
European white stork
Golden-winged sunbird
Gray go-away-bird
Gray wagtail
Gray woodpecker
Great cormorant
Great crested grebe
Greater flamingo

Greater painted snipe
Green woodhoopoe
Hammerhead
Helmeted guineafowl
Hoopoe
House sparrow
Leaf-love
Osprey
Ostrich
Peregrine falcon
Red-billed oxpecker
Rock pigeon
Rosy-breasted longclaw
Ruddy turnstone
Sacred ibis
Secretary bird
Shoebill
Small buttonquail
Southern ground-hornbill
Southern red bishop
Spotted flycatcher
Square-tailed drongo
Stonechat
Village weaver
White-helmet shrike
Wilson's storm-petrel
Yellow-fronted tinkerbird
Zitting cisticola

THAILAND

Arctic warbler
Asian fairy-bluebird
Australasian lark
Barn swallow
Barred eagle-owl
Baya weaver
Black bulbul
Black-and-red broadbill
Black-naped monarch
Black-winged stilt
Cattle egret
Common cuckoo
Common iora
Common myna
Coppersmith barbet
Crested tree swift

Dollarbird
Fiery minivet
Fire-breasted flowerpecker
Gray nightjar
Gray wagtail
Great cormorant
Greater painted snipe
Greater racket-tailed drongo
Green magpie
Helmeted hornbill
Hooded pitta
Hoopoe
Malaysian honeyguide
Northern lapwing
Northern wryneck
Orange-breasted trogon
Osprey
Peregrine falcon
Pheasant-tailed jacana
Purple sunbird
Rock pigeon
Ruby-cheeked sunbird
Ruddy turnstone
Rufous-collared kingfisher
Small buttonquail
Spotted munia
Stonechat
White-throated fantail
Zitting cisticola

TOGO
African jacana
African palm swift
African paradise-flycatcher
Barn swallow
Black tern
Black-winged stilt
Cattle egret
Collared pratincole
Common bulbul
Eurasian bittern
European bee-eater
European roller
Gray parrot
Gray woodpecker
Great blue turaco

Greater painted snipe
Green woodhoopoe
Hammerhead
Helmeted guineafowl
Hoopoe
Leaf-love
Northern wryneck
Osprey
Peregrine falcon
Rose-ringed parakeet
Ruddy turnstone
Sacred ibis
Secretary bird
Small buttonquail
Spotted flycatcher
Square-tailed drongo
Village weaver
White-helmet shrike
Wilson's storm-petrel
Yellow-fronted tinkerbird
Zitting cisticola

TRINIDAD AND TOBAGO
Blue-crowned motmot
Gray potoo
Hairy hermit
Oilbird
Rufous-tailed jacamar

TUNISIA
Barn swallow
Black-winged stilt
Collared pratincole
Common bulbul
Corncrake
Crag martin
Dunnock
Egyptian vulture
Eurasian bittern
European bee-eater
European roller
European starling
Gray wagtail
Great cormorant
Great crested grebe

Greater flamingo
Greater hoopoe-lark
Hoopoe
House sparrow
Northern gannet
Northern lapwing
Northern raven
Northern wryneck
Peregrine falcon
Rock pigeon
Ruddy turnstone
Small buttonquail
Spotted flycatcher
Stonechat
Winter wren
Zitting cisticola

TURKEY
Barn swallow
Black tern
Cattle egret
Chaffinch
Collared pratincole
Common bulbul
Common cuckoo
Corncrake
Crag martin
Dunnock
Egyptian vulture
Eurasian bittern
Eurasian dipper
Eurasian golden oriole
European bee-eater
European roller
European starling
Gray wagtail
Great bustard
Great cormorant
Great crested grebe
Great tit
Greater flamingo
Hoopoe
Horned lark
House sparrow
Mallard
Mute swan

Northern gannet
Northern lapwing
Northern raven
Northern wryneck
Nuthatch
Peregrine falcon
Red crossbill
Red-throated loon
Rock pigeon
Snow finch
Spotted flycatcher
Stonechat
Winter wren
Zitting cisticola

TURKMENISTAN

Barn swallow
Black-winged stilt
Cattle egret
Chaffinch
Collared pratincole
Common cuckoo
Common myna
Crag martin
Egyptian vulture
Eurasian bittern
Eurasian golden oriole
European bee-eater
European roller
European starling
Gray hypocolius
Great cormorant
Great crested grebe
Great tit
Hoopoe
Horned lark
House sparrow
Mallard
Northern lapwing
Northern raven
Nuthatch
Peregrine falcon
Red-throated loon
Rock pigeon
Spotted flycatcher

Winter wren

UGANDA

African broadbill
African jacana
African palm swift
African paradise-flycatcher
African pitta
African snipe
Bar-breasted mousebird
Barn swallow
Black-winged stilt
Buff-spotted flufftail
Cattle egret
Collared pratincole
Common bulbul
Common cuckoo
Common waxbill
Corncrake
Egyptian vulture
Eurasian golden oriole
European roller
European white stork
Golden-winged sunbird
Gray parrot
Gray woodpecker
Gray-crowned crane
Great blue turaco
Great cormorant
Great crested grebe
Greater painted snipe
Green woodhoopoe
Hammerhead
Helmeted guineafowl
Hoopoe
Leaf-love
Northern wryneck
Osprey
Ostrich
Peregrine falcon
Red-billed oxpecker
Rose-ringed parakeet
Sacred ibis
Secretary bird
Shoebill

Small buttonquail
Southern red bishop
Spotted flycatcher
Village weaver
White-helmet shrike
Yellow-fronted tinkerbird
Zitting cisticola

UKRAINE

Barn swallow
Black tern
Black-winged stilt
Chaffinch
Collared pratincole
Common cuckoo
Corncrake
Dunnock
Eurasian bittern
Eurasian golden oriole
European bee-eater
European roller
European starling
European white stork
Gray wagtail
Great bustard
Great cormorant
Great crested grebe
Great tit
Hoopoe
Horned lark
House sparrow
Mallard
Mute swan
Northern lapwing
Northern raven
Northern wryneck
Nuthatch
Osprey
Peregrine falcon
Red crossbill
Red-throated loon
Rock pigeon
Snow bunting
Spotted flycatcher
Spotted nutcracker

Stonechat
Winter wren

UNITED ARAB EMIRATES
Crab plovers
Egyptian vulture
European roller
Greater hoopoe-lark
Hoopoe
House sparrow
Northern lapwing
Osprey
Purple sunbird
Rock pigeon
Ruddy turnstone
Stonechat
Wilson's storm-petrel

UNITED KINGDOM
Barn owl
Barn swallow
Canada goose
Chaffinch
Common cuckoo
Common loon
Common murre
Corncrake
Dunnock
Eurasian bittern
Eurasian dipper
Eurasian golden oriole
European roller
European starling
Gray wagtail
Great auk
Great cormorant
Great crested grebe
Great tit
House sparrow
Mallard
Manx shearwater
Mute swan
Northern gannet
Northern lapwing

Northern raven
Northern wryneck
Nuthatch
Osprey
Peregrine falcon
Puffin
Red crossbill
Red-throated loon
Rock pigeon
Ruddy turnstone
Snow bunting
Spotted flycatcher
Stonechat
Willow ptarmigan
Winter wren

UNITED STATES
American anhinga
American avocet
American cliff swallow
American dipper
American goldfinch
American mourning dove
American robin
American white pelican
Anna's hummingbird
Apapane
Arctic skua
Arctic warbler
Baltimore oriole
Barn owl
Barn swallow
Belted kingfisher
Bishop's oo
Black rail
Black tern
Black-and-white warbler
Black-capped chickadee
Black-capped vireo
Black-winged stilt
Blue jay
Blue-gray gnatcatcher
Brown creeper
Brown pelican
Bushtit

Cactus wren
California condor
Canada goose
Cattle egret
Cedar waxwing
Chimney swift
Common loon
Common murre
Crested caracara
Eastern bluebird
Eastern phoebe
Eastern screech-owl
European starling
Gray catbird
Great auk
Great blue heron
Great cormorant
Great kiskadee
Greater roadrunner
Gyrfalcon
Harris's hawk
Hawaiian honeycreepers
Horned lark
House sparrow
House wren
Ivory-billed woodpecker
Killdeer
King eider
Kirtland's warbler
Laysan albatross
Laysan finch
Limpkin
Loggerhead shrike
Long-billed curlew
Magnificent frigatebird
Mallard
Manx shearwater
Mute swan
Northern bobwhite quail
Northern fulmar
Northern gannet
Northern raven
Osprey
Peregrine falcon
Plain chachalaca
Puffin

Red crossbill
Red-breasted nuthatch
Red-cockaded woodpecker
Red-throated loon
Red-winged blackbird
Rock pigeon
Roseate spoonbill
Rose-throated becard
Ruddy turnstone
Sandhill crane
Savanna sparrow
Snow bunting
Song sparrow
Sprague's pipit
Verdin
Western grebe
Western scrub-jay
Whip-poor-will
White-tailed tropicbird
Wild turkey
Willow ptarmigan
Wilson's storm-petrel
Winter wren
Wood duck
Wood stork
Wrentit
Yellow-bellied sapsucker
Yellow-breasted chat

URUGUAY
American anhinga
American cliff swallow
Barn owl
Baywing
Black-winged stilt
Cattle egret
Crested caracara
Gray potoo
Great kiskadee
Greater thornbird
Harris's hawk
House sparrow
King vulture
Limpkin
Magellanic penguin
Manx shearwater

Peregrine falcon
Red-legged seriema
Rock pigeon
Roseate spoonbill
Ruddy turnstone
Rufous hornero
Wilson's storm-petrel
Wood stork

UZBEKISTAN
Barn swallow
Black-winged stilt
Chaffinch
Collared pratincole
Common cuckoo
Common myna
Crag martin
Egyptian vulture
Eurasian bittern
Eurasian dipper
Eurasian golden oriole
European bee-eater
European roller
European starling
Great bustard
Great cormorant
Great crested grebe
Great tit
Hoopoe
Horned lark
House sparrow
Mallard
Northern raven
Pallas's sandgrouse
Peregrine falcon
Rock pigeon

VENEZUELA
Amazonian umbrellabird
American anhinga
Baltimore oriole
Barn owl
Barn swallow
Barred antshrike
Belted kingfisher
Black tern

Black-and-white warbler
Black-capped donacobius
Black-winged stilt
Blue-black grassquit
Blue-crowned motmot
Brown pelican
Cattle egret
Common trumpeter
Crested caracara
Gray antbird
Gray potoo
Great kiskadee
Greater flamingo
Guianan cock-of-the-rock
Hairy hermit
Harris's hawk
Highland tinamou
Hoatzin
Horned screamer
King vulture
Limpkin
Magnificent frigatebird
Oilbird
Osprey
Peregrine falcon
Red-billed scythebill
Roseate spoonbill
Ruddy turnstone
Rufous-browed peppershrike
Rufous-tailed jacamar
Scarlet macaw
Sharpbill
Spangled cotinga
Sparkling violet-ear
Sunbittern
Sungrebe
White-necked puffbird
Wilson's storm-petrel
Wire-tailed manakin
Wood stork

VIETNAM
Arctic warbler
Asian fairy-bluebird
Australasian lark
Barn swallow

Baya weaver
Black bulbul
Black-and-red broadbill
Black-crowned barwing
Black-naped monarch
Black-winged stilt
Cattle egret
Common cuckoo
Common iora
Common myna
Coppersmith barbet
Crag martin
Crested tree swift
Dollarbird
Eurasian bittern
Fire-breasted flowerpecker
Gray nightjar
Gray wagtail
Great cormorant
Great tit
Greater painted snipe
Greater racket-tailed drongo
Green magpie
Hoopoe
Northern wryneck
Orange-breasted trogon
Osprey
Peregrine falcon
Pheasant-tailed jacana
Purple sunbird
Rock pigeon
Ruby-cheeked sunbird
Ruddy turnstone
Saunder's gull
Small buttonquail
Spotted munia
Stonechat
White-throated fantail
Zitting cisticola

YEMEN

African palm swift
Cattle egret
Crab plovers
Crag martin
Egyptian vulture

European roller
Gray wagtail
Greater hoopoe-lark
Hammerhead
Hoopoe
House sparrow
Osprey
Peregrine falcon
Rock pigeon
Ruddy turnstone
Stonechat
Wilson's storm-petrel

YUGOSLAVIA

Common cuckoo
Corncrake
Crag martin
Egyptian vulture
Eurasian dipper
European bee-eater
European roller
European white stork
Gray wagtail
Great cormorant
Great crested grebe
Hoopoe
Horned lark
Mallard
Northern lapwing
Peregrine falcon
Rock pigeon
Snow bunting
Zitting cisticola

ZAMBIA

African broadbill
African jacana
African palm swift
African paradise-flycatcher
African pitta
African snipe
Bar-breasted mousebird
Barn swallow
Black-winged stilt
Buff-spotted flufftail

Cattle egret
Collared pratincole
Common bulbul
Common cuckoo
Common waxbill
Corncrake
Eurasian golden oriole
European bee-eater
European roller
European white stork
Gray go-away-bird
Gray-crowned crane
Great cormorant
Greater flamingo
Greater painted snipe
Green woodhoopoe
Hammerhead
Helmeted guineafowl
Hoopoe
House sparrow
Osprey
Ostrich
Peregrine falcon
Red-billed oxpecker
Rosy-breasted longclaw
Sacred ibis
Secretary bird
Shoebill
Small buttonquail
Southern ground-hornbill
Southern red bishop
Spotted flycatcher
Square-tailed drongo
Stonechat
Village weaver
White-helmet shrike
Yellow-fronted tinkerbird
Zitting cisticola

ZIMBABWE

African broadbill
African palm swift
African paradise-flycatcher
African pitta
African snipe
Bar-breasted mousebird

Barn swallow
Black-winged stilt
Buff-spotted flufftail
Cape batis
Cattle egret
Collared pratincole
Common bulbul
Common cuckoo
Common waxbill
Corncrake
Eurasian golden oriole
European bee-eater
European roller
European white stork

Gray go-away-bird
Gray-crowned crane
Great cormorant
Greater painted snipe
Green woodhoopoe
Hammerhead
Helmeted guineafowl
Hoopoe
House sparrow
Osprey
Ostrich
Peregrine falcon
Red-billed oxpecker
Rock pigeon

Rosy-breasted longclaw
Sacred ibis
Secretary bird
Shoebill
Small buttonquail
Southern ground-hornbill
Southern red bishop
Spotted flycatcher
Stonechat
Village weaver
White-helmet shrike
Yellow-fronted tinkerbird
Zitting cisticola

Index

Italic type indicates volume number; **boldface** type indicates entries and their pages; (ill.) indicates illustrations.

American black rails, 2: 315

American cliff swallows, 4: 919–21, 919 (ill.), 920 (ill.)

American dippers, 4: 1005, 1007–9, 1007 (ill.), 1008 (ill.)

American goldfinches, 5: 1282–84, 1282 (ill.), 1283 (ill.)

American mourning doves, 3: 513–14, 513 (ill.), 514 (ill.)

American pearl kites, 1: 212

American redstarts, 4: 792

American robins, 4: 1014, 1015, 1022–23, 1022 (ill.), 1023 (ill.)

American white pelicans, 1: 139–41, 139 (ill.), 140 (ill.)

Amytornis striatus. See Striated grasswrens

Anas platyrhynchos. See Mallards

Anatidae. *See* Ducks; Geese; Swans

Andean condors, 1: 177

Andean flamingos, 1: 201, 202

Andean stilts, 2: 423

Andigena hypoglauca. See Gray-breasted mountain-toucans

Anhima cornuta. See Horned screamers

Anhimidae. *See* Screamers

Anhinga anhinga. See American anhingas

Anhingas, 1: 98, 99, **116–24**

Anis, 3: **545–51**

Anna's hummingbirds, 3: 636–38, 636 (ill.), 637 (ill.)

Anseriformes, 2: **241–45**

Ant thrushes, 4: **836–44**

Antbirds. *See* Ant thrushes

Antcatchers. *See* Ant thrushes

Anthreptes species, 5: 1209

Anthus spragueii. See Sprague's pipits

Anting behavior, 4: 1005

Antiphonal duets, 5: 1361

Antpittas. *See* Ant thrushes

Antshrikes. *See* Ant thrushes

Antwrens. *See* Ant thrushes

Apapanes, 5: 1289, 1291–92, 1291 (ill.), 1292 (ill.)

Aphelocoma californica. See Western scrub-jays

Apodidae. *See* Swifts

Apodiformes, 3: **610–14**

Apolinar's wrens, 4: 1039

Apostlebirds, 5: 1360

Aptenodytes forsteri. See Emperor penguins

Apterygidae. *See* Kiwis

Apteryx australis. See Brown kiwis

Ara macao. See Scarlet macaws

Arabian babblers, 4: 1026

Arabian ostriches, 1: 39

Arachnothera, 5: 1209

Aramidae. *See* Limpkins

Aramus guarauna. See Limpkins

Araripe manakins, 4: 866

Archer's larks, 4: 905

Arctic skuas, 2: 479–80, 479 (ill.), 480 (ill.)

Arctic terns, 2: 396

Arctic warblers, 4: 1058–59, 1058 (ill.), 1059 (ill.)

Ardea herodias. See Great blue herons

Ardeidae. *See* Bitterns; Herons

Arenaria interpres. See Ruddy turnstones

Artamidae. *See* Woodswallows

Artamus cyanopterus. See Dusky woodswallows

Ascension frigatebirds, 1: 110

Ash's larks, 4: 905

Asian dowitchers, 2: 454

Asian fairy bluebirds, 4: 960–61, 960 (ill.), 961 (ill.)

Asian frogmouths, 3: 586, 587

Asities, 4: **801–6**; 5: 1209

Astley's leiothrix, 4: 1027

Astrapia mayeri. See Ribbon-tailed astrapias

Astrapias, ribbon-tailed, 5: 1391–92, 1391 (ill.), 1392 (ill.)

Asynchronous hatching, 2: 476

Atoll fruit doves, 3: 505, 509

Atrichornis rufescens. See Rufous scrub-birds

Atrichornithidae. *See* Scrub-birds

Attagis gayi. See Rufous-bellied seedsnipes

Auckland Island teals, 2: 241

Audubon, John James, 4: 852, 933

Auklets, 2: 486

Auks, 2: 397, **486–95**

Auriparus flaviceps. See Verdins

Australasian figbirds, 5: 1340–41, 1340 (ill.), 1341 (ill.)

Australasian larks, 4: 906–7, 906 (ill.), 907 (ill.)

Australian brush-turkeys, 2: 270

Australian chats, 4: **1087–92**

Australian chestnut-backed buttonquails, 2: 328

Australian creepers, 5: **1145–50**

Australian diamond doves, 3: 504

Australian fairy-wrens, 4: **1070–78**

Australian frogmouths, 3: 585–86, 587

Australian greater painted snipes, 2: 408, 409, 410, 412

Australian honeyeaters, 4: 1087; 5: 1124, **1225–34**

Australian magpie-larks, 5: 1360, 1361, 1362–64, 1362 (ill.), 1363 (ill.)

Australian magpies, 5: 1372–74

Australian masked owls, 3: 557

Australian owlet-nightjars, 3: 592, 593

Australian pelicans, *1*: 98, 134

Australian pratincoles, *2*: 436, 437, 442–43, 442 (ill.), 443 (ill.)

Australian robins, *5*: **1123–29**

Australian warblers, *4*: **1079–86**

Australian whipbirds, *4*: 1099, 1101

Avocets, *2*: **423–30**

B

Babblers, *4*: **1025–35**

    See also Pseudo babblers

Bachman's warblers, *5*: 1260

Bahama swallows, *4*: 915

Balaeniceps rex. See Shoebills

Balaenicipitidae. See Shoebills

Bald eagles, *1*: 209; *2*: 295

Balearica regulorum. See Gray crowned cranes

Baltimore orioles, *5*: 1270–71, 1270 (ill.), 1271 (ill.)

Banded cotingas, *4*: 874

Banded stilts, *2*: 423

Banded wattle-eyes, *4*: 1062

Banding birds, *4*: 852

Bannerman's turacos, *3*: 539

Bar-breasted mousebirds, *3*: 639, 641–43, 641 (ill.), 642 (ill.)

Barbados yellow warblers, *5*: 1260

Barbets, *3*: 708–9, 725–29, 747–56, 766, 768

Barn owls, *3*: **557–63**, 564, 565

Barn swallows, *4*: 913, 916–18, 916 (ill.), 917 (ill.)

Barred antshrikes, *4*: 836, 840–41, 840 (ill.), 841 (ill.)

Barred buttonquails, *2*: 317

Barred eagle-owls, *3*: 570–71, 570 (ill.), 571 (ill.)

Barrow, Mary Reid, *2*: 247

Bates' sunbirds, *5*: 1209

Batis capensis. See Cape batises

Batrachostomus. See Asian frogmouths

Bay-winged cowbirds. *See* Baywings

Baya weavers, *5*: 1313–14, 1313 (ill.), 1314 (ill.)

Baybirds, *5*: 1269

Baywings, *5*: 1275–76, 1275 (ill.), 1276 (ill.)

Beach thick-knees, *2*: 431, 432, 434–35, 434 (ill.), 435 (ill.)

Beaks. *See* Bills and beaks

Bearded reedlings, *4*: 1026, 1027

Bearded wood-partridge, *2*: 305

Becards, rose-throated, *4*: 854–55, 854 (ill.), 855 (ill.)

Bee-eaters, *3*: 653, 654, 655–56, **682–90**, 768

Bee hummingbirds, *3*: 630

Bellbirds, *4*: 872; *5*: 1131, 1132

Belted kingfishers, *3*: 654, 666–68, 666 (ill.), 667 (ill.)

Bengal florican bustards, *2*: 319

Bernier's vangas, *4*: 972, 975

Berrypeckers, *5*: 1194–95

    crested, *5*: 1196

    fan-tailed, *5*: 1199–1201, 1199 (ill.), 1200 (ill.)

    scarlet-collared, *5*: 1196

    Visayan, *5*: 1196

Bewick's wrens, *4*: 1037

Bhai tapaculos, *4*: 847

Biak gerygones, *4*: 1081

Bills and beaks, *1*: 146

    See also specific species

BirdLife International, *1*: 62

Birds of paradise, *4*: 789; *5*: **1389–97**

Birds of prey, diurnal, *1*: **207–11**; *3*: 555; *5*: 1346

Bishops, *5*: 1306

    red, *5*: 1309

    southern red, *5*: 1315–16, 1315 (ill.), 1316 (ill.)

    yellow-crowned, *5*: 1309

Bishop's oos, *5*: 1229–30, 1229 (ill.), 1230 (ill.)

Bitterns, *1*: 143, 146, **149–59**

Black-and-red broadbills, *4*: 798–800, 798 (ill.), 799 (ill.)

Black-and-white warblers, *5*: 1263–64, 1263 (ill.), 1264 (ill.)

Black-bellied dippers, *4*: 1010

Black-bellied plovers, *2*: 446

Black-belted flowerpeckers, *5*: 1196

Black-billed wood ducks, *2*: 259

Black-breasted buttonquails, *2*: 328

Black bulbuls, *4*: 945, 952–53, 952 (ill.), 953 (ill.)

Black-capped chickadees, *5*: 1167–69, 1167 (ill.), 1168 (ill.)

Black-capped donacobius, *4*: 1047–49, 1047 (ill.), 1048 (ill.)

Black-capped vireos, *5*: 1238–40, 1238 (ill.), 1239 (ill.)

Black catbirds, *4*: 998

Black-cinnamon fantails, *4*: 1105

Black-crowned barwings, *4*: 1028–29, 1028 (ill.), 1029 (ill.)

Black cuckoos. *See* Anis

Black-faced sheathbills, *2*: 469, 472–73, 472 (ill.), 473 (ill.)

Black guans, *2*: 284–85, 284 (ill.), 285 (ill.)

Black-headed weavers. *See* Village weavers

Black herons, *1*: 150

Black larks, *4*: 903

Black-legged seriemas, *2*: 383

Black-naped monarchs, *5*: 1120–22, 1120 (ill.), 1121 (ill.)

Black-necked cranes, *2*: 319

Chlidonias niger. See Black terns

Choco tinamous, *1:* 7

Choughs, white-winged, *5:* 1360

Chowchillas, *4:* 1093–98

Christmas frigatebirds, *1:* 110

Cicinnurus regius. See King birds of paradise

Ciconia ciconia. See European white storks

Ciconiidae. *See* Storks

Ciconiiformes, *1:* 143–48

Cinclidae. *See* Dippers

Cinclosoma punctatum. See Spotted quail-thrushes

Cinclus cinclus. See Eurasian dippers

Cinclus mexicanus. See American dippers

Cinerous wattled birds. *See* Kokakos

Cinnamon-tailed fantails, *4:* 1109

Cinnyris asiaticus. See Purple sunbirds

Cissa chinensis. See Green magpies

Cisticola juncidis. See Zitting cisticolas

Cisticolas, zitting, *4:* 1053–54, 1053 (ill.), 1054 (ill.)

CITES (Convention on International Trade in Endangered Species)
on eclectus parrots, *3:* 528
on helmeted hornbills, *3:* 721

Clarion wrens, *4:* 1039

Cliff swallows, *4:* 913, 919–21, 919 (ill.), 920 (ill.)

Climacteridae. *See* Australian creepers

Climacteris rufa. See Rufous treecreepers

Cobb's wrens, *4:* 1039

Cobeldick, William, *5:* 1355

Cocks-of-the-rock, Guianan, *4:* 879–80, 879 (ill.), 880 (ill.)

Cockerell's fantails, *4:* 1109

Coleridge, Samuel Taylor, *1:* 46

Colibri coruscans. See Sparkling violet-ears

Colies. *See* Mousebirds

Coliidae. *See* Mousebirds

Coliiformes. *See* Mousebirds

Colinus virginianus. See Northern bobwhite quails

Colius striatus. See Bar-breasted mousebirds

Collared pratincoles, *2:* 437, 439–41, 439 (ill.), 440 (ill.)

Collared sunbirds, *5:* 1209

Collocalia species, *3:* 613

Colombian grebes, *1:* 92

Colombian tinamous, *1:* 7

Colonial nesters, *2:* 396
See also specific species

Columba livia. See Rock pigeons

Columbidae. *See* Doves; Pigeons

Columbiformes, *3:* 504–7

Common barn owls, *3:* 557, 560–62, 560 (ill.), 561 (ill.)

Common bulbuls, *4:* 938 (ill.), 943, 944, 947–49, 947 (ill.)

Common buttonquails, *2:* 328

Common cuckoos, *3:* 545, 547–48, 547 (ill.), 548 (ill.); *4:* 1061

Common diving-petrels, *1:* 67, 68, 69–70, 69 (ill.), 70 (ill.)

Common ioras, *4:* 956, 958–59, 958 (ill.), 959 (ill.)

Common loons, *1:* 87–89, 87 (ill.), 88 (ill.)

Common murres, *2:* 489–91, 489 (ill.), 490 (ill.)

Common mynas, *5:* 1329–30, 1329 (ill.), 1330 (ill.)

Common potoos. *See* Gray potoos

Common redshanks, *2:* 454

Common sunbird-asities, *4:* 801, 802, 803, 804–5, 804 (ill.), 805 (ill.)

Common trumpeters, *2:* 379–81, 379 (ill.), 380 (ill.)

Common waxbills, *5:* 1299–1300, 1299 (ill.), 1300 (ill.)

Communal breeding, *5:* 1140
See also specific species

Condors, *1:* 143, 146, 175, 176
Andean, *1:* 177
California, *1:* 147, 177, 181–82, 181 (ill.), 182 (ill.)

Congo bay owls, *3:* 565

Congo swifts, *3:* 617

Convention on International Trade in Endangered Species. *See* CITES

Cooling mechanisms, *1:* 187

Coorong gerygones, *4:* 1081

Coots, *2:* 316, 356–65

Coppersmith barbets, *3:* 750–51, 750 (ill.), 751 (ill.)

Coppery-chested jacamars, *3:* 732, 735–36, 735 (ill.), 736 (ill.)

Coracias garrulus. See European rollers

Coraciidae. *See* Rollers

Coraciiformes, *3:* 653–57

Coracina typica. See Mauritius cuckoo-shrikes

Cormorants, *1:* 99, 100, 101, 116–24

Corncrakes, *2:* 364–65, 364 (ill.), 365 (ill.)

Cortaplantas. *See* Plantcutters

Corvidae. *See* Crows; Jays

Corvus corax. See Northern ravens

Corvus species, *5:* 1398

Corythaeola cristata. See Great blue turacos

Corythaixoides concolor. See Gray go-away-birds

Cotarramas. *See* Plantcutters

Cotinga cayana. See Spangled cotingas

Great kiskadees, 4: 850, 856–57, 856 (ill.), 857 (ill.)

Great snipes, 2: 455

Great spotted cuckoos, 3: 545

Great spotted kiwis, 1: 29, 30

Great-tailed grackles, 5: 1268

Great tits, 5: 1170–72, 1170 (ill.), 1171 (ill.)

Greater adjutant storks, 1: 166

Greater anis, 3: 545, 546

Greater flamingos, 1: 203–5, 203 (ill.), 204 (ill.)

Greater hoopoe-larks, 4: 908–9, 908 (ill.), 909 (ill.)

Greater melampittas, 4: 1100

Greater painted snipes, 2: 407, 408–9, 410–12, 410 (ill.), 411 (ill.)

Greater racket-tailed drongos, 5: 1350–51, 1350 (ill.), 1351 (ill.)

Greater rhabdornis, 5: 1188, 1190

Greater rheas, 1: 13

Greater roadrunners, 3: 545, 549–50, 549 (ill.), 550 (ill.)

Greater scythebills, 4: 832

Greater thornbirds, 4: 827–29, 827 (ill.), 828 (ill.)

Grebes, 1: **90–97**

Green ioras, 4: 957

Green magpies, 5: 1398, 1405–6, 1405 (ill.), 1406 (ill.)

Green peafowl, 2: 266

Green woodhoopoes, 3: 710–12, 710 (ill.), 711 (ill.)

Greenbuls, 4: 944, 945–46

Grenadier weavers. *See* Southern red bishops

Griffon vultures, 1: 207

Grooming feathers, 1: 126

Grosbeak weavers, 5: 1306

Ground antbirds, 4: 836

Ground cuckoo-shrikes, 4: 935, 936

Ground-hornbills
  Abyssinian, 3: 653–54

southern, 3: 717–19, 717 (ill.), 718 (ill.)

Ground jays, Hume's, 5: 1398

Ground-rollers, 3: 691, 692, 693

Grouse, 2: 298

Gruidae. *See* Cranes

Gruiformes, 2: **315–19**

Grus canadensis. See Sandhill cranes

Grus japonensis. See Red-crowned cranes

Guácharos. See Oilbirds

Guadalupe storm-petrels, 1: 43

Guam boatbills. *See* Guam flycatchers

Guam flycatchers, 5: 1116

Guam rails, 2: 318, 359

Guam swiftlets, 3: 617

Guans, 2: **279–87**

Guianan cocks-of-the-rock, 4: 879–80, 879 (ill.), 880 (ill.)

Guillemots, 2: 486, 487

Guineafowl, 2: **268–69, 288–93**

Gulls, 2: **395–98, 475–85**

Gymnogyps californianus. See California condors

Gyrfalcons, 1: 229, 234–35, 234 (ill.), 235 (ill.)

H

Haast brown kiwis. *See* Haast tokoeka kiwis

Haast tokoeka kiwis, 1: 29, 32, 33

Haematopodidae. *See* Oystercatchers

Haematopus unicolor. See Variable oystercatchers

Hairy hermits, 3: 632–33, 632 (ill.), 633 (ill.)

Hamerkops. *See* Hammerheads

Hammerheads, 1: **143, 146, 160–65**, 162 (ill.), 163 (ill.)

Happy family. *See* Gray-crowned babblers

Harpactes oreskios. See Orange-breasted trogons

Harris's hawks, 1: 213, 217–18, 217 (ill.), 218 (ill.)

Hatching, asynchronous, 2: 476
  See also specific species

Hawaiian creepers, 5: 1288

Hawaiian crows, 5: 1400

Hawaiian finches, 5: 1288

Hawaiian honeycreepers, 5: 1209, **1288–95**

Hawks, 1: 207, 208, 209, **212–22**, 230

Hedge sparrows, 4: **991–96**

Heliornis fulica. See Sungrebes

Heliornithidae. *See* Sungrebes

Helmet shrikes, 4: 962, 964

Helmet vangas, 4: 972, 973, 975

Helmeted guineafowl, 2: 291–92, 291 (ill.), 292 (ill.)

Helmeted hornbills, 3: 720–21, 720 (ill.), 721 (ill.)

Hemiprocne coronata. See Crested tree swifts

Hemiprocnidae. *See* Tree swifts

Hermits, hairy, 3: 632–33, 632 (ill.), 633 (ill.)

Herons, 1: 143, 144, 145, 146, **149–59**, 186

Highland tinamous, 1: 8–10, 8 (ill.), 9 (ill.)

Himalayan accentors, 4: 992

Himalayan vultures, 1: 212

Himantopus himantopus. See Black-winged stilts

Himatione sanguinea. See Apapanes

Hirundinidae. *See* Swallows

Hirundo pyrrhonota. See American cliff swallows

Hirundo rustica. See Barn swallows

Hoatzins, 2: **310–14**, 312 (ill.), 313 (ill.)

Hobbies, 1: 229

Honeycreepers, Hawaiian, 5: 1209, **1288–95**

Honeyeaters, Australian, 4: 1087; 5: 1124, **1225–34**

Honeyguides, 3: 725–26, 727–28, **766–73**

Hood mockingbirds, 4: 998, 1001–3, 1001 (ill.), 1002 (ill.)

Hooded cranes, 2: 319

Hooded crows, 5: 1399

Hooded pitohuis, 5: 1132

Hooded pittas, 4: 810–11, 810 (ill.), 811 (ill.)

Hooded plovers, 2: 446

Hook-billed vangas, 4: 972, 973

Hoopoe-larks, greater, 4: 908–9, 908 (ill.), 909 (ill.)

Hoopoes, 3: 653–57, **701–6**, 702 (ill.), 703 (ill.), 768

Hornbills, 3: 653–54, 655, 656, **714–24**

Horned larks, 4: 901, 910–12, 910 (ill.), 911 (ill.)

Horned screamers, 2: 263–64, 263 (ill.), 264 (ill.)

Horneros. *See* Ovenbirds

Horsfield's bronze-cuckoos, 4: 1071, 1089

House sparrows, 5: 1319, 1320–22, 1320 (ill.), 1321 (ill.)

House wrens, 4: 1038, 1039, 1043–44, 1043 (ill.), 1044 (ill.)

Huias, 5: 1354–55

Hume's ground jays, 5: 1398

Hummingbirds, 3: 610–14, **630–38**, 669; 5: 1208

Hurricanes, 1: 104

Hyacinth macaws, 3: 522

Hydrobatidae. *See* Storm-petrels

Hydrophasianus chirurgus. See Pheasant-tailed jacanas

Hypocolius, gray, 4: 979, 980, 985–86, 985 (ill.), 986 (ill.)

Hypocolius ampelinus. See Gray hypocolius

Hypothymis azurea. See Black-naped monarchs

Hypsipetes madagascariensis. See Black bulbuls

I

Ibisbills, 2: 423, 424

Ibises, 1: 143–47, **192–99**

Icteria virens. See Yellow-breasted chats

Icteridae. *See* New World blackbirds; Orioles

Icterus galbula. See Baltimore orioles

Ifrits, 4: 1099, 1100, 1101

Iiwis, 5: 1288

Indian bustards, 2: 318

Indicator archipelagicus. See Malaysian honeyguides

Indicatoridae. *See* Honeyguides

Insecticides, 1: 135

International Ecotourism Society, 1: 68

International Shrike Working Group, 4: 964

Ioras, 4: 955, 956–57
    common, 4: 956, 958–59, 958 (ill.), 959 (ill.)
    great, 4: 955
    green, 4: 957
    Marshall's, 4: 956

Irena puella. See Asian fairy bluebirds

Irenidae. *See* Fairy bluebirds; Leafbirds

Itombwe nightjars, 3: 577, 604

IUCN Red List of Threatened Species. *See* World Conservation Union (IUCN) Red List of Threatened Species

Ivory-billed woodpeckers, 3: 786–87, 786 (ill.), 787 (ill.)

J

Jacamars, 3: 725, 726, 727, 730–37, 738

Jacanas, 2: 397, **399–406**

Jacanidae. *See* Jacanas

Jackdaws, 5: 1398

Jacky winters, 5: 1125–26, 1125 (ill.), 1126 (ill.)

Jaegers, 2: 475–77

Jamaican todies, 3: 669; 4: 988

James's flamingos, 1: 202

Japanese cranes. *See* Red-crowned cranes

Japanese waxwings, 4: 979

Japanese white-eyes, 5: 1222–23, 1222 (ill.), 1223 (ill.)

Java sparrows, 5: 1298

Javan plovers, 2: 446

Javanese lapwings, 2: 446

Jays, 4: 789; 5: **1398–1410**

Jefferson, Thomas, 4: 998

Jerdon's pratincoles, 2: 438

Jesus birds. *See* Jacanas

Jewel-babblers, 4: 1099, 1101

Jewel thrushes. *See* Pittas

Jewels of the forest. *See* Pittas

Jynx torquilla. See Northern wrynecks

K

Kagus, 2: 316, 317–18, **349–55**, 353 (ill.), 354 (ill.)

Kalinowski's tinamous, 1: 7

Kangaroo emus, 1: 27

Keel-billed motmots, 3: 678

Kemp's longbills, 4: 1052

Kestrels, 1: 208, 229

Killdeer, 2: 447–49, 447 (ill.), 448 (ill.)

King birds of paradise, 5: 1395–97, 1395 (ill.), 1396 (ill.)

King eiders, 2: 256–57, 256 (ill.), 257 (ill.)

King Island emus, 1: 27

King vultures, 1: 175, 176, 178–80, 178 (ill.), 179 (ill.)

Kingbirds, 4: 852

Mousebirds, *3:* 639–43

Moustached tree swifts, *3:* 624

Moustached woodcreepers, *4:* 832

Mudnest builders, *5:* **1360–65**

Munias, spotted, *5:* 1303–4, 1303 (ill.), 1304 (ill.)

Murrelets, *2:* 397, 488

Murres, *2:* **486–95**

Muscicapa striata. See Spotted flycatchers

Muscicapidae. See Old World flycatchers

Musophagidae. See Plantain eaters; Turacos

Musophagiformes. See Plantain eaters; Turacos

Mute swans, *2:* 243, 249–51, 249 (ill.), 250 (ill.)

Mycteria americana. See Wood storks

Mynas, *5:* 1306, **1326–36**

N

Namaqua sandgrouse, *3:* 499–500, 499 (ill.), 500 (ill.)

Narrow-billed todies, *3:* 669, 672

Nectarinia, *5:* 1208–9

Nectariniidae. See Sunbirds

Needle beaks. *See* Rufous-tailed jacamars

Neodrepanis coruscans. See Common sunbird-asities

Neophron percnopterus. See Egyptian vultures

Nesomimus macdonaldi. See Hood mockingbirds

Nests
    burrow, *2:* 414
    snakeskin, *5:* 1390
    See also specific species

New Caledonian crows, *5:* 1399

New Caledonian owlet-nightjars, *3:* 593

New Guinea forest rails, *2:* 356

New Guinea logrunners, *4:* 1093, 1094, 1095

New South Wales National Park, *4:* 1077

New World blackbirds, *5:* **1268–77**

New World finches, *5:* **1244–57**

New World quails, *2:* **303–9**

New World toucans, *3:* 654

New World vultures, *1:* 143–48, **175–85,** 187

New World warblers, *5:* **1258–67**

New Zealand dotterels, *2:* 446

New Zealand storm-petrels, *1:* 62

New Zealand wattlebirds, *5:* **1353–59**

New Zealand Wildlife Service, *5:* 1355

New Zealand wrens, *4:* **815–20**

Newtonias, red-tailed, *4:* 1062

Nicators, yellow-spotted, *4:* 945

Niceforo's wrens, *4:* 1039

Nighthawks, *3:* 602

Nightingale wrens, *4:* 1037

Nightingales, *4:* 789, 1014, 1016

Nightjars, *3:* 555, **574–78,** 602–9

Nimba flycatchers, *4:* 1062

Nocturnal birds, *2:* 432
    See also specific species

Noisy scrub-birds, *4:* 895–97

Non-passerines, *4:* 791

Nonnula ruficapilla. See Rufous-capped nunlets

Nordmann's greenshanks, *2:* 456

Norfolk Island gerygones, *4:* 1081

North African ostriches, *1:* 35

North American Chimney Swift Nest Research Project, *3:* 620

North Island brown kiwis, *1:* 29

North Island kokakos, *5:* 1356–57, 1356–58

North Island saddlebacks, *5:* 1355

Northern bobwhite quails, *2:* 306–8, 306 (ill.), 307 (ill.)

Northern cassowaries, *1:* 20

Northern creepers, *5:* 1189

Northern fulmars, *1:* 58–60, 58 (ill.), 59 (ill.)

Northern gannets, *1:* 127–29, 127 (ill.), 128 (ill.)

Northern hawk owls, *3:* 565

Northern house wrens, *4:* 1038, 1039

Northern lapwings, *2:* 450–51, 450 (ill.), 451 (ill.)

Northern logrunners, *4:* 1094

Northern Pacific albatrosses, *1:* 45

Northern ravens, *5:* 1398, 1409–10, 1409 (ill.), 1410 (ill.)

Northern saw-whet owls, *3:* 565

Northern screamers, *2:* 262

Northern wrynecks, *3:* 777–78, 777 (ill.), 778 (ill.)

Notharchus macrorhynchos. See White-necked puffbirds

Nothocercus bonapartei. See Highland tinamous

Nucifraga caryocatactes. See Spotted nutcrackers

Nukupuus, *5:* 1288

Numida meleagris. See Helmeted guineafowl

Numididae. See Guineafowl

Nunlets, rufous-capped, *3:* 744–45, 744 (ill.), 745 (ill.)

Nutcrackers, spotted, *5:* 1407–8, 1407 (ill.), 1408 (ill.)

Nuthatches, *5:* **1173–81,** 1179 (ill.), 1180 (ill.)

Nyctea scandiaca. See Snowy owls

Red-backed shrikes, *4:* 962

Red-billed buffalo-weavers, *5:* 1307, 1308–9

Red-billed oxpeckers, *5:* 1334–36, 1334 (ill.), 1335 (ill.)

Red-billed queleas, *5:* 1309

Red-billed scythebills, *4:* 833–35, 833 (ill.), 834 (ill.)

Red-billed tropicbirds, *1:* 103

Red birds of paradise, *5:* 1390

Red bishops, *5:* 1309

Red-breasted cacklers. *See* Gray-crowned babblers

Red-breasted nuthatches, *5:* 1176–78, 1176 (ill.), 1177 (ill.)

Red-breasted plantcutters, *4:* 881–82, 883

Red-breasted pygmy parrots, *3:* 522

Red-browed treecreepers, *5:* 1145

Red-cockaded woodpeckers, *3:* 781–83, 781 (ill.), 782 (ill.)

Red-collared widowbirds, *5:* 1306–7

Red crossbills, *5:* 1285–87, 1285 (ill.), 1286 (ill.)

Red-crowned cranes, *2:* 319, 341–42, 341 (ill.), 342 (ill.)

Red-eyed bulbuls, *4:* 944

Red-eyed vireos, *4:* 792

Red-faced mousebirds, *3:* 639

Red-headed rockfowl. *See* Gray-necked picathartes

Red-headed weavers, *5:* 1308

Red-kneed dotterels, *2:* 445

Red larks, *4:* 905

Red-legged seriemas, *2:* 384–86, 384 (ill.), 385 (ill.)

Red List of Threatened Species. *See* World Conservation Union (IUCN) Red List of Threatened Species

Red-lored whistlers, *5:* 1132

Red-shouldered vangas, *4:* 974–75

Red-tailed newtonias, *4:* 1062

Red-tailed vangas, *4:* 972

Red-throated loons, *1:* 85–86, 85 (ill.), 86 (ill.)

Red-vented bulbuls, *4:* 944

Red-whiskered bulbuls, *4:* 944

Red-winged blackbirds, *5:* 1269, 1272–74, 1272 (ill.), 1273 (ill.)

Reed warblers, *4:* 1051

Reedlings, bearded, *4:* 1026, 1027

Regent bowerbirds, *5:* 1380

Remizidae. *See* Penduline titmice

Resplendent quetzals, *3:* 649–51, 649 (ill.), 650 (ill.)

Réunion cuckoo-shrikes, *4:* 937

Réunion flightless ibises, *1:* 193

Réunion solitaires, *3:* 517

Rhabdornis, *5:* 1188–93

Rhabdornis mysticalis. See Stripe-headed rhabdornis

Rhabdornithidae. *See* Philippine creepers

Rheas, *1:* 2, 3, **11–17**

Rheidae. *See* Rheas

Rhinocryptidae. *See* Tapaculos

Rhinoplax vigil. See Helmeted hornbills

Rhipidura albicollis. See White-throated fantails

Rhipidura leucophrys. See Willie wagtails

Rhipiduridae. *See* Fantails

Rhynochetidae. *See* Kagus

Rhynochetos jubatus. See Kagus

Ribbon-tailed astrapias, *5:* 1391–92, 1391 (ill.), 1392 (ill.)

Ribbon-tailed birds of paradise, *5:* 1390

Riflebirds, Victoria's, *5:* 1393–94, 1393 (ill.), 1394 (ill.)

Riflemen, *4:* 816, 817–19, 817 (ill.), 818 (ill.)

The Rime of the Ancient Mariner, 1: 46

Ring ouzels, *4:* 1015

Rio de Janeiro antwrens, *4:* 838

River-martins, white-eyed, *4:* 914–15

Roadrunners, 3: 545–51

Roatelos, 2: 320–25

Robin accentors, *4:* 992

Robins, 4: 1038; 5: 1124
American, *4:* 1014, 1015, 1022–23, 1022 (ill.), 1023 (ill.)
Australian, 5: 1123–29

Rock pigeons, *3:* 511–12, 511 (ill.), 512 (ill.)

Rock thrushes, *4:* 1014, 1015

Rockfowl, *4:* 1025
See also Gray-necked picathartes

Rockwarblers, *4:* 1079

Rodrigues solitaires, *3:* 517–18

Rollers, 3: 653, 654, 655, 691–99

Rondonia bushbirds, *4:* 838

Rooks, *5:* 1398

Rose-ringed parakeets, *3:* 524–25, 524 (ill.), 525 (ill.)

Rose-throated becards, *4:* 854–55, 854 (ill.), 855 (ill.)

Roseate spoonbills, *1:* 196–97, 196 (ill.), 197 (ill.)

Rostratula benghalensis. See Greater painted snipes

Rostratulidae. *See* Painted snipes

Rosy-breasted longclaws, *4:* 930–31, 930 (ill.), 931 (ill.)

Rotten meat, *1:* 176

Ruby-cheeked sunbirds, *5:* 1211–12, 1211 (ill.), 1212 (ill.)

Rudd's larks, *4:* 905

Ruddy turnstones, *2:* 461–62, 461 (ill.), 462 (ill.)

Ruffs, 2: 455

Rufous babblers, 5: 1139, 1140

Rufous-bellied seedsnipes, 2: 466–67, 466 (ill.), 467 (ill.)

Rufous-breasted hermits. See Hairy hermits

Rufous-browed peppershrikes, 5: 1241–43, 1241 (ill.), 1242 (ill.)

Rufous-capped nunlets, 3: 744–45, 744 (ill.), 745 (ill.)

Rufous-collared kingfishers, 3: 664–65, 664 (ill.), 665 (ill.)

Rufous fantails, 4: 1106, 1107, 1108

Rufous horneros, 4: 822, 823, 824–26, 824 (ill.), 825 (ill.)

Rufous-necked wood-rails, 2: 357

Rufous potoos, 3: 596

Rufous scrub-birds, 4: 895–900, 898 (ill.), 899 (ill.)

Rufous-tailed jacamars, 3: 732, 733–34, 733 (ill.), 734 (ill.)

Rufous-tailed plantcutters, 4: 881–82, 883

Rufous treecreepers, 5: 1146, 1147, 1148–50, 1148 (ill.), 1149 (ill.)

Rufous vangas, 4: 976–77, 976 (ill.), 977 (ill.)

Rupicola rupicola. See Guianan cocks-of-the-rock

Rusty-belted tapaculos, 4: 848–49, 848 (ill.), 849 (ill.)

S

Sacred ibises, 1: 193, 194–95, 194 (ill.), 195 (ill.)

Saddlebacks, 5: 1353, 1354, 1355

Saffron toucanets, 3: 759

Sagittariidae. See Secretary birds

Sagittarius serpentarius. See Secretary birds

St. Helena plovers, 2: 446

San Clemente loggerhead

shrikes, 4: 970

Sandgrouse, 3: 497–503

Sandhill cranes, 2: 334, 339–40, 339 (ill.), 340 (ill.)

Sandpipers, 2: 397, 453–63

Sandstone shrike-thrushes, 5: 1132

Sangihe shrike-thrushes, 5: 1132

São Tomé sunbirds, 5: 1208

Sarcoramphus papa. See King vultures

Sarothrura elegans. See Buff-spotted flufftails

Sarus cranes, 2: 315

Satanic-eared nightjars, 3: 577, 604

Satin bowerbirds, 5: 1383–85, 1383 (ill.), 1384 (ill.)

Satyr tragopans, 2: 300–301, 300 (ill.), 301 (ill.)

Saunder's gulls, 2: 481–82, 481 (ill.), 482 (ill.)

Savanna sparrows, 5: 1255–57, 1255 (ill.), 1256 (ill.)

Saw-whet owls, northern, 3: 565

Saxicola torquata. See Stonechats

Sayornis phoebe. See Eastern phoebes

Scarlet-collared berrypeckers, 5: 1196

Scarlet macaws, 3: 532 (ill.), 533–34, 533 (ill.)

Schetba rufa. See Rufous vangas

Schlegel's asities, 4: 801, 802, 803

Scimitar babblers, 4: 1025

Scissor-tailed flycatchers, 4: 850

Sclater's larks, 4: 905

Sclerophyll forests, 4: 1095

Scolopacidae. See Sandpipers

Scopidae. See Hammerheads

Scopus umbretta. See Hammerheads

Screamers, 2: 241–45, 261–65

Screaming cowbirds, 5: 1276

Screaming pihas, 4: 872

Screech-owls, 3: 553, 567–69, 567 (ill.), 568 (ill.)

Scrub-birds, 4: 895–900; 5: 1146

Scrub-jays, western, 5: 1403–4, 1403 (ill.), 1404 (ill.)

Scrub robins, 5: 1123, 1127–28 (ill.), 1127 (ill.), 1128 (ill.)

Scythebills
    greater, 4: 832
    red-billed, 4: 833–35, 833 (ill.), 834 (ill.)

Sea eagles, 1: 212

Seabirds, 1: 101

Secretary birds, 1: 207, 223–28, 225 (ill.), 226 (ill.)

Seed-eaters, 5: 1288
    See also specific species

Seedsnipes, 2: 396, 464–68

Semnornis ramphastinus. See Toucan barbets

Semper's warblers, 5: 1260

Senegal thick-knees, 2: 431

Sequential polyandry, 2: 327

Seriemas, 2: 316, 317, 318, 382–86

Seychelles sunbirds, 5: 1208

Seychelles swiftlets, 3: 617

Shakespeare, William, 3: 555; 5: 1327

Shanks, 2: 454

Sharp-tailed sandpipers, 2: 455

Sharpbills, 4: 860–63, 862 (ill.), 863 (ill.)

Shearwaters, 1: 43, 53–60

Sheathbills, 2: 396, 469–74

Shoebills, 1: 143, 145, 186–91, 188 (ill.), 189 (ill.)

Shore plovers, 2: 445, 446

Shorebirds. See Charadriiformes

Short-eared owls, 3: 554

Shovel-billed kingfishers, 3: 655

Yellow-crowned bulbuls, *4:* 945

Yellow-crowned gonoleks, *4:* 962

Yellow-eyed penguins, *1:* 73

Yellow-fronted tinkerbirds, *3:* 752–53, 752 (ill.), 753 (ill.)

Yellow-headed vultures, *1:* 175–76

Yellow-legged tinamous, *1:* 7

Yellow-rumped honeyguides, *3:* 768

Yellow-rumped thornbills, *4:* 1082–83, 1082 (ill.), 1083 (ill.)

Yellow-spotted nicators, *4:* 945

Yellow-streaked bulbuls, *4:* 944

Yellow-throated leafbirds, *4:* 956

Yellow tits, *5:* 1166

Yellow wagtails, *4:* 929

Yellowheads, *4:* 1084–85, 1084 (ill.), 1085 (ill.); *5:* 1132

Yemen accentors, *4:* 993

Z

Zapata wrens, *4:* 1039

Zebra finches, *5:* 1298, 1301–2, 1301 (ill.), 1302 (ill.)

Zenaida macroura. See American mourning doves

Zitting cisticolas, *4:* 1053–54, 1053 (ill.), 1054 (ill.)

Zosteropidae. *See* White-eyes

Zosterops japonicus. See Japanese white-eyes

Zuberbühler, Klaus, *3:* 539